W9-BSI-606

FILM
and the
LIBERAL
ARTS

Theodore Lownik Library
Illinois Benedictine College
Lisle, Illinois 60532

FILM
and the
LIBERAL
ARTS

T. J. Ross
FAIRLEIGH DICKINSON UNIVERSITY

Holt, Rinehart and Winston, Inc.
New York   Chicago   San Francisco
Atlanta   Dallas   Montreal   Toronto

Copyright © 1970 by Holt, Rinehart and Winston, Inc.
All rights reserved
Library of Congress Catalog Card Number: 78-104815
SBN: 03-081104-X
Printed in the United States of America
9 8 7 6 5 4 3 2 1

ACKNOWLEDGMENTS

For permission to reprint copyrighted materials,
the editor is indebted to the following:

James Agee, "The Bride Comes to Yellow Sky" (shooting script). From
AGEE ON FILM: VOL. II by James Agee, "The Bride Comes to Yellow
Sky" by James Agee. Copyright © 1958 by Theasquare Productions,
Inc. Reprinted by Permission of the publisher, Grosset & Dunlap, Inc.,
New York.

Daniel Fuchs, "Writing for the Movies," *Commentary,* February 1962, pp.
104–116. Reprinted from *Commentary,* by permission; Copyright © 1962
by the American Jewish Committee. With permission of the author.

Sergei Eisenstein, "Dickens, Griffith, and the Film Today." From *Film Form*
by Sergei Eisenstein, translated by Jay Leyda, copyright, 1949, by
Harcourt, Brace & World, Inc. and reprinted with their permission.

Jan Kott, "Shakespeare—Cruel and True," from *Shakespeare Our Contemporary* by Jan Kott, translated by Boleslaw Taborski, pp. 229–236. Copyright © 1964 by Panstwowe Wydawnictwo Naukowe. Reprinted by
permission of Doubleday & Company, Inc., New York, and Methuen
& Co. Ltd., London.

Arnold Hauser, "Surrealistic Art and the Film." From *The Social History
of Art,* vol. 4, by Arnold Hauser. Published 1951, 1958 by Alfred A.
Knopf, Inc. Reprinted by permission of Alfred A. Knopf, Inc., and of
Routledge & Kegan Paul Ltd., London.

Joseph von Sternberg, "Film as a Visual Art." Reprinted with permission of
The Macmillan Company from *Fun in a Chinese Laundry* by Joseph
Von Sternberg, pp. 309–325. Copyright © 1965 by Joseph Von Sternberg.

Oscar Levant, "A Cog in the Wheel." From *A Smattering of Ignorance* by
Oscar Levant, pp. 89–92, 98–100, 105–106, 107–112. Copyright 1939, 1940 by
Oscar Levant. Reprinted by permission of Doubleday & Company, Inc.

Susan Sontag, "The Imagination of Disaster." Reprinted with permission of
Farrar, Straus & Giroux from *Against Interpretation* by Susan Sontag.
Copyright © 1965 by Susan Sontag.

Pauline Kael, "Movies on Television." From *Kiss Kiss Bang Bang* by Pauline
Kael, by permision of Atlantic–Little, Brown and Co. Copyright © 1965,
1966, 1967, 1968 by Pauline Kael, originally appeared in *The New Yorker.*

Marshall McLuhan, "Movies: The Reel World." From *Understanding Media*
by Marshall McLuhan, pp. 284–288. Copyright © 1964 by Marshall
McLuhan. Used with permission of McGraw-Hill Book Company.

Jack Kerouac, "Nosferatu," *New Yorker Film Society Notes,* January 9, 1960,
pp. 1–4. Copyright © 1960 by New Yorker Film Society Notes. Reprinted
by permission of The Sterling Lord Agency.

"The Art of the Director: Godard Interviews Antonioni," by Jean-Luc Godard, *Cahiers du Cinema in English,* January 1966, pp. 19–30. Reprinted by permission of Cahier Publishing Co., Inc.

Luis Buñuel, "A Statement," *Film Culture,* Summer 1960, pp. 41–42. Reprinted by permission of the editors.

Nicola Chiaromonte, "Priests of the Highbrow Cinema," *Encounter,* January 1963, pp. 40–41, 42–43. First published in *Tempo Presente,* June 1962. Excerpt reprinted by permission of the author and *Encounter.*

J. B. Priestley, "The Mad Sad World," *New Statesman,* January 31, 1964. Reprinted by permission of the editors.

Kingsley Amis, "A Decade of New Heartbreakers," *Mademoiselle,* January 1960, pp. 75, 6, 8. Reprinted by permission of A. D. Peters & Company.

Catherine Sugy, "Black Men or Good Niggers?" *Take One,* 1:8 (1968), pp. 18–20. Reprinted by permission of the editors.

Dmitri Tiomkin, "Composing for Films," *Films in Review,* November 1951, pp. 17–22. Reprinted by permission of the editor.

George Antheil, "New Tendencies in Composing for Motion Pictures," *Film Culture,* Summer 1955, pp. 16–17. Reprinted by permission of the editors.

Page Cook, "Film Music as Noise," from "The Sound Track," *Films in Review,* March 1968, pp. 162, 163, 166. Reprinted by permission of the copyright owners.

David Riesman, "The Oral Tradition, the Written Word, and the Screen Image," from David Riesman, *The Oral Tradition, The Written Word and the Screen Image* (Yellow Springs, Ohio: The Antioch Press, 1955), pp. 30–39. Reprinted by permission of the author.

George N. Fenin and William K. Everson, "Contents and Moral Influence of the Western," from George N. Fenin and William K. Everson, *The Western* (New York: Grossman Publishers, Inc., 1962), pp. 25–30, 40–41, 44–49. Reprinted by permission.

Robert Warshow, "The Gangster as Tragic Hero," from *The Immediate Experience* (New York: Doubleday & Company, Inc., 1962), pp. 89–107. Reprinted by permission of Paul Warshow.

Rudolph Arnheim, "Art Today and the Film," *Film Culture,* Fall 1966, pp. 43–46. Reprinted by permission of the editors.

T. J. Ross, "Gipsies and Gentlemen," *The Massachusetts Review,* Spring 1968, pp. 359–369. Reprinted by permission of the editors.

Philip French, "All the Better Books," *Sight and Sound,* Winter 1966–1967, pp. 38–41. Reprinted by permission of the editors.

Richard Wilbur, "A Poet and the Movies," from W. R. Robinson and George Garrett (eds.), *Man and the Movies* (Baton Rouge, La.: Louisiana State University Press, 1967), pp. 223–226. Reprinted by permission.

Parker Tyler, "The Film Sense and the Painting Sense," *Perspectives USA,* April 1955, pp. 95–104. Reprinted by permission of the author.

Dwight Macdonald, "Our Elizabethan Movies," *The Miscellany,* December 1929. Reprinted by permission of Dwight Macdonald. A shortened version appeared in *Film Society Review,* 1:1 (1963), pp. 15–17.

J. Blumenthal, " 'Macbeth' into 'Throne of Blood,' " *Sight and Sound,* Autumn 1965, pp. 190–195. Reprinted by permission of the editors.

George Bluestone, "The Limits of the Novel and the Limits of the Film," from George Bluestone, *Novels into Film* (Baltimore, Md.: The Johns Hopkins Press, 1957), pp. 1–6. Reprinted by permission.

André Malraux, "A Sketch of the Rhetoric of the Sound Film," translated from the French by Joseph Satin, from André Malraux, *Equisse d'une Psychologie du Cinema* (Paris: Editions Gallimard, 1947). © Editions Gallimard 1947.

André Bazin, "The Evolution of the Language of Cinema," from André Bazin, *What Is Cinema?* edited by Hugh Gray (Berkeley, Calif.: University of California Press, 1967), pp. 23–40. Reprinted by permission of The Regents of the University of California.

O. B. Hardison, "The Rhetoric of Hitchcock's Thrillers," from W. R. Robinson and George Garrett (eds.), *Man and the Movies* (Baton Rouge, La.: Louisiana State University Press, 1967), pp. 137–139. Reprinted by permission.

Raymond Durgnat, "The Impossible Takes a Little Longer," *Films and Filming,* September 1968, pp. 13–16. Reprinted by permission of A. D. Peters & Company.

Erwin Panofsky, "On Movies," *Bulletin of the Department of Art and Archaeology, Princeton University,* 1934. Reprinted by permission of Mrs. Gerda Panofsky.

PREFACE

Film plays a dominant role in our culture. The intensive discussions aroused in recent years by outstanding films, ranging from *Breathless* to *Bonnie and Clyde*, from *La Dolce Vita* to *2001*, from *A Hard Day's Night* to *The Graduate*, attest to the extent to which film—more than any of the other media—touches home; it reaches us all.

On the campus, there has developed an increasingly vital and inquiring interest in film, an interest held in common by teachers and students. This means that film as a subject lends itself to immediate and engaged discussion, to a ready sharing and exchange between teacher and student of viewpoints and tastes and expectations. Since film is a medium which partakes of all the more traditional arts, revealing special kinships with literature, with the visual arts, and with music, it lends itself to a purview which bridges over into these areas, and into allied liberal arts areas like rhetoric, sociology, and psychology. The advantage to the student of an orientation keyed to the multiple nature of the cinema, such as this book offers, is that it also introduces him to the multiple concerns and possibilities of communications and culture in general. And the teacher is provided with various approaches from a central base for class discussion and writing.

The essays in this book use film as a common core, but not in isolation. Rather, each set of essays revolves around film and one or more of the liberal arts: first, film and rhetoric, to highlight the special language of film, its mode of communication; then an extensive section on film and literature followed by briefer ones on film and the visual arts, and film and music, to examine the elements film shares with each of these forms; the next section on film and society offers in-depth appraisals of the cinema in its response to, and presentation of, social styles and values; a final section on film and esthetics considers aspects of the film-making process as these relate to evaluation of film and its achievement as an art form. This in overview is the sequence of the book; the topics of each section, however, are self-contained and may be taken up and used in any order.

Each essay is followed by three types of exercises: exercises on the content of the essay; exercises which invite the reader to compare his own film experience with that of the essayist under consideration; and exercises on the essay's structure and language as guides to discussion of effective writing. An appendix at the end of the volume lists a number of films related to the section topics and the distributing companies through which they may be obtained. A selected bibliography is also included.

Although a number of the selections are of manifest topical appeal, I have sought articles written from a point of view which has proved to be, or seems likely to be, of continuing pertinence. In line with this, I have favored writing whose implication and argument can be readily followed whether or not one is directly familiar with the work which served as the author's point of departure. Further, to provide a basis for independent opinion and response I have in several instances brought together contrasting, as well as cognate, views on the same topic. Ranging in tone and style from the breezy to the earnest, from the poetically evocative to the toughly analytical, the essays present a variety of modes of lively and graceful prose. They also exemplify—like any educational experience of value—the varying degrees of pressure and judgment which can be brought to bear on a given topic.

In the preparation of this volume, I owe special thanks to Phillip Leininger for his steady editorial help and encouragement.

Madison, New Jersey   T.J.R.
December 1969

CONTENTS

Postlude: Film and the Liberal Arts **373**

FILM
and
RHETORIC

We may apply the term "rhetoric" to the means we use to clarify, dramatize, or otherwise add to the point of what we have to say. The so-called rhetorical devices we employ—whether the suspended rhythms of a periodic sentence or the patient accumulation of examples, a lengthy simile or blunt expletive—we employ as an expressive means. Rhetoric can serve us in effectively shaping our material; and the more effectively we shape our material, the more do we succeed in bringing it to life. Rhetoric, then, may be thought of as the animating presence in language; as such, it is inseparable from our idea of language, that is, of expression at a distinctively human level.

Whatever is rhetorical is shaped to a purpose, and our understanding of any mode of rhetoric will seek to embrace both the means employed and the purpose implicit in the choice of means. In the corrupt rhetoric of a demagogue, there will be evident a bad or equivocal purpose; in the arch and padded rhetoric of, say, the Tarzan stories of Edgar Rice Burroughs, we recognize a wholly escapist motive and the language of pipe dreams. On the other hand, the mastery of the modes of rhetoric of John Milton or Abraham Lincoln is integral to the power of their noblest statements in writing or speech. Whatever the purpose or motive, from the demagogue's to the comedian's to the poet's, rhetoric connotes the artistry of an individual. This is the point of the film historian and critic André Bazin when he remarks: "The great directors are first creators of form: if you wish, they are rhetoricians."

The more practiced a writer or speaker, the more will his "rhetorical flourishes"—his way of touching in a definition here, filling out an analogy there, or leading up to a clinching point—come to seem "natural," as much a part of his second nature as the loops of his signature. Students of the cinema have begun to discover similar recognizable directorial touches in movies, as they have begun seriously to consider the way movies are made and the way they work on us in the audience. Later sections of this volume include essays which show how we may to some extent "read" a film as we read a poem, how, that is, we may pinpoint some of the characteristics of a director's style in much the same way we might define the revealing touches of metaphor and manner in a poet with whose work we were thoroughly familiar. As an art which testifies to the expressive grace of human beings, the cinema too has its "rhetoric."

From varying perspectives, each of the following selections adds to our understanding of how the formal (rhetorical) properties of a film affect its content. The opening essays by Malraux and Bazin are both general in scope and extensive in coverage; between them they examine some of the key technical features and advances in the cinema from its burgeoning period to the present. With the brilliance and Olympian shorthand characteristic of his criticism in other fields, Malraux covers a great deal of ground in a few closely packed paragraphs. His remarks in passing on ". . . special moments that each art form may make use of" or "contrapuntal images" suggest possibilities of approach which the student may find it useful to define and explore further on his own. Bazin traces similar developments in the cinema in a more detailed and equally suggestive way. The student should note, however, the differences in emphasis and tone between the two writers which would seem to point to a difference in the ultimate expectations of each concerning film as an art form. It is also on the score of expectations that O. B. Hardison considers the style and appeal of the films of Alfred Hitchcock.

The next pair of selections should be considered as a single unit. Stephen Crane's "The Bride Comes to Yellow Sky" is a short story classic; its treatment by James Agee is a superior example of film script form. Placed together, story and script exemplify concretely the main theoretical lines of the previous essays, showing how the multiple nature of the film medium re-creates a written work in its own terms, and offer an instructive exercise in comparison and contrast.

In Bazin's phrase, the developments and possibilities considered in this opening set of selections trace an "evolution in the language of the cinema" and so belong in a category which defines itself as a "rhetoric of vision."

A SKETCH
OF THE RHETORIC
OF THE SOUND FILM

André Malraux

The sound film inevitably changed the state of the film medium, although not, as some say, by "perfecting" the silent film. The sound film is no more a perfecting of the silent film than the elevator is a perfecting of the skyscraper. The skyscraper was born of the discovery of reinforced concrete and the elevator; the modern film was born not out of the possibility of hearing words spoken aloud from the once silent screen, but out of the possibilities of expression, wherein sound and image are joined together. As long as sound in films remained merely phonographic it was as pointless as the silent film was while it remained photographic. It became an art when directors understood that the ancestor of sound in talking films was not the phonograph record but radio techniques.

When creative artists redesigned *The Meeting of 9 Thermidor*[1] for radio they first had to work out a new genre whose text was shaped by new-required techniques of reproduction. It was not a

---

[1] The French revolutionaries changed the calendar and renamed the eleventh month (July 19 to August 17) Thermidor. 9 Thermidor (July 27, 1794) marked the fall of Maximilien Robespierre, an idealist turned terrorist, and the end of the Reign of Terror.

mere matter of having actors read lines into a monitor, but, first of all, to convert into the "shorthand" of the monitor certain moments of that famous meeting, to make a montage of it. The detailed actual account of the Thermidor meeting which has come down to us is tedious, as are all shorthand accounts, because of its length.

We are inclined to believe that every incident offers the following choices: there exist, as on the night Robespierre fell, special moments that each art form may make use of. It seems, at first glance, that selective elements in every crisis, in every life, become the primary material of each art form and that the leftover elements remain forever blurred and suppressed. There lies the distinction between historical language and the allusive, significant, properly "artistic" moment. To be sure, a number of special moments exist in every crisis, but those which are used are determined by precisely which of the arts must communciate that crisis. At the moment when Robespierre can no longer make himself understood, the decisive emphasis for radio would perhaps be his failing voice. But for the film it would perhaps be a distraction on the part of one of the guards, busy that very instant throwing out one of the teenagers or looking for his tinder box.

In the twentieth century, for the first time, art forms have been created which are inseparable from mechanical means of expression; they are not only capable of reproduction but are expressly designed for it. The finest sketches can already be reproduced with a perfection of detail; without doubt paintings will be too, well before the end of the century. But neither sketches nor paintings were created *in order to be reproduced*. They are ends in themselves. So is the split second which converts a filmed scene with living actors into photography, and into that alone, or that which converts a radio skit into a phonograph record to be sent out over a microphone.

Lastly, the power of expression of recorded sounds, weak when transmitted only by phonograph record via radio, becomes tremendously amplified when it finds its contrapuntal image. The inspiration of contrast (i.e., juxtaposition of sound and image) becomes a perfecting; then the sound film becomes to the silent film what painting is to sketching.

From André Malraux, *Esquisse d'une Psychologie du Cinema.* © Editions Gallimard 1947.

EXERCISES

on film and rhetoric

1. For Malraux the rhetoric of film is "*expression,* wherein sound and image are joined together." Explain, using examples, what he means by this definition.
2. Compare the rhetoric of radio with the rhetoric of film, according to Malraux.
3. How does Malraux see historical language differing from the language of the film?
4. In the next to the last paragraph Malraux seems to be saying that twentieth-century art is mechanical; yet, contradictorily, he adds that for a split second it is not. What potentialities of expression does this "split second" open up for film makers?

on film

1. Discuss films you have seen in terms of Malraux's definition of expression.
2. Criticize, on the basis of films you have seen, his definition of expression. How would you define the rhetoric of film?

on structure and language

1. Show how the motif of "perfecting" runs through this entire essay.
2. What does Malraux mean by "shorthand" in this essay? Give examples.
3. Comment on the use Malraux makes of these paired comparisons: film and radio; painting and sketching.

THE EVOLUTION OF THE LANGUAGE OF CINEMA

André Bazin

By 1928 the silent film had reached its artistic peak. The despair of its elite as they witnessed the dismantling of this ideal city, while it may not have been justified, is at least understandable. As they followed their chosen aesthetic path it seemed to them that the cinema had developed into an art most perfectly accommodated to the "exquisite embarrassment" of silence and that the realism that sound would bring could only mean a surrender to chaos.

In point of fact, now that sound has given proof that it came not to destroy but to fulfill the Old Testament of the cinema, we may most properly ask if the technical revolution created by the sound track was in any sense an aesthetic revolution. In other words, did the years from 1928 to 1930 actually witness the birth of a new cinema? Certainly, as regards editing, history does not actually show as wide a breach as might be expected between the silent and the sound film. On the contrary there is discernible evidence of a close relationship between certain directors of 1925 and 1935 and especially of the 1940's through the 1950's. Compare for example Erich von Stroheim and Jean Renoir or Orson Welles, or again Carl Theodore Dreyer and Robert Bresson. These more or less clear-cut affinities demonstrate first of all that the gap separating the 1920's and the 1930's can be bridged, and secondly that certain cinematic values actually carry over from the silent to the sound film and, above all, that it is less a matter of setting silence over against sound than of contrasting certain families of styles, certain basically different concepts of cinematographic expression.

Aware as I am that the limitations imposed on this study restrict me to a simplified and to that extent enfeebled presentation of my argument, and holding it to be less an objective statement than a working hypothesis, I will distinguish, in the cinema between 1920 and 1940, between two broad and opposing trends: those directors who put their faith in the image and those who put their faith in reality. By "image" I here mean, very broadly speaking, everything that the representation on the screen adds to the object there represented. This is a complex inheritance but it can be reduced essentially to two categories: those that relate to the plastics of the image and those that relate to the resources of montage, which, after all, is simply the ordering of images in time.

Under the heading "plastics" must be included the style of the sets, of the make-up, and, up to a point, even of the performance, to which we naturally add the lighting and, finally, the framing of the shot which gives us its composition. As regards montage, derived initially as we all know from the masterpieces of Griffith, we have the statement of Malraux in his *Psychologie du cinéma* that it was montage that gave birth to film as an art, setting it apart from mere animated photography, in short, creating a language.

The use of montage can be "invisible" and this was generally the case in the prewar classics of the American screen. Scenes were broken down just for one purpose, namely, to analyze an episode according to the material or dramatic logic of the scene. It is this logic which conceals the fact of the analysis, the mind of the spectator quite naturally accepting the viewpoints of the director which are justified by the geography of the action or the shifting emphasis of dramatic interest.

But the neutral quality of this "invisible" editing fails to make use of the full potential of montage. On the other hand these potentialities are clearly evident from the three processes generally known as parallel montage, accelerated montage, montage by attraction. In creating parallel montage, Griffith succeeded in conveying a sense of the simultaneity of two actions taking place at a geographical distance by means of alternating shots from each. In *La Roue* Abel Gance created the illusion of the steadily increasing speed of a locomotive without actually using any images of speed (indeed the wheel could have been turning on one spot) simply by a multiplicity of shots of ever-decreasing length.

Finally there is "montage by attraction," the creation of S. M. Eisenstein, and not so easily described as the others, but which may be roughly defined as the reenforcing of the meaning of one image by association with another image not necessarily part of the same episode—for example the fireworks display in *The General Line* following the image of the bull. In this extreme form, montage by attraction was rarely used even by its creator but one may consider as very near to it in principle the more commonly used ellipsis, comparison, or metaphor, examples of which are the throwing of stockings onto a chair at the foot of a bed, or the milk overflowing in H. G. Clouzot's *Quai des orfèvres*. There are of course a variety of possible combinations of these three processes.

Whatever these may be, one can say that they share that trait in common which constitutes the very definition of montage, namely, the creation of a sense or meaning not proper to the images themselves but derived exclusively from their juxtaposition. The well-known experiment of Kuleshov with the shot of Mozhukhin in which a smile was seen to change its significance according to the image that preceded it, sums up perfectly the properties of montage.

Montage as used by Kuleshov, Eisenstein, or Gance did not give us the event; it alluded to it. Undoubtedly they derived at least the greater part of the constituent elements from the reality they were describing but the final significance of the film was found to reside in the ordering of these elements much more than in their objective content.

The matter under recital, whatever the realism of the individual image, is born essentially from these relationships—Mozhukhin plus dead child equal pity—that is to say an abstract result, none of the concrete elements of which are to be found in the premises; maidens plus appletrees in bloom equal hope. The combinations are infinite. But the only thing they have in common is the fact that they suggest an idea by means of a metaphor or by an association of ideas. Thus between the scenario properly so-called, the ultimate object of the recital, and the image pure and simple, there is a relay station, a sort of aesthetic "transformer." The meaning is not in the image, it is in the shadow of the image projected by montage onto the field of consciousness of the spectator.

Let us sum up. Through the contents of the image and the resources of montage, the cinema has at its disposal a whole arsenal of means whereby to impose its interpretation of an event on the spectator. By the end of the silent film we can consider this arsenal to have been full. On the one side the Soviet cinema carried to its ultimate consequences the theory and practice of montage while the German school did every kind of violence to the plastics of the image by way of sets and lighting. Other cinemas count too besides the Russian and German, but whether in France or Sweden or the United States, it does not appear that the language of cinema was at a loss for ways of saying what it wanted to say. . . .

It seems to us that the decade from 1940 to 1950 marks a decisive step forward in the development of the language of the film. If we have appeared since 1930 to have lost sight of the trend of the silent film as illustrated particularly by Stroheim, F. W. Murnau, Robert Flaherty, and Dreyer,* it is for a purpose. It is not that this trend seems to us to have been halted by the talking film. On the contrary, we believe that it represented the richest vein of the so-called silent film and, precisely because it was not aesthetically tied to montage, but was indeed the only tendency that looked to the realism of sound as a natural development. On the other hand it is a fact that the talking film between 1930 and 1940 owes it virtually nothing save for the glorious and retrospectively prophetic exception of Jean Renoir. He alone in his searchings as a director prior to *La Règle du jeu* forced himself to look back beyond the resources provided by montage and so uncovered the secret of a film form that would permit everything to be said

---

* A trend which Bazin describes as realism achieved by making time and space literal realities and by the piling up of revealing realistic detail.

without chopping the world up into little fragments, that would reveal the hidden meanings in people and things without disturbing the unity natural to them.

It is not a question of thereby belittling the films of 1930 to 1940, a criticism that would not stand up in the face of the number of masterpieces, it is simply an attempt to establish the notion of a dialectic progress, the highest expression of which was found in the films of the 1940's. Undoubtedly, the talkie sounded the knell of a certain aesthetic of the language of film, but only wherever it had turned its back on its vocation in the service of realism. The sound film nevertheless did preserve the essentials of montage, namely discontinuous description and the dramatic analysis of action. What it turned its back on was metaphor and symbol in exchange for the illusion of objective presentation. The expressionism of montage has virtually disappeared but the relative realism of the kind of cutting that flourished around 1937 implied a congenital limitation which escaped us so long as it was perfectly suited to its subject matter. Thus American comedy reached its peak within the framework of a form of editing in which the realism of the time played no part. Dependent on logic for its effects, like vaudeville and plays on words, entirely conventional in its moral and sociological content, American comedy had everything to gain, in strict line-by-line progression, from the rhythmic resources of classical editing.

Undoubtedly it is primarily with the Stroheim-Murnau trend—almost totally eclipsed from 1930 to 1940—that the cinema has more or less consciously linked up once more over the last ten years. But it has no intention of limiting itself simply to keeping this trend alive. It draws from it the secret of the regeneration of realism in storytelling and thus of becoming capable once more of bringing together real time, in which things exist, along with the duration of the action, for which classical editing had insidiously substituted mental and abstract time. On the other hand, so far from wiping out once and for all the conquests of montage, this reborn realism gives them a body of reference and a meaning. It is only an increased realism of the image that can support the abstraction of montage. The stylistic repertory of a director such as Hitchcock, for example, ranged from the power inherent in the dénouement as such, to superimpositions, to large close-ups. But the close-ups of Hitchcock are not the same as those of C. B. de Mille in *The Cheat* (1915). They are just one type of figure, among others, of his style. In other words, in the silent days, montage evoked what the director wanted to say; in the editing of 1938, it described it. Today we can say that at last the director writes in film. The image—its plastic composition and the way it is set in time, because it is founded on a much higher degree of realism— has at its disposal more means of manipulating reality and of modifying it from within. The film-maker is no longer the competitor of the painter and the playwright, he is, at last, the equal of the novelist.

EXERCISES

on film and rhetoric

1. Bazin sees sound films developing in two directions, which he defines as image and reality. How does the rhetoric of film adapt itself to image? to reality?
2. How according to Bazin does 1940–1950 mark "a decisive step forward in the development of the language of the film"?
3. How do the films of 1930–1940 represent a plateau in rhetorical development?
4. Bazin concludes his essay with a description of the highest level of rhetorical excellence, that found in modern films. Define that level in your own words, and give examples.

on film

1. Discuss films you have seen which exemplify the rhetoric of image; of reality.
2. Which in your opinion are better films? Which are more entertaining? Do "better" and "more entertaining" necessarily go hand in hand?

on structure and language

1. Bazin's essay traces step by step the growth and development of film as a result of the advent of sound. Outline the essay and then comment on the logic of his reasoning.
2. How does Bazin define invisible, parallel, and accelerated montage? montage by attraction?
3. According to Bazin, "The talkie sounded the knell of a certain aesthetic of the language of the film." How does he define the aesthetic of the silent film? How would you define it?

THE RHETORIC OF HITCHCOCK'S THRILLERS

O. B. Hardison

We can start from the axiom that Alfred Hitchcock is one of the great professionals in the movie business—probably the greatest. I use the word professional in its most favorable sense: movies are entertainment, and no one entertains more and more consistently than Hitchcock. What the Lincoln Continental is to the Fairlane 500 the Hitchcock film is to the standard production-model Hollywood thriller. The public recognizes this. Hitchcock is one of a very few producers whose name is more important at the box office than the names of his stars. But professionalism has its limits, too. Nobody would seriously compare Hitchcock to a dozen directors and producers who have used the film medium as an art form. Eisenstein, Chaplin, Ford, Bergman, Olivier, Fellini—the list could be expanded—have qualities undreamed of in the world of cops and robbers and pseudo-Freudian melodrama, which is the world where Hitchcock reigns supreme.

Consider the professional a rhetorician. The purpose of art, says Aristotle, is to give pleasure. Not any kind of pleasure, but the sort that comes from learning. The experience of art is an insight, an illumination of the action being imitated. Rhetoric, on the other hand, is oriented toward the marketplace. Its purpose is not illumination but persuasion, and its governing concept is that the work produced must be adjusted to the mind of the audience. Rhetorical art succeeds by saying what the audience has secretly known (or wanted to know) all along. Its language is disguised flattery, its norm fantasy, and its symbols surrogates for unconscious cravings. Given the passionate desire that everyone has to suspend disbelief, almost anything works, as witness the comic book and the exploits of Mike Hammer and James Bond; but some kinds of rhetoric work better than others. Just as there is good and bad art, there is good and bad rhetoric.

A work of art produces insight. To experience it is to become different. If not wiser, at least more human. Since a work of rhetoric is shaped by its audience, it cannot *cause* insight, but its data, when analyzed, can lead to certain useful understandings. We study a work of art aesthetically, but the study of professional entertainment is a branch of sociology. Professional entertainment, that is to say, goes according to formula. A formula is simply a way of doing things that works—that has been tried and found successful in the marketplace and is therefore repeated as long as it retains its appeal. Seen in this way, a formula is a psychological category created by social and economic conditions, usually tensions. Crude rhetorical art, like that of Mickey Spillane or Ian Fleming, is almost pure formula, and it is fantastic because it approximates the mode of uninhibited daydream. Adolescents, by and large, can take their fantasy straight. They provide the economic base for the comic book industry and its relatives. Grown-ups, on the other hand, want their fantasy to be credible simply because they so desperately want it to be true, and it is their needs that both shape and support Hitchcock's work. To put it differently, adults can ejoy Hitchcock without being *ashamed,* whereas they feel apologetic or vaguely guilty about enjoying what their children like. Intellectuals, by the way, tend to be the most inhibited of all groups. In the thirties movies were definitely non-U, and one still occasionally meets individuals who refuse to buy television sets. The current fad for formula entertainment with built-in satre—*The Man from U.N.C.L.E. or Batman*—shows that the predicament of the intellectual is widespread and quite serious. It is, in effect, a mild schizophrenia, since the entertainment it summons into being must provide both a fantasy to which one can surrender and a hostile critique of this fantasy. The values that the individual has learned are at war—and the psychological cost of this war should not be underestimated—with the needs that he has inherited from his culture.

How does one become a master rhetorician? There are doubtless any number of ways, but two or three things definitely help. First, it is good to know your audience. It is best, in fact, to have been one of them. There is a famous passage in "The Art of Fiction" in which Henry James tells how a lady artist (I believe it was George Eliot) was able to deduce the whole milieu of French Protestantism from a glimpse of some young Protestants finishing a meal with their *pasteur*; but James was talking about art and, in particular, about a moment of insight. A rhetorician does not need moments of insight. To the extent that a moment of insight suggests departure from formula, it may even prove an embarrassment. What the rhetorician needs is a sense of the formulas themselves, and this sense will be surest if he has grown up amid the conditions that produced them. Being ingrained, it will seem to emerge spontaneously in later life as talent. But talent is not enough. It must be shaped and filed by experience, and for the rhetorician the only relevant experience is the marketplace. Mastery of rhetoric, like mastery of any other skill, comes slowly. The rhetorician needs a long career allowing for experimentation, some failure, but mostly a polishing and bringing to perfection of the formulas that work and a pruning away of the ones that do not.

EXERCISES

on film and rhetoric

1. Rhetoric, says Hardison, is "oriented toward the marketplace." Explain what he means by this and comment.
2. What differences does Hardison find between "crude rhetorical art" and the art of a "master rhetorician"? What factors make Hitchcock a master rhetorician?
3. Compare Hardison's definition of "rhetoric" with Malraux's "expression" and with Bazin's "languages of image and reality."

on film

1. Discuss films you have seen which exemplify crude rhetorical art.
2. Discuss films which exemplify masterful rhetoric. Which type do you prefer? Why?

on structure and language

1. The line of development of this essay is based upon special assumptions and definitions set forth by the author. How many of these do you find? Comment upon each from your own point of view.
2. How does Hardison define the experience of art?
3. Would he consider Hitchcock's films to be art?

THE BRIDE COMES TO YELLOW SKY

Stephen Crane

I

The great Pullman was whirling onward with such dignity of motion that a glance from the window seemed simply to prove that the plains of Texas were pouring eastward. Vast flats of green grass, dull-hued spaces of mesquit and cactus, little groups of frame houses, woods of light and tender trees, all were sweeping into the east, sweeping over the horizon, a precipice.

A newly married pair had boarded this coach at San Antonio. The man's face was reddened from many days in the wind and sun, and a direct result of his new black clothes was that his brick-colored hands were constantly performing in a most conscious fashion. From time to time he looked down respectfully at his attire. He sat with a hand on each knee, like a man waiting in a barber's shop. The glances he devoted to other passengers were furtive and shy.

The bride was not pretty, nor was she very young. She wore a dress of blue cashmere, with small reservations of velvet here and there, and with steel buttons abounding. She continually twisted her head to regard her puff sleeves, very stiff, straight, and high. They embarrassed her. It was quite apparent that she had cooked, and that she expected to cook, dutifully. The blushes caused by the careless scrutiny of some passengers as she had entered the car were strange to see upon this plain, under-class countenance, which was drawn in placid, almost emotionless lines.

They were evidently very happy. "Ever been in a parlor-car before?" he asked, smiling with delight.

"No," she answered; "I never was. It's fine, ain't it?"

"Great! And then after a while we'll go forward to the diner, and get a big lay-out. Finest meal in the world. Charge a dollar."

"Oh, do they?" cried the bride. "Charge a dollar? Why, that's too much—for us—ain't it, Jack?"

"Not this trip, anyhow," he answered bravely. "We're going to go the whole thing."

Later he explained to her about the trains. "You see, it's a thousand miles from one end of Texas to the other; and this train runs right across it, and never stops but four times." He had the pride of an owner. He pointed out to her the dazzling fittings of the coach; and in truth her eyes opened wider as she contemplated the sea-green figured velvet, the shining brass, silver, and glass, the wood that gleamed as darkly brilliant as the surface of a pool of oil. At one end a bronze figure sturdily held a support for a separated chamber, and at convenient places on the ceiling were frescos in olive and silver.

To the minds of the pair, their surroundings reflected the glory of their marriage that morning in San Antonio; this was the environment of their new estate; and the man's face in particular beamed with an elation that made him appear ridiculous to the negro porter. This individual at times surveyed them from afar with an amused and superior grin. On other occasions he bullied them with skill in ways that did not make it exactly plain to them that they were being bullied. He subtly used all the manners of the most unconquerable kind of snobbery. He oppressed them; but of this oppression they had small knowledge, and they speedily forgot that infrequently a number of travelers covered them with stares of derisive enjoyment. Historically there was supposed to be something infinitely humorous in their situation.

"We are due in Yellow Sky at 3:42," he said, looking tenderly into her eyes.

"Oh, are we?" she said, as if she had not been aware of it. To evince surprise at her husband's statement was part of her wifely amiability. She took from a pocket a little silver watch; and as she held it before her, and stared at it with a frown of attention, the new husband's face shone.

"I bought it in San Anton' from a friend of mine," he told her gleefully.

"It's seventeen minutes past twelve," she said, looking up at him with a kind of shy and clumsy coquetry. A passenger, noting this play, grew excessively sardonic, and winked at himself in one of the numerous mirrors.

At last they went to the dining-car. Two rows of negro waiters, in glowing white suits, surveyed their entrance with the interest, and also the equanimity, of men who had been forewarned. The pair fell to the lot of a waiter who happened to feel pleasure in steering them through their meal. He viewed them with the manner of a fatherly pilot, his countenance radiant with benevolence. The patronage, entwined with the ordinary deference, was not plain to them. And yet, as they returned to their coach, they showed in their faces a sense of escape.

To the left, miles down a long purple slope, was a little ribbon of mist where moved the keening Rio Grande. The train was approaching it at an angle, and the apex was Yellow Sky. Presently it was apparent that, as the distance from Yellow Sky grew shorter, the husband became commensurately restless. His brick-red hands were more insistent in their prominence. Occasionally he was even rather absent-minded and faraway when the bride leaned forward and addressed him.

As a matter of truth, Jack Potter was beginning to find the shadow of a deed weigh upon him like a leaden slab. He, the town marshal of Yellow Sky, a man known, liked, and feared in his corner, a prominent person, had gone to San Antonio to meet a girl he believed he loved, and there, after the usual prayers, had actually induced her to marry him, without consulting Yellow Sky for any part of the transaction. He was now bringing his bride before an innocent and unsuspecting community.

Of course people in Yellow Sky married as it pleased them, in accordance with a general custom; but such was Potter's thought of his duty to his friends, or of their idea of his duty, or of an unspoken form which does not control men in these matters, that he felt he was heinous. He had committed an extraordinary crime.

Face to face with this girl in San Antonio, and spurred by his sharp impulse, he had gone headlong over all the social hedges. At San Antonio he was like a man hidden in the dark. A knife to sever any friendly duty, any form, was easy to his hand in that remote city. But the hour of Yellow Sky—the hour of daylight—was approaching.

He knew full well that his marriage was an important thing to his town. It could only be exceeded by the burning of the new hotel. His friends could not forgive him. Frequently he had reflected on the advisability of telling them by telegraph, but a new cowardice had been upon him. He feared to do it. And now the train was hurrying him toward a scene of amazement, glee, and reproach. He glanced out of the window at the line of haze swinging slowly in toward the train.

Yellow Sky had a kind of brass band, which played painfully, to the delight of the populace. He laughed without heart as he thought of it. If the citizens could dream of his prospective arrival with his bride, they would parade the band at the station and escort them, amid cheers and laughing congratulations, to his adobe home.

He resolved that he would use all the devices of speed and plains-craft in making the journey from the station to his house. Once within that safe citadel, he could issue some sort of a vocal bulletin, and then not go among the citizens until they had time to wear off a little of their enthusiasm.

The bride looked anxiously at him. "What's worrying you, Jack?"

He laughed again. "I'm not worrying, girl; I'm only thinking of Yellow Sky."

She flushed in comprehension.

A sense of mutual guilt invaded their minds and developed a finer tenderness. They looked at each other with eyes softly aglow. But Potter often laughed the same nervous laugh; the flush upon the bride's face seemed quite permanent.

The traitor to the feelings of Yellow Sky narrowly watched the speeding landscape. "We're nearly there," he said.

Presently the porter came and announced the proximity of Potter's home. He held a brush in his hand, and, with all his airy superiority gone, he brushed Potter's new clothes as the latter slowly turned this way and that way. Potter fumbled out a coin and gave it to the porter, as he had seen others do. It was a heavy and muscle-bound business, as that of a man shoeing his first horse.

The porter took their bag, and as the train began to slow they moved forward to the hooded platform of the car. Presently the two engines and their long string of coaches rushed into the station of Yellow Sky.

"They have to take water here," said Potter, from a con-stricted throat and in mournful cadence, as one announcing death. Before the train stopped his eye had swept the length of the plat-form, and he was glad and astonished to see there was none upon it but the station-agent, who, with a slightly hurried and anxious air, was walking toward the water-tanks. When the train had halted, the porter alighted first, and placed in position a little tem-porary step.

"Come on, girl," said Potter, hoarsely. As he helped her down they each laughed on a false note. He took the bag from the negro, and bade his wife cling to his arm. As they slunk rapidly away, his hang-dog glance perceived that they were unloading the two trunks, and also that the station-agent, far ahead near the baggage-car, had turned and was running toward him, making gestures. He laughed, and groaned as he laughed, when he noted the first effect of his marital bliss upon Yellow Sky. He gripped his wife's arm firmly to his side, and they fled. Behind them the porter stood, chuckling fatuously.

II

The California express on the Southern Railway was due at Yellow Sky in twenty-one minutes. There were six men at the bar of the Weary Gentleman Saloon. One was a drummer, who talked a great deal and rapidly; three were Texans, who did not care to talk at that time; and two were Mexican sheep-herders, who did not talk as a general practice in the Weary Gentleman Saloon. The bar-keeper's dog lay on the board walk that crossed in front of the door. His head was on his paws, and he glanced drowsily here and there with the constant vigilance of a dog that is kicked on occa-sion. Across the sandy street were some vivid green grass-plots, so wonderful in appearance, amid the sands that burned near them in a blazing sun, that they caused a doubt in the mind. They exactly resembled the grass mats used to represent lawns on the stage. At the cooler end of the railway station, a man without a coat sat in a tilted chair and smoked his pipe. The fresh-cut bank of the Rio Grande circled near the town, and there could be seen beyond it a great plum-colored plain of mesquit.

Save for the busy drummer and his companions in the saloon, Yellow Sky was dozing. The new-comer leaned gracefully upon the bar, and recited many tales with the confidence of a bard who has come upon a new field.

"—and at the moment that the old man fell down-stairs with the bureau in his arms, the old woman was coming up with two scuttles of coal, and of course—"

The drummer's tale was interrupted by a young man who suddenly appeared in the open door. He cried: "Scratchy Wilson's drunk, and has turned loose with both hands." The two Mexicans at once set down their glasses and faded out of the rear entrance of the saloon.

The drummer, innocent and jocular, answered: "All right, old man. S'pose he has? Come in and have a drink, anyhow."

But the information had made such an obvious cleft in every skull in the room that the drummer was obliged to see its importance. All had become instantly solemn. "Say," said he, mystified, "what is this?" His three companions made the introductory gesture of eloquent speech; but the young man at the door forestalled them.

"It means, my friend," he answered, as he came into the saloon, "that for the next two hours this town won't be a health resort."

The barkeeper went to the door, and locked and barred it; reaching out of the window, he pulled in heavy wooden shutters, and barred them. Immediately a solemn, chapel-like gloom was upon the place. The drummer was looking from one to another.

"But say," he cried, "what is this, anyhow? You don't mean there is going to be a gun-fight?"

"Don't know whether there'll be a fight or not," answered one man, grimly; "but there'll be some shootin'—some good shootin'."

The young man who had warned them waved his hand. "Oh,

there'll be a fight fast enough, if any one wants it. Anybody can get a fight out there in the street. There's a fight just waiting."

The drummer seemed to be swayed between the interest of a foreigner and a perception of personal danger.

"What did you say his name was?" he asked.

"Scratchy Wilson," they answered in chorus.

"And will he kill anybody? What are you going to do? Does this happen often? Does he rampage around like this once a week or so? Can he break in that door?"

"No; he can't break down that door," replied the barkeeper. "He's tried it three times. But when he comes you'd better lay down on the floor, stranger. He's dead sure to shoot at it, and a bullet may come through."

Thereafter the drummer kept a strict eye upon the door. The time had not yet been called for him to hug the floor, but, as a minor precaution, he sidled near to the wall. "Will he kill anybody?" he said again.

The men laughed low and scornfully at the question.

"He's out to shoot, and he's out for trouble. Don't see any good in experimentin' with him."

"But what do you do in a case like this? What do you do?"

A man responded: "Why, he and Jack Potter—"

"But," in chorus the other men interrupted, "Jack Potter's in San Anton'."

"Well, who is he? What's he got to do with it?"

"Oh, he's the town marshal. He goes out and fights Scratchy when he gets on one of these tears."

"Wow!" said the drummer, mopping his brow. "Nice job he's got."

The voices had toned away to mere whisperings. The drummer wished to ask further questions, which were born of an increasing anxiety and bewilderment; but when he attempted them, the men merely looked at him in irritation and motioned him to remain silent. A tense waiting hush was upon them. In the deep shadows of the room their eyes shone as they listened for sounds from the street. One man made three gestures at the barkeeper; and the latter, moving like a ghost, handed him a glass and a bottle. The man poured a full glass of whisky, and set down the bottle noiselessly. He gulped the whisky in a swallow, and turned again toward the door in immovable silence. The drummer saw that the barkeeper, without a sound, had taken a Winchester from beneath the bar. Later he saw this individual beckoning to him, so he tiptoed across the room.

"You better come with me back of the bar."

"No, thanks," said the drummer, perspiring; "I'd rather be where I can make a break for the back door."

Whereupon the man of bottles made a kindly but peremptory gesture. The drummer obeyed it, and, finding himself seated on a box with his head below the level of the bar, balm was laid upon his soul at sight of various zinc and copper fittings that bore a resemblance to armor-plate. The barkeeper took a seat comfortably upon an adjacent box.

"You see," he whispered, "this here Scratchy Wilson is a wonder with a gun—a perfect wonder; and when he goes on the war-trail, we hunt our holes—naturally. He's about the last one of the old gang that used to hang out along the river here. He's a terror when he's drunk. When he's sober he's all right—kind of simple—wouldn't hurt a fly—nicest fellow in town. But when he's drunk—whoo!"

There were periods of stillness. "I wish Jack Potter was back from San Anton'," said the barkeeper. "He shot Wilson up once—in the leg—and he would sail in and pull out the kinks in this thing."

Presently they heard from a distance the sound of a shot, followed by three wild yowls. It instantly removed a bond from the men in the darkened saloon. There was a shuffling of feet. They looked at each other. "Here he comes," they said.

III

A man in a maroon-colored flannel shirt, which had been purchased for purposes of decoration, and made principally by some Jewish women on the East Side of New York, rounded a corner and walked into the middle of the main street of Yellow Sky. In either hand the man held a long, heavy, blue-black revolver. Often he yelled, and these cries rang through a semblance of a deserted village, shrilly flying over the roofs in a volume that seemed to have no relation to the ordinary vocal strength of a man. It was as if the surrounding stillness formed the arch of a tomb over him. These cries of ferocious challenge rang against walls of silence. And his boots had red tops with gilded imprints, of the kind beloved in winter by little sledding boys on the hillsides of New England.

The man's face flamed in a rage begot of whisky. His eyes, rolling, and yet keen for ambush, hunted the still doorways and windows. He walked with the creeping movement of the midnight cat. As it occurred to him, he roared menacing information. The long revolvers in his hands were as easy as straws; they were moved with an electric swiftness. The little fingers of each hand played sometimes in a musician's way. Plain from the low collar of the shirt, the cords of his neck straightened and sank, straightened and sank, as passion moved him. The only sounds were his terrible invitations. The calm adobes preserved their demeanor at the passing of this small thing in the middle of the street.

There was no offer of fight—no offer of fight. The man called to the sky. There were no attractions. He bellowed and fumed and swayed his revolvers here and everywhere.

The dog of the barkeeper of the Weary Gentleman Saloon had not appreciated the advance of events. He yet lay dozing in front of his master's door. At sight of the dog, the man paused and raised his revolver humorously. At sight of the man, the dog sprang up and walked diagonally away, with a sullen head, and growling. The man yelled, and the dog broke into a gallop. As it was about to enter an alley, there was a loud noise, a whistling, and something spat the ground directly before it. The dog screamed, and, wheeling in terror, galloped headlong in a new direction. Again there was a noise, a whistling, and sand was kicked viciously before it. Fear-stricken, the dog turned and flurried like an animal in a pen. The man stood laughing, his weapons at his hips.

Ultimately the man was attracted by the closed door of the Weary Gentleman Saloon. He went to it, and, hammering with a revolver, demanded drink.

The door remaining imperturbable, he picked a bit of paper from the walk, and nailed it to the framework with a knife. He then turned his back contemptuously upon this popular resort, and, walking to the opposite side of the street and spinning there on his heel quickly and lithely, fired at the bit of paper. He missed it by a half-inch. He swore at himself, and went away. Later he comfortably fusilladed the windows of his most intimate friend. The man was playing with this town; it was a toy for him.

But still there was no offer of fight. The name of Jack Potter, his ancient antagonist, entered his mind, and he concluded that it would be a glad thing if he should go to Potter's house, and by bombardment induce him to come out and fight. He moved in the direction of his desire, chanting Apache scalp-music.

When he arrived at it, Potter's house presented the same still front as had the other adobes. Taking up a strategic position, the man howled a challenge. But this house regarded him as might a great stone god. It gave no sign. After a decent wait, the man howled further challenges, mingling with them wonderful epithets.

Presently there came the spectacle of a man churning himself into deepest rage over the immobility of a house. He fumed at it as the winter wind attacks a prairie cabin in the North. To the distance there should have gone the sound of a tumult like the fighting of two hundred Mexicans. As necessity bade him, he paused for breath or to reload his revolvers.

IV

Potter and his bride walked sheepishly and with speed. Sometimes they laughed together shamefacedly and low.

"Next corner, dear," he said finally.

They put forth the efforts of a pair walking bowed against a strong wind. Potter was about to raise a finger to point the first appearance of the new home when, as they circled the corner, they came face to face with a man in a maroon-colored shirt, who was feverishly pushing cartridges into a large revolver. Upon the instant the man dropped his revolver to the ground, and, like lightning, whipped another from its holster. The second weapon was aimed at the bridegroom's chest.

There was a silence. Potter's mouth seemed to be merely a grave for his tongue. He exhibited an instinct to at once loosen his arm from the woman's grip, and he dropped the bag to the sand. As for the bride, her face had gone as yellow as old cloth. She was a slave to hideous rites, gazing at the apparitional snake.

The two men faced each other at a distance of three paces. He of the revolver smiled with a new and quiet ferocity.

"Tried to sneak up on me," he said. "Tried to sneak up on me!" His eyes grew more baleful. As Potter made a slight movement, the man thrust his revolver venomously forward. "No; don't you do it, Jack Potter. Don't you move a finger toward a gun just yet. Don't you move an eyelash. The time has come for me to settle with you, and I'm goin' to do it my own way, and loaf along with no interferin'. So if you don't want a gun bent on you, just mind what I tell you."

Potter looked at his enemy. "I ain't got a gun on me, Scratchy," he said. "Honest, I ain't." He was stiffening and steadying, but yet somewhere at the back of his mind a vision of the Pullman floated: the sea-green figured velvet, the shining brass, silver, and glass, the wood that gleamed as darkly brilliant as the surface of a pool of oil—all the glory of the marriage, the environment of the new estate. "You know I fight when it comes to fighting, Scratchy Wilson; but I ain't got a gun on me. You'll have to do all the shootin' yourself."

His enemy's face went livid. He stepped forward, and lashed his weapon to and fro before Potter's chest. "Don't you tell me you ain't got no gun on you, you whelp. Don't tell me no lie like that. There ain't a man in Texas ever seen you without no gun. Don't take me for no kid." His eyes blazed with light, and his throat worked like a pump.

"I ain't takin' you for no kid," answered Potter. His heels had not moved an inch backward. "I'm takin' you for a —— fool. I tell you I ain't got a gun, and I ain't. If you're goin' to shoot me up, you better begin now; you'll never get a chance like this again."

So much enforced reasoning had told on Wilson's rage; he was calmer. "If you ain't got a gun, why ain't you got a gun?" he sneered. "Been to Sunday-school?"

"I ain't got a gun because I've just come from San Anton' with my wife. I'm married," said Potter. "And if I'd thought there was going to be any galoots like you prowling around when I brought my wife home, I'd had a gun, and don't you forget it."

"Married!" said Scratchy, not at all comprehending.

"Yes, married. I'm married," said Potter, distinctly.

"Married?" said Scratchy. Seemingly for the first time, he

saw the drooping, drowning woman at the other man's side. "No!"
he said. He was like a creature allowed a glimpse of another
world. He moved a pace backward, and his arm, with the revolver,
dropped to his side. "Is this the lady?" he asked.

"Yes; this is the lady," answered Potter.

There was another period of silence.

"Well," said Wilson at last, slowly, "I s'pose it's all off now."

"It's all off if you say so, Scratchy. You know I didn't make
the trouble." Potter lifted his valise.

"Well, I 'low it's off, Jack," said Wilson. He was looking at the
ground. "Married!" He was not a student of chivalry; it was
merely that in the presence of this foreign condition he was a
simple child of the earlier plains. He picked up his starboard
revolver, and, placing both weapons in their holsters, he went
away. His feet made funnel-shaped tracks in the heavy sand.

THE BRIDE COMES TO YELLOW SKY
(shooting script)

James Agee

FADE IN
EXT. MAIN STREET OF YELLOW SKY—DUSK

Late summer dusk; sound of church bell O.S. PULL DOWN onto Potter's little home, of which the second story is a jail—barred windows. Jack Potter comes out his door, dressed for travel, carrying a bag. He walks a few steps, then glances back around at his house.

PRISONER (in upper window) So long, Marshal. Don't do nothing I wouldn't do.

POTTER Don't you do nothing I wouldn't, s'more like it. You lock yourself in right after mealtimes.

PRISONER You can trust me, Marshal.

POTTER I don't need to. I done tole Laura Lee to keep an eye on you. (pause; shyly) Well, so long. I'll be back in a couple of days.

He walks away.

PRISONER (calling after) Give my howdy to the gals in San Antone!

POTTER You do that when you git out. I ain't no hand fer it.

PRISONER Oh, I doan know, Marshall. They tell me still waters run deep.

Potter doesn't answer. He walks on away.

DOLLY SHOT *—POTTER AND DEACON SMEED

Deacon Smeed falls in with him. CAMERA DOLLIES along with them. The following dialogue interrupted two or three times by eminently respectable people converging on the church. All treat Potter respectfully but a little remotely.

SMEED Evening, Mr. Potter.

POTTER Evening, Deacon.

SMEED Leaving town so soon again?

POTTER It's been most two months.

SMEED Oh *has* it indeed, indeed. Hm. And what's going to happen to your prisoner, if I may ask?

POTTER Laura Lee's gonna take care of him.

SMEED Mrs. Bates? (Potter nods) She'll bring him his meals?

POTTER He'll let himself out for 'em.

SMEED Do you think that—ah—looks right?

POTTER (quietly) Afraid I ain't worryin' *how* it looks, Deacon. It's the easiest way, and you know as well as I do, he ain't gonna make no trouble.

SMEED I'm afraid you don't care how *anything* looks, Mr. Potter.

POTTER Oh now, Deacon, don't start on that church business again!

SMEED I'm sorry, Marshal, but every respectable person in Yellow Sky agrees with me. If only for appearance' sake, you ought to come to church.

POTTER Looky here, Deacon. We never did get nowheres with that argument, and we never will. I ain't got nothin' against churchgoin'; I just don't hold with it fer myself.

SMEED And then all these mysterious trips to San Antonio lately—

They pause in front of church.

POTTER Now looky here, Deacon—if you mean light women and such, you know I ain't a man to fool around with them.

SMEED Oh, you *misconstrue me*, Marshal, *indeed* you do. But . . . Caesar's wife, you know . . .

The church bell stops ringing.

---

* A dolly is a wheeled vehicle for a camera. Dollying means moving the camera so that it accompanies the action.

POTTER How's that?

SMEED She must be *above* suspicion.

POTTER Well, who's suspicious? You?

SMEED Of course not, Marshal. Perish the thought. Only you never *say* *why* you're going to San Antonio.

POTTER (after a pause) Just business. Goodnight, Deacon.

SMEED Goodnight, Mr. Potter.

Potter walks ahead; he blows out his cheeks; his eyes focus gratefully on:

VIEWPOINT SHOT *—"THE WEARY GENTLEMAN" SALOON   CUT TO
POTTER AS BEFORE

He checks his watch and speeds up out of shot.   CUT TO

MEDIUM SHOT—DEACON

He pauses at the church door, sees Potter enter the "Weary Gentleman", and goes into church, over sound of first hymn.   CUT TO

INT. "WEARY GENTLEMAN"—DUSK

There is a typical western bar, behind which Laura Lee, a woman in her fifties, is presiding as bartender. CAMERA PANS † Potter to bar. He leaves his bag on a table near the door.

POTTER Evenin', Laura Lee.

LAURA LEE (behind bar) Hi, Jack.

JASPER Jack.

ED Howdy, Marshal.

POTTER Jasper,—Ed.

ED Leavin' town again?

POTTER That's right.

ED San Antone?

POTTER (nods; drinks) Laura Lee, you tell Frank no drinks, no foolin' around. Just come right straight here and eat and get right

---

* A long prespective shot which establishes the whereabouts of all the elements of a scene.
  † Horizontal camera movement in order to cover a wide area.

back again. 'Cause it's got the Deacon bothered, him goin' out at all.

LAURA LEE Aw, Smeed. I tell you, Jack, when you waded in here and cleaned the town up, it wasn't just a favor you done us. Everything's gettin' too blame respectable.

POTTER It was my job.

LAURA LEE I don't hold it agin you. But if things get too tame around here, you'll up an' quit town fer good.

POTTER Uh, uh. I aim to be buried here. Besides, long as ole Scratchy busts loose now an' then, things won't never get *too* tame.

OVER mention of Scratchy, Laura Lee's eyes focus on something o.s.

LAURA LEE (a little absently) Here's *to* 'im.

Potter's eyes follow hers.

MEDIUM SHOT—ALONG BAR—FROM THEIR ANGLE

A half-finished glass of beer, no customer.

CLOSE SHOT—POTTER

A glance from the beer to Laura Lee, a look of slightly concerned inquiry, meaning, "Is that Scratchy's?"

CLOSE SHOT—LAURA LEE
nodding.

LAURA LEE It don't work holding him to nothing, Jack. I figured maybe beer, on 'lowance . . .

POTTER Don't hear me hollerin', do you? It's worth tryin'. Only thing bothers me is if I'm out of town.

LAURA LEE He ain't due for another tear yet.
POTTER Ain't sure we can count on him hittin' 'em regular, no more. He's gettin' rouncier all the time.

JASPER (breaking a pause) What ye doin' in San Antone, Jack?

Laura Lee gives him a cold glance.

POTTER Just a business trip.

OVER this last, Scratchy comes in through a side door and up to bar, to a half-finished glass of beer.

POTTER Howdy, Scratchy.

Scratchy doesn't answer. Potter and others are quietly amused.

LAURA LEE What's wrong with ye, Scratchy? Cat got yer tongue?

Scratchy drinks glass down.

LAURA LEE (continuing) Yer last one tonight. Rather wait fer it?

SCRATCHY Just draw me my beer.

POTTER Ain't still sore, are ye, Scratchy?

SCRATCHY You know it was all in fun. What d'ye go an' plug me fer?

POTTER 'Tain't fun, Scratchy. Not skeerin' the daylights out o' folks
    that ain't used to gun-play.

SCRATCHY You're a fine one to talk about gun-play. Mean, sneakin'
    skunk!

POTTER Sneakin'? It was fair and above board, like it always is.

LAURA LEE He just beat ye to the draw, an' you know it.

SCRATCHY That don't make my leg no happier.

POTTER Mendin' a'right, Scratchy?

SCRATCHY Oh, *I* git around.

POTTER Just mind where ye git *to*, that's all I ask.

SCRATCHY Next time, I'll make *you* dance.

POTTER Better not be no next time. 'Cause next time, instead o' the
    meat o' the leg, I might have to pop you in the kneecap.

SCRATCHY You wouldn't do that.

POTTER I wouldn't want to. But I might have to Scratchy, just to learn
    you. You don't know it but you're gettin' dangersome when
    you drink, lately.

SCRATCHY Me—dangersome? A good man with a gun's a safe man
    with a gun, an' I'm the best they is.

LAURA LEE When you're in yer likker, yeah. But you don't drink fer
    fun no more, Scratchy. You kinda go out o' yer head.

POTTER That's right, Scratchy. One o' these days you're gonna shoot
    to kill, an' swing fer it, an 'then all of us'll be sorry.

SCRATCHY I don't need to kill nobody more—I got my notches, an' to
    spare—(he pats his gun)

POTTER That was all right, agin the kind o' varmints that used to be
    around here in the old days—You come in right handy. Sort

of a scavenger, like a turkey-buzzard. But you can't go shootin' up law-abidin' citizens an' git away with it.

SCRATCHY (with extreme contempt) Who wants to shoot a law-abidin' citizen!

UNDER the above, Potter finishes his drink, pays, starts out.

POTTER Well . . .

SCRATCHY You leavin' town again?

POTTER 'Bye, Laura Lee. See you day after tomorrow. (to Scatchy) You watch yer drinkin' while I'm gone.

SCRATCHY I'll save it all up fer you, Jack. 'Tain't nobody else is wuth the hangover.

Potter exits.

JASPER Reckon what he's up to, all these trips to San Antone?

LAURA LEE Never you mind, it's his business.

ED You ain't sweet on Jack, are ye, Laura Lee?

LAURA LEE (a cold look at him) Only man I ever was, he's in his grave ten year.

SHE HEARS the train draw out, pours and drinks.

LAURA LEE (continuing) But if I was, that's the only one *man* enough since.

CUT TO

INT. DAY COACH—CLOSE SHOT—POTTER—NIGHT

He finishes rolling a cigarette, lights it and, elbow on windowsill, settles into the tired posture of night travel, gazing out of window. CAMERA SLOWLY PANS, losing his face, then his reflected face, squaring on the dark land flooding past.

FADE OUT

FADE IN
INT. PARLOR CAR

CAMERA LOOKS SQUARELY through window at fast-moving daylit land, reversing direction of preceding shot; then in a SLOW PAN picks up the reflection of Bride's face in window; then the face itself; then PULLS AWAY into:

TWO-SHOT *—POTTER AND BRIDE

For a few moments we merely HOLD on them, as though this were a provincial wedding portrait of the period. (Circa 1895) He has an outdoor clumsiness in his new suit, which is a shade tight and small for him. Her very new-looking hat and dress are in touchingly ambitious, naive taste.

Between their heads, in the seat just behind theirs, the head of a "sophisticated" man turns slowly, slyly watching, filled with patronizing amusement. Potter, gradually aware, turns and looks him in the eye; the guy shrivels and turns away fast.

HOLD on Bride and Potter a moment. Bride looks at something o.s.†

MEDIUM SHOT–TWO WOMEN

watch her, whispering and giggling.

MEDIUM SHOT—CENTERING POTTER AND BRIDE—FROM VIEWPOINT OF WOMEN

The Bride smiles very sweetly, looking straight into the CAMERA, and we HEAR O.S. a more intense giggling and whispering and a few inaudible words.

The Bride looks a little puzzled, her smile fading; then she smiles again, sure there can be no malice toward her; then looks straight ahead of her. Both are glowing and intensely shy. His large, spread hands englobe his knees; hers are discreet in her lap. He stares straight ahead, his eyes a little unfocused. She keeps looking around. With almost the manner of a little girl, she draws a deep breath and utters a quiet sigh of joy, at the same time slightly raising, then relaxing, the hands on her lap. He hears her happy sigh; he looks at her; he watches her shyly and with a certain awe. He slowly shakes his head in the manner of one who can scarcely believe his good fortune. He lifts his own hands from his knees; decides they were where they belong; carefully replaces them. When he finally speaks he tries to be light and tender and it is clear that the loudness of his voice startles and embarrasses him, and in the b.g.‡ heads flinch slightly.

POTTER WELL, MRS. POTTER!

BRIDE (by reflex) Shh!

Both are terribly embarrassed.

POTTER (quick and low) Sorry! Frog in my throat.

---

* A shot almost fully occupied by two characters.
† Outside.
‡ Background.

BRIDE (ditto) I'm sorry, I didn't mean to shush you. It just made me jump's all.

POTTER You shush me any time yer a mind to.

BRIDE (after a pause; with shy daring) You *call* me that, any time yer a mind to. 'Cause I like to hear you say it. Only not so loud.

POTTER (after a pause, whispering it, very shy) Mrs. Potter . . .

Overwhelmed by his daring, he blushes and looks away. She shivers with quiet delight; she glances up at him, then all around, with shy pride; then, as delicately as if it were asleep, she moves her hands in her lap as to uncover her wedding ring, and slowly, almost unbelievingly, lowers her eyes and looks at it. Then she looks around again, speculatively.

BRIDE Think they can tell we just got m— (she speaks the word almost sacredly) married?

POTTER Don't see how they would. We ain't treatin' 'em to no lovey dovey stuff or none o' that monkey business.

BRIDE (whisper) Jack!

POTTER 'Scuse me.

BRIDE It's all right.

POTTER No it ain't neither. It ain't fittin' I talk to you like that.

BRIDE Yes it is, Jack. I reckon it just kinda crep up on me from behind.

Silent, they look out the window. They have run out of talk. They have plenty to think about, but soon he feels he has to make conversation.

POTTER This-yer train sure does gobble up the miles, don't it?

BRIDE My yes. Just goes like the wind.

POTTER It's a thousand mile from one end o' Texas to the other, and it don't only stop but four times.

BRIDE My land!

POTTER It only stops for water at Yaller Sky.

BRIDE Oh.

POTTER Hope you ain't gonna mind. What I mean, it's a good town, but it might look awful puny, side o' San Antone.

BRIDE Oh *no*. I never did like a big town. I like it where ever'body *knows* ever'body else.

POTTER You'll like it there then.

They run out of talk again. She looks around with more and more appreciation of the opulence and splendor of the car. CAMERA PANS around Pullman car.

BRIDE'S VOICE (o.s.) I just can't get over it! (pause) It's all so handsome and rich-lookin'!

POTTER'S VOICE (o.s.) Yeah. They do it in style, sure enough, don't they?

BRIDE'S VOICE (o.s.) It's just like it was a palace or sumpin'. Even the ceilin'!

MEDIUM SHOT—A FANCY CEILING OIL PAINTING—CUPIDS, ETC.

POTTER'S VOICE (o.s.) Gee. You sure do notice things. I never even seen it.

CLOSE SHOT—POTTER

who has been looking up.

POTTER (continuing) Ever rode a parlor car before?

BRIDE No.

POTTER Me neither. One of these days we'll go on a trip overnight.

Both are quietly aghast with embarrassment.

POTTER (struggling) I mean, I always did have a hankerin' to see what them Pullman berths are like.

BRIDE (helping him) This is wonderful enough.

POTTER Shucks. This ain't *nothing*. After a while we'll go forward to the diner and get a big layout. Ever et in a diner?

BRIDE No. I always took me along some lunch.

POTTER Finest meal in the world. Charge a dollar.

CLOSE THREE SHOT *—POTTER, BRIDE AND SOPHISTICATED MAN

Sophisticated man registers, "God, what rubes!"

BRIDE A dollar? Why that's too much—for us—ain't it Jack?

POTTER Not this trip, anyhow. We're gonna do the whole thing.

He swells up, a little like a nabob, and looks away so she can look at him admiringly.   DISSOLVE TO

---

* A closeup shot almost fully occupied by three characters.

INSERT:

INT. SCRATCHY'S HOUSE (ADOBE)—DAY

EXTREME CLOSE SHOT

Sighting above the bore of a long-barreled, blue-black revolver, against a raggedly-curtained window.

INSERT:

The smoothly spinning cylinder of the revolver. Scratchy's other hand, with a rag, wipes the weapon clear of cleaning oil; the weapon is turned this way and that, lovingly, catching the light; then is sighted along, aiming it at Indians on a calendar, and is dry fired, with a click of the tongue and a whispered, "Got ye that time, ye dog!"; then it is laid delicately down on a patchwork quilt. CAMERA PANS with Scratchy's hand to a pint whiskey bottle on the floor by the bed. (Next to it is another bottle, empty.) Hand and bottle move out of shot; SOUND of drinking; bottle is returned, a good inch lower; hand unwraps a second revolver from a worn, fine old napkin. Then a rag, then a little can of cleaning oil and a little rod. The hands start cleaning revolver.

OVER THIS ENTIRE SCENE, Scratchy Wilson's voice is HEARD, deeply and still tranquilly drunk, humming as much as singing, "Brighten The Corner". The singing is of course interrupted; by his muttered line; by occasional shortness of breath; by his drinking and a sharp cough afterward; and just as it resumes after the drinking, the voice is raw. But in overall mood it is as happy and innocent as a baby talking to itself in its crib. Over hand cleaning revolver,   CUT TO

INT. PARLOR CAR—DAY

MEDIUM SHOT—CENTERING POTTER AND BRIDE

The dining steward walks through SHOT fast, hitting chimes.

STEWARD Fust call for dinnah! Fust call!

Only Potter and Bride react. A quick exchange of glances and they get up and follow steward out of shot.

INT. DINING CAR—DAY

MEDIUM SHOT

Shooting past waiters ranked ready beside empty tables as Potter and Bride enter the car, registering abrupt dismay at all the service, whiteness, glitter and loneliness.

VIEWPOINT SHOT—THREE WAITERS

solicit them, with knowing glances.

MEDIUM SHOT—DOLLY

The waiter nearest them tries to steer them toward a two-some table. Potter, in a replying spasm of independence, steers Bride to a 4-chair table opposite. The two sit down side by side as CAMERA DOLLIES sidelong into a

TWO SHOT

POTTER (low) Looks like we're the only customers.

Instantly a hand plants a large menu in Potter's hand, blocking off his face, and then the same to the Bride.

WAITER'S VOICE (juicy, o.s.) There you are sir! An' how're *you*-all today!

Potter slowly lowers menu, looks to waiter. Bride, ditto, looks to Potter.

POTTER Gone up on yer prices, ain't ye?

WAITER'S VOICE (o.s.) Things are costin' more all ovah, these days. (oily) Matter o' fact, though, we can 'commodate folks of more moderate means. (his finger reaches down and points out on menu) There's a nice gumbo, good sandwiches . . .

POTTER (across him) We'll have the dollar and a quarter dinner.

The Bride watches him with admiration.

WAITER Yes indeed, sir. The chicken or the ham, sir? The ham is *mighty* delicious today, sir.

POTTER Chicken.

WAITER Yes, *sir!*

They unfold their napkins. Potter glances about.

VIEWPOINT UP-SHOT

Several waiters pretend not to watch.

BRIDE AND POTTER AS BEFORE

As Bride settles her napkin in lap, he starts tucking his high into his vest.

DISSOLVE TO

EXT. "WEARY GENTLEMAN" SALOON—DAY

DOLLY SHOT

Following the nattily dressed Drummer through swinging doors into INT. "WEARY GENTLEMAN" SALOON, we pause and shoot past him as he hesitates and looks around at Jasper, Laura Lee and Frank. All glance at him casually and resume talking.

FRANK Not even a small beer?

LAURA LEE (sliding a tall one toward Jasper) Not even that, Frank. What's more, it's high time you locked yourself back in. 'Cause Jack Potter's treatin' you white, an' its up to you to treat him the same. Now git along with ye.

CLOSE SHOT—DRUMMER

Over "lock yourself back in," he registers sharp interest, glancing keenly back and forth between Frank and Laura Lee.

FRANK'S VOICE (o.s.) He'd treat me a whole lot whiter if he'd get back when he said he would.

LAURA LEE'S VOICE (o.s.) He ain't but a day late.

FRANK'S VOICE (o.s.) A day's a long time when you spend it in jail.

Drummer registers curiosity and consternation and looks exclusively at Frank.

NEW ANGLE—LAURA LEE AND FRANK

LAURA LEE Read them magazines he give ye.

CAMERA PANS with Frank as he starts toward door, HOLDING on Drummer.

FRANK Done read 'em four or five times. Git tired of it, all that bang-bang stuff. (to Drummer) Howdy, stranger.

He walks on out.

DRUMMER (belated and odd) Howdy.

CAMERA PANS with his walk up to the bar.

DRUMMER (to Laura Lee) Did I hear that man correctly, ma'am? Is he a *jail-bird?*

LAURA LEE If you want to put it that way.

DRUMMER (looks to Jasper who is wholly neutral) Well! (he looks to both; both are neutral) Well!

LAURA LEE What'll ye have, mister?

DRUMMER Beer, please, a big head on it.

Laura Lee draws and hands it to him, sizing him up.

LAURA LEE Big head.

DRUMMER Nice little town.

LAURA LEE It'll pass.

DRUMMER Oh, I've had quite a profitable morning's work. (he sips)

LAURA LEE That'll be a nickel, mister.

He pays and sips again.

DRUMMER Matter of fact, I'm a Drummer.

LAURA LEE I can see that.

DRUMMER That's right. I travel in stockings. "Exquisite" stockings. (hustling his sample case to bar) Paris to your doorstep, that's our slogan. Now if you're willing to spare a moment of your time, I can *promise* you, a lady of your taste and refinement, you just won't be able to *resist!*

LAURA LEE (across him) Don't trouble yourself, mister, I don't—

But the drummer is already lifting the lid of the case. She leans her arms on it, nipping his fingers.

LAURA LEE (continuing)—Now, looky here, young feller; I ain't even a'goin' to *look* at them fool stockin's, let alone *resist* 'em.

OVER THIS, two Mexican sheepherders enter quietly by the rear door and sit at a table.

LAURA LEE (to Mexicans) What's yours, Narciso Gulliermo Diorisio Mario?

1st MEXICAN Cervezas

The second Mexican nods.

DRUMMER (sucking his fingers) That hurt, ma'am.

LAURA LEE (drawing beer) Wouldn't be surprised.

JASPER Seen Scratchy around, Laura Lee?

LAURA LEE Not since t'other night.

JASPER Gittin' so ye can't count on him fer nothin'. He was 'sposed to clair out my cess-pool yesterday. Never showed up.

LAURA LEE (pause—quietly) Can't say as I blame him, Jasper; that's a job ye do yourself—and nobody ought to have to do it for him.

JASPER Well—sometimes ye gotta take what ye can git.

She is silent.

JASPER (continuing) All I hope is, he ain't a-tyin' one on.

CLOSE SHOT—LAURA LEE

LAURA LEE If I had to do a job like that fer you, I might tie on a few myself.

CAMERA PANS as she takes beer to end of bar. First Mexican pays and takes them. She sits on her stool, looking at nobody.

A NEW ANGLE—JASPER

He watches her, nettled, and a little malicious.

JASPER Hey, Laura Lee.

LAURA LEE Yeah.

JASPER Reckon what Jack Potter's *up* to in San Antone.

LAURA LEE Reckon what business 'tis o' yourn.

JASPER Just figured he might of *told* you.

LAURA LEE (quiet and stern) Jack Potter ain't tied to *my* apron strings, nor nobody's.

FAST WIPE * TO

---

* Fast transition from one scene to another, wherein a line moves across the screen wiping off one scene and bringing in the other.

INT. DINING CAR—DAY

Potter and Bride are finishing their desserts opposite a wooden, middle-aged married couple (the car is now full of people).

We INTER-CUT CLOSE SHOT as Potter and the man meet glances; Bride and woman do same. Potter glances secretively down at his lapel and, privately as he can, scratches with his thumb-nail at a food stain.

Their voices are low:

BRIDE Don't worry. I can get that off in a jiffy.

POTTER Ain't likely I'll wear it much, nohow.

BRIDE Why, you'll wear it a-Sundays, church an' all.

POTTER (uneasy) I ain't never been much of a hand for church.

BRIDE You don't ever go?

Potter uneasily shakes his head.

BRIDE (continuing; uneasy) I don't know what I'd do, for lonesomeness, without no church to go to.

WAITER'S VOICE (o.s.) Look what I done brung yah both! An extra pot of nice fresh coffee.

VIEWPOINT UP-SHOT cuts into his line.

He leans over, setting down pot, beaming, proprietary, working for a big tip.

NEW ANGLE—POTTER AND BRIDE

Mild embarrassment reactions; they murmur appreciations ad lib.

POTTER No thanks.

She pours for herself. The sugar is not in easy reach.

POTTER (formally, to other man) Pass the sugar, please.

MAN (glumly) Certainly.

POTTER (to Bride) Sugar?

BRIDE Sure you won't have some more coffee?

POTTER All right. Thanks. Thank you.

BRIDE Certainly.

She leans to pour for him, much enjoying serving him, and knocks her napkin from the edge of the table to the floor between them. Both quickly stoop to reach for it.

INSERT:

Their hands touch accidentally and fly apart as if they had struck a spark.

BOTH 'Scuse me!

TWO SHOT—POTTER AND BRIDE AS BEFORE

As they straighten up quickly, Potter bumps the table making a clatter and the bride slops a little of the coffee from the pot in her other hand onto their clothes.

TOGETHER: POTTER (to everyone) 'Scuse me.

            BRIDE (to him) Gee, I'm sorry.

REVERSE ANGLE

The two older people exchange unsmiling glances and pretend nothing is happening.

POTTER AND BRIDE AS BEFORE

He with his handkerchief, she with his napkin, they gently dab coffee off each other; they are embarrassed but not at all at odds.
As the waiter's arm presents the check to Potter, the CAMERA LIFTS AND TILTS, DOLLYING gently in to center his right hand near his trousers pocket. The hand makes the odd, helpless gesture of putting aside a holster which isn't there.

BRIDE'S VOICE (o.s.) What's the matter?

POTTER'S VOICE (o.s.) Just habit I reckon. Fust time in years I ain't totin' a gun.

CAMERA ZOOMS, centering.   FAST DISSOLVE * TO

INT. SCRATCHY'S—DAY—CLOSE VIEWPOINT SHOT

Scratchy's loaded cartridge belt lies heavy and lethal across his knees. He thumbs in the last cartridge and lays aside the belt. The CAMERA, as Scratchy rises to his feet, goes into a short SPINNING BLUR IN AND OUT OF FOCUS.

---

    * Transition from one scene to another, wherein the first fades away and the second gradually emerges.

SCRATCHY'S VOICE (o.s.) Whoa there.

CAMERA proceeds into a slow, wobbly DOLLYING PAN, past window and bureau to pegs where Scratchy's hand fumbles among his few clothes. Most of them are old and poor but his hands select and get off the hook a violently fancy pseudowestern shirt on which CAMERA comes into ULTRA SHARP FOCUS. Then one hand, as CAMERA CREEPS IN, FOCUS DITTO, reaches for a real shocker of a necktie, muffs it, and as CAMERA comes into EXTREME CLOSE SHOT, drags it drunkenly, snakily, slithering from its hook. All this time Scratchy is muttering and humming. OVER the slithering tie we   IRIS OUT

IRIS IN *

INT. PARLOR CAR—DAY

Center CAMERA on Potter's more conservative tie. Tense and uneasy, he adjusts it.

TWO SHOT—POTTER AND BRIDE

He is tense; she is content. He takes out and looks at a thick hunter watch. Watching him, she realizes his uneasiness. She checks her own watch with his.

BRIDE Mine's slow.

POTTER Nope: I trust yourn. She's a seventeen jeweller.

Behind them, the "sophisticated" man slopes an amused eye.

BRIDE Gracious.

Potter corrects his watch, pockets it and avoids her eyes. She watches him. An uneasy silence. He looks at his watch again.

BRIDE (continuing) Jack.

POTTER Hmm.

BRIDE Somethin's eatin' at you.

POTTER Me?

She nods—a pause.

_____

* Placing a filter over the camera lens in order to dim the light.

POTTER Nuthin' much. Only I wisht I'd sent a telegram.

BRIDE Thought you did, there at the depot.

POTTER I just tore it up.

Silence.

BRIDE (shyly) Was it—about us—gittin' married this morning?

POTTER I oughta told 'um, back in Yaller Sky. That's all. You see, they're so used to me bein' a bachelor an' all. They ain't gonna take it no way good, me never tellin' 'em—an' all of a sudden I come home married—(an inarticulate pause; ashamed)—Reckon I'm just plain bashful.

BRIDE (very shy) Reckon I feel the same.

He looks at her, unbelieving. She corroborates her statement with a little nod. They are so relieved they awkwardly resist an impulse to join hands and both face rigidly front, their tension growing.

                                                    FAST DISSOLVE TO

INT. SCRATCHY'S HOUSE—DAY

A lurching CLOSE PAN to a broken, distorting mirror. The CAMERA is on Scratchy, and the reflection is his. He is wearing a fancy shirt, both revolvers and the cartridge belt and he has to stoop to see himself. He is in a reeling slouch, glaring, stinking drunk. He draws closer, making savage faces which are still more savagely distorted in the mirror. He becomes momentarily fascinated by these distortions. He draws both guns and lurches into EXTREME CLOSEUP, growling low:

SCRATCHY All right, Jack Potter. Yore time has come!

CAMERA PULLS BACK centering hands getting, from his dresser drawer, a newish hat as phony as the shirt. The hands lift this through the shot as valuably as the Holy Grail and CAMERA again LEANS for mirror reflection as he preens the hat on his head.   DISSOLVE TO

INT. "WEARY GENTLEMAN"—DAY

CLOSE SHOT—THE DRUMMER

His eyes fixed almost on the lens in the cold manner of a snake charming a bird. CAMERA PULLS AWAY along his fully extended, shirt-sleeved, and fancily sleeve-gartered arm. It is clothed to the armpit in a super-sheer, elaborately clocked dark stocking.

DRUMMER (soft and almost lascivious) Speaks louder than words, doesn't it! (he shifts his eye o.s.) *You* tell her, gentlemen; in *all your experience*, did you ever meet a lady that wouldn't *swoon* just to look at it? (eyes back to center) Sheer as twilight air. And just look at that clocking! (he points it out, then his subtle hand impersonates a demi-mondaine foot) Nothing like it ever contrived before, by the most inspired continental designers, to give style to the ankle and moulding to the calf. (he runs fingers up his arm to the armpit, his eyes follow) And they run all the way up —opera length. (he casts his eyes down, then returns to off-center and gives his eyes all he's got. With a trace of hoarseness, almost whispering) How about it, madam? (He gives her an homme-fatale smile. A grand pause.)

TWO SHOT—JASPER AND ED

They look toward him with quiet disgust.

TWO SHOT—TWO MEXICANS

They glance at each other and toward Laura Lee.

CLOSE SHOT—LAURA LEE

She gives the merchandise one more cold, fascinated once-over, then looks the Drummer in the eye.

LAURA LEE All right son. I'm still resistin'. So, fork over that dollar.

DRUMMER But madam, you haven't given the Exquizzit—

LAURA LEE (across him) Save yer breath young feller. Why, if my husband had caught me in a pair o' them things, he'd 'a' broke my jaw. You're in the *wrong territory*, son. 'Cause this is a man's country. It's hard country.

A young man comes in quickly.

YOUNG MAN Scratchy Wilson's drunk an' he's turned loose with both hands.

Both Mexicans set down their unfinished beers and fade out the rear door. The Drummer views with mystification; nobody pays any attention to him. They're as quick and efficient as a well-rehearsed fire-drill. Jasper and Ed go out the front door and close the window shutters. The young man bolts the rear door. Laura Lee bars the window on her side and goes center, swinging shut one leaf of the plank door. As Jasper and Ed return, Jasper swings the other shut and bars his window and Ed brings from the corner the bar for the main door and helps Laura Lee put it in place. Laura Lee returns to her place behind the bar. In the sudden, solemn, chapel-like gloom, the Drummer is transfixed; his eyes glitter.

DRUMMER Say, what *is* this?

A silent reaction from the men.

DRUMMER (continuing) Is there going to be a gun-fight?

JASPER (grimly) Dunno if there'll be a fight or not, but there'll be some shootin'—some good shootin'.

YOUNG MAN Oh, there's a fight just *waitin'* out there in the street, if anyone wants it.

Jasper and Ed nod solemnly.

DRUMMER (to young man) What'd ye say his name was?

ALL Scratchy Wilson.

The Drummer does a fast multiple take, person-to-person.

DRUMMER What're you goin' to do?

Grim silence.

DRUMMER (continuing) Does he do this often?

More silence.

DRUMMER (continuing) Can he break down that door?

LAURA LEE No: he's give that up. But when he comes you'd better lay down on the floor, stranger. He's dead sure to *shoot* at that door, an' there's no tellin' what a stray bullet might do.

The Drummer, keeping a strict eye on the door, begins carefully removing the stocking from his arm.

DRUMMER Will he kill anybody?

The men laugh low and scornfully.

JASPER He's out to shoot, an' he's out fer trouble. Don't see no good *experimentin'* with him.

DRUMMER But what do you *do* in a case like this? What do you do?

YOUNG MAN Why, he an' Jack Potter—

JASPER AND ED (across him) Jack ain't back yet.

YOUNG MAN (suddenly frightened) *Lordy!*

DRUMMER Well who's he? What's *he* got to do with it?

YOUNG MAN He's Marshal.

LAURA LEE Comes to shootin', he's the only one in town can go up agin him.

Far off, o.s. we HEAR a wild Texas yell, a shot, another yell. Everyone becomes very still and tense.

DRUMMER (half whispered) That must be him comin', hey?

The men look at him in irritation and look away again. They wait, their eyes shining in the gloom. Jasper holds up three fingers. Moving like a ghost, Laura Lee gets out three glasses and the bottle. The Drummer lifts one forlorn finger; she adds another glass. They pour. In unison they snap the drinks down at a gulp and walk to windows to look through chinks. The Drummer quietly puts a coin on the bar. Laura Lee just looks at it, at him, and away.

He shamefacedly takes back his coin. She silently takes a Winchester from beneath the bar and breaks it.

DRUMMER (whispered) You goin' to *shoot* him?

Silence; everyone looks at him bleakly.

LAURA LEE (low) Not if I can help it. I ain't a good enough shot. Might kill him.

DRUMMER Well, it'd be pure self defense if you did, wouldn't it?

No answer.

DRUMMER (continuing) Well, *wouldn't* it? Good riddance *too, I'd* say.

LAURA LEE closes the breech.

LAURA LEE (low) Mister, Scratchy Wilson's an old friend. Nobody'd harm a hair of his head if they's any way out—let alone kill him. You see, trouble is, he's a wonder with a gun. Just a wonder. An' he's a terror when he's drunk. So when he goes on the war trail, we hunt our holes—naturally.

DRUMMER But—why do they allow him—what's he doin' in a town like this?

LAURA LEE He's the last of the old gang that used to hang out along the river here.

A silence. Then nearer, but distant, a howl is HEARD. The Drummer reacts, jittery.

LAURA LEE (continuing) You better come back o' the bar. I kinda fixed
        it up.

DRUMMER (ashamed) No thanks, I'll—

LAURA LEE (with a peremptory gesture) Come on.

He does. He squats low in the front angle of the bar and examines, with
some relief, the various plates of scrap metal with which she has armored it.
o.s., nearer, we HEAR another shot and three yowls. There's a shuffling of
feet. They look at each other.

MEN (quietly) Here he comes!

PAN SHOT

We DOLLY with Laura Lee, carrying her gun, to look through a chink in the
shutter, and through the chink see Scratchy round the corner at the far end
of the empty street, yelling, a long heavy blue-black revolver in either hand.
We HEAR his words, distant, but preternaturally powerful, as he strides to
the middle of the street and stops dead, both guns alert, threatening and
at bay.

SCRATCHY *Yaller Sky, hyar I come!*

MEDIUM SHOT—SCRATCHY

He holsters a revolver, extracts a pint bottle from his belt, cocks it vertically
and drains it, and tosses it high and glittering into the sunlight, in mid-air;
then shoots it into splinters, left-handed, and does a quick 360-degree whirl,
drawing both guns, as if against enemies ambushing him from the rear. He
raises a small tornado of dust. CUT to a HEAD CLOSEUP into which he
finishes his pivot, glaring. His eyes are glittering, drunk, mad, frightening.
He is eaten up with some kind of interior bitter wildness.

SCRATCHY (a low growl) Got ye, ye yaller-bellies!

PULL DOWN AND AWAY. He gives a lonely Texas yowl; the echoes die. He
glares all about him; his eyes, focusing on something o.s., take on sudden
purpose.

SCRATCHY (loud) Jack Potter!

MEDIUM SHOT—WITH STILL CAMERA—POTTER'S HOUSE—FREEZE

CLOSER SHOT—SCRATCHY

trying to adjust his eyes to this oddity.

SCRATCHY (louder) Jack Potter!

MED. SHOT—POTTER'S HOUSE—AS BEFORE

SCRATCHY'S VOICE (o.s.) You heared me, Jack Potter. Come on out an' face the music. Caze it's time to dance.

CLOSE SHOT—SCRATCHY

Dead silence.

He is puzzled.

SCRATCHY 'Tain't no ways like you Potter, asullin' there in yer house. You ain't no possum. I treated ye fair an' square. I saved it all up for ye, like I told ye. Now you play square with me.

FRANK'S VOICE (o.s., scared) Hey, Scratchy.

SCRATCHY (puzzled, looking around) How's that? Who *is* that?

POTTER'S HOUSE—PAST SCRATCHY

FRANK'S VOICE Hit's me. Frank.

SCRATCHY Why don't ye say so. Whar ye at?

FRANK'S VOICE I'm up yere in the jail.

SCRATCHY Well *show* yerself! What ye skeered of?

FRANK'S VOICE You.

SCRATCHY Me? Shucks. Only man needs to be skeered o' me is Jack Potter, the yaller hound.

FRANK'S VOICE Jack ain't here, Scratchy.

SCRATCHY What ye mean he ain't here?

FRANK'S VOICE He ain't got back yet, that's what I mean. That's what I was tryin' to tell you.

SCRATCHY Ain't back! Don't gimme none o' that. He come back yesterday when he promised he would.

FRANK'S VOICE No he didn't.

SCRATCHY You lie to *me*. Frank Gudger, I'll give ye what *fer*.

He shoots, striking a bar and ringing a musical note.

FRANK'S VOICE: Scratchy! Don't do that! Hit's dangersome.

SCRATCHY Not if ye keep yer head low it ain't.

FRANK'S VOICE 'Tis too. Ye can't tell *whar* them bullets'll rebound.
SCRATCHY Don't you dast tell me how to shoot, ye pore wall-eyed
                woods colt. *Is* Jack Potter back or *ain't* he?

FRANK'S VOICE: No he ain't and that's the honest truth.

SCRATCHY Don't you *sass me*.

CLOSE SHOT

Scratchy shoots another bar, ringing a different musical note, which is followed by a shattering of glass.

SCRATCHY (continuing) Is he back?

FRANK'S VOICE Quit it, Scratchy. Ye done busted my lamp chimbley.

SCRATCHY *Is* he back or *ain't* he?

FRANK'S VOICE All right, have it yer own way. He's back if you say
                so.

SCRATCHY Well, why didn't you tell me so straight off?

No answer.

SCRATCHY (continuing) Why don't he come on out then?

FRANK'S VOICE Reckon he would if he was inside.

SCRATCHY Oh, he ain't inside, huh?

FRANK'S VOICE Not that I know of.

SCRATCHY Well, that leaves just one other place for him to be.

He turns toward the "Weary Gentleman," hikes his trousers, reaches for the bottle which is no longer there.

SCRATCHY (growling and starting) Dad burn it. Never seed it yet I
                didn't run out just at the wrong time.

He walks fast past the respectable houses, the churches and so on, and DOLLYING, SHOOTING PAST HIM, we see they all have an unearthly quietness. As he walks, he talks, now to himself, now shouting.

SCRATCHY (continuing) But that's all right. Just lay low. 'Caze quick as I wet my whistle, I'm gonna show ye some shootin'!

He stops in front of Morgan's house.

SCRATCHY (continuing) You, Jasper Morgan. Yeah, and that snivellin' woman o' yourn, too! Too dainty to do like ordinary folks. Too high an' mighty! Git yerself a lot o' fancy plumbing, an' ye ain't man enough to clean out yer own cess-pool. "Let Scratchy do it." Ain't nuthin' so low but Scratchy'll do it for the price of a pint.

He glares around for a target. He spies a potted fern suspended from the porch ceiling. He shoots the suspension chain and the whole thing drops to the porch floor with a foomp. There! Clean that up! He turns, Deacon's house is opposite.

SCRATCHY (continuing; a horrible travesty of a sissy voice) *Deacon!* Oh *Deacon Smee-eed!* (he makes two syllables of Smeed) You home, Deacon? Kin I pay ye a little call? *Most* places in town, ye just *knock* an' walk *in,* but that ain't *good* enough for a *good* man, *is* it, Deacon? Oh *no!* No—*no!* Pay a little call on the Deacon, ye got to shove a 'lectric bell, real special. (a hard shift of tone) All right, Smeed, start singin' them psalms o' yourn. You'll be whangin' 'em on a harp, few mo' minutes, you an' yer missuz, too. Can't stop in right now, I'm a mite too thirsty. But I'll be back, Deacon. Oh, I'll be back. (he studies the house) Here's my callin' card.

He takes careful aim, and

INSERT

Hits the doorbell, so fusing it that it rings continuously. We HEAR a woman scream hysterically.

CLOSE SHOT OF SCRATCHY

SCRATCHY Ah, quit it. Don't holler 'til yer hurt.

INT. DEACON'S HOUSE—DEACON AND WIFE

Past Deacon and his wife, through the curtained window, we see Scratchy pass.

The Deacon has an arm around his wife. He is trying pathetically to resemble an intrepid doomed frontiersman in an Indian fight.

DEACON He'll pay for this. By the Almighty, he'll pay dearly. I'm not
        going to stand for it, I'm simply not going—

MRS. SMEED Oh hush. For goodness sake, stop that horrid *bell!*

He looks at her, goes into the hallway with wounded dignity, and jerks a wire loose. Just as the bell stops, there is a shot and the stinging sound o.s. of the church bell being shot at. The Deacon reacts to this latest outrage.

MEDIUM SHOT—UPWARD—CHURCH BELL—FROM SCRATCHY'S VIEW-POINT

CLOSE SHOT—SHOOTING DOWN—SCRATCHY

looking up at bell, both pleased and angry, and shooting again at the church bell.

SCRATCHY (he bellows) Come on out and fight if you dast—only you
        don't dast.

He starts glancing all around; the revolvers in each hand are as sensitive as snakes; the little fingers play in a musician-like way; INTER-CUT with still facades of details of greater stillness; a motionless curtain of machine-made lace with a head dimly silhouetted behind; a drawn shade, with an eye and fingertips visible at the edge.

SCRATCHY (continuing) O no! You know who's *boss* in *this* town.
        Marcellus T. Wilson, that's who. He ain't fittin' to wipe
        yer boots on, no-sirree, he's the lowest of the low, but he's
        boss all the same. 'Caze *this* is a boss, (gesturing with a
        revolver) an' *this* is a boss, (another) an' this is the feller
        that can boss the both of 'em better'n any other man that's
        left in this wore-out womanizin' country. An' there ain't
        hardly a man of ye dast *touch* a gun, let alone come up
        again a *man* with one. Oh no! Got lil' ole honeybunch to
        worry about, lil' ole wifey-pifey, all the young 'uns, make
        ye some easy money runnin' a store, doctorin', psalm-
        singing, fix ye a purty lawn so Scratchy kin cut it for ye,
        if ye can't get a Mex cheap enough. Oh, I—(he searches
        helplessly, then half-says)—hate—I could wipe every one
        of ye offen the face o' the earth, a-hidin' behind your

women's skirts, ever' respectable last one of ye! Come out an' fight! Come on! Come on! Dad *blast* ye!

He glares all around again. There is no kind of response at all. His attention shifts; his eyes focus on something o.s., he becomes purposeful.

EXT. "WEARY GENTLEMAN" SALOON—BARRICADED—DAY

DOLLY SHOT over Scratchy's shoulder as he advances on door.

CUT TO

MEDIUM CLOSE SHOT—SCRATCHY

He comes to door and hammers on it with gun butt.

SCRATCHY Laura Lee. (pause) Laura Lee. (pause)

Now he hammers with both revolvers.

SCRATCHY (continuing; yelling) *Laura Lee!* (no answer) You can't fool me. I know you're there. Open up. I want a drink. (no answer) All I want's a little drink.

Now he hammers harder than ever. Over SOUND of hammering, CUT INSIDE

TO CLOSE SHOTS IN THIS ORDER

CLOSE SHOT—LAURA LEE

low behind bar, her rifle ready if need be, thumb on safety.

CLOSE SHOT—THREE LOCAL MEN

on floor, watching the door fixedly.

CLOSE SHOT—THE DRUMMER

behind the bar, plenty scared.

CLOSE SHOT—BACK TO SCRATCHY

finishing his hammering. He is rather tired. He glares at the door a moment, then:

SCRATCHY All right then. All right.

He looks around him, sore. He sights a scrap of paper in the dirt, picks it up, and with a vicious and cruel thrust, nails it to the door with a knife. Then he turns his back contemptuously on the saloon, walks to the far side of the street and, spinning quickly and lithely, fires at the sheet of paper.

INSERT

The bullet misses by half an inch.

SCRATCHY AS BEFORE

SCRATCHY Well, I, Gah . . . gittin' old in yer old age, Scratchy.

He takes careful aim and fires.

INSERT

The bullet splits the haft of the knife; the blade clatters down; the paper follows, fluttering; a hole appears in the door.

CLOSE SHOT—INT. "WEARY GENTLEMAN"

Jasper is on floor, between a chair and a spittoon. Bullet flicks wood from chair, ricochets with appropriate SOUNDS, puncturing spittoon from which dark liquid oozes. Jasper, with slow horror, looks at it.

FROM SCRATCHY'S VIEWPOINT

the paper finishes settling.

CLOSE SHOT—SCRATCHY

He is satisfied; he turns and starts walking grandly away. Suddenly he cries out:

SCRATCHY Hey! (and stops and faces the saloon again) Hey, tell Jack
         Potter to come on out o' there like a man!

REVERSE ANGLE—OVER SCRATCHY

No answer.

SCRATCHY (continuing; yelling) *Jack!* JACK POTTER?

CLOSE SHOT—INT. SALOON

LAURA LEE Jack Potter ain't here, Scratchy, an' *you know it!* 'Cause if he was, he'd be out thar arter ye.

CLOSE SHOT—SCRATCHY

He hesitates, thinks it over.

SCRATCHY (uncertainly) You wouldn't fool me, would ye, Laura Lee?

LAURA LEE'S VOICE (o.s.) I never did, did I?

SCRATCHY Well don't never you try it. 'Caze I ain't the man'll stand fer it. (suddenly sore) That lyin' no-'count Frank! I'll fix *him!* I'll cook *his* goose!

HE STARTS OUT FAST UP THE STREET—there is the sound of a distant train whistle o.s. Over it   DISSOLVE TO

INT. PARLOR CAR—DAY

SOUND of dying wail of whistle o.s. Throughout scene, SOUND of slowing train.

TWO SHOT—POTTER AND BRIDE

Tension and emotion increase in their faces.

POTTER (with desperate finality) Well—

She looks to him anxiously—he meets her eyes briefly and both smile, then lower their eyes pathetically. He gratefully thinks of something to do.

POTTER (continuing) Better git down our truck.

With day-coach reflex, he stands up, reaching for the non-existent baggage rack, realizes his mistake, and pretends he is only tidying his clothes.

PORTER'S VOICE (o.s., loud and glad) Don't you bother, mister—

                                                        CUT TO

CLOSE SHOT—PORTER

grinning.

PORTER (continuing)—I got it all ready an' waitin'!

FULL SHOT

Some amused heads turn.

BRIDE AND POTTER AS BEFORE

He sits down abashed. Train SOUND is much slower. Their time is short.

POTTER (smiling and wretched) Home at last.

BRIDE (uneasy) Mm-hmm.

A silence.

CLOSE SHOT—POTTER

in real desperation, o.s. SOUND of train bell.

POTTER (sweating; rapidly) Say listen. You ain't goana like me fer this an' I don't blame ye, but I just can't face 'em if we can help it, not right yet. What I want, I want to sorta *sneak* in, if we can git away with it, an' make home without nobody seein' us, an' then study what to do about 'em. I figure we got a chance if we kinda skin along the hind side o' Main Street. We got cover 'til about sixty foot from my door. Would ye do it?

CAMERA PULLS AND PANS into TWO SHOT—POTTER AND BRIDE

BRIDE (fervent) Oh gee, if only they don't ketch us!

POTTER (incredulously grateful) You don't hate me fer it?

BRIDE (with all her heart) *Hate* you?

They look at each other with entirely new love. The train is stopping. They get up fast and leave the shot.   CUT TO

EXT. STATION YELLOW SKY—DAY

As train pulls to a stop, PAN AND DOLLY into CLOSE UP-SHOT of train steps. The Porter descends first and leaves the shot. Potter, with Bride behind and above him, peers anxiously forward along the station platform.

LONG SHOT—HIS VIEWPOINT

The empty platform.

MEDIUM SHOT—PANNING

POTTER (over shoulder) Come on girl. Hurry.

He steps to platform, she follows unassisted. He grabs up both bags and, looking back to her, collides with the untipped, dismayed Porter.

POTTER Oh.

He sets down bags. A fumbling rush for change. He hands out a coin.

POTTER (continuing) Much obliged.

He picks up bags and starts walking, the Bride alongside.

POTTER Let's git outa here.

PORTER (across him) Much obliged to you, sir.

Potter walks away so fast that she has to hustle to keep alongside. Both are eagle-eyed—he with anxiety, she with that and with simple interest.

REVERSE ANGLE SHOT

We glimpse an empty segment of street.

BRIDE'S VOICE (o.s.) Gee, I don't see *nobody*.

BRIDE AND POTTER AS BEFORE

POTTER Just the hot time o' day, let's not risk it.

They walk still faster around rear corner of station and out of sight.

CUT TO

CLOSE SHOT—CELL WINDOW IN POTTER'S HOUSE

It is empty; very, very slowly a little mirror rises to eye level above the sill —and jerks down fast.

CLOSE SHOT

between the rear of two buildings toward the vacant Main Street. Potter's head comes CLOSE INTO SHOT, then the Bride's.

POTTER (whispering) All right.

They dart noiselessly across the gap.

POTTER (continuing) Good girl.

They laugh, low and sheepish, and steal ahead. CAMERA PANS WITH THEM l. to r.

POTTER (still whispering) Next corner, dear, an' I can show you our home.

BRIDE (same) Oh, Jack.

She stops. Her eyes are damp. He stops.

POTTER (whispering) Sumpin' the matter?

VERY CLOSE SHOT—BRIDE

BRIDE The way you said that!

POTTER'S VOICE (o.s.) Said what?

BRIDE (moved) Our home!

She smiles very shyly. He is moved and says, in a most embarrassed voice:

POTTER Come on then, girl.—Let's get there.

ANOTHER ANGLE

They start walking fast and quiet; we PAN with them, approaching the frame corner of a house.

POTTER (continuing) Now right the next second, you can see it!

They continue. WE LEAD THEM slightly as they circle the corner and come face to face with a CLOSE SHOT OF SCRATCHY. He is leaning against the wall, just around the corner, reloading. Instantly he drops this revolver, whips the other from its holster, and aims it at Potter's chest.
A deadly silence.

REVERSE ANGLE—OVER SCRATCHY ONTO POTTER AND BRIDE

The Bride grabs Potter's right arm. He drops both bags and exhibits the desperate reflex of a man whose fighting arm has never before been encumbered. He reaches for the gun that is not there. He sweeps her behind him.

CLOSEUP—SCRATCHY

CLOSE SHOT—THE BRIDE

Her face looks crumpled with terror; she gazes at the gun as at an apparitional snake.

CLOSE SHOT—POTTER

He looks up from the gun into Scratchy's eyes.

CLOSE SHOT—THE REVOLVER

CAMERA RISES SLOWLY TO BRING IN SCRATCHY IN EXTREME CLOSE-UP.

His eyes are cold and mad; his face is almost solemn.

SCRATCHY (almost reproachfully) Tried to sneak up on me. Tried to
    sneak up on me!

TWO SHOT OF THE MEN—THE BRIDE BEHIND POTTER

Potter makes a slight movement; Scratchy thrusts his revolver venomously
forward; CAMERA LUNGES FORWARD CORRESPONDINGLY.

CLOSE SHOT OF SCRATCHY

SCRATCHY (he smiles with a new and quiet ferocity) No' don't ye do
    it, Jack Potter. Don't you move a finger towards a gun just
    yet. Don't you bat an eyelash. The time has come fer me to
    settle with you, so I aim to do it my own way, an' loaf
    along without no interferin'. So if ye don't want a gun bent
    on ye, or a third eye right now, just mind what I tell ye.

He slowly raises his revolver to eye level, so that it is pointing a little
upward, DEAD INTO THE LENS

CLOSE SHOT—POTTER—PAST GUN

He is looking directly down the barrel. He is not at all a cowardly man but
he is looking directly into the eye of death. Sweat breaks out on his face.

EXTREME CLOSE SHOT

looking down the pistol barrel.

EXTREME CLOSE SHOT—POTTER

then,

THE BRIDE'S FACE, saying "our home" (without sound) and smiling.

RETURN TO POTTER

His eyes, a little dizzily out of focus, restore to normal.

POTTER (quietly) I ain't got a gun, Scratchy. Honest I ain't. You'll have to do all the shootin' yerself.

CLOSE SHOT—SCRATCHY—PAST POTTER

He goes livid and steps forward and lashes his weapon to and fro.

SCRATCHY Don't you tell me you ain't got no gun on you, you whelp. Don't tell me no lie like that. There ain't a man in Texas ever seen you without no gun. Don't take me fer no kid.

His eyes blaze with light; his throat works like a pump.

CLOSE SHOT—POTTER—PAST SCRATCHY

POTTER I ain't takin' you fer no kid. I'm takin' you fer a damned fool. I tell you I ain't got a gun an' I aint. If you're gonna shoot me up, ya better do it now; you'll never get a chance like this again.

PULL AWAY INTO TWO SHOT—Scratchy calms a little.

SCRATCHY (sneering) If you ain't got a gun, why ain't you got a gun? Been to Sunday school?

POTTER You know where I been. I been in San Antone. An' I ain't got a gun because I just got married. An' if I'd thought there was goin' to be any galoots like you prowlin' around, when I brought my wife home, I'd a had a gun, an' don't you fergit it.

SCRATCHY (says the word with total, uncomprehending vacancy) Married?

POTTER Yes, married. I'm married.

SCRATCHY (a little more comprehension) Married? You mean, you? (he backs off a pace; the arm and pistol drop) No. (he studies Potter cagily and shakes his head)

Then literally for the first time, he sees the Bride.

SCRATCHY (continuing) What's that ye got there? Is this the lady?

POTTER Yes, this is the lady.

A silence.

SCRATCHY Well, I 'spose it's all off now.

POTTER It's all off if you say so, Scratchy. You know I didn't make the trouble.

He picks up both valises.

NEW SHOT—SCRATCHY—OVER POTTER

He studies Potter up and down, slowly, incredulously. Then he looks at the ground.

SCRATCHY Well, I 'low it's off, Jack. (he shakes his head) *Married!*

He looks up with infinite reproach, sadness and solitude. He picks up his fallen revolver. He hefts it and turns both revolvers in his hands, looking at them, then puts them with finality into their holsters. Then he again meets Potter's eyes.

SCRATCHY (continuing; almost inaudibly) G'bye, Jack.

CLOSE SHOT—POTTER

He begins to comprehend; he is moved.

POTTER 'Bye, Scratchy.

REVERSE ANGLE—SCRATCHY

He looks at Potter a moment, then turns around and walks heavily away.

TWO SHOT—POTTER AND BRIDE

She emerges from behind him, whimpering, glancing from man to man, hugging his arm. His eyes on Scratchy o.s., he is hardly aware of her.

INSERT

A lace curtain is plucked aside and Deacon's wife looks out.

CLOSE SHOT

A front door opens cautiously, squeakily; and cautiously, a man we don't know emerges.   CUT TO

INT. "WEARY GENTLEMAN"—DAY

The doors open; Jasper, Ed, the Young Man, and finally Laura Lee, followed by the Drummer, emerge onto the porch, looking up the street.

LONG SHOT—POTTER, BRIDE AND SCRATCHY

through this group as a few people timidly venture into the space between.

REVERSE ANGLE—GROUP SHOT—FAVORING LAURA LEE AND DRUMMER

DRUMMER (smug) You were saying, ma'am—this is a *hard* country?

She gives him a look and looks again toward Scratchy and company.

LONG SHOT—PAST ED AND DRUMMER

The Deacon trots out to Potter, frantically effusive.

PANTOMIME introductions.

ED Drummer: looks like ye got ye a new customer.

Drummer registers certainty and anticipation.

DRUMMER (to Laura Lee) And how about you, ma'am?

CLOSE SHOT—LAURA LEE

She turns on him, colder than ever.

LAURA LEE (in measured tones) I wouldn't wear them things if it killed me.

Then she realizes she is dead. Her eyes fall, tragic and defiant, to a neutral angle. In b.g., Jasper, watching her, realizes a little of the meaning. He is sympathetic.

ED'S VOICE (o.s.) Well look at that!

LONG SHOT—PAST ALL OF THEM

Potter is walking toward home with Deacon and the Bride as if between custodians. They stop. The Deacon, extra effusive, peels off and toddles for home.

CLOSE MOVING SHOT—POTTER AND BRIDE WALKING

She glances back toward the filling, watchful street, which we see past them. Potter is looking toward Scratchy o.s.

BRIDE Sure looks like the cat's outa the bag.

POTTER More like a wild-cat.

He stops. So do Bride and CAMERA.

POTTER (continuing) You know? There's somethin' I always wanted to do.

He sets down the suitcases and looks her up and down, business-like. She is willing but mystified. He picks her up.

BRIDE (surprised and grateful) Oh, Jack . . .

As he carries her forward out of the shot, he looks sadly again toward Scratchy o.s. while she, loving and puzzled, looks at him.

MEDIUM SHOT—FRANK

at the window.

FRANK Howdy Marshal! Proud to know ye Miz Potter! Welcome home!

With the attempted velocity of a fast baseball, he slams down handsful of improvised confetti. PULL CAMERA DOWN. Potter and Bride walk to door amid showering confetti.

CONTINUE PULLING DOWN as Potter shoves door open with his shoe, enters, Bride in arms, and shoves door shut.

DOLLY IN—STILL PULLING DOWN TO

CLOSE SHOT showing that Scratchy has shot the lock to pieces.

END PULL DOWN—vertical to the doorstep as last confetti flutters down. Salient are the torn pictures of the murderous faces and weapons of early western fiction.

VERY LONG SHOT—SCRATCHY

Very small, he walks heavily away toward a solitary, still more distant hovel; empty earth and sky all around. A LONG HOLD; then CAMERA PULLS DOWN TO

CLOSE SHOT—the funnel-shaped tracks of his feet in heavy sand.

THE END

EXERCISES

on film and rhetoric

1. In what ways does Agee provide for movement in his treatment of this story? for visual imagery?
2. Show how Agee uses camera angles for dramatic effect; to point up meaning; to help establish character.
3. On the basis of Agee's use of dialogue, describe the characters of Scratchy, Potter, and Potter's bride. Compare these characterizations with those of Crane, and account for the differences you find.
4. Agee adds several situations to the original plot, such as the muted conflict between Laura Lee and Potter's bride, and several characters, such as Deacon Smeed. Cite as many additions made by Agee as you can, and show how they belong significantly to the rhetoric of film as determined by its visual framework; its heavy reliance upon spoken language; its function as entertainment.
5. The time sequence is juggled in each of these works. Crane does so by use of flashbacks. Agee tells his story chronologically, but switches back and forth between the train and Yellow Sky, thus presenting time in disjointed spurts. Explain why each method of manipulating time is especially appropriate to the rhetoric of the medium employed.
6. Agee moves much closer to the actual language of the original story toward the end of his film treatment. Why do you think he does so?
7. The language of the two works is closer at their conclusions; yet those conclusions contain subtle and searching differences. Try to account for those differences on the basis of differences between the rhetoric of fiction and the rhetoric of film.

on film

1. Discuss the rhetoric of films you have seen on the basis of their movement; dialogue; visual imagery; characterization; in terms of their total "rhetorical" effect.

on structure and language

1. Compare Agee's extended exposition (not in the Crane story) with Crane's beginning in the middle of things. Why is each method especially appropriate to its own form?
2. Compare the uses Crane and Agee make of spoken language. Account for the differences you find on the basis of short story structure versus film script structure.
3. Compare the diction and uses of Crane's descriptions with those of Agee. Show how each is a product of its medium; of its time. (The Crane story was published in 1898.)

FILM
and
LITERATURE

In the essay in this section by George Bluestone, the author begins by quoting remarks by Joseph Conrad and D. W. Griffith in which both artists state their passion to make their audiences "see." Conrad's oft-quoted remark, ". . . to make you feel—before all, to make you *see,*" puts the stress, as does Griffith, on the moment when sight becomes insight. The way Conrad puts his priorities reminds us that the capacity to see with perception—to perceive—depends on an emotional readiness. Feeling empowers seeing with perception, even as breadth of insight depends on generosity of outlook. It is through this relationship of feeling and perception, of generosity and vision, that we attain to integrity of response. Thus King Lear cries to Poor Tom as he begins to awake from his own emotionally narrow and hence blinkered condition:

> Let the superfluous and lust-dieted man
> That slaves your ordinance, that will not see
> Because he does not feel, feel your power quickly.

Here precisely is a shared aim of those novelists and film-makers whose work grips us to such a degree that we care to study it: to lead us from awakened sympathies to fuller perceptions of reality.

Bluestone notes this motive common to literature and films in order to suggest, however, that we not look to them for quite the same thing, for quite the same quality of emotion or the same kind of insight. This despite the fact that, as Bluestone informatively points out, films have fed steadily and ravenously on every type of literary fare for source material.

One difference would seem to lie in the relatively primitive and broad treatment of the emotions in film. Nearly all the writers of this group of essays keep returning us to the matter of the emotional in motion pictures, and they seem especially responsive to, and prefer to single out, effects of the most "breathtaking" kind—the grand, the pathetic, the hectic, the cruel—effects which project emotions "in the raw." The novelist Daniel Fuchs describes his adventures in learning to write scripts for highly charged effects. (This essay on writing for films is also one of the best ever written on living in Hollywood.) J. Blumenthal admires Kurosawa's film on *Macbeth* for the immediate force of the film's images, whose impact he seeks to distinguish from those he would consider more "literary." Both Dwight Macdonald and Jan Kott draw striking parallels between the film form and one of the most emotionally open and free-wheeling of dramatic forms: the Elizabethan play. And when Richard Wilbur seeks to recount the influence of the movies on his own art as a poet, he turns, not to a serious "adult," "message" film but to *Dracula*. His essay describes the process through which elements of the film, and his experience of the film, were assimilated into a fine and highly subtle poem. (Interestingly, the other poet who appears in this volume, Jack Kerouac, is drawn to writing on another horror film, *Nosferatu*.)

The inescapable question is how far the film's properties allow for the transmutation of raw elements to a complex level of thought and vision: how far can the film succeed in integrating intellectual with emotional force? And how complex a depiction of emotions may we expect from films? Consider the intensity of feeling of a dramatic monologue by T. S. Eliot. This intensity derives from the weight of various elements which Eliot found the monologue capable of containing. Do you find in films like Antonioni's *L'Avventura* or Godard's *Contempt* a weight and pressure comparable to that in poems like "The Love Song of J. Alfred Prufrock" or "The Hollow Men"? This question is well worth working through in your own writing on it. (You may, of course, wish to substitute other works or combinations of works.)

The value of comparative reflections of this nature is that our inquiry into the boundaries of either art serves to extend our sense of both. Eisenstein's essay on Griffith and Dickens is valuable not only for what it says about Griffith as a film-maker but also for the light it sheds on Dickens' literary technique. Kott's discussion of the cinematic qualities of *Titus Andronicus* adds to our sense of the myriad elements the Shakespearean structure contains. A similar double function is served by the literary analogies in the Ross essay on the film *Accident.* When Ross cites Henry James in discussing a film in which lust and violence play a notable part, the citation qualifies not only our idea of the film, but also our idea of James' fiction, which may possess much more of a raw side than it has ordinarily been credited with.

The essay by Philip French on the recent abundant appearance in —and actual discussion of—books in films surely belongs in this section. It is an apt reminder of the number of book-reading, print-oriented people who now comprise an increasingly large and enthusiastic part both of the film-making scene and of the general film audience.

WRITING
FOR THE MOVIES

Daniel Fuchs

Dear Editors:

Thank you for your kind letter and compliments. Yes, your hunch was right, I would like very much to tell about the problems and values I've encountered, writing for the movies all these years. I'm so slow in replying to you because I thought it would be a pleasant gesture—in return for your warm letter—to send you the completed essay. But it's taken me longer than I thought it would. I've always been impressed by the sure, brimming conviction of people who attack Hollywood, and this even though they may never have been inside the business and so haven't had the chance of knowing how really onerous and exacerbating the conditions are. But for me the subject is more disturbing, or else it is that I like to let my mind wander and that I start from a different bias, or maybe I've just been here to long.

When I came to California twenty-five years ago, I was taken with the immense, brilliantly clean sunshine which hovered over everything. I wrote troubled pieces about Hollywood—a diary which I actually kept, an article titled "Dream City or The Drugged Lake" The studio where I worked, RKO on Gower Street, seemed drenched and overpowered by the sun. The studio paths were empty; you heard a composer somewhere listlessly working up a tune for a musical picture: "Oh, I ADORE you, ADORE you, ADORE you—you WONDERFUL thing!" The people stayed hidden inside their offices, and what they did there, I didn't know. I was made welcome to the community with a grace I somehow hadn't expected—by the wonderful Epstein brothers, who broke the way for me and looked out for me; by Dorothy Parker, who telephoned and introduced me to a glittering group of people, or a group I thought glittering; by John Garfield, with his honest and whole-hearted happy spirits; and by a man named Barney Glazer, now dead, at one time head of Paramount Studios. Mr. Glazer had a beautiful home on Chevy Chase Drive in Beverly Hills. It was surrounded by carefully tended grounds—gardens and strawberry patches, patios, a championship enclosed tennis court, a championship swimming pool, dressing rooms, a gymnasium. After the week's work, starting with Saturday afternoon, guests assembled there and a sort of continuous party went on until Monday morning. Mr. Glazer trotted through the assemblage, ignoring the entertainment and the championship tennis court, bent on his own pursuits. He was interested in fine china and *objets d'art,* in carpentry work, in watching over his dogs who were getting old and decrepit and kept falling into the swimming pool; the dogs, when they hurt themselves, would huddle motionless and just wait until Mr. Glazer came hurrying up, to scold and take care of them. With his open generosity, he took pains to make sure I felt easy among the company at those parties, and I visited his home often, appearing on most of the week-ends. Many kinds of people were there, but mainly the old-timers, men who were firmly a part of the movie business—grizzled and heavy-eyed, patient, pestered by arthritis, sciatica, and other vexations. They smiled at me. They were amused by my inexperience and newness to their community. They liked me and I think they wanted to be liked. But they would never parry my questions. They wouldn't respond to my inquiries and doubts. They knew that if I was to learn anything about their way of living and working, it would be no good unless I found it out by myself. "I would argue with you," one of them said to me, "but if I win the argument, what do I win?" They had their minds set on other things, and the time was short.

Not long after I came to Hollywood, I was asked by my studio —not RKO, another studio—to help work on a picture which was shot and done, which was in its rough cut, but which had gone awry along the road. The picture was a mystery-spy thriller, the kind of story the English write so expertly. Our English novelist was one of the best; his novel had been adapted by an able, conscientious screen-writer; the producer and director were also thoroughly seasoned and professional. The trouble lay in the star. If you examine these English spy-thrillers, you find that they're almost invariably concerned with an innocent: the hero is guileless and sweet; he is suddenly assaulted by a bewildering collection of circumstances; he gropes, is buffeted; he holds on, out of a perverse stubbornness; he digs in, perseveres; little by little the truths are revealed to him; he is chastened, matured, and the picture is over. That's how these stories go. But our star would have nothing to do with innocence. He adamantly refused to play the part as written. There was no use in blaming him. He had built up a personal identity over the years as a trench-coated, hard-boiled character who knew the world; he believed in this characterization and had prospered with it; and from his point of view it would have been senseless to jettison everything for the sake of a single picture. Nor could you fairly blame the studio management —there are just so many stars around and you take the best one you can get. So I could understand the star, I could understand the studio; I was inside the business now, and knew these were realities that had to be met. But this essential conflict between the star and his part produced a chaos—when the picture was put together—that was amazingly complex and convoluted. Every story value was bewitched. The film raced on its sprocket holes; people glided about, as in dreams; telling points were certainly being made, except that you didn't know what they told, you didn't know what you were supposed to think or feel. I was confounded. I didn't know even how to begin. To add to my predicament, by a quirk of fortune, I was thrown into this assignment by the studio, required to work in tandem with a collaborator who was no less than one of perhaps the ten most important literary figures in the world. I was paralyzed by awe. It happened that I had a deep, long-time admiration for this man and his achievement. I couldn't blurt out my esteem. It was almost impossible for me to hold conferences with him, to exchange notions and story ideas in the free, knock-about way which is our practice in the studios. I stuttered and fumbled. I couldn't meet his eyes in his presence, and kept looking down at the floor. I addressed him as Mr. Soinso, not as Al or Tom.

"I know why you don't cozy to me," he said softly to me one day, seeing that things were going badly. "You don't cozy to me because you think I'm anti-Semitic."

"Yes," I said. I was dismayed to hear myself saying, "How about that?"

"Well, it's troo-oo," he said, searching within himself and perplexed. "I don't like Jews—but I don't like Gentiles neither."

The director, a fastidious gentleman, as so many of them in our city are, was no help. He wore a smart, hand-embroidered cowboy suit, cowboy boots, a scarf at his throat, and had recently married a girl one-third his age—he was sixty and not easy to approach. At our first meeting, he lifted an eyelid, took a good look at my collaborator and me, saw there was nothing coming from us, and disappeared. I can't recall that he ever said a single word to either one of us. The producer was similarly out of reach. He was in hiding, incommunicado. Our star insisted on a scene in which he was given the Congressional Medal of Honor—Cagney had received one, in *Yankee Doodle Dandy,* the camera shooting from behind President Roosevelt's head, and our star threatened bodily harm unless the producer rewarded him in the same way at the conclusion of our picture. The producer, in consequence, stayed clear of his office and did his work in whatever sound stages happened to be idle around the lot. So my collaborator and I were left strictly to ourselves. I floundered. Scenes had to be written; some key had to be found which would toss the combinations magically aright; the re-takes were waiting to be shot. And the deadlines were coming nearer and nearer.

"Where do you sneak off to every night?" my collaborator said to me one evening, drawing up softly, out of nowhere.

I stared at him. I didn't know what he was talking about.

"Comes about nightfall," he said, sly and glinting, drawing up closer—*what did I have stashed away? What illicit bargainings was I up to, what devious chicaneries?* "Comes about nightfall, I look out my window, and there I see you on the path scooting along—where do you go?"

"Where do I go?" I said. "I go no place—I go home."

"Home?" he said. "Home? *Every* night?"

I felt disheartened and lost, ignominious or ludicrous as the terms of the situation might be. I was bereft. I liked my collaborator, and was failing him. I had seen enough of the people at Mr. Glazer's home to be genuinely respectful. I was touched by their quality; I wondered at them and was attracted and wanted some day to be part of them. And yet they were failing me, or I was failing them. Out of my helplessness and distress, I became furtive. I started keeping out of sight. I slipped off the lot. They say the first delivery is the hardest, but in our case with my wife and me, it was the second—we were having a new baby at the time. I received sudden emergency calls, and bolted. Toward the end I stayed close to the hospital and was gone from the studio for days at a stretch. And then abruptly, miraculously, everything was calm. The fever was over. Everything that needed to be done was done. The scenes had been photographed; the picture was re-assembled; the front office was pleased. Suddenly, late one Saturday afternoon, I found myself with my collaborator sitting in the producer's office, the producer there thanking us for our contributions to the job, still apologizing because he had unavoidably neglected us. All endings are sad, no matter what they are the endings to, and few places are as peaceful and benign as a movie lot when the work has halted and everyone has left. The producer was mellow, worn and humble in spirit, as we are after crisis.

"I'll think of you," he said to my collaborator—my collaborator was leaving us, on his way back to his home in the heart of the nation.

"I'll think of you too," my collaborator said, eyeing us both somberly, thinking no doubt of the turmoil, the business with the sound stages, my peculiar behavior, and the mysterious phone calls. "I'll think of you too," he said, implacable and without mercy to the last, "in the middle of the night."

The wonder was the picture. It was whole now, sound—the myriad nerve-lines of continuity in working order, the conglomeration of effects artfully re-juggled, brisk and full of urgent meaning. With the unsettling irrelevance of life everywhere, when I was in the Navy some years later, during the war, I was assigned to the OSS, the intelligence agency, and on one of the first days this old spy-thriller movie was duly shown to us in the official course of our orientation. My collaborator, talented but benighted, had been distrustful. He had been discomfited by the things we had seen, was affronted and disapproving, and passed on. But for me what had taken place was now in the nature of a phenomenon. I knew a massive exertion had been put forth. I knew it was a head-breaking feat of will and strength, a feat certainly beyond me. I thought of the producer, overworked and beset on all sides, doggedly bearing down on his task, never once letting himself lose heart. My mind went back to the director, with his scarf, with his erect, courtly posture and reticence, with his accumulation of who knew what special lore within him. "Isn't Fitzwilliam wonderful?" his bride had burst out impetuously to a group of us waiting in the anteroom, that morning of our first meeting. She was entranced, glowing. "He's shooting his next picture in Tahiti, and he's taking me along. He's so good to me. Oh, I love him. He is the only man in the world I could ever care for." He was sixty; he lived, I had heard, in a mansion under dark pines near the mansions of Hearst and Doheny, raced thoroughbreds from Ireland, had been to sea and had wrangled horses in Wyoming in his youth. Working in private, disregarding sightseers, outsiders, and all other distractions, this elegant, strange man had struggled with the film with a dedication and intensity which I could well imagine but couldn't fathom, and hadn't rested until he had conquered it.

We tested our pictures in Huntington Park, in out of the way small towns, towns still undeveloped and straggling. This was what the studios went by—the audience's reaction. It was bedrock for them, holy writ—the rest, all other criteria, they waved aside with a blunt, contemptuous indifference. Banks of lights were set up on top of the marquee: MAJOR STUDIO PREVIEW TONIGHT, and the people would come gathering in the chill of evening, drifting up to the theater, to the blaze of light, in their jeans and stiff cotton house dresses, their eyes wavering and uncertain. They were field-hands, workers in the citrus groves; they were miscellaneous day laborers, filling-station attendants, people newly resettled from Oklahoma and Arkansas. I saw them in our great drugstores, wandering through the gaudy aisles, staring in silence at the gewgaws and confections on the shelves, spending their money on objects which, when they took them home, they must have surely realized were unneeded and a waste. I used to stand in front of the theater and look at their loose, yielding faces, and wonder what kind of pictures could be given to them; if it was possible to reach them in any important, meaningful way; if it even made sense to try. And yet, once they were inside the movie house, a transformation occurred. Others have remarked on it. In the dark, forming a mass, they lost their individual disabilities and insufficiencies. They became informed; they became larger than themselves; a separate entity appeared, an entity that was knowing and complete. Unfamiliar and demanding as the material might be, no matter how deeply probing or delicate and sophisticated the treatment, if the picture was good, they were unfailingly affected by it and gave it its full measure of appreciation. I witnessed it again and again, with the unlikeliest pictures, so that I was soon able to understand why the studios put such store on these sneak previews, so that I began to share their faith, so that I myself have now come secretly to believe—secretly, since I know it isn't so—that good pictures will always command a mass audience, that if a picture fails to find this mass following, then it is in reality spurious and without substance. In an interview in *Life* magazine, Joseph L. Mankiewicz said (I quote freely, from memory): "The most electrifying thing happens in the movie-house when you give the audience the truth." I knew exactly what he meant. You could almost tell the instant the picture took hold. An excitement filled into the theater, a thralldom. The people forgot they were sitting on the seats; they forgot themselves, their bodies. They lived only in the film. They were tumbled, swept along, possessed. Of course Mr. Mankiewicz didn't mean it could be just any truth. It had to be a carefully selected truth, carefully aligned and ordered. It had to be a truth that was worthy and could legitimately engage an audience. It had to have an opulence; or an urbanity; or a gaiety; a strength and assurance; a sense of life with its illimitable reach and promise. As a matter of fact, it didn't even have to be the truth. Properly stated, the sentence should have read: "The most electrifying thing happens in the movie-house when you give the audience—."

No one knew. Wizardry was involved. The studio people, with their unrelenting practicality, held solely with the instinct of the audience. These standards were basic, material, solid; everything else was frippery and phoniness. The product here was tested, exposed. There was no opportunity for illusion or deception. You *saw* the proof. And yet the exasperating dilemma remained that what you were to give the audience was a quantity really indefinable, ephemeral, everlastingly elusive. Here was the heart of the problem, the problem which was to plague and occupy me in all my time in the studios. It lay at the bottom of the commotion that went on in these places. It accounted for much of the puzzling behavior—the excesses, the hi-jinks, the strife and alarms, the wild, demented flights. It was a tantalizing, almost constantly frustrating pursuit, and the movie people gave themselves over to it with a tenacity that amounted to a kind of devotion.

We screenwriters shifted about from studio to studio, staying on one lot for a spell until a disenchantment set in and we were let go or left of our own volition and moved on to the next. Traveling around the studios, listening to the gossip at the different writers' tables in the commissaries, I heard stories about a certain outstanding movie executive who soon caught hold in my imagination and with whom I eventually became entangled. He was one of the industry's pioneers, had built his studio from the street up. Like the courtly director to whom for the sake of convenience I gave the fictitious name Fitzwilliam, he also had come out of a dim, adventurous background. He had been a bootlegger, a prizefighter, had participated in mean, degrading enterprises, had also roamed through the solitary towns of the Far West fifty years back. The studios, most of them, were not prepossessing establishments; they had been put together haphazardly over the years, additions stuck on to existing structures, projection rooms interspersed among the wardrobe and accounting departments, the whole clutter connected by a maze of stairways, ramps, crosswalks, balconies—and this movie executive prowled restlessly at all hours through the maze at his studio, looking for employees to pounce upon, for lights that should have been turned out and were left burning, to make trouble in general. He was a low-slung, pugnacious man, thoroughly hated, grasping, and always dissatisfied. "Your husband's just like me, we both don't care for money," he said to my wife one evening at a party—this was later, when I had become mixed up with him and he and I knew each other—and my wife shrieked with glee from the shock. It was a totally unexpected, bizarre remark, coming from him. "He put more people in the cemetery than all the rest of them combined," a man once told me about him, sincerely marveling, big-eyed and solemn. The way I came to meet him, I was calling on a friend of mine, a much sought-after director who was making a picture at his studio; my friend and I were weaving through the maze of staircases, going out to the street, when the movie executive, coursing on his rounds there, saw us and promptly nabbed us. It was my friend's birthday that day, and the executive—courting him aggressively at the time, the disenchantment not yet having set in—insisted on celebrating the occasion, on having a drink with him, and so he dragged us back up to his office, I tagging along. Upstairs in the office he was rattling around the room, working on my friend and putting on a show, when he suddenly broke off and turned to me. "What kind of a writer are you anyway?" he said harshly, hurriedly, getting it in. "Some people tell me you're good, other people tell me you stink."

I winced, confused and dazed, not so much offended—confused to think, in the flurry of the moment, that he had heard of me, that he knew who I was, and let down because he had expressed himself so dismally. He went right on with his shenanigans, but he had seen that wince on my face and it irked him, I could tell—it was in him to be affected because I was disappointed in him, that he had been rushed and hadn't been able to do well by himself. It stayed in his mind and rankled. From that meeting on, he kept having me brought over to his office to offer me a number of picture assignments, assignments which for one reason or another were unsuitable and I couldn't accept. He put himself out for my benefit. He became impish, teased me, revealed the softer side to his nature. "Keep quiet," he said to the coterie of assistants who surrounded him, shushing them. He wanted to do all the talking. "He didn't come up here to hear you. He heard the legend—now let him see the man," he said, and turned and faced me, grinning.

"What's the matter, you don't like my money?" he chided me, as I passed up his assignments. "You got a better job some place else? What are you trying to prove to me, that you're a fine rabbi? You giving me the con, getting me fat and sweet, and then you'll move in and make a killing?" He couldn't believe a writer would turn down an assignment just because the material was unsuitable. He thought there had to be a deeper, intricate motivation. He thought I was maneuvering. "Everybody that walks into this office is a prostitute," he said. "They don't come in here unless they're out for something. Everybody cares only for their self-interest. Here, I'll show you—I got it right in my desk. . . ." He pulled the paper out. It was a garish act of betrayal by some close relative, a son or a brother. They had manipulated stock against him, had labored in an effort to push him out of his company. The betrayal had occurred many years ago, but he always kept the letter of dismissal with him—it was a comfort, he needed to believe that people were base and abject.

The funny thing was there was some substance to his suspicions about me. His studio owned a story, the basis of a story, which I liked very much and kept secretly angling for. During those turbulent interviews in his office, in the ebb and rise, I would persistently refer to this story property, mentioning what a fine picture I thought it would make, murmuring how I would be pleased to be allowed to work on it.

"You don't want to do that story," he ground out at me. "You just want to hit me for a big pot of money. If you really want to write it, if you got your heart and soul so set on it, then why don't you write it—who's stopping you?"

He had me. I didn't know how to answer him, and one day, after a difficult session, sawing back and forth, listening to his explosions and the flow of his bitter cynicisms, I finally agreed to go in with him in some loose, percentage arrangement, proceeding more or less on a speculative basis; and so that was how I came to work for him; that was why he told my wife I didn't care for money. I did, in fact, have my heart in the story. I sometimes think a successful motion picture story is so complex and impossibly constituted that you don't really write them—that they already exist and that you *find* them, that they're either there, somewhere, or else you're doomed. This was one of those stories, touched with grace and blessed. It went kindly. It became vigorous and spunky with life. I found, and firmly, the dramatic incubus, that enveloping cloud of anxiety against which a man moment by moment pits himself and which thereby gives a story its never-ceasing, insidious thrust. I found the theatrical image of my hero, the humor—that dancing bundle of slants, deceits, stratagems by which a man conceals his despair and which gives him an instantaneous hold on the attention of the audience. Best of all, what delighted me, was a lyricism—I caught, and was able to show, those innermost dreams and raptures the steady dissolution of which infuses a man's despair with meaning and a piercing, significant emotion.

"It's a wonderful story," he told me, when I had finished it and had turned it in. He had stayed up all night with the script, I knew; he had studied it meticulously, section by section. I sang inside of me. He knew the story perfectly, savored each value, each shading. "It's the story of you and your wife," he twitted me. "It's autobiographical. You can't make up things like this. They have to happen. It's the best story I ever read," he said, crashing down on me. "I wouldn't touch it with a ten-foot pole—it'll be a colossal flop."

He wouldn't touch it because nobody was interested in horse-race betting (if we assume the subject of this story had to do with the horses), but he flung that out carelessly, on the run; because it was different, flukey; because it wasn't enough for a picture to be original—just because a picture was new and different, it didn't necessarily mean it would go; because it was ambitious and hard to manage and fragile; because if a story like this one miscarried, it would splatter and become a hideous, total fiasco; because a screen-play was nothing but a blueprint, a declaration of hopes and intentions; because it needed actors, handlers, diviners who would know surely what to do with it and who could be counted on to bring it off. "Get me a big star," he said, in spite of his arguments, reversing himself, "and I'll do it. Get me a big director," he told his subordinates, and they in turn came hurrying to tell me; and it struck me, so that it remains with me still, how this harsh, rampaging man, who was universally detested, whose fingers were fearfully twisted with arthritis, who just recently had undergone surgery for cancer (a secret, which I knew only through the indiscretion of a friend, a doctor), although, oddly, it was a heart seizure that took him off a year and a half later—it struck me how he fiercely persevered with his obsession, asking no quarter, staying up all night in the dead quiet of his studio.

While I was at the studio on this bout, it happened that an old acquaintance was simultaneously working there. He was brought in on a one-picture deal, a picture which he had initiated and was to produce for the management. As could be predicted, he quickly became embroiled with the executive, and I had an inside view of their curious, intensive battle over the stretch of months. This acquaintance was a man I knew from earlier days in New York; he was a brilliant Broadway producer with a distinguished record of successes, who also at intervals busied himself in motion pictures and who—I never clearly understood why, because he said I reminded him of all his uncles—had befriended me and took a continuing, fitful interest in my welfare. He was a vivid individual, with a surging, autocratic style. He had made fortunes, had lost them, acted on fancy and was always on the move. He would come swooping down on me in Hollywood, find out what I was doing, immediately rant and lash out at me for wasting my time; he would call up my agent and fire him, call up the heads of the studios where I was working (people who most often didn't even know I was in their employ), drub them in the most forceful, intemperate language—"He's working for *you?* You should be working for *him*"—hang up and go spinning off again, to resume his journeyings. "Don't, *don't* write short stories about me," he would say, grimacing with distaste, after he had read in a magazine some piece of disguised fiction I had written about him, "—novels, novels!" He lived in a cocoon. "A son is a fantasy," he would say, his eyes shining, believing in children, in whatever would enhance life. "You don't have to excite yourself and try to show me how bright, how talented you are—just listen," he would say, when I would think of something to add to the conversation. He wanted to do all the talking too. "Read *Life on the*

Mississippi." "Never write about people who can't manipulate their destinies." And he would hustle out to the airport, get himself settled in his sleeping berth on the plane, take a dose of sleeping tablets, tuck the blankets tidily around him, and be wafted off to London or Peru.

But during this period I'm writing of, he was anchored, in disgrace with fortune, obliged to work out a term at the studio, and so this made two of them, my friend and the executive. They went at it hammer and tongs, the executive with a grinning relish, almost grateful, it seemed to me, to have such a willing, supple adversary at hand. They fought over the casting, over hairdressers, over gowns, over lines of dialogue, over each separate word. I watched them cut each other up almost daily when they met at lunch in the studio private dining room. But underneath the clash of wills and the tumulting, what was really provoking them, if the truth was known, was the old basic problem of the picture, the familiar welter of uncertainties and indecisions. The mind became cauterized; it was a torment to hold on to the over-all vision of the picture—the lines of the continuity, the component sequences, the proper working place of everything in the design. It wasn't enough to go on hope or intuition or instinct. You could take nothing on sufferance. You had to *know* every moment what was happening in the picture; you had perpetually to control and understand each stroke and effect—and it was easier for them to hack away at themselves in these senseless spasms than to go on wrestling with the riddles. Just as Mr. Louis B. Mayer over at Metro had a sentimental attachment to chicken-noodle soup and provided it at less than cost at his studio's commissary, so, similarly, pickles meant something to our executive; once a week or once every two weeks, whichever it was, the great black truck from the pickle-works drew up to the curb with its terrible smell, bringing us fresh supplies—and my friend, boring in assiduously, fiendishly belabored the executive on the score of this human frailty, taking a ruthless advantage of every opening. "You're common. You fill yourself with junk. You come from a low-class, first-generation tenement life and you're still stuck away there in that Yiddish *pippik*. That's why you're worth only a measly five or six million. You have no taste, no sense of literature." At the time the contracts were worked up, there had been a hard wrangle over the control of the picture—my friend was determined not to let the executive have the say-so over him. The executive had craftily agreed, conceding the point, stipulating only that he, the executive, was to be brought in as arbiter in cases where my friend had differences with the other principals—the stars, the director. It proved to be a peculiarly constraining condition—a strait jacket, an affliction. My friend, who thought that he and only he alone saw the picture true, was unable to flash fire and impose orders; he had to cajole, plead—there were even excruciating instances when he had to give ground. His chest broke out in a profusion of boils. I can remember the sight of him, hurtling blindly from wall to wall in the murky maze of the staircases. I can see him now as he once went skimming over the pavement of the parking lot, panting and clawing at his chest, vowing that he wouldn't be beaten, that he would stick it out no matter what the cost. "I'll get along with everyone," he affirmed breathlessly, lost in his fervor. "Nobody'll be able to say I'm temperamental. I'll be sweet. I'll be charming—they won't even recognize it's me." As the weeks rolled on, his madness broke loose and he went past all rational behavior. He communicated with the executive in a series of wicked, fanatically labored-over, anti-Semitic memos. As the picture neared completion and everyone could see it would be at last a wonderful, resplendent hit, as the New York office of the film company tried to entice him and keep him at the studio for further commitments, he flared out into the most searing, impossible demands—that the executive was to be forbidden ever to speak to him, that the executive was to keep himself out of view. "If I walk into the private dining room and he's sitting there eating, he has to get up and leave." He wanted that put into the contract. But the New York office, in courting him, in trying to keep him at the studio, was only speaking for the executive; it was the executive who was really courting him—in spite of the vilification, in spite of the pickles and the wretched memos.

It was a strange preoccupation they had, and it chivvied them in countless ways, without let-up. Passing along through the studios in the game of musical chairs we played, I continually met with this ferment, with this reckless expenditure of energy and clamor. I never knew Mr. Mayer, was only introduced to him three or four times; but he was of course a stalwart figure, no doubt the most obstreperous of the breed, and I often glimpsed him in action, moving here and there with his retinue, vigilantly attending to everything. He walked like a czar. Jules Dassin—then beginning as a director, treading carefully—once made a photographic study of his leading lady, shading her face with the flickering play of leaves; and Mr. Mayer swiftly had him on the carpet for the shot, upbraiding him for the shadows, wanting nothing that would mar the clear, crystalline beauty of his company's stars. He lectured Jules severely on the point, so that Jules told me of the incident, startled by the older man's vehemence, by his notions, by his odd possessive insistence. It was a deep, personal involvement with Mr. Mayer, a seemingly life and death concern. When I returned to Metro on an assignment after the war, they were making *The Postman Always Rings Twice*, a picture of the violent category to which Mr. Mayer was powerfully opposed; and I was seriously cautioned for my own good never to speak of this picture aloud—it was in production on the lot and we were all to behave as though it wasn't there, he wasn't to hear of it. Years later, when the dice had taken another roll and he was out of the studio, fallen from favor, I saw him one evening at a party —idling by himself on the fringes now, no one any longer obliged to listen to him. I was again introduced to him, Miss Lillian Burns plucking me by the sleeve and bringing me over to him. He smiled graciously, in spite of adversity; he started to offer me his hand; and then Miss Burns, a vivacious lady with an impudent, mischievous bent, went on to mention the name of a picture I was at that particular time associated with, a big hit which was also of the category he despised—and he instantly took his hand back, turned on his heel and stalked off, still haughty, still fierce, indomitable. . . . I knew of a certain director, a veteran, master movie-maker, well-tempered and suave, who one day—in the heat and struggle—suddenly went raving wild at his writer (thank God, not me), raging that the writer didn't know his craft, that he hadn't applied himself, that he hadn't been willing to dig into the *bones* of the work, that he hadn't broken his head enough at those devastating sneak previews which were our testing grounds.

I remember a curious experience with Billy Wilder: I had seen his *Sunset Boulevard* twice, was greatly moved by this work of art, sent him a fan letter. A little while later it happened that I met him for the first time, and to my astonishment he spent the greater part of our meeting inquiring into a section of the film—the section where the hero first wanders into that gauzy, soft-lit mansion of Norma Desmond, the faded movie star. The picture was out, playing in the houses, acclaimed, but the sequence still vexed Mr. Wilder. He didn't know what was working there, why it should be sound. He wasn't on top of it, couldn't rationalize it; and he worried away at the problem, probing and trying to reassure himself. In another case, not far from the studio where *Sunset Boulevard* was made, a writer-director—who had finally rationalized his picture, who knew in his heart he controlled and was on top of it— was nevertheless engaged in a furious, running feud with the head of his studio (always the same pattern, always somehow that grueling, drawn-out battle between the two). "I'm so sure this will be the biggest disaster we've ever had in the history of the studio, that I'm putting it in writing," the head of the studio wrote him, dating and signing his memo. The writer-director swept on, uncaring. They tested their picture in some small town up north, Sausalito or San Anselmo—and the audience howled it down, they ripped it to pieces. Everything went wrong. The writer-director disappeared for days. No one knew where he was or what was happening to him. But then there he was back at the studio again, locked up in the cutting room, working over the movieola, grim and spinning and searching, never pausing until he got it right. He won out in the end—the picture became one of the all-time classics, the studio was festooned with honors. . . . It was always surprising how underneath the outcries and confusion the work steadily went on. They never slackened; fighting the *malach ha-moves* and the dingy seepage of time, they beat away to the limits of their strength and endowments, striving to get it right, to run down the answers, to realize and secure the picture. I was once brought in with a producer and director, a famous mismatched pair who were noted for their rows and the rigors of their professional efforts, and so this time I was in the eye of the storm, caught up in the middle between them. This producer's trouble was his compassion, his kindliness and understanding. He had lived five lifetimes in one, was intelligent, sensitive, and had a ready, inundating sorrow. "Darling, sweetheart, why are you blue?" he would beseech his gifted partner, pursuing him. "Do you want my beach house? Do you want my boat, my car?" In retaliation, the director —who was the one I was supposed to work with—savagely turned himself inside out to think up new ways of torturing him. He was harrowed enough with the dilemmas of the script—"they expect us to work up a screenplay out of a ketchup label." He contrived mean, elaborate practical jokes. We took off in all directions, traveling by train and plane—ostensibly for purposes of research, to scout locations. We criss-crossed the country. We were gone for weeks and the weeks turned into months. The director entertained royally wherever we went, holding big drinking parties every day before and after dinner, sitting down thirty and forty guests at a clip for dinner, everything charged to the producer. The producer wept and fumed at long range, laying the blame on me.

"That's why I put you in with him—to watch out and be a restraining influence," he reproached me piercingly over the phone, all hot and scrambled. "Him we knew for a lunatic, that was foregone. But you are a family man, with responsibilities— why do you conspire with him against me?"

"I'll speak to him," the director said to me that day in the hotel room, taking the phone from me. "Ben," he declaimed into the mouthpiece, speaking in his hearty, royal way, "how are you?"

"Don't ask me how I am; never mind how I am!" the producer railed at him, his voice whirling aloft, and for a minute or two I could hear him carrying on there in his frenzy three thousand miles away.

"Ben, I've got good news for you and bad," the director boomed, unperturbed.

"Don't tell the bad!" the producer wailed. "Bad news I got, all I can use. I don't need more. Only tell me the good—what is the good?"

"Ben, we are leaving New Orleans tonight."

"Darling, sweetheart!" the producer cried, ecstatic, gushing, everything changed—bygones would be bygones; they would forget what transpired; they would go forward now only in harmony. "So what is the bad news—what can be bad?"

"We're going to New York," the director said.

It went on like that on that trip and on other trips, for a number of years, in great capitals and over four continents. I dropped out, to work for other directors and producers, but they skirmished along, harassing each other day by day, the director systematically making the producer's life a hell, the two of them evolving in the meantime between them a group of the most beguilingly rare, iridescent productions—until at last the director shamed himself irreparably before the producer and was forced to bring their relationship to a permanent end. "Darling, sweetheart," I can still hear the producer crying, desolate and engulfed, his eyes hungering to forgive, to forget, to let bygones be bygones. But the director had offended too deeply and there was no going back for him. "If I could only find an honest Ben Soinso," he often mutters to himself, pining for his friend, disconsolate and wretched.

They knew the wandering lassitude of the will, the essential human servitude and unworthiness. They knew how loathesome it was to be obliged to transgress, to commit iniquity and betray, and that the pity was with the wrongdoer. They were a chastened crew, with a wry, flickering wisdom. Coming out of their raw, bustling background, combing the earth with their energy and avid need for pleasure, they had the kind of education you get in the prize-ring—not from hearsay or from precept. They knew the *guderim*. Isn't it true that a good deal of what we know of the world comes from these men—from their pictures, from their lore? Isn't it true that they have had an amazingly penetrating effect, people in countries all over the globe running eagerly to see their pictures, to share in their virility, in their realism and gusto and command of life? I think it is a foolish scandal that we have the habit of deriding these men and their industry, that it is the mode. Is it fitting to pass by so indifferently the work of Ford, Stevens, Wilder, Mankiewicz, Huston, Zinnemann, William Wellman, Howard Hawks, Sam Wood, Clarence Brown, Victor Fleming, William Van Dyke, King Vidor, Raoul Walsh, Henry Hathaway, Henry King, Chaplin, Lubitsch, Goldwyn, Selznick, Milestone,

Capra, Wyler, Cukor, Kazan? They were a gaudy company, ram-
bunctious and engrossed. What they produced, roistering along in
those sun-filled, sparkling days, was a phenomenon, teeming with
vitality and ardor, as indigenous as our cars or skyscrapers or
highways, and as irrefutable. Generations to come, looking back
over the years, are bound to find that the best, most solid creative
effort of our decades was spent in the movies, and it's time someone came clean and said so.

There is no RKO any longer. The studio on Gower Street is
given over to other pursuits. The child who was born that day,
when I was struggling with the mystery-thriller, with my distinguished collaborator, is now full grown, busy with his own affairs,
away from home. In the middle of the night the phone rings and
we rouse from sleep. "It's Adele," my wife says to me, carefully
covering the mouthpiece with her hand to spare the caller's feelings, and then she removes her hand and they go on talking over
the phone. Adele is a once famous star, now inactive, unwanted,
the years having flown. We don't know Adele and she doesn't
know us. Originally she was looking for some people named
Ridgway, a family who used to live in our house. She knows the
Ridgways aren't here, my wife tells her; but she likes the sound of
my wife's voice, it is a solace, and in the dead hours of the night
she continues to phone, prolonging this curious friendship that
has formed between them. "Is this Mr. Ridgway's residence?" she
begins shyly, and my wife says no, soft and solicitous, and they
commune.

How illusory is the nature of desire; how wonderfully strange
and various are the strivings of the hidden heart. Long ago, I was
assigned (by the same diligent, untiring producer who was
involved in the mystery-thriller upset, not that it matters) to help
with a story of backstage life which was supposed to be fictitious
but was actually based on the true experiences of another star, an
actress then at the height of her success, fresh and vibrant, with
that incredible shining beauty they have. When she was fourteen
years old, she had been tampered with by a passing entertainer.
Her aunt, with whom she lived, was an ambitious woman. She
immediately took hold of the opportunity; forced the entertainer

to marry her niece; left her own husband and latched on; and in this way the two of them, the aunt and the niece, escaped from their depression-ridden New England industrial town and gained a foothold in show business. The entertainer, burdened with a wife he didn't want and with this overbearing aunt in the bargain, ducked and weaved, eventually managed to shake free; he drifted off. The two went on by themselves. The girl scored, going straight to the top in one of those dazzling overnight leaps. The entertainer made a rapid turnabout, clamored after his wife, publicly protested he was being abandoned, slashed his wrists a little. A settlement was arranged; the matter was taken care of.

This was the story behind the star's rise to fame. These were the facts, bedraggled and humanly forlorn, as they were commonly known, as we had them to deal with. We improvised. We glossed. We inserted a few nobilities. The entertainer became a tragic figure, genuinely in love, genuinely bereaved; when he attempted suicide, he succeeded. The fourteen-year-old—now seventeen—was purely a victim, innocent and unthinking. We changed New England to Oklahoma; we made the aunt a sister, so that she might be more readily cast, sisters being less aged than aunts. We were having enough trouble trying to cast the leading role. For a long time we were stumped, it seemed altogether impossible to find the right actress. Acting on a sudden, desperate brainstorm, we decided to offer the part to the star herself. She read the script—astonishingly, it went straight past her. She never recognized herself in the drama. "You know," she said to us at lunch, as we were wooing her, "this might almost be the story of me and my aunt."

She turned us down, the part disturbing her, and in any case she was much too grand in those days for our modest project; the picture went out with another player. But the years passed by, twelve or fourteen, and it happened that we fell in with one another again, the actress appearing in another picture I was concerned with, amenable now, subdued. She knew by this time the backstage story had been about her—someone had told her or she had come to it herself; I often caught her glance upon my face—rueful, bemused. "Do you want to know what really happened, sonny?" she said to me one day on the set, when there was a lull in the activity, when we all stood by and everything idled.

She was dead game, conceding nothing to time. The legs were

muscled, hard and used, the hard, unkind lines showing. That pearly, short-lived radiance was gone. I remembered the stories I knew about her, how when she used to make public appearances in the big movie houses, she would go darting up to the balcony between shows with a companion, to look at the picture, to neck.

There had been no tampering, no seduction. No one had had his way with her. There had been no hasty marriage. It had been all her own idea, on her own initiative. It was odd how the facts were scrambled. The entertainer had been a friend of the family, was going with an older cousin, was engaged. When she was fourteen years old, she had watched the courtship from the distance, had quietly set her cap for him. "I thought he was the handsomest man I had ever seen in my life," she told me that afternoon. "I wanted him. I made up my mind. I went for him. I got him. I knew how. And then, later. . . ." She shrugged, her voice fell away; she turned aside, smiling and helpless, dreaming. "You change," she said. "Time passes. . . ." She wandered off and left me—someone called her name. It was the time of day on the set when the mood grows gray, when the electricians and grips yawn and the work goes soft, when extras and bit-players—out of monotony, to beguile the moments away—face one another and start jiggling on their feet, dancing by themselves in this unspoken, sleepy mockery, the faces of the girls flushed and wicked and tempted, when the air is filled with longing and the promise of better things seems just around the bend.

EXERCISES

on film and literature

1. In this essay Fuchs delays a long time before discussing writing for the films. What does he suggest by means of this delay about writing for films? about film writing as literature?
2. Show how Fuchs' anecdotes about the star, the director, and the coauthor are all oblique commentary about film writing as a literary form.
3. What is the paradox contained in the final half of this essay? How much, in your opinion, does the film script have to do with the creation of that paradox?

on film

1. Which films have you seen that strike you as being particularly well written? Can you remember the names of their authors?
2. Compare the importance, in films you have enjoyed, of film star and film script.

on structure and language

1. Unlike the previous essays in this collection, the style of this one is informal. What devices does Fuchs use to achieve his familiar, informal tone?
2. A key word in this essay is the word "wizardry." How does Fuchs define the word? Does he succeed in defining it precisely? If not, why not?

THE LIMITS OF THE NOVEL
AND THE LIMITS
OF THE FILM

George Bluestone

Summing up his major intentions in 1913, D. W. Griffith is reported to have said, "The task I'm trying to achieve is above all to make you see." Whether by accident or design, the statement coincides almost exactly with an excerpt from Conrad's preface to *Nigger of the Narcissus* published sixteen years earlier: "My task which I am trying to achieve is, by the power of the written word, to make you hear, to make you feel—it is, before all, to make you *see*." Aside from the strong syntactical resemblance, the coincidence is remarkable in suggesting the points at which film and novel both join and part company. On the one hand, that phrase "to make you see" assumes an affective relationship between creative artist and receptive audience. Novelist and director meet here in a common intention. One may, on the other hand, see visually through the eye or imaginatively through the mind. And between the percept of the visual image and the concept of the mental image lies the root difference between the two media.

Because novel and film are both organic—in the sense that aesthetic judgments are based on total ensembles which include both formal and thematic conventions—we may expect to find that differences in form and theme are inseparable from differences in media. Not only are Conrad and Griffith referring to different ways of seeing, but the "you's" they refer to are different. Structures, symbols, myths, values which might be comprehensible to Conrad's relatively small middle-class reading public would, conceivably, be incomprehensible to Griffith's mass public. Conversely, stimuli which move the heirs of Griffith's audience to tears, will outrage or amuse the progeny of Conrad's "you." The seeming concurrence of Griffith and Conrad splits apart under analysis, and the two arts turn in opposite directions. That, in brief, has been the history of the fitful relationship between novel and film: overtly compatible, secretly hostile.

On the face of it, a close relationship has existed from the beginning. The reciprocity is clear from almost any point of view: the number of films based on novels; the search for filmic equivalents of literature; the effect of adaptations on reading; box-office receipts for filmed novels; merit awards by and for the Hollywood community.

The moment the film went from the animation of stills to telling a story, it was inevitable that fiction would become the ore to be minted by story departments. Before Griffith's first year as a director was over, he had adapted, among others, Jack London's *Just Meat (For Love of Gold)*, Tolstoy's *Resurrection,* and Charles Reade's *The Cloister and the Hearth.* Sergei Eisenstein's essay, "Dickens, Griffith, and the Film Today," demonstrates how Griffith found in Dickens hints for almost every one of his major innovations. Particular passages are cited to illustrate the dissolve, the superimposed shot, the close-up, the pan, indicating that Griffith's interest in literary forms and his roots in Victorian idealism provided at least part of the impulse for technical and moral content.

From such beginnings, the novel began a still unbroken tradition of appearing conspicuously on story conference tables. The precise record has never been adequately kept. Various counts range from 17 to almost 50 per cent of total studio production. A sampling from RKO, Paramount, and Universal motion picture output for 1934–35 reveals that about one-third of all full-length features were derived from novels (excluding short stories). Lester Asheim's more comprehensive survey indicates that of 5,807 releases by major studios between 1935 and 1945, 976 or 17.2 per cent were derived from novels. Hortense Powdermaker reports, on the basis of *Variety's* survey (June 4, 1947) that of 463 screenplays in production or awaiting release, slightly less than 40 per cent were adapted from novels. And Thomas M. Pryor, in a recent issue of the *New York Times*, writes that the frequency of the original screenplay, reaching a new low in Hollywood, "represented only 51.8 per cent of the source material of the 305 pictures reviewed by the Production Code office in 1955." Appropriate modifications must be made in these calculations, since both Asheim and Powdermaker report that the percentage of novels adapted for high-budgeted pictures was much higher than for low-budgeted pictures.

The industry's own appraisal of its work shows a strong and steady preference for films derived from novels, films which persistently rate among top quality productions. Filmed novels, for example, have made consistently strong bids for Academy Awards. In 1950, *Time* reported the results of *Daily Variety's* poll of 200 men and women who had been working in the industry for more than twenty-five years. *Birth of a Nation* was considered the best silent film; *Gone with the Wind* the best sound film and the best "all time film." Originally, both were novels. The choice of *Gone with the Wind* was a happy meeting of commercial and artistic interests. For when, some five years later, *Time* reported *Variety's* listing of Hollywood's "all time money makers," Miss Mitchell's title stood ahead of all others with earnings of some $33.5 million. More important, of the ten most valuable film properties, five had been adapted from novels. The high percentage of filmed novels which have been financially and artistically successful may be more comprehensible when we remember how frequently Pulitzer Prize winners, from *Alice Adams* to *All the King's Men*, have appeared in cinematic form.

Just as one line of influence runs from New York publishing house to Hollywood studio, another line may be observed running the other way. Margaret Farrand Thorp reports that when *David Copperfield* appeared on local screens, the demand for the book was so great that the Cleveland Public Library ordered 132 new copies; that the film premiere of *The Good Earth* boosted sales of that book to 3,000 per week; and that more copies of *Wuthering Heights* have been sold since the novel was screened than in all the previous ninety-two years of its existence. Jerry Wald confirms this pattern by pointing out, more precisely, that after the film's appearance, the Pocket Book edition of *Wuthering Heights* sold 700,000 copies; various editions of *Pride and Prejudice* reached a third of a million copies; and sales for *Lost Horizon* reached 1,400,000. The appearance, in 1956, of such films as *Moby Dick* and *War and Peace*, accompanied by special tie-in sales of the novels, has continued this pattern.

But when Jean Paul Sartre suggests that for many of these readers, the book appears "as a more or less faithful commentary" on the film, he is striking off a typically cogent distinction. Quantitative analyses have very little to do with qualitative changes. They tell us nothing about the mutational process, let alone how to judge it. In the case of film versions of novels, such analyses are even less helpful. They merely establish the fact of reciprocity; they do not indicate its implications for aesthetics. They provide statistical, not critical data. Hence, from such information the precise nature of the mutation cannot be deduced.

Such statements as: "The film is true to the spirit of the book"; "It's incredible how they butchered the novel"; "It cuts out key passages, but it's still a good film"; "Thank God they changed the ending"—these and similar statements are predicated on certain assumptions which blur the mutational process. These standard expletives and judgments assume, among other things, a separable content which may be detached and reproduced, as the snapshot reproduces the kitten; that incidents and characters in fiction are interchangeable with incidents and characters in the film; that the novel is a norm and the film deviates at its peril; that deviations are permissible for vaguely defined reasons—exigencies of length or of visualization, perhaps—but that the extent of the deviation will vary directly with the "respect" one has for the original; that taking liberties does not necessarily impair the quality of the film, whatever one may think of the novel, but that such liberties are somehow a trick which must be concealed from the public.

What is common to all these assumptions is the lack of awareness that mutations are probable the moment one goes from a given set of fluid, but relatively homogeneous, conventions to another; that changes are *inevitable* the moment one abandons the linguistic for the visual medium. Finally, it is insufficiently recognized that the end products of novel and film represent different aesthetic genera, as different from each other as ballet is from architecture.

The film becomes a different *thing* in the same sense that a historical painting becomes a different thing from the historical event which it illustrates. It is as fruitless to say that film A is better or worse than novel B as it is to pronounce Wright's Johnson's Wax Building better or worse than Tchaikowsky's *Swan Lake*. In the last analysis, each is autonomous, and each is characterized by unique and specific properties.

EXERCISES

on film and literature

1. What according to the author is the root difference between the film and the novel?
2. What differences exist between the public for a novel and the public for a film? How do those differences affect the content of each form?
3. What evidences of "reciprocity" exist between film and novel? Show how those evidences are superficial only.

on film

1. Cite some films you have seen based upon novels you have read. From your own point of view explain how each form is different from the other.
2. Can you give an example of a film that is better than the novel upon which it is based? of a novel better than its filmed version? Why, in each case?

on structure and language

1. The author makes heavy use in this essay of documentation, example, and statistics. How does each technique add to his main contentions?

2. Compare the style of the final three paragraphs. Show how the clichés in the first of the three create a special tone and implication. Show how, and why, the intellectual tone of the second is especially effective. Comment on the author's use of analogies in the final one.

DICKENS, GRIFFITH,
AND THE FILM TODAY

Sergei Eisenstein

Dickens's nearness to the characteristics of cinema in method, style, and especially in viewpoint and exposition, is indeed amazing. And it may be that in the nature of exactly these characteristics, in their community both for Dickens and for cinema, there lies a portion of the secret of that mass success which they both, apart from themes and plots, brought and still bring to the particular quality of such exposition and such writing.

What were the novels of Dickens for his contemporaries, for his readers? There is one answer: they bore the same relation to them that the film bears to the same strata in our time. They compelled the reader to live with the same passions. They appealed to the same good and sentimental elements as does the film (at least on the surface); they alike shudder before vice, they alike mill the extraordinary, the unusual, the fantastic, from boring, prosaic and everyday existence. And they clothe this common and prosaic existence in their special vision.

Illumined by this light, refracted from the land of fiction back to life, this commonness took on a romantic air, and bored people were grateful to the author for giving them the countenances of potentially romantic figures.

This partially accounts for the close attachment to the novels of Dickens and, similarly, to films. It was from this that the universal success of his novels derived. . . . Dickens's tours as a reader gave final proof of public affection for him, both at home and abroad. By nine o'clock on the morning that tickets for his lecture course were placed on sale in New York, there were two lines of buyers, each more than three-quarters of a mile in length:

> The tickets for the course were all sold before noon. Members of families relieved each other in the queues; waiters flew across the streets and squares from the neighboring restaurant, to serve parties who were taking their breakfast in the open December air; while excited men offered five and ten dollars for the mere permission to exchange places with other persons standing nearer the head of the line!

Isn't this atmosphere similar to that of Chaplin's tour through Europe, or the triumphant visit to Moscow of "Doug" and "Mary," or the excited anticipation around the première of *Grand Hotel* in New York, when an airplane service assisted ticket buyers on the West Coast? The immense popular success of Dickens's novels in his own time can be equaled in extent only by that whirlwind success which is now enjoyed by this or that sensational film success.

Perhaps the secret lies in Dickens's (as well as cinema's) creation of an extraordinary plasticity. The observation in the novels is extraordinary—as is their optical quality. The characters of Dickens are rounded with means as plastic and slightly exaggerated as are the screen heroes of today. The screen's heroes are engraved on the senses of the spectator with clearly visible traits, its villains are remembered by certain facial expressions, and all are saturated in the peculiar, slightly unnatural radiant gleam thrown over them by the screen.

It is absolutely thus that Dickens draws his characters—this is the faultlessly plastically grasped and pitilessly sharply sketched gallery of immortal Pickwicks, Dombeys, Fagins, Tackletons, and others. . . .

The visual images of Dickens are inseparable from aural images. The English philosopher and critic, George Henry Lewes, though puzzled as to its significance, recorded that "Dickens once declared to me that every word said by his characters was distinctly *heard* by him. . . ."

We can see for ourselves that his descriptions offer not only absolute *accuracy of detail*, but also an absolutely *accurate drawing of the behavior* and actions of his characters. And this is just as true for the most trifling details of behavior—even gesture, as it is for the basic generalized characteristics of the image. Isn't this piece of description of Mr. Dombey's behavior actually an exhaustive regisseur-actor directive?

> He had already laid his hand upon the bell-rope to convey his usual summons to Richards, when his eye fell upon a writing-desk, belonging to his deceased wife, which had been taken, among other things, from a cabinet in her chamber. It was not the first time that his eye had lighted on it. He carried the key in his pocket; and he brought it to his table and opened it now—having previously locked the room door–with a well-accustomed hand.

Here the last phrase arrests one's attention: there is certain awkwardness in its description. However, this "inserted" phrase: *having previously locked the room door*, "fitted in" as if recollected by the author in the middle of a later phrase, instead of being placed where it apparently should have been, in the consecutive order of the description, that is, before the words, *and he brought it to his table*, is found exactly at this spot for quite unfortuitous reasons.

In this deliberate "montage" displacement of the time-continuity of the description there is a brilliantly caught rendering of the *transient thievery* of the action, slipped between the preliminary action and the act of reading another's letter, carried out with that absolute "correctness" of gentlemanly dignity which Mr. Dombey knows how to give to any behavior or action of his.

This very (montage) arrangement of the phrasing gives an exact direction to the "performer," so that in defining this decorous and confident opening of the writing-desk, he must "play" the closing and locking of the door with a hint of an entirely different shade of conduct. And it would be this "shading" in which would also be played the unfolding of the letter; but in this part of the "performance" Dickens makes this shading more precise, not only with a significant arrangement of the words, but also with an exact description of characteristics.

> From beneath a heap of torn and cancelled scraps of paper, he took one letter that remained entire. Involuntarily holding his breath as he opened this document, and 'bating in the stealthy

action something of his arrogant demeanour, he sat down, resting his head upon one hand, and read it through.

The reading itself is done with a shading of absolutely gentlemanly cold decorum:

> He read it slowly and attentively, and with a nice particularity to every syllable. Otherwise than as his great deliberation seemed unnatural, and perhaps the result of an effort equally great, he allowed no sign of emotion to escape him. When he had read it through, he folded and refolded it slowly several times, and tore it carefully into fragments. Checking his hand in the act of throwing these away, he put them in his pocket, as if unwilling to trust them even to the chances of being reunited and deciphered; and instead of ringing, as usual, for little Paul, he sat solitary all the evening in his cheerless room.

This scene does not appear in the final version of the novel, for with the aim of increasing the tension of the action, Dickens cut out this passage on Forster's advice; in his biography of Dickens Forster preserved this passage to show with what mercilessness Dickens sometimes "cut" writing that had cost him great labor. This mercilessness once more emphasizes that sharp clarity of representation towards which Dickens strove by all means, endeavoring with purely cinematic laconism to say what he considered necessary. (This, by the way, did not in the least prevent his novels from achieving enormous breadth.)

I don't believe I am wrong in lingering on this example, for one need only alter two or three of the character names and change Dickens's name to the name of the hero of my essay, in order to impute literally almost everything told here to the account of Griffith.

From that steely, observing glance, which I remember from my meeting with him, to the capture *en passant* of key details or tokens—indications of character, Griffith has all this in as much a Dickens-esque sharpness and clarity as Dickens, on his part, had cinematic "optical quality," "frame composition," "close-up," and the alteration of emphasis by special lenses.

Analogies and resemblances cannot be pursued too far—they lose conviction and charm. They begin to take on the air of machination or card-tricks. I should be very sorry to lose the conviction of the affinity between Dickens and Griffith, allowing this abundance of common traits to slide into a game of anecdotal semblance of tokens.

All the more that such a gleaning from Dickens goes beyond the limits of interest in Griffith's individual cinematic craftsmanship and widens into a concern with film-craftsmanship in general. This is why I dig more and more deeply into the film-indications of Dickens, revealing them through Griffith—for the use of future film-exponents. So I must be excused, in leafing through Dickens, for having found in him even—a "dissolve." How else could this passage be defined—the opening of the last chapter of *A Tale of Two Cities*:

> Along the Paris streets, the death-carts rumble, hollow and harsh. Six tumbrils carry the day's wine to La Guillotine. . . .
> Six tumbrils roll along the streets. Change these back again to what they were, thou powerful enchanter, Time, and they shall be seen to be the carriages of absolute monarchs, the equipages of feudal nobles, the toilettes of flaring Jezebels, the churches that are not my Father's house but dens of thieves, the huts of millions of starving peasants!

How many such "cinematic" surprises must be hiding in Dickens's pages!

However, let us turn to the basic montage structure, whose rudiment in Dickens's work was developed into the elements of film composition in Griffith's work. Lifting a corner of the veil over these riches, these hitherto unused experiences, let us look into *Oliver Twist*. Open it at the twenty-first chapter. Let's read its beginning:

Chapter XXI [1]

1. It was a cheerless morning when they got into the street; blowing and raining hard; and the clouds looking dull and stormy.

The night had been very wet: for large pools of water had collected in the road: and the kennels were overflowing.

There was a faint glimmering of the coming day in the sky; but it rather aggravated than relieved the gloom of the scene: the sombre light only serving to pale that which the street lamps afforded, without shedding any warmer or brighter tints upon the wet housetops, and dreary streets.

There appeared to be nobody stirring in that quarter of the town; for the windows of the houses were all closely shut; and the streets through which they passed, were noiseless and empty.

2. By the time they had turned into the Bethnal Green Road, the day had fairly begun to break. Many of the lamps were already extinguished;

[1] For demonstration purposes I have broken this beginning of the chapter into smaller pieces than did its author; the numbering is, of course, also mine.

a few country waggons were slowly toiling on, towards London,

and now and then, a stage-coach, covered with mud, rattled briskly by:

the driver bestowing, as he passed, an admonitory lash upon the heavy waggoner who, by keeping on the wrong side of the road had endangered his arriving at the office, a quarter of a minute after his time.

The public-houses, with gas-lights burning inside, were already open.

By degrees, other shops began to be unclosed; and a few scattered people were met with.

Then, came straggling groups of labourers going to their work;
then, men and women with fish-baskets on their heads:
donkey-carts laden with vegetables;
chaise-carts filled with live-stock or whole carcasses of meat;
milk-women with pails;
and an unbroken concourse of people, trudging out with various supplies to the eastern suburbs of the town.

3. As they approached the City, the noise and traffic gradually increased;

and when they threaded the streets between Shoreditch and Smithfield, it had swelled into a roar of sound and bustle.

It was as light as it was likely to be, till night came on again; and the busy morning of half the London population had begun. . . .

4. It was market-morning.
The ground was covered, nearly ankle-deep, with filth and mire;
and a thick steam, perpetually rising from the reeking bodies of the cattle,
and mingling with the fog,
which seemed to rest upon the chimney-tops, hung heavily above. . . .
Countrymen,
butchers,
drovers,
hawkers,
boys,
thieves,
idlers,
and vagabonds of every low grade,
were mingled together in a dense mass;

5. the whistling of drovers,
the barking of dogs,
the bellowing and plunging of oxen,
the bleating of sheep,

the grunting and squeaking of pigs;
the cries of hawkers,
the shouts, oaths and quarrelling on all sides;
the ringing of bells
the roar of voices, that issued from every public-house;
the crowding, pushing, driving, beating,
whooping and yelling;
the hideous and discordant din that resounded from every corner of the market;
and the unwashed, unshaven, squalid, and dirty figures constantly running to and fro, and bursting in and out of the throng; rendered it a stunning and bewildering scene, which quite confounded the senses.

How often have we encountered just such a structure in the work of Griffith? This austere accumulation and quickening tempo, this gradual play of light: from burning street-lamps, to their being extinguished; from night, to dawn; from dawn, to the full radiance of day (*It was as light as it was likely to be, till night came on again*); this calculated transition from purely visual elements to an interweaving of them with aural elements: at first as an indefinite rumble, coming from afar at the second stage of increasing light, so that the rumble may grow into a roar, transferring us to a purely aural structure, now concrete and objective (section 5 of our break-down); with such scenes, picked up *en passant*, and intercut into the whole—like the driver, hastening towards his office; and, finally, these magnificently typical details, the reeking bodies of the cattle, from which the steam rises and mingles with the overall cloud of morning fog, or the close-up of the legs in the almost ankle-deep filth and mire, all this gives the fullest cinematic sensation of the panorama of a market.

EXERCISES

on film and literature

1. Explain the significance of Eisenstein's point that in Dickens's novels "commonness took on a romantic air." Would Eisenstein say the same of Griffith's films?

2. Eisenstein feels that the "secret" of the novel and film in appealing to large audiences is similar. What is the "secret" of their appeal?
3. What are some of the social and moral values Eisenstein finds common to both a Griffith movie and a Dickens novel?

on film

1. Can the cinema deal as well with interior life as with external action? Can you think of films which have dealt successfully with the life of a philosopher or other type notable for his intellectual achievement?
2. What in your opinion contributed to the merits of those films? Do you find that their subject matter leads to any disadvantage?

on structure and language

1. There is no question of Eisenstein's enthusiasm for the work of Griffith and Dickens. How does he transmit his enthusiasm to the reader?
2. Although Eisenstein pays close and instructive attention to the techniques of the artists he discusses, what topics draw his primary interest?
3. Consider how this essay reflects Eisenstein's own concerns as an artist. From a reading of this selection alone, what might you guess would be some of the characteristics of his own films?

OUR ELIZABETHAN MOVIES

Dwight Macdonald

This century, so indifferent to the poet and the painter, so warped and feeble in creative power, has strangely given birth to a new form of art that has already produced its masterpieces. If our writers are uninspired and our musicians impotent, at least the directors of our moving pictures have done work comparable to that of the past in emotional power and in beauty of form. On them has fallen the mantle of those great magicians of the Renaissance who called into being the thousand and one shapes of human passion and destiny. Our movie directors, some of them at least, seem to possess the touch that makes their creations both moving and beautiful, existing both as a thing in nature and as a formal expression of art. Their movies live as the paintings of Leonardo, the dramas of Shakespeare live—though perhaps not in the same degree—because they are deeply concerned with human life. This does not make them aesthetically good: the degenerate theatre of our times is also concerned with life—too much so, indeed. But when extreme beauty of form blends with this interest in the emotions and destinies of men, there result such masterpieces as *Greed, The Cruiser Potemkin, The Lash of the Czar, Stark Love, The Wedding March, The Case of Lena Smith,* and *The End of St. Petersburg.*

111

Historically, it is to be expected that the movies should give us our highest type of aesthetic expression. Long ago the other arts reached, and passed, their climaxes in respect to technique: letters and the plastic arts in the Renaissance, music in the late eighteenth century. Their possibilities have long been known, their remoter provinces explored more and more intensely. A new departure in technique must today appear somewhat forced, as, for example, in the modern theatre the expressionist drama of Germany and the experiments of O'Neill in *The Great God Brown* and *Strange Interlude.* So thoroughly have the main technical resources of painting, drama, and the rest been developed that he who would discover new ones must travel far into the regions of the eccentric and the unnatural. In a word, the modern painter or musician arrives on the scene a century or two after the major battles in his art have been fought. Not so the movie director. Fifty years ago his medium did not exist; twenty-five years ago it was in the crudest state imaginable. And films only five years old can easily be detected from their now antiquated technique. The talkies, of course, have been in existence scarcely a year, bringing with them new problems and possibilities in technique before those of the silent film have been half exhausted. The movie director is in the happy position of a man who has come into a fortune and whose chief concern is how to spend it. A wealth of untouched and unexploited means of expression lies at hand. He has but to take advantage of this new material with all his ingenuity and imagination.

In being a young art, the movies are fortunate in a subtler way as well: in their relation to the public. Like the plays of Elizabeth's reign, our movies are not generally considered "art" at all. Often, indeed, pedants consider them the very antithesis of art, just as Elizabethan-latinists contemned the popular drama of their time. Movies are created for the enjoyment of the people, not the delectation of the connoisseur or the dilettante. It is well known that the greatest Elizabethan dramatists did not consider their plays of permanent value enough to see them through the press—Ben Jonson, of course, was a striking exception. Today a movie has the same ephemeral life: once it is played, it exists no longer, to the public at least. It may reappear as a "revival" a year later but only those strange persons who haunt the small "art" theatres will be interested. There is the same vast production— hundreds of plays, hundreds of movies a year—and the same confusion, or rather complete chaos of good, bad, and mediocre. Shakespeare was highly regarded by the public of his time— and so were several gentlemen whose very names are long forgotten. Though von Sternberg's *Underworld,* a remarkable film, was the greatest box office success in the year it appeared, who knows what piece of folly and stupidity pleased the customers the next year? On the same program at a cheap movie house I once saw a Tom Mix "Western", one of the most vapid and infantile forms of art ever conceived even by the brain of a Hollywood movie producer, and *The Lash of the Czar*, a Russian film of the greatest subtlety and sophistication. That such a combination was incongruous probably occurred to no one in the theatre. A movie is a movie, and people cannot be bothered about aesthetic distinctions when they are in search of enjoyment.

Nor indeed can they be so bothered any other time. Painful as it may be, it is a fact that not one person in a thousand understands, or is even interested in, aesthetic values. They read novels, look at paintings, hear music, but they are seeking to be excited, instructed, distracted from their troubles, anything except aesthetically moved. And yet, though the public taste is not impeccable, and though the people do not understand, or even perceive, many of his finest effects, the artist seems to draw strength from contact with his fellow men as Antaeus was refreshed by touching his mother earth. It is better that the public should respond to work of genius though it may respond equally to the charlatan—better for the man of genius. In other fields of art today the distinction is only too rigidly drawn between what is good and what is popular. A great source of strength for the movies lies in the fact that this distinction has not yet come to be made in that field. Therefore the movie director communicates his creations to a public as broad and inclusive as that of the modern painter, for instance, is small, narrow, specialized. The soil is deep enough to nourish the highest trunks, the most abundantly spreading branches. Some such communication, or at least the feeling of it, would seem almost essential to the development of the highest artistic productions. Religion, the ancient immemorial meeting place of the great and the small, the powerful and the weak, has also long served as common ground for the artist and the layman. Through this medium the Greek tragedians, Dante, Milton, Bach, and the painters, sculptors, architects of almost every age reached their fellow men. Entertainment is another such meeting place: Homer, the Elizabethans, Moliere, and now the motion picture directors, approach the public through that channel. These last are the fortunate creators in this age, since they feel that connection with their fellows without which no creative work can grow rounded and full-bodied.

There are other interesting parallels between our movies and the plays of Elizabeth's reign. Both have achieved masterpieces within a few decades of their birth: from *Gordobuc* (1561) to *Tamburlaine the Great* (1587) and *Dr. Faustus* (1588) is about the same stretch as from *The Great Train Robbery* (1904) to *The Cruiser Potemkin* (1926). Incidentally, the two earliest masters, Christopher Marlowe and Serge Eisenstein, are curiously alike: the inhuman brilliance of their technique dominates the slight philosophical content of their work. Compared to the mature appreciation of human values that marks a Shakespeare, a Chaucer, or a Protozanov, they are gifted barbarians. Not only does Eisenstein resemble Marlowe in the fact that his technique dominates but also in the nature of this technique. The same vigorous, pulsating rhythm driving without hesitation towards its climax can be felt in the speeches of Tamburlaine, the conqueror, and in the film sequence showing the "Potemkin" preparing for the approaching battle. The movement of later, more mature works is not so direct. In *Macbeth* and in *The Lash of the Czar* there is more hesitation to the blank verse and to the sequences, the hesitation of the mature artist who must qualify, explain, and analyze the actions of his people. The powerful rhythms of Marlowe and Eisenstein are unbroken by this need for philosophical reflection.

Rapid development has caused in the old plays and in our movies a generous, warm, turbulent flowing of vitality. Too much premeditation, whether of one man for hours or of a race for generations, has a chilling, reducing effect on art. If the creator reflects too long on what he is about, he will find it increasingly hard to see in it any beauty or meaning. And the longer he reflects, the more will his ambitions dwindle, until his epic has shrunk to a cautious sonnet. The directors of our movies have had little time for such hesitation, too little in fact, both as a generation and individually. They have been forced to be as prolific in creation as any poor devil playwright turning out plays from the pot-house, from the garret, from the prison itself for some insatiable theatre manager. The attitude of Henslowe and such Elizabethan entrepreneurs toward the plays they ground out of their writers to feed to the public is repeated today in Adolf Zukor, Carl Laemmle, Sam Goldwyn, and the rest.

The continual pressure from theatre managers, together with the impatience of a young and self-confident art, produced plays that, often hasty and crude, none the less moved actively towards ambitious goals. The situation is repeated in the movies of today. For example, a recent talking picture of no unusual merit, William Wellman's production, *Woman Trap,* lustily attacks a dramatic theme of sizable proportions: a complete change in the behavior of the hero, a detective who suddenly becomes as stern as he originally is easy-going. His change of heart, the scenario decrees, comes when he accidentally blinds his mother. To further embarrass Mr. Wellman: the scenario writer, or Mr. Zukor, or the Devil, or whoever contrives movie fables, has insisted that the hero shall cause the arrest and execution of his sweetheart's brother, and that his sweetheart in revenge shall bring about the arrest (by the hero) of the hero's brother and his subsequent suicide. This is all quite hectic, reminding one somewhat of Shirley and Webster. In cold blood one might well hesitate before such a theme, but Mr. Wellman has not hung back an instant. His scenes move along swiftly and vigorously, carrying off the melodramatic plot by the briskness of their attack. Though he does not succeed in transmuting the melodrama into something finer, as did Von Sternberg in *Underworld,* at least he renders it effective in itself. The settings—a drab room in a boarding house, a warehouse at night, etc., are uncompromisingly realistic, and the characters act out their drama with all the force of passion of real people. Finally, Mr. Wellman, a talented director, has embellished his tawdry story with many effective bits of composition in which he gets dramatic effects with moving light and form. His direction has a turbulent vitality that conquers the unpromising material with which he must work.

This triumph of the director over his scenario presents another parallel to Elizabethan drama. It is a commonplace that the Elizabethans cared little about the sources of their plays. They casually accepted tales from Plutarch, Holinshed, Boccaccio, wherever they found a certain amount of color and life. The original tale was unimportant because they completely transmuted it when they cast it into dramatic form. How foreign is this attitude to later literary custom can be appreciated if one imagines Thackeray or Thomas Hardy thus casually adopting some old fable as the basis for a novel.

This indifference to the original story reappears in our movies. Many of them are in one way or another based on a play or novel; the rest are turned out by hack scenario writers. The plays and novels are almost invariably second-rate; the products of the Hollywood scenarists (excepting only the brilliant Ben Hecht) are not even that. Yet the directors take this stuff and, by some potent alchemy, make it into fine moving pictures. The genius of D. W. Griffith made a ham novel, Thomas Dixon's *The Clansman,* into *The Birth of a Nation,* a production that remains great after years of the most rapid technical development. When it is put down in cold words, the plot of almost any movie (as of almost any Elizabethan play) sounds overstrained, melodramatic, sentimental, absurd. The only occupation worse than writing scenarios would be having to read them. It is the treatment the director gives these unimpressive stories that lifts them at times into the realm of art.

Whatever the sins of the old plays and of our own movies, they are not those of omission. The spacious domain that the Elizabethan playwright took for his own—all the vast extent of human passions, supernatural beings of land and air, the widest range of geography, and an even wider range between ribald humor and the blackest tragedy, subtlety and childishness, heroism and villainy, delicacy and coarseness, tenderness and brutality, and almost every other imaginable antithesis—this also is the domain of the movie director. Elizabethan delight in pomp and circumstance reappears in the stirring Corpus Christi procession in *The Wedding March,* and the equally Elizabethan relish for the racy humors of the kitchen and the barnyard is reflected in the realistic butcher shop and the dishevelled brothel in the same picture. Our movies repeat the Elizabethan contrasts in human behavior. Once more people are moved by intense emotions and impulses that seem inconsistent to the intellect, that can only be understood through artistic presentation. Prince Niki in *The Wedding March,* for example, resembles Prince Hamlet in the contradiction of his moods: he is sometimes the tender lover, sometimes the gross, cynical man of the world. Like the Elizabethans, our directors exploit with equal gusto the romantic and the realistic, or rather they do not recognize any such silly distinctions. In *The Cruiser Potemkin,* Eisenstein shows us impartially the maggot-infested meat and some lovely glimpses of the calm morning harbor.

Not only do antithetical qualities and opposed types of beauty flourish side by side in the same production, but the confusion is increased by a wild mixture of the sublime and the banal. Included in Marlowe's *Dr. Faustus* are routine scenes of low comedy in which fire-crackers are set off under people, and such perfect lyrical utterances as the invocation to Helen of Troy. The popular influence is responsible for this incongruous mixture: the crowd wants horse play and sentimental lovers and deeds of blood. This demand the talented playwright sometimes satisfied in perfunctory episodes, as in the above instance, writing the rest of his play to suit himself; or else he took it for the basis of his whole play and performed the miracle of getting something good out of it. Shakespeare used the latter method, giving the groundlings their moonlight serenades in *Romeo and Juliet,* their bloody deeds in *Hamlet* and *Macbeth,* their horse play in *The Taming of the Shrew,* and so on.

Today, to satisfy the crowd is the *raison d'être* of every picture—though not necessarily the aim of its director—and the crowd still wants, as in Elizabethan times, comedy, love-making, action. It is not difficult to satisfy these demands, for the crowd is not discriminating. Most directors, like most of the old dramatists, have been content to feed the crowd its romance and action without going beyond the time-honored, labor-saving banalities. This is only to say that most artists, whether they work in the Hollywood of 1929 or in the London of 1600, are mediocrities and satisfied with mediocrity. There are, however, certain men of talent among our movie directors, and they have gone beyond merely meeting the public demands, and created works of art.

Venerable among ham movie formulae is that of the Handsome Young Aristocrat and the Lovely Bourgeois Girl. This has stood the test of time, for it represents an overpowering combination of romance, sentiment, and "human interest." Once your Aristocrat is rigged out in a tight-fitting officer's uniform and your Bourgeoise is robed in simple burgher costume, your work as director is practically over: the movie will unfold itself of its own momentum. Last winter this hopeless theme was developed by two of our best directors, Erich von Stroheim and Josef von Sternberg. The resulting pictures were *The Wedding March* and *The Case of Lena Smith,* films that have been equalled only by the Russians.

For those who can see beneath the surface banality, the movies hold drama and beauty. Drama, because they are concerned with the most basic and moving aspects of life: with ambition, with love, with heroism, with sin, with passion, with failure, with birth and death. Unlike the modern theatre, the movies are interested in human beings for their own sake, not because they fit into some neat intellectual framework constructed by a Shaw or a Galsworthy. There are no "problem movies." The theme of the movie director is character in action, nor does he shrink from the boldest, most moving variations on it. His understanding of character may be crude, but it is robust, with vitality and emotional depth compared to the piddling superficialities of our playwrights. Beauty, too, the movies offer, a beauty of form that is their chief distinction. Not only are one's emotions stirred by the human drama they unfold, but also one's eye finds a wholly aesthetic pleasure in following the interplay of form on the screen. Moving picture technique is as complex as that of music or painting. It includes the static composition of each "shot," the relation of one moving form to another, gesture and facial expression, the angle of the camera, together with its distance from the object photographed and sometimes its line of motion, lighting effects, and, most vital of all elements, the "mounting" (cutting the newly developed film into separate units and reassembling them in a desired order). By this last process the director determines the sequence in which the various parts of the film shall appear, and hence the rhythm and emphasis of the whole. There are many other elements of movie technique, no doubt, but their number is not the point. The thing to be observed here is that these technical elements are of the first importance in the modern movie. Directors are constantly studying the technical basis of their art: the relationship of moving forms. The result is that it would be possible to get aesthetic satisfaction out of a movie even though one completely disregarded its content. Only a work of art meets this test. It is met by almost no modern plays or novels. Chaplin's genius, for example, is almost wholly one of form: his pantomime is what amuses us and not the fact that he drops ice cream down a fat lady's back or is pursued by hordes of Keystone cops—the form, in short, and not the content is the essential.

This beauty of form is the greatest aesthetic distinction of the movies. It is also the most significant parallel between them and Elizabethan drama. The authors of *The Maid's Tragedy* take a hackneyed theme that can be stated in three words: "Men are deceivers," and elaborate it, in the mouth of their character, Aspatia, into:

> Then, my good girls, be more than women, wise;
> At least be more than I was; and be sure
> You credit anything the light gives light to,
> Before a man. Rather believe the sea
> Weeps for the ruined merchant, when he roars;
> Rather the wind courts but the pregnant sails
> When the strong cordage cracks; rather the sun
> Comes but to kiss the fruit in wealthy autumn
> When it falls blasted . . .

And thus for another twenty lines. As Beaumont and Fletcher used words, so do the directors use images:[1] not to imitate reality but to create, by means of formal groupings of words, or images, a beauty that is beyond and above reality. These formal groupings, also, are of interest in themselves apart from any meaning or emotion they may express. In its youth every art is marked by this beauty of form. Its technique is still new to its practitioners: they delight in the play of purely formal relations because the combinations have not yet been exhausted. The movie director restrains

---

[1] "Image" means here the basic unit of the movie film, namely: the individual picture. When a series of these pictures, each showing the action in a slightly more advanced stage that that shown by its predecessor, is run through the projection machine at a certain rate, the illusion of movement is produced on the screen. The "image" in movies roughly corresponds to the word in literature.

his camera as little as the dramatist restrained his fluent, eager pen. Both play exuberantly with form: witness, the Elizabethan delight in puns (formal combinations of words), and the glimpses of statuary in Russian films (experiments in image-sequence). No such freedom and variety of expression, born of mastery over new forms rich in untried possibilities, is to be found in literature since the Renaissance. In the eighteenth century it appeared in the music of Bach and especially in that of Mozart, whose fluent expression leaps and runs like a swiftly flowing stream. Cézanne and his followers recaptured it in the nineteenth century in their bold and restless experimentation with form and color. And today this command over the material of his art—perhaps "persuasion" would be closer than "command"—belongs to the movie director, as it belonged to his closest relative in art, the Elizabethan playwright.

That the movies should be distinguished by great beauty of form is all the more striking in that precisely this element is weakest in the modern theatre. While the plays of our time have degenerated into an infantile mimicking of reality, the movies have more and more tended to express reality in terms of art, which is quite another thing. That nine out of ten movies are cheap, banal, drearily shallow means nothing except that, as every one knows, nine out of ten attempts at artistic creation are failures. The tenth film justifies the rest. This is important: that the general background out of which the movies come makes it at least *possible* for the tenth film to be produced, just as the general state of the English theatre made it possible for *The Duchess of Malfi* and a few score of other masterpieces to be produced.

EXERCISES

on film and literature

1. What similar patterns does Macdonald find in the historical development of the modern cinema and the Elizabethan drama?
2. What aspect of movie technique, in its affinity with other arts, does Macdonald stress?

3. What is the difference between his approach to literary and film forms and Eisenstein's?

on film

1. According to Macdonald, how important is the narrative element of a film?
2. Who does he assume is the key figure in the creation of a movie? Why? Defend his assumption on the basis of movies you have seen.

on structure and language

1. Macdonald carefully distinguishes between the type of movie he likes and the type he doesn't. And he seems to base his distinctions on what he calls "philosophical content," and also on "form." Is he contradictory in his application of these standards?
2. Perhaps no contributor to this section is more sensitive to questions—and levels—of taste. Cite examples from Macdonald's diction which contribute to the tone of his remarks, while revealing his sensitivity to matters of taste.
3. First published in 1929, this essay is one of Macdonald's earliest writings on film. Cite any emphases or references which seem especially to reflect the time when it was written. Which points in the essay seem most relevant to present-day attitudes and thinking about film and about the arts in general?

"MACBETH"
INTO "THRONE OF BLOOD"

J. Blumenthal

As easy as it may be to film a play, it is quite another thing to make
a film out of one. Orson Welles, who has shown a genius for both
media, is a good case in point. He has tried making films out of two
of Shakespeare's plays and has failed—miserably with *Macbeth*,
gracefully with *Othello*—both times. His *Othello*, beautiful as it is,
fails because most of its cinematic flourishes are gratuitous. His
toying with the medium remains toying for all its mastery. Welles
is too often guilty of serving up chunks of pure Shakespeare that
have been sugar-coated with an unusual camera angle or composition, or nicely sliced up by a bold cut. Although this is all very
fascinating to look at, the experience of looking is empty at the
centre. It is film as hobby, or ornament, but not as expression.[1] No
matter from what angle one photographs it, or the number of cute
little pieces into which one cuts it, the material in its original form
(the play, the individual scene with dialogue intact) remains
essentially what it was. In such cases the filming is a more or less
gratuitous decoration of the subject and not what it must be: an
inevitable articulation of it.

122

THE FOREST

This takes us to *Throne of Blood*. At the same time, it takes us to Kurosawa's profound commitment to creating meaning by the manipulation of material reality. No doubt this is for him just as much an involuntary response to experience as it is a commitment; but whatever its sources, the form it takes in this film is revealing. To begin with, Kurosawa is doing much more here than simply letting us see the things that Shakespeare's characters describe, and the places where the action is set. This time-honoured but very limited device for filming plays is far from his only resource.[2] The point is that Kurosawa actually thinks by manipulating material reality. Birnam Wood, for example, which has only a few lines of vague description devoted to it in the play, becomes in Kurosawa's hands a physical presence that is potent enough to embody the film's very complex network of themes. The forest in *Throne of Blood* was born with Kurosawa's conception of the film. It is not the result of a makeshift adaptation, nor is it even a fancy visualisation of the play. It is rather an offspring of the metamorphosis from play to film, and it is to a great degree responsible for charging *Throne of Blood* with an inner principle of motion, for making it an autonomous work of art.

It might help to look at the problem from Kurosawa's point of view. He feels deeply sympathetic to the theme of *Macbeth* and is moved to make a film out of it. The play is about a noble and highly ambitious warrior faced with the dire task of gaining control over his own vivid but treacherous imagination. He needs to prove himself to himself and can do so only by acting out his most horrible visions, wholly embracing whatever evil he encounters in his own soul. Self-control and self-destruction soon become identical, and this is the tragedy. As Kurosawa must have seen it, the crucial problem was to find a natural means of externalising, of objectifying, Macbeth's thoughts. By "natural" I mean that the object chosen had to appear to exist in the real world just as Macbeth did, living and growing there. For it is not enough that Macbeth's thoughts can be photographed; photographing them must bring them to life.

Birnam Wood, a marginal symbol from the original work, was perfect for the part. Even in the play, it is only when the forest defies the laws of nature (just as Macbeth subverts the moral order) that Macbeth's fate becomes explicit and he realises that the kind of self-control he sought was suicidal. In the film, however, the forest is more than a marginal objective correlative of the theme. It is both the battleground where the conflict rages and the very incitement to conflict. If this sounds like a fair description of what is called the "world" of a work of art, we are on the point. For this is precisely the role that the forest plays. It is the life at the centre of the film, what we always look for but seldom find in film versions of anyone's plays.

A sizeable portion of *Throne of Blood* is devoted to the terrifying spectacle of Washizu (Macbeth) waging war on the forest. In an extended sequence near the beginning he and Miki (Banquo) thunder through a dense, murky forest on horses no less frightened than they. (The forest is referred to as "The Labyrinth" and much is made, here and later in the film, of the difficulty of finding one's way out of it.) Washizu is clearly the leader: *he* will find a way out, for he cannot bear the sense of dread and helplessness he feels before the blind paths, the unidentifiable shrieks and moans, the thunder, lightning, and fog. He starts at what he thinks an evil spirit, unsheathes his sword, and letting out a blood-curdling cry, half defiant and half hysterical, he plunges into the dark with Miki following him. The reality of this forest is overwhelming. It breathes, and sweats, and twitches, and speaks in the unknown tongue. It is easily as powerful a presence as Washizu himself; and this is exactly what it must be, since for Washizu this first encounter with the forest is nothing less than a headlong plunge into the self.

In this sequence Washizu and Miki are on their way to Forest Castle, where their lord is waiting to reward them for leading the victorious battle against the rebel forces. Control of this castle soon becomes Washizu's obsession, and already he is struck by the thought that one would be truly invulnerable if he could control the forest, which is the only means of access to the castle. In a moment the crazed horses burst through the underbrush on to a small clearing that glows with an unholy light. Here, surrounded by heaps of carcases and bones, a chalk-white, sexless, ageless demon sits spinning a loom and chanting the prophecies that eventually drive Washizu on to the ultimate dare. "I must paint the forest with blood!" he will cry. The forest is Washizu's mind. As his ambitions reveal, it is no longer controlled by his lord. His lord is therefore vulnerable, but no more so than the doomed Washizu, whose position is ironically similar.

Kurosawa has at least this much in common with most other great film-makers: his ability to imbue a place with such deep moral meaning that the place often seems to take charge and structure the narrative on its own. I am not suggesting that the place equals the film. It is simply necessary that the place come alive and help shape the film. If it generates no conflict, if it does not partake of the reality of the characters' experiences, place remains meaningless. And if the place is meaningless, so is the film. A very painful example of this failing is the painted-backdrop universe of Olivier's *Henry V*. It is as if a novelist had tried to preserve *The Ring of the Niebelungen* by objectively reporting all the action, characters, dialogue, and scenery exactly as they appear on the stage. And then concluded his lark with a request that we actually read his work.

In *Throne of Blood*, however, place becomes an autonomous reality. The horses gallop through the forest and Kurosawa, always behind a maze of gnarled trunks and barren branches, gallops with them.[3] The whole—the men and their horses, the composition of the frame, the narrative, and the theme itself—is galvanised by the hellish milieu. This applies equally to the interiors, whose simple theatricality constitutes a world within that of the all-encompassing forest. Behind the flimsy walls man makes to seal himself off from an amoral nature, there is a lucid, quiet geometry that is assaulted throughout the film and, in the end, shattered. Toward the end, before the forest moves, a futile war council between Washizu and his captains is thrown into confusion by a flock of squealing bats which suddenly comes flapping into the hall from the forest. Washizu understands only too well what this means. He screams for his horse (*à la* Richard III) and rides for the last time to that unholy clearing seeking the assurances he could not obtain from others. The forest, which is the objectification of Washizu's mind, both controls and contains the action of the film.

Finally, there are the tumultuous comings and goings of the men and their horses which function so importantly as the narrative link between castle and forest. They enable the director to tell his story with great economy and force and deserve a little section to themselves.

THE HORSES

I am reminded here of those two sleepy creatures who might conceivably have served as the drunken chamberlains but were forced instead to labour as mounts for Macbeth and Banquo at the beginning of Welles' film on the subject. Not that Welles should have made Kurosawa's film, but we do have some right to expect that a flair for phantasmagoria will show up in more than flashy editing and pretentiously symbolic sets—in the life surrounding the characters, for example.

> ROSS
> And Duncan's horses—a thing most strange and certain—
> Beauteous, and swift, the minions of their race,
> Turned wild in nature, broke their stalls, flung out,
> Contending 'gainst obedience, as they would
> Make war with mankind.
>
> OLD MAN
> 'Tis said, they eat each other.

I grant that the old man's footnote would present problems. Ross's description, though, is the work of an excellent scenarist, and one whose talent Kurosawa did not fail to notice. From a lingering shot of Washizu and his wife retiring as the chaos loosed by the murder seems finally to have subsided, there is a jolting cut to the next morning, and we see the king's horses "contending 'gainst obedience," much as Duncan's did. The entire castle is aroused again as the horses, in their frantic rush to flee the thing they have sensed, stampede through a row of huge banners which flap resoundingly as they are dragged off towards the forest.

The sequence is typically Kurosawa in the calculated violence of its execution. All the action is shot from a worm's-eye view and up close; a few rapid-fire shots of the rebellious steeds and the stunned, helpless men and we move on immediately to the film's loose counterpart of Macduff, Noriashu, who is making off under cover of the excitement to warn Miki of his suspicions. The narrative takes an important step forward and nothing is left hanging.

The brief turmoil here is anything but a decorative cinematic effect. We already know from the forest sequence at the beginning that Kurosawa is modelling his world on that of Shakespeare. The whole of nature is sensitive to moral traumas in this type of world, and the moral traumas themselves are often of such magnitude as to unhinge the whole of nature. Kurosawa's great gift is that he has the power as a film-maker to make us experience this world. If he had tried to abstract from the process the thing that Shakespeare, working as a dramatist, did—if he had given us a reaction to the event instead of the event itself—everything would have been lost. We would have neither play nor film.

Let me give another telling example, one for which Kurosawa did not have Shakespeare's potential genius as a scenarist to serve as inspiration. (Isn't this, by the way, at the heart of the matter? That Kurosawa relies on Shakespeare only as a scenarist whose vision is consonant with his own, and never as a maker of pentameters?) Miki decides, because of the prophecies, to throw in his lot with Washizu even though he is certain of Washizu's guilt.[4] He is now a guest at Washizu's new residence, Forest Castle. The sequence opens in Washizu's chamber, with Lady Washizu playing the role of evil counsellor. She does not trust Miki and knows that Washizu doesn't either, so she gives voice to what he desires yet dreads even to think of: another murder. We cut immediately from Washizu's speechless, petrified face to the courtyard, where Miki's horse, normally gentle, seems to be going mad. It is charging around the courtyard and refuses to let the groom saddle it. Miki's son interprets this as a bad omen and pleads with his father not to ride forth that afternoon but to stay for the banquet and tend to his affairs the next morning. Miki laughs this off as childishness, but no sooner does he move to saddle the horse himself than we cut to a shot of the courtyard taken from the ramparts of the castle. It is night, and still, and the courtyard, far away and off in the lower lefthand corner of the frame, is deserted. Miki's men are seated up here in a circle discussing in hushed tones the strange turn of events during the last few days. Suddenly they fall silent. They hear something in the distance. It becomes louder and finally identifies itself as the sound of a galloping horse. The shot is held a moment longer, just long enough for Miki's beautiful white stallion to come racing into the courtyard, riderless. The cut is to

Washizu at the banquet. Washizu, of course, is paying no attention to the entertainment or his guests; he cannot stop gaping at the one empty seat in the hall.

This passage, which lasts no more than three or four minutes, is film narrative at its most eloquent. Kurosawa edits with an unerring instinct for clipping each action at its climax so that it will reverberate throughout the whole, and movement and placement within the frame are always obliquely at the service of the story. But the sequence is also noteworthy because it allows us to catch Kurosawa in the act of narrating what Shakespeare dramatised, and in doing so it reveals how greatly film narrative depends on the material components of the world being depicted.

Kurosawa builds the entire sequence around the reactions of Miki's horse. The movements of this short-circuited creature are responsible for all the characteristic ellipses in the narrative; they say everything that has to be said until Washizu's own body and face take over again at the banquet. At the same time, they necessitate doing away with much of the play. The elaborate preparations with the murderers, and even the murder itself (presumably excellent cinematic material), are discarded. Kurosawa has no use for even the murder because the world he is creating already contains its own narrative potential. It is a world of morally sensitised objects (the forest, the horses, the bodies and faces of the characters) which throughout the film lead a life of their own. And in their autonomy they demand that the film-maker adhere to their logic. If the film-maker is really making a film, and not just filming a play, he is only too willing to accede.

All appearances to the contrary, I am not arguing for the horse-opera notion of film aesthetics. Silver, too, neighs when there is trouble in the air, but who hasn't had the urge to strike him mute? One does not need horses, or chases, or even the unleashing of stupendous natural forces whose mass can be hurtled across the screen, in order to make filmic films. One thing that is indispensable, though, is the ability to convince the spectator that the surfaces of body, face, and place, bristle with nerve-ends, and that the synapses between the three generate the meaning and control the structure of the film.[5] Kurosawa does this again and again in *Throne of Blood*. I hope it is clear that what he does bears no relation to such things as Olivier's desperate attempt at the end of

Henry V to add a dash of "cinema" to the recipe in the form of an equine extravaganza.

THE CHARACTERS

Probably the most radical result of this transformation from play to film is the total absence from the latter of Shakespeare's diction. That Kurosawa's characters in *Throne of Blood* speak Japanese is only half the point. The other and more important half is that they speak only when they can't communicate in any other way, and then in language that is terse, unadorned, brutally functional. As far as one can tell from the subtitles, Shakespeare's poetry is gone

not just translated and trimmed, but gone.[6] In our discussion of the forest and the horses we saw some of the things that take its place. There it was best to concentrate on the fundamental similarity of the problems facing Macbeth and Washizu. But the film's scrupulous avoidance of Shakespeare's verse is closely related to some equally fundamental differences in plot and characterisation. These differences deserve attention because they take us deeper into the question of how character is developed in a film, and they may even provide some basis for a speculation on what types of character, if any, are most suitable to the medium.

> LADY MACBETH
> I have given suck, and know
> How tender 'tis to love the babe that milks me—
> I would while it was smiling in my face
> Have plucked my nipple from his boneless gums,
> And dashed the brains out, had I so sworn as you
> Have done to this.

Such is the chilling eloquence that Shakespeare uses to build the character of Lady Macbeth. Lady Washizu, however, is denied this mode of self-expression. She is endowed instead with a purely physical power, one that reaches far beyond (although it includes) the immediately visible gesture. A short time before the action of the film opens, she conceives Washizu's child. This pregnancy becomes the pitchfork with which she goads her husband into carrying out his evil intentions, and she needs few words to exploit her advantage. The child, who was to have been the ultimate beneficiary of the plot to kill the king and Miki, becomes with

Lady Washizu's miscarriage one of its victims, and by the same token an incarnation of the plot itself. After Washizu gains control of Forest Castle, Lady Washizu acts out this perverse fertility rite by dancing, insane with joy, in the room where the king was murdered. But the pressures of approaching failure soon bring on the miscarriage, which in turn precipitates Lady Washizu's nervous breakdown. (The cause of Lady Washizu's madness is one of Kurosawa's most brilliant additions to the story.) In the mad scene she simply huddles in the middle of her empty chamber, scrubbing her hands and whimpering. We neither see nor hear of her again.

Earlier I mentioned the hero's vivid but treacherous imagination. Yet one would be hard pressed to find much evidence of a vivid imagination in what he says. What we are given is a barrage of gapes, grunts, shrieks, and snorts; and the taut motions of a trapped but still powerful animal. Washizu cannot articulate his nightmarish visions, but there is no doubt that he has them. Some of this we encountered in his reaction to the forest. There is more. When Miki's ghost appears to him at the banquet—that it does appear is also germane to the question at hand—he staggers all the way across the hall and back, the spasmodic thudding of his feet threatening at any moment to splinter the thin wooden floor. The delicate Japanese architecture is used throughout as a sounding board for the man's tremendous violence. He crashes into the wall, gasping for breath, his eyes half out of their sockets. The banquet soon ends and one of the murderers reports that Miki's son has escaped. The stricken Washizu kills him on the spot without saying a word; he screams, flings the sword away, and reels out of the room. We are meant to feel here that the powers of the forest are assaulting the fragile order of interiors that are not really interiors at all, but merely veneer, flimsy defences against the bestiality within. Although the faculty of speech eludes him, this is what Washizu feels (and expresses) with every bone in his body.

We are never allowed to forget the hero's primitive physicality. When Washizu finally glimpses the forest moving, he shudders and crouches in a corner of the ramparts unable to believe his eyes. With great effort he musters the courage to try to embolden his men. Pacing the rampart like a caged lion, he roars down into the terrified crowd. (The camera is placed well beneath him here and pans unsteadily back and forth, imitating his nervous motion.) But his men have had enough. The forest has moved and this creature's doom screams at them with his every gesture, no matter how brazen. They draw their bows and turn them on their master, denying him the honour of dying, as Macbeth did, with "harness on his back." The result is gruesome, for it is some time before Washizu, howling and writhing, with dozens of arrows stuck in him, is caught in the neck.[7] He falls (in slow motion) into the courtyard and his body, which seems as if it will never stop bouncing, raises huge clouds of dust. The entire army backs off, fearing that the demon may not have been completely exorcised. It has, though, and when the body finally comes to rest, the film ends.

It seems to me that the main consequence of these various transformations is that the grotesque *rapprochement* between the human and animal kingdoms common to both works is more complete in *Throne of Blood* than in *Macbeth*. Essentially the same thing happens to both heroes, but this could not have been expressed filmically unless Macbeth were transformed into a more instinctive, more physical, creature; one for whom the moral dimension of behaviour exists but seldom crosses the threshold of conceptualisation into verbal poetry, or into philosophy. Washizu is no less sensitive than Macbeth, and no less moral. But because there is no place in the film (in any film, for that matter) for Shakespeare's poetry, he must of course be less of a poet, and less of a philosopher, and perhaps not quite the classical tragic hero that Macbeth is in the play.

Even at the news of the miscarriage and at the sight of his deranged wife, even in his attempt at the end to rally his men, meanings for him remain locked in their physiological symptoms. Given Macbeth's eloquence, Washizu might have succeeded in dying more nobly, with "harness on his back." But this is to confuse the two characters. For Washizu's character is controlled in this important respect by the requirements of the medium. His men turn on him because his body and face, awesome as they are in this final attempt to command, cannot conceal his awareness of his imminent destruction. Washizu is simply not articulate enough to mediate, in the lofty manner of the classical tragic hero, between his perceptions and his gestures. If he were, he would not present the powerful film image that he does.[8] It is fitting that Kurosawa should exploit this by placing him on the ramparts in full view of everyone and at the mercy of those to whom he cannot help but reveal himself.

All this is not to say that Washizu cannot think. The point is that he thinks in another medium. When Macbeth hears of his wife's death he delivers the famous speech beginning "Tomorrow, and tomorrow, and tomorrow . . ." Washizu, looking into his wife's chamber, sees part of the result of his folly huddled in the centre of the room; his whole being sags and he moves off heavily to his own chamber. We follow him there. He enters the room and lets his limp body drop to the floor. "Fool!" he cries. "Fool!" These are the only words he speaks. Occupying the frame with his seated figure, however, are two other objects: his sword, and the throne. Kurosawa holds this eloquent shot for a long time. It is as good an indication as any that Washizu is not a brutish man incapable of reflection. He is rather the spirit of Macbeth distilled to almost pure materiality. Lady Washizu is the spirit of Lady Macbeth distilled in the same fashion. These distillations are the lifeblood of the film. Without them a meaningful and moving narrative would have been impossible.[9]

As for the lesser characters, they receive much the same kind of treatment. Macduff (Noriashu) is an interesting example because in the process he loses not only his eloquence but also his glorious role as avenger. Although he is presumably among the forces attacking Forest Castle at the end, after he ineffectually warns Miki of his suspicions we never see him again. One result of this is that the effects of the central action on the body politic are not dwelt upon as they are in *Macbeth*. We may be thankful for the absence of all the tedious business between Macduff and the mealy-mouthed Malcolm, but we do demand that the social implications of the tragedy, which are integral, find some expression in the film. And this they find not in subtle political machinations, but in the monstrous betrayal that Washizu's men are forced to perform at the end. This is indeed a primal social situation. It can be seen (without stretching the point, I believe) as a re-enactment of the ritual replacement of the old king. In this the film seems even closer to the Dionysian roots of tragedy than the play; and seems also to descend, in its own way, just as deeply into the darker side of human nature and relationships. In his search for the surfaces he needed as a film-maker, Kurosawa had to chip some of the crust of civilisation off the drama. Macduff (and Malcolm) were part of that crust.

A final question arises. Are there certain types of character that are not really fit for film narrative? Let me venture into these deep waters with the speculation that no film-maker could help but grossly distort or over-simplify a character such as Hamlet's. I am not talking here about the problems that Olivier encountered in trying to preserve a theatrical performance of the role, but about those that would be involved in trying to create the character filmically. And the problem is not Hamlet's complexity, for Macbeth, too, is a very complex character and Kurosawa was able to recreate him filmically by means of a distillation that neither distorted nor simplified the fundamental meaning of his experience. Hamlet would be untranslatable because of the verbality of his experience. One can be verbal without one's experience being so. Macbeth, who is at bottom a man of action, is also a great poet, and therefore a good example of this. The verbal experience is typical of those who never wholly enter their experience, those who can only act at acting. It is typical of the theatrical, role-playing personality, which is *par excellence* Hamlet's. Macbeth, on the other hand, always lives his experiences, and thereby provides Kurosawa with the irreducible core of raw, unquestioned reality that is the first premise of most great films.

Polonius asks Hamlet what he is reading. "Words, words, words," Hamlet answers. A pun of this calibre should be able to withstand the strain of one more meaning. I submit it as a description of exactly the kind of self-conscious verbal construct that is the basic form of Hamlet's own character and experience. It is the theatre that has always nourished this sensibility and it seems therefore destined to remain outside the mainstream of film-making.[10]

Notes

1. The image of Iago caged and being returned to the castle, with which Welles frames the action of the film, and the brilliant sequence in the sewers, are among the exceptions to this.

2. As it is, for example, for Max Reinhardt (*A Midsummer Night's Dream,* 1935), whose enchanted forest inhabited by real people, and whose cardboard castle, merely underscore the intractability of his material.

3. Kurosawa's imitators have succeeded in making a cliché of this image, but that is their problem.

4. The changes in the plot will be dealt with at greater length in the next section.

5. This sounds very much like Kracauer's definition of what a film should be (see his *Theory of Film*), but his notion of film as "the redemption of physical reality," dependent as it is on what he calls the "stream of life," would leave little room for *Throne of Blood.* He would probably have severe reservations about its tight plot and medieval setting.

6. In what I suppose is an attempt to be faithful to Shakespeare, a recent Russian film version of *Othello* went so far as to use English-speaking actors. This kind of piety is not one of Kurosawa's virtues.

7. Kurosawa had real arrows shot at the actor here. As Anderson and Richie point out in *The Japanese Film,* "His interest was not in using the real thing simply because it was real but that the effect on film was greatest when real arrows were really aimed at Mifune." The same might be said of the forest.

8. Even the sophisticated, terriby self-conscious characters in Antonioni's films are usually at a loss for words to express their plight (when they aren't too weary to do so). This verbal lethargy and frustration are important sources of the often tremendous impact of these figures as film images.

9. If this statement seems too strong, have a look at Judith Anderson's Lady Macbeth in George Schaefer's film version of the play. Shakespeare's diction was meant to be rendered theatrically—it cannot be rendered well any other way—and at this Miss Anderson is expert. On the screen, however, her excellent theatrical performance becomes operatic and therefore ludicrous. The film-maker who tries to preserve a theatrical experience ends up sacrificing the best virtues of both media.

10. In his recent book, *Metatheater,* Lionel Abel convincingly traces

the modern theatrical sensibility ("life seen as a dream, the world as a stage") back to *Hamlet*. This sensibility has had very little influence on the great film-makers.

EXERCISES

on film and literature

1. What does the author assume to be the basic differences between a film and a play?
2. The author points out how far Kurosawa's film departs from being a literal transcription of *Macbeth*. Why does he feel that this paradoxically helps Kurosawa get closer to the spirit of Shakespeare's play than he otherwise might have?
3. In general, what does Blumenthal find to be the relationship between literature and film? Is his point of view similar to or different from that of Macdonald?

on film

1. What are Blumenthal's main objections to film versions of Shakespeare? According to your experience of films based on Shakespeare, do you agree with Blumenthal's criticism of such films, or do you find intrinsic merits in them?
2. What does Blumenthal see as Kurosawa's greatest "virtue" as a director?

on structure and language

1. The essay is organized chiefly through the use of comparison and contrast. Note some examples in the essay of this.
2. What is the main purpose of the footnotes the author appends to his essay: To cite sources of information? to add information? or to reinforce the argument of his essay?
3. What is the tone of the essay? Is the tone in keeping with its purpose? How does the division of the piece into parts headed "The Forest," "The Horses," and "The Characters" serve its overall purpose?

SHAKESPEARE— CRUEL AND TRUE[1]

Jan Kott

If *Titus Andronicus* had six acts, Shakespeare would have had to take the spectators sitting in the first row of the stalls and let them die in agony, because on the stage no one, except Lucius, remains alive. Even before the curtain rose on the first act, twenty-two sons of Titus had died already. And so it goes on all the time, until the general slaughter at the end of Act V. Thirty-five people die in this play not counting soldiers, servants and characters of no importance. At least ten major murders are committed in view of the audience. And most ingenious murders they are. Titus has an arm chopped off; Lavinia has her tongue and hands cut off; the nurse gets strangled. On top of that we have rape, cannibalism and torture. Compared with this Renaissance drama, the "black" American literature of our day may seem a sweet idyll.

Titus is by no means the most brutal of Shakespeare's plays. More people die in *Richard III; King Lear* is a much more cruel play. In the whole Shakespearean repertory I can find no scene so revolting as Cordelia's death. *King Lear* and *Richard III* are both masterpieces. In reading, the cruelties of *Titus* seem childish. I have recently re-read it, and found it ridiculous. I have seen it on

[1] The Shakespeare Memorial Theatre Company in *Titus Andronicus*. Produced by Peter Brook. Performed in Warsaw—June, 1957.

the stage, and found it a moving experience. Why? Is it only because Sir Laurence Olivier is a tragedian of genius, and Mr. Brook a great producer? I think there is more to it than that.

When a contemporary play seems to us in reading flat and childish, while in the theatre it thrills and overpowers us, we say that it makes good theatre. But to say of Shakespeare that he makes good theatre is rather funny. And there is little doubt that *Titus Andronicus* is a play by Shakespeare, or rather a play adapted by him. But so is *Hamlet* for that matter. The difference being that in *Titus* Shakespeare had been just beginning to shape the dramatic material found in his model. He had already been forming great characters, but was unable as yet to make them fully articulate. They stammer, or—like Lavinia—have their tongues cut off. *Titus Andronicus* is already Shakespearean theatre; but a truly Shakespearean text is yet to come.

Brook and Olivier have both declared that they were encouraged to produce *Titus* on realizing that this play contained—though still in a rough shape—the seed of all great Shakespearean tragedies. No doubt *Titus*' sufferings foretell the hell through which Lear will walk. As for Lucius, had he—instead of going to the camp of the Goths—gone to the university at Wittenberg, he would surely have returned as a Hamlet. Tamora, the queen of the Goths, would be akin to Lady Macbeth, had she wished to look inside her own soul. She lacks the awareness of crime, just as Lavinia lacks the awareness of suffering that plunged Ophelia into her madness. Watching *Titus Andronicus,* we come to understand—perhaps more than by looking at any other Shakespeare play—the nature of his genius: he gave an inner awareness to passions; cruelty ceased to be merely physical. Shakespeare discovered the moral hell. He discovered heaven as well. But he remained on earth.

Peter Brook saw all this in *Titus Andronicus.* But he was not the first to discover the play. It is true that for two centuries it had been regarded as an uncouth and imperfect work; a Gothic work, as classicists called it. But it had pleased the Elizabethan audience and was one of the most frequently performed plays. Mr. Brook did not discover *Titus.* He discovered Shakespeare in *Titus.* Or rather—in this play he discovered Shakespearean theatre. The theatre that had moved and thrilled audiences, terrified and dazzled them.

If we were to ask the question who in our time has shown the true Shakespeare the most persuasively, the answer would clearly be Sir Laurence Olivier. The living Shakespeare of our time has been presented, first and foremost, in film. Compared to Olivier's great films—*Hamlet, Henry V, Richard III*—even the best theatrical performances seem flat, conventional, meaningless and boring.

Film has discovered the Renaissance Shakespeare. In the production brought to us by the Shakespeare Memorial Theatre Company it is the return to the true Shakespeare in the theatre through the experiences of film that amazes us most. This is something worth reflecting on, since it is this fact that will help us to understand the Renaissance Shakespeare who is also modern.

In what settings and costumes should Shakespeare be performed? I have seen Shakespeare played on a huge staircase and with a background of cubist prisms; among rachitic crooked trees (so popular with Polish stage designers), and in a wood so true to life that you could see every leaf rustle; in so-called fantastic settings with fish scales, floating gauze and armour hired from the Opera; in decor striking in its pomp, or in its pseudo-noble functionalism.

Some were better than others, but all of them were bad. Only film has shown that one way to transmit Shakespeare's vision could be the great paintings of the Renaissance and the Baroque; or tapestries, as in *Richard III*. Of course, this had to be a point of departure, not imitation. A starting point for gesture, visual composition, costume. In Shakespearean tragedies, Romans should not be dressed in artificially contrived, stylized costumes that do not belong to any period; on the other hand, their costumes must not be accurate museum copies. They must be Romans as seen and painted by the Renaissance.

This is the way chosen by Mr. Brook. Like a true artist, he does not copy, or impose an artificial unity. He has freely taken a full range of yellows from Titian, dressed his priests in the irritating greens of Veronese. The Moor, in his black-blue-and-gold costume, is derived from Rubens. The scene in the camp of the

Goths where Aaron is tortured and tormented in a cage made up of big ladders also looks Rubensian.

It does not matter whether the colours have really been derived from the Venetians; or whether the dramatic visual compositions of characters are more indebted to El Greco or to Rubens. What matters is that it is painting as seen through film experience. There is nothing of the *tableau vivant* and the opera about it. The scenes are composed like film shots and follow each other like film sequences.

Once Shakespeare's plays began to be filmed, action became as important as speech. All Shakespeare's plays are great spectacles abounding in clatter of arms, marching armies, duels, feasts and drunken revels, wrestling contests, clowning, winds and storms, physical love, cruelty and suffering. Elizabethan theatre was—like the Chinese opera—a theatre for the eyes. Everything in it was really happening. The audience believed that they were watching a tempest, a sinking ship, a king with his retinue setting out for a hunt, a hero stabbed by hired assassins.

The beginnings of Elizabethan tragedy were very similar to the beginnings of film. Everything that was at hand could be included in a tragedy. Everyday events, tales of crime, bits of history, legends, politics and philosophy. It was a news-reel and an historical chronicle. Elizabethan tragedy did not follow any rules; it snapped at any subject. Just as films do now, it fed on and digested crime, history and observation of life. Everything was new, so everything could be adapted. The great Elizabethans often remind one of film producers looking, above all, for an attractive subject. It is enough to mention Marlowe, Ben Jonson, or Shakespeare.

When the theatre abandoned Elizabethan convention, it also lost the spectacular quality and full-bloodedness of Shakespeare. It lacked technical means, or had too many of them. I have seen Shakespeare played on a revolving stage and against back-drops, with signs being lowered to show the place of action. In both instances, it was not a true Shakespeare. Theatre has alternated between illusionism and convention. Illusionism has been flat, naturalistic or childish and operatic; convention has been abstract and formalistic, or obtrusive. Illusionism and convention alike have managed to deprive Shakespeare of awe and poetry.

Four men meet. One of them begins to abuse the other three. Swords are drawn. One of the four is murdered. The others disperse. Friends have become enemies. A civil war or a rebellion has begun. All this lasted two minutes. The fate of a kingdom has been decided in a dozen exchanges.

Lad throws girl a flower. She picks it up. Their eyes meet. She happens to be the daughter of his enemy. Three speeches—on the sun, the stars, and young tigers. She is passionately in love. At this instant the fate of two families has been decided.

Try to play both these scenes naturalistically or conventionally. You will butcher Shakespeare. Shakespeare is truer than life. And one can play him only literally. Olivier's films have achieved this literal meaning and super-truth more than any theatre has. They have created a new Shakespearean language where no word is meaningless.

An actor brought up on the nineteenth-century theatre cannot fall in love in thirty seconds; or come to hate in the course of two short speeches; or cause the fall of a kingdom in ten. A film actor passes directly from a great love scene to madness. He has killed a man, put his sword into the scabbard, and ordered his servant to bring him a cup of wine. He has hardly drunk it when the news comes that his son has been killed. He will suffer, but for not more than thirty seconds. How has this come about? The "empty spaces" have been edited out. A great film—like a Shakespearean play—is composed only of meaningful scenes.

The fact that the action of Shakespeare's plays is so condensed requires a particular kind of acting. The text is intense, metaphorical. Like a film director, Shakespeare makes frequent use of close-ups. Soliloquies are spoken directly "to the camera", i.e., on the apron stage, directly to the audience. Shakespearean soliloquy is like a close-up. A stage actor of the old school stands helpless in such moments. In vain does he try to give the soliloquy some probability. He continues to be conscious of the whole stage around him, while in fact he is meant to be alone with the audience.

Shakespeare's plays have been divided in the theatre into a number of scenes according to the places of action. After the theatre had abandoned the Elizabethan convention, it tried in vain to put the scenes together to form some sort of entity. A scenario is not divided into scenes, but into shots and sequences. Shakespeare's plays are also composed of shots and sequences. Shakespearean scholars and some modern producers have known this for a long time. But only Olivier's films have demonstrated the fluency, homogeneity and rapidity of action in Shakespeare's plays.

Mr. Brook has composed his *Titus Andronicus* not of scenes, but of shots and sequences. In his production tension is evenly distributed, there are no "empty places". He has cut the text but developed the action. He has created sequences of great dramatic images. He has found again in Shakespeare the long-lost thrilling spectacle.

The film convention of imperceptible changes of time and place is the simplest, the least obtrusive for a modern audience. In *Richard III* Sir Laurence opens with the great coronation scene which is followed by a sequence of metaphors. Pages carry the crowns of the King's brothers on scarlet cushions; the crowns of those who are to die. This is typical film narration, but is inherent in Shakespeare's text itself. One can imagine this scene also on the proscenium stage: the pages passing by, the crowns falling. It is a film effect that can easily be taken over by the theatre. And then how truly Shakespearean is the metaphor of Richard's shadow leaning over the King's shadow like a huge spider. It foretells the drama and creates an atmosphere of terror at the same time. This is the great film scenario, contained in the text, and yet so seldom brought out properly by the theatre.

Mr. Brook introduces film conventions into theatre. Intervals of time are marked by black-outs. Scenes fade, one into the other, as in a film. The audience do not seem to notice the convention; they accept it. It is then that Shakespeare is taken in literally. The King really sets out for a hunt; Tamora and Aaron really meet in a forest; Lavinia is really raped.

Such a Shakespeare belongs to the Renaissance, and at the same time is most modern indeed. He is violent, cruel and brutal;

earthly and hellish; evokes terror as well as dreams and poetry; he is most true and improbable, dramatic and passionate, rational and mad; eschatological and realistic.

There is something else that amazes us in the production. Mr. Brook's art is based in the same degree on modern film experience and on the achievements of the new Shakespearean school of Stratford on Avon. This modern Shakespeare, the "film Shakespeare", is presented on a stage, which in its essentials returns to the old Elizabethan tradition. As in Shakespeare's day the play is performed on the proscenium and on a threefold stage, the middle part of which has two levels. The interior of a large wooden column with folding sides is the family tomb, the forest, Titus's chamber. Thanks to this arrangement Mr. Brook achieves an admirable unity and logic in the development of the action.

There is no Shakespeare without great actors. Sir Laurence is recognized today as the greatest modern tragedian. His interpretation of Titus is based not merely on the imperfect text of this play by young Shakespeare. He has taken in the passion and suffering of all great Shakespearean characters. He is Titus who has been through the ordeal of King Lear. He, too, is super-real. He uses the full register of his voice and gesture; is not afraid of ridicule, pathos, groan or whisper. It is difficult to describe a genius. One can only admire him.

Close-up in film is super-real. It condenses and magnifies expression. In this English production, dramatic encounters and soliloquies stand apart from crowd scenes, like big close-ups. The whole attention has been concentrated on a given character, who seems to grow and come nearer to the audience; as if a film camera were tracking from Titus to Lavinia, from Tamora to Aaron.

EXERCISES

on film and literature

1. "Film has discovered the Renaissance Shakespeare." What does Kott mean by this?

2. What is Kott's point in comparing the attitude of the film producer with that of the Elizabethan dramatist?
3. What does Kott believe to be the key to Peter Brook's staging of *Titus Andronicus?*

on film

1. Why does Kott believe screen versions of Shakespeare are likely to be closer to the rhythms and structure of his plays than stage productions?
2. How does the technique of the close-up work to the film's advantage in adapting Shakespeare?

structure and language

1. The tone of Kott's essay on drama and film is itself highly dramatic. Consider, for example, the opening sentence. In what does its impact consist? Cite other passages in the selection which carry a similar "punch."
2. Kott tends to move rapidly from one point to another, without pausing to develop any one point extensively. How does this make his style similar to the style he admires in films and theater. Note his contrast between the pace of the "nineteenth-century theatre" and that of the modern. Besides his rapid-fire movement from point to point, in what other ways does his own writing style suggest the modern as opposed to the nineteenth-century manner?

GIPSIES AND GENTLEMEN

T. J. Ross

> *. . . And it may be useful to remind ourselves that the struggle for sexual freedom, at least in the lives of individual persons, requires considerable stepping over the bodies of others and that it is not only in political revolutions that crimes are committed in the name of liberty.*
>
> —*Steven Marcus,* The Other Victorians

> *"No gentleman can or should be always a gentleman. Some get more ungentlemanly than others, though."*
>
> —*Kingsley Amis,* The Anti-Death League

For all its sedate and enticing surface of a picture-book Oxford, *Accident* begins with the menacing roar of a machine out of control, a roar which comes out of a darkness toward whose heart the film's hero will be drawn for a characteristically Loseyan self-confrontation among a whirl of colliding egos and the splintered furies of the will. Like the surface of his other films—like, say, the prison and its environs of *The Criminal* or the Chelsea house and streets of *The Servant* or the Venetian haunts of *Eva*—the glamor-ized Oxford of *Accident* provides the metaphors of a psychic terrain. Though its incidental sociological shots are fairly steady, this isn't the film to go to for a plain look at the data and processes of academic life. The main interest has to do with Sex and Power, especially with the more equivocal aspects of their merger as sex-and-power. It is a subject which Losey and Pinter in various of their separate works, as in their collaborations on this film and on *The Servant,* have been mapping out with the verve and aptness of an E. M. Forster teaching an earlier generation how the abstract question of Good and Evil could become dangerously real when you spelled it good-and-evil.

A philosophy don, Dirk Bogarde, is nagged by a sense of the relative mutedness of his existence: a sense exacerbated by the presence of a colleague who has won success on the side as a novelist and television personality. Affecting a wide boy style, the other man, Stanley Baker, wades into things unhesitatingly. Bogarde is self-conscious, contained, irritable. He is the type of person who doesn't like making scenes though he would like to make the scene. Lacking the insistent force of a champion in any field, he nonetheless keeps a shaded eye cocked on the spoils of victory. Which is to say he is an average crafty gentleman, accustomed to watching the game from the sidelines. Not that Baker has that much on him, for all his more hectic activity. More go-getting than inspired, he is a bull-dozing careerist, typical and up-to-date. In this matching of types we have the Complete Scholar's Syndrome as Losey and Pinter see it. It figures that each of our dons should be married to a wife who is rich, unremarkable, and on edge. The Baker menage includes three children; Bogarde has two, with another on the way to keep things even.

Both men are at the point of facing what the French call "the crisis of being forty," and the plot itself recalls a vintage French drama of adultery, intrigue, and come-uppance. Like the picture-book placidity of the decor, such a plot too would seem to be out of this world. In fact, the plot serves to bring us, and its characters, into the rhythms, the life, of our moment while evoking as well what are commonly thought to be the less urbane, less tentative, structures of feeling and value of a preceding time—those values each generation looks back to as "traditional." The vintage plot, then, serves the purposes of both perspective and sentiment. (The matter of adultery has recently served these purposes in films otherwise so different as Truffaut's *The Soft Skin*, Godard's *A Married Woman*, and Fellini's *Juliet of the Spirits*.)

In the tacit struggle between the dons a main pawn is student Michael York—thick-lipped, tow-headed, rugged-seeming, and impish:

> "I don't have many friends."
> "You're an aristocrat."

Although a bit more sympathetically portrayed, the aristocratic youth is of a kind with the James Fox character—the fatuous bourgeois playboy—of *The Servant*. With a heedlessness which is both Olympian and cherubic, such characters tend to get involved in dangerous situations with which they prove unable to cope, since they lack the temperamental requisites for surviving in a world as careworn as it is cautious—a world composed more of scavenging opportunists than high-flying good sports. "You were made to be killed," says Bogarde. "Naturally, since I'm immortal." A sad remark and out of character in its perceptiveness, for the boy is saying that all he can hope for is to end up as a myth.

The roar out of the night with which the film opens is the roar of fatality—whose sound is heard from the road outside Bogarde's house, drawing to crescendo pitch the closer it draws to the house. Then a crashing pile-up.

Bogarde races from his house to find dead in the car the aristocrat, on whose face the car's other occupant steps as she climbs out of the wreck. "You're stepping on his face!" Bogarde shrieks, witness to, and now leading actor in, the scene of an accident which has left in his grip the girl he had himself long had his eye on, brought to him like a gift by the dead god in the machine.

It is not till the closing scenes of the film that we gain more fully a sense of the range of relationships and conflicts "brought to a head" by the crash which opens the picture. Flashbacks, and flash-forwards out of the flashbacks, are intercut in such a way that each moment shown is invested with the charge of its implied future. One dip back to the past brings us to the aristocrat's palatial home, where he sparks a game of dining-hall rugby. Among the guests is Bogarde, whom his host presses into the game as goalie. Amidst the marble pillars and smiling blasé spectators— deb-types, dames and elderly men—the young blades pummel one another with increasing ferocity as they warm up to the sport. The aristocrat takes an especially severe mauling in his eagerness to score off goalie Bogarde; he fails to pass the don, instead is buried in a pile-up; disentangling himself, a player steps on the aristocrat's face.

Balancing this scene is the Sunday the youth had been invited to spend at his tutor's house. Present also—and main motive for the gathering—is Bogarde's other student, Jacqueline Sassard. Hailing from Middle Europe's most *mittel-europäisch* Austria, she enters the scene as exotic bird, the "foreign body" which serves in Losey's films as catalyst to the action. The men swoop around her, united, drawn close in competition.

Baker, who has already begun an affair with the girl, comes on the party uninvited—to complete a familiar arrangement in the films, of Wide Boy and Exotic Bird entering a cosily insulated house to get things going to a violent finale.

In *The Servant*, the title-figure (who will later be joined by his mistress acting as maidservant) moves in on a gentleman's house and takes over; in the same way a gipsy, later followed by her lover who doubles as stable-hand, moves in on the manor of the young lord in *The Gipsy and the Gentleman*. In *The Sleeping Tiger* we have an approximating pattern when a youthful thief is hauled out of the night by a psychiatrist and invited to live, on an experimental basis, in the latter's suburban home; the psychiatrist's wife is brought into complicity with the thief when she becomes his mistress. She would be in temperamental cahoots with the underworld character, in any case, since her own origins, in contrast to her English husband's, are exotically American and plebeian. Like those interloping teams, Baker and Sassard use their host's house to make love in; and as the gipsy and the thief are shown rifling the files of their respective hosts, Baker in one instance peremptorily reads Bogarde's mail.

It will be clear that—as much as for Raymond Williams—for Losey the idea of the "clash of cultures" assumes the clash of class. The stray gipsies of his films, who emerge out of a world of night and storm to confront and threaten the style and tenuous stability of a daytime established realm, are compelled by the goads of sexual and social aggression. Nor is it in their melodramatized class-consciousness alone that Losey's films "read" a little like Victorian novels; for, equally in line with the Victorian manner, the class emphasis is balanced and given edge by a conservative cautionary moral, by an adherence to the values of "self-knowledge" and "self-control" if not, quite, "self-reverence." Thus *The Sleeping Tiger* ends in a car accident in which the impassioned wife is slain; *The Gipsy and the Gentleman* ends with a coach careening over the side of a bridge into a river where the gipsy,

locked in the grip of the gentleman, is drowned with him. Both
the psychiatrist's wife and the gipsy's lord are virtual suicides.
Having lost to their obsessions all power over themselves, they
have nowhere to go but into the nearest wall.

The most interesting of the playboy-gentleman-aristocrat
types who are turned on to the point of self-destruction is the hero
of *The Gipsy and the Gentleman*. He himself is shown to be no
stranger to underworlds: we meet him in the cellar of a gaming-
house where he wins a bet by wrestling down a greased pig and
holding on to it for several seconds. As he says to his fiancée's
father, who is escorting him back to the daytime respectable
world: "I've been underground but I've had a good run." But when
he tangles with a "greased pig" like the gipsy, Melina Mercouri,
the result is the stalemate of an embrace to the death.

In *Accident*, the "greased pig" is Sassard: should Bogarde try
to dominate her, he will find himself in a class with the gentlemen
and lords of the other films, in a class in fact with Michael York
in this film—and so doomed.

Accident begins at the climactic point to which *The Sleeping
Tiger* and *The Gipsy and the Gentleman* build: the explosive con-
cision of its opening scene signals a play of time-sequence, a distortion of chronology for the purpose of lending to each frame the
force of a simultaneity of implication involving past, present and
future. The three time-levels are merged in a nice exemplification
of the ". . . present in time future / And time future contained in
time past."

For T. S. Eliot, the redeeming dimension is beyond time;
Losey, who holds to a more humanist line, emphasizes the fateful
choices—and compulsions—of the individual in the present;
another way of saying that he weights each scene with its implied
future, which in turn is a way of noting that the structural basis of
the film is moral.

The quest in time after certain of the springs of human nature
allows for a full measure of melodramatic suspensefulness and
shocks—all of which here depend on the choices and reactions of
the gentleman on the scene. Unlike the heroines of *The Gipsy and
the Gentleman* or *Eva*, once the Sassard character has set things in
a whirl by her presence, she remains in a passive secondary role:
so that the much-criticized woodenness of her playing is of small

matter. The film is paced according to the days in the gentleman's life. The center is his, as we accompany him across the Oxford sward or to London. We are made intimately aware of, and kept in suspense about, his moods and moves, and from his viewpoint we meet the other figures.

In the Sunday sequence we see him at home vis-à-vis both his family and the students and confrère in whose intrigues he has been caught up. Both students, York from the start, and Sassard by the finish, look to him for the Word. What York wants above all is his mentor's full approbation and blessings; this would mean victory and it is in the course of speeding to him for a final word that the boy is killed. Sassard appears bemused at the prospects of an affair with the subdued don—chiefly as a further move in a game in which she, as the bohemian passing through, is the challenger. The Baker character, who holds, and is possessed by, the spoils, is banal and predictable. He represents, however, one possibility in Bogarde's present, even as Alexander Knox, who shares a scene with the hero at the sidelines of a cricket match, defines a future prospect. The provost of the college, he is presented as the perennial near-sighted spectator and, in this flat sense, he is invulnerable. Although he is concerned about his daughter in the City (another character, as will be seen, sadly fixed in her orbit), he remains as much in the dark about her as about the rest of the action raging around him, hardly able to hear what Bogarde says. The administrator as Mr. Magoo.

Also awaiting a Word, and also seen, perforce, on the sidelines of the scene along with their children and dog, is the hero's pregnant wife. During their Sunday, she can do little more than hang around or do a routine trick or two, rather like the family dog: she serves drinks, she prepares a lunch. From a chair placed outside the mesh wires of their court, she momentarily watches the others play tennis. A shot on her empty chair, after she has loped off back to the kitchen, strongly evokes her isolation, her sense of being cornered yet "out of it," her baffled good faith. (As she did with her wife-in-distress role in *Alfie*, Vivian Merchant here again walks away with every scene she is in, giving a great demonstration of how to hold the foreground while playing a subdued character, a feat at which Bogarde himself is no slouch.)

Equally fine are the scenes devoted to the don's weekday in

the City. He had been summoned by a producer interested in his appearing on a television show. Amidst the steel-and-glass blankness of an industrial compound, he scurries up and down the obstacle-course network of stairways till he finds the producer's office, to face—the producer being laid up in hospital—a busy associate who fluffs him off.

Their anti-interview reminds the associate (played with relish by Pinter) of his superior in sick-bed, whom he rushes off to see; and reminds the don of a former mistress—none other than the Provost's daughter—dug in in the City. She had been mentioned in passing by the television man, who had also, one gathers, "known" her. So Delphine Seyrig enters the picture as the complaisant friend who will serve as less than perfect solace for our gentleman's comedown in missing a chance to get one past televisionwise Baker. His mood will have been affected too by the turmoil roused in him by Sassard, and by his domestic blues over the widening silence between himself and his wife.

In no sequence is the dialogue more spare; the focus is on the characters as they "go through the motions," from his call from the awkward and stifling isolation of a phone booth to the still, grey isolation of her apartment, to their dinner among the jazzy red decor of a restaurant for whose style they are rather too ponderously mature, to their return to the emptiness of her apartment and bed. What dialogue there is, is of an elemental formality: to Seyrig's vulgarly demure prattle about "getting too fat," Bogarde's return of "You're not too fat," is delivered at just the right pitch of cozening and smug ardor inherent in the physiology of the moment. Translated, this exchange would go:

> "Do you really want to?"
> "I do."

In this meeting scooped out of the chasm of time, neither can have anything in mind, anything to share, but sex.

Objectively—without interpretation—the sequence can stand as a classic in the way it captures one of the most common, and most forlorn, types of sexual engagement; but our interest here is to note how it works in the context of the film and so sound its theme.

With Seyrig, the don enjoys the one time of his day when he

is "in power." After a series of buffetings which have left him in a mood to murder the world, he has his turn to "take it out" on someone else. Sex, as a compensation for spleen, rather than being a further possession of experience, is a further dislocation from it. With a thwarted power-drive as its chief motive, the sexual act becomes the final mode of alienation—for our hero, the final one of his day's defeats. This wind-up to the first half of the film points to the key moment of the concluding part when the don, with Sassard in his power, must decide how to act. Losey and Pinter have taken literally, in order to examine critically, the ordinary notion of, and reference to, the sexual act as a "conquest."

Before the set-to with Sassard, a flash-forward from a scene between Bogarde and his wife shows him confronting Baker's wife in a melancholy rain which curtains both the shape of her features and her voice. She stands beseeching, stalwart, and futile, knowing her husband to be out in the storm at a point beyond summoning. The extent to which Bogarde will be drawn out into the storm "remains to be seen." Here he faces in effect the questions of his own wife and life.

The final scenes take us past the moment of the accident to what occurred directly after. Since the girl had been at the wheel of the car, she is herself in something of a fix. Before, with the head office man away in hospital, Bogarde had been left to deal with a swollen-up assistant throwing his weight around; now, with Bogarde's wife away in maternity ward, Sassard is left to square off against Bogarde in his empty house, the occasion ripe for him to come on strong. He makes a scene, wrestles her round the room. As she fitfully demurs, he pushes her, in his anger, with enough force to cause her to fall back on the floor. A close-up shot from an angle which shows Bogarde "towering over" the girl at his feet gives us the pose in which the villain of a piece, the club wielder, is usually set. The bird who before had been seen stepping on another's face looks up at Bogarde deadpan. No need to show expression, both know she is at his mercy. The question is whether he will place himself at hers.

The pose—and implication—set here is constant in Losey's work. When the playboy of *The Servant* leans in to the maid in the kitchen of his house, he in effect speeds the process of yielding himself to the power of her lover, the title-figure who, in several shots of the film, is shown looming over the collapsed form of his master. In *The Gipsy and the Gentleman*, Mercouri, who arrives out of a storm into the manor of the lord whom she proceeds to bring to heel, is herself shown in one instance at the feet of her peasant lover, after he had shoved her to the ground during a quarrel. When the hoodlum of *The Sleeping Tiger* first meets his host's wife, he has to look up to her from the foot of a flight of stairs as, riding crop in hand, she stands aloof and above him; he soon gets his own back by tripping up the housemaid and looming above her as she sprawls in terror among the smashed tea-things. In *Blind Date*, detective Stanley Baker looms darkly over the suspect whom, in a sudden loss of control, he had shoved to the floor of a station house. In *The Big Night* a barkeep is shown on his knees on the floor of his saloon before a cane-wielding character named Judge, portrayed outrightly as a sadist.

In a spectrum of intensities ranging from the psychopathic to the genteel (from *The Big Night* to the present film), we are shown those intertwinings and frictions of the drives to sex and power which ignite in the "accidents" of violence, in the lurchings and thrusts of sadistic self-expression. To have power is to use it eventually like a club. While the consequence of being driven by nothing but the pursuit, or the behests, of power is the loss of power over self, the fall to one's fix, signalled by the reflex of lashing out.

Gipsy Mercouri uses her sex as her one means to self-assertion and power. She seeks to dominate the world of a manor whose manners, however, she disdains; in consequence, she grows wilder the closer she moves to victory. Increasingly disoriented in her own sexuality and identity, she commences to smash the furniture and lay about her with her riding crop. The wife in *The Sleeping Tiger* is in a similar bind of class and sexual anxiety.

In the course of solving a murder case, the detective hero of *Blind Date* is led to confront his own class- and sexual-restiveness. The victim in the case is a svelte and luxuriously-kept courtesan; the chief suspect, a young painter of working-class background with whom she had had an extra-contractual affair. Himself an earnest Welshman who had slogged his way out of what the British habitually refer to as "the muck," the detective maintains an aggressive aloofness toward his suspect and toward the deca-

dent mess in which the latter had become involved. It is a manner
of overstated self-protection, for it is evident that the detective's
attitude is complicated by the naggings of erotic envy. A further
complication—in face of the power-establishment's eagerness that
the suspect be sent up without delay—is the detective's hunger for
a long-awaited promotion. But he remains in control, and despite
personal and professional goads, finds the real guilty party. In this,
he is like the psychiatrist who, despite pressure from the police to
hand him over, sticks by his thief-patient to succeed finally in
releasing the latter from his self-destructive compulsions. Both the
painter and the hoodlum are able to walk away from their scenes
as free men—through the auspices of men relatively free, in control of, their own pile-driving natures, and who show that freedom
in a loyalty to professional principles.

The don's actions put him finally in a class with these stead-
fast professionals. He steps back—looking "askance" as used to
be said—from his sprawled prey: in the next shot, Bogarde and
Sassard face each other, the space between them running down
the center of the frame defining the irrecoverable distance—the
whole past depicted in the film—at which they stand from one
another. That the don "has" the bird before the fadeout of the
previous scene is not so much to the point as his consequent
restraint, a restraint by which he recognizes her discrete existence,
accepts his, and so acknowledges as well that of the slain youth.
It is no longer a matter of victory but of recognition. Thus the key
shot is that of the couple's separated, motionless figures. Able to
yield the spoils, the don remains able to act. He sends Sassard
safely on her way from Oxford to pastures new, and supports a
collapsed and inert Baker as the latter falls back to his leash on
the lawns of academe. Like the detective and the psychiatrist in
their different (and less ambiguously drawn) situations, Bogarde
holds, despite his own sexual and cultural disturbance, to the lore
of his books, and so earns the right to his pipe.

To be sure, the script seeks to offer a view of human nature
"as it is" without a sermon of comments; the moralizing slant is
in the camera's angle, is chiefly Losey's. And from this angle, the
film may seem impossibly tentative or crass or skittish or "decadent," especially to those impatient anyway with the inherent
vulgarity of a medium to whose fiction-features the melodramatics

and duplicities of the soap opera or thriller are indispensable. Or one's impatience may be with the times in general, whose spirit so much combines a moral tentativeness with a cool vulgarity. Certainly the films of Losey, like those of the most esteemed European directors, reflect and speak especially to, that part of the public composed of hipsters and their hippie offspring. The majority of the audience, those comprising, to adapt Hazlitt's distinction, the less "philosophical part," have responded to recent films like *Accident* or *Blow-Up* (which they had initially been drawn to see through a combination of advance publicity teasers and culture-boom imperative) with a red-eyed perplexity. It is, after all, in a minority enclave like Oxford that Losey's films have been most admired and taken up; and his latest feature is in the way of a return salute to film enthusiasts there. Among such minority audiences, in the schools and out, there seems to be developing a return to modes of inquiry aimed at defining the content of their so far hazily itemized "new morality."

Thus a film like *Accident* adds up to a good deal more than another camp romp; its pathological overtones are both interestingly used in, and assimilated by, its moral scheme. There is probably already in the works somewhere an enormous tome on "The Homosexual Vision" in the contemporary arts. Losey's films will belong in it, since a play on homoerotic tensions among their characters, and a related emphasis in the arrangement of situation and setting, do determine to a degree the films' tone and slant; yet simply to see them in this way would be as limiting as, say, so to tag and file away such works as *Twelfth Night* or *The Longest Journey*. Although it has become heretical in the purest and narrowest writing on films to drop any literary references, these references have been made here precisely to suggest the more general cultural interest and appeal of Losey's achievement.

Indeed the name that first comes to mind when thinking of Losey is of that other artist who brought an American sensibility to the English scene in order to create a unique hothouse world suited to getting over his sense of things, a world in which characters triumph through yielding up the spoils they had been compelled by, and whose heroes prove capable of actions as crass as that of the hero of *The Wings of the Dove* when he virtually blackmails his raven-haired, deadpan fiancee into spending one night

with him. This occurs in the course of a relationship which cul-
minates when both stand motionless, separated, shocked to a
recognition of the existence of the dead blonde goddess—their
hostess—whom they had betrayed. Henry James would have
enjoyed Losey's films—none more than *Accident*.

EXERCISES

on film and literature

1. Toward the end of his essay, Ross notes that the "melodramatics and duplicities of soap opera" are also characteristic
   of most feature films. What is melodramatic and duplicitous
   about soap opera?
2. Do the soap opera elements of *Accident* mean that the film (as
   described in the essay) is to be considered on the same artistic
   level as a television "soaper"? You may find useful pointers on
   the subject of melodrama in the chapter on this included in
   Eric Bentley's *The Life of the Drama*.
3. Besides those of the soap opera, Ross also finds in the film
   certain attitudes and slants characteristic of the Victorian
   novel. What are some of these? Is the novel form itself—even
   on its most "serious" levels—wholly free of soap opera elements? Discuss, with examples.

on film

1. In his discussion, does Ross emphasize the film's script more,
   or its direction? What does this suggest about the relative
   importance he would place on the writer and the director in
   the creation of a film?
2. Cite a recent film you have seen which seemed to you entirely
   on the level of soap opera.

on structure and language

1. What is the purpose of the opening paragraph? How does it
   prepare the reader for the essay's general approach and
   emphasis?

2. What is the connotation of the slang term "wide boy"? Do you find the use of expressions of this kind effective? What dangers may there be for the writer who resorts frequently to colloquial and slang expressions?
3. Hazlitt's phrase concerning the "philosophical part" of an audience is cited in order to distinguish levels of audience response and interest. What distinction is being made? What other words more common today might have been used in place of Hazlitt's?

ALL THE BETTER BOOKS

Philip French

DORE SCHARY: "I want to tell the audience the narration is from the book. A lot of people don't know this is a book. I want to be blunt with them. Put them in a more receptive mood. I want to tell them they're gonna see a classic, a great novel."
—Quoted by Lillian Ross in PICTURE

Hollywood has not on the whole set out to woo the reading public. As an industry it was established to provide entertainment for the semi-literate urban masses. To buy a book in Hollywood meant to acquire the film rights, at which point it became a "property" presenting problems that had to be "licked". When studios hired writers they were generally reduced to lowly regarded (if highly paid) cogs in the production machine. Within movies themselves a bespectacled book-lover was traditionally a person without a Saturday date, lonely and frustrated—eventually either to be left in the lurch or to throw away book and glasses for more rewarding pursuits such as making love or money. If, as Dorothy Parker said, men seldom make passes at girls who wear glasses, women rarely give second looks to men who read books. Not that books were totally disregarded—merely that they belonged in anonymous leather bindings on the shelves of the rich. Only a few licensed eccentrics, like Leslie Howard, were allowed to take them down.

In a vague sort of way books were respected for their prestige (as authors were before they signed studio contracts) provided they didn't have to be read. "I would rather take a fifty-mile hike than crawl my way through a book," wrote Jack L. Warner in his autobiography. This ambivalence is caught in William Inge's play *Picnic,* when the footloose Hal is "impressed" (stage direction) by the pathetic younger sister having read "a *whole* book in an afternoon," and says: "I wish I had more time to read books. That's what I'm going to do when I settle down. I'm gonna read all the better books—and listen to all the better music. A man owes it to himself." The part of Hal in the film was of course taken by William Holden, who a few years before had played the embittered writer in *Sunset Boulevard* and, as the intellectual journalist in *Born Yesterday*, had donned horn-rimmed spectacles to give Judy Holliday a crash course in civics.

This nexus of attitudes has by no means been confined to Hollywood; on the contrary it is a reflection of the working assumptions of those functioning in the mass media throughout the world. Currently, however, European films are full of references to other arts, to books, paintings, plays, and music. Some are significant and personal, others merely modish—or meaningless. This tendency is a product of many factors: the general drift of our culture; the kind of people who make films; the strata of society with which movies now deal and toward which they are directed; the decline in straight narrative cinema and the consequent emphasis upon individual rather than generalised décor; the growing acceptance by audiences of the unexplained and the elliptical.

One cannot point to a particular date when this tendency first began to show itself, but in retrospect and in view of their subsequent influence the appearance of both *Breathless* and *L'Avventura* in 1960 is worth noting. In the former Godard includes a specific, if rather tangential, discussion of Faulkner's *The Wild Palms*, the events and themes of which have much in common with his film. This was but one among many references to literature, music, art, and other movies. *Breathless* was the beginning of a sort of personal culture-collage that has tended to preoccupy Godard and, especially in *Une Femme Mariée* and *Pierrot le Fou*, even to form the infrastructure of his movies.

In *L'Avventura*, Antonioni also referred to an American novel. But its function in the film can be more easily isolated. It is when a copy of *Tender is the Night* is discovered along with the Bible in the luggage of the missing Anna. Naturally her father seizes upon the Bible as an indication that she has not committed suicide. The audience however has been made aware of his lack of understanding of her situation, and Fitzgerald's novel is surely a clue to the state of Anna's mind through an identification with the neurotic spoilt rich-girl, Nicole Diver. At the same time there are obvious parallels between the career of the film's ruined architect Sandro and the novel's corrupted psychiatrist, Dick Diver.

One would neither demand nor expect this level of sophistication from the straight commercial cinema, yet something has begun to percolate through. In his chapter on Hollywood and the novel in *Waiting for the End*, Leslie Fiedler asked: "How many scenes involving books remain in the memory out of the films of the last thirty years, excepting those shelves of meaningless books in libraries, obviously bought by the gross like furniture?" But then, said Fiedler, "Who, for instance, can imagine the great figures who survive from movie to movie reading a book? Think of . . . John Wayne, Steve McQueen or Mickey Mouse entering a library or standing before a bookshelf with any serious intent in mind." For that matter one might ask just how much time Captain Ahab or Huck Finn spent haunting libraries.

Dr. Fiedler, however, raised these questions in 1964, and regretted that no American director used books the way Antonioni had done. As a leading investigator of the arcane processes of cultural osmosis, he would no doubt appreciate the irony of Steve McQueen withstanding a deadly knife assault in *Nevada Smith* by having a copy of McGuffey's Practical Reader concealed beneath his shirt. Equally he might note with approval the well-stocked shelves of George and Martha in the film version of *Who's Afraid of Virginia Woolf?* (not to mention the fact that the title wasn't changed to *Campus Fury*). No random job-lot of "meaningless books" here: the complete Thomas Mann, well-thumbed, behind the bed, Günter Grass and David Storey in the living-room, *Paris Review* on the coffee table, and so on. It might indeed be . . . well, Dr. Fiedler's own house.

One doesn't want to make too much of these films, but they are instances from expensive studio productions of books operating on the one hand (albeit pretty crudely) on a functional level, on the other hand in terms of décor. The theme of *Nevada Smith* is the way in which a man survives to carry out a self-appointed task through his willingness to learn. In this light the reading primer is not only a device to preserve him (which might have been a snuff-box or a medallion) but also an emblem. In the case of *Virginia Woolf* the books are only fine set decoration. I say "only", but the rightness of the choice is an instance of the care that can be taken over such matters.

Naturally one might be wrong about *Virginia Woolf*—maybe every one of those books has some dramatic meaning beyond that of providing a convincing setting for a university couple. It is not a problem we have in the theatre, where we just see crowded bookshelves. On the stage, when George reads aloud from a book (a scene omitted in the film), many critics assumed it was a passage from Spengler, whereas it was an invention of Albee's. (Similarly, many people thought that singing the title of the play to the tune "Here We Go Round the Mulberry Bush" was intended to invoke Eliot's "The Hollow Men", when in fact it was done to avoid infringing the copyright in the original music held by Walt Disney.) In the film we would have had to see the book from which George was reading.

Only from the front of the stalls can stage décor be seen in any detail, and only when the production is extremely dull does one inspect it with care. Thus in *The Owl and the Pussycat* boredom drove me to examine the hero's bookshelves and to wonder how this San Francisco intellectual happened to possess so many English book club editions and why all his postcards came from the Tate Gallery. Unimportant perhaps, but it can break the mood, as in an even more striking way did a curious anomaly in the Denver hospital sequence of *Lolita*. How had Humbert Humbert come by a copy of the Penguin edition of *Portrait of the Artist as a Young Man* in the Rocky Mountains? From a branch of the same store perhaps that sold Lolita's mother the English-style Gordon's Gin bottle in New England.

In the movies everything is brought up before our faces, and in the higher reaches of the cinema, ever since audiences came reeling out of *Citizen Kane* after raking every frame for a clue to the identity of Rosebud, we're often inclined to see significance where none is intended. As a comment on the increased visual awareness and sophistication of cinemagoers it might be pointed out that many people back in the early Forties searched for Rosebud in vain. Far off indeed seem the days when critics could state with admiration that the wedding scene in *Greed* was so compelling that no one noticed the discrepancy between the turn of the century interior and the 1920's life going on outside in the street.

These references to the other arts raise a number of important points about the cinema, only a few of which I have space to deal with and a number of which I haven't fully resolved. Initially there is a distinction to be drawn between those which are self-contained and those which refer one outside the film. This can only be a rough distinction; because even in the most obvious cases there is always some outside reference where a specific work is used. When Clive Donner accurately places a David Hockney on the rising executive's office wall in *Nothing But the Best* it is not necessary to recognise the painting to appreciate its effect. It has no personal meaning for Donner of the kind that, say, Renoir and Velasquez have for Godard in *Pierrot le Fou*. But before going further I'd like to mention and dispense with the three categories of film that actually concern artists.

The first of these is where works of identifiable authorship are attributed to fictional characters. Elizabeth Frink's sculptures attributed to Viveca Lindfors in Losey's *The Damned* raise no issues that go beyond the immediate thematic context of the film. When Ray Walston "composes" little-known Gershwin songs in *Kiss Me, Stupid*, we are amused and charmed. In the film version of *The Horse's Mouth*, however, our view of Gulley Jimson's genius is conditioned by our own response to the paintings of John Bratby; we react quite differently to the first-person narrative of Joyce Cary's novel.

In the second category, where real work is produced by actors portraying artists in film biographies, our main attention is given to the extent to which an actor measures up to our notion of the artist he portrays, and the conviction that he brings to the circumstances of creation. Thus Charles Laughton conveys some idea of the identity of Rembrandt; Cornel Wilde falls rather short of suggesting the sensibility of Chopin, etc.

The third category is where fake works are turned out by fictional characters. For example the ghastly paintings that supposedly make Dick Van Dyke the toast of Paris in *The Art of Love* are obviously less carefully planned (though no less indicative of the maker's intentions) than Richard Macdonald's paintings (sort of instant Josef Hermanns) run up for Hardy Kruger in Losey's *Blind Date*. In the case, say, of a fictitious novelist the burden of convincing the audience falls entirely upon the film actor—he must *be* a novelist in a way that no author in real life is obliged to.

These films however raise problems that I'm not particularly concerned with here. Rather, my interest centres upon the use of identifiable works, where what is at stake is neither the nature of their creation nor the personality of their creators, but the use that directors make of them.

The risks of misunderstanding, as I've already suggested, are immense. Let me give a couple of illustrations of what I mean. The first of these does not actually concern a work of art, though it brings up the same point. The critic of *The Guardian*, in a general slating of *Cul-de-Sac*, took Polanski to task for a reference to "Vince's shirts". This critic took it as an indication of the fact that Polanski was not as *au fait* with current Carnaby Street fashions as he might think. Now it is possible that the situation had changed since Polanski wrote the script, or that Polanski *did* realise the present standing of Vince's and consequently intended that the girl should be provincial and out-of-touch. It is equally feasible that the girl ad-libbed the line on the set. Whichever way you look at it, it seems singularly unimportant, and would anyway have little meaning of any kind outside a very small section of London life. But I say this because my knowledge of fashion is non-existent; the natural tendency is to discount the significance of references to fields of which we have little knowledge.

My other illustration follows on from this and is a good deal more important. It concerns the meaning that Antonioni attached to Hermann Broch's *The Sleepwalkers* in *La Notte*. Ian Cameron in his valuable monograph on Antonioni refers to it as "a vast egghead volume," but I doubt if Antonioni intends that we should see Valentina (Monica Vitti) merely as the sort of girl who sits around ostentatiously reading books at parties. On the contrary, I imagine that Antonioni is a great admirer of Broch and that he has been influenced by this Austrian writer, with whom he has certain affinities. It would seem that Valentina is intended to share Broch's beliefs in, if I understand it correctly, a metaphysical redemption from social problems rather than any possibility of their resolution. She is thus a person of superior awareness of her situation who has come to terms with alienation. This would tie in with the visit that Giovanni (Marcello Mastroianni) makes at the beginning of the film to a dying friend whose last work is an essay on the German Marxist critic T. W. Adorno, who greatly influenced the writing of Thomas Mann's *Dr. Faustus*. It would be possible, however, to come to the same conclusion about Valentina without being in any way acquainted with Broch. Certainly Antonioni could count on very few people recognising *The Sleepwalkers*—far fewer than those who would know *Tender is the Night*.

The obvious difference between playing a piece of music or exhibiting a painting and showing a book is that the former is the thing itself and the latter can only have a meaning if the spectator knows it. Whatever may be said about Buñuel's use of Handel in *Viridiana*, no one would suggest that the choice of music was obscure. In the case of only a very few books can the general audience be expected to recognise the director's meaning immediately and relatively unambiguously. The Bible is perennially one of them; others vary with time and place. In the 1940s for instance there were numerous occasions (e.g. *Dear Octopus, Passport to Pimlico*) when an easy laugh was obtained by having someone unpack a case which contained *No Orchids for Miss Blandish*. *Lady Chatterley's Lover* or *Fanny Hill* would presumably serve the same purpose today.

With other books the director needs to take account of the possibilities of non-recognition, or of the variable subjective responses of his audience. One assumes that in *Some Came Running* Vincente Minnelli believed the audience would accept Dave Hirsch (Frank Sinatra) as a novelist in the main tradition of 20th Century fiction when he shows him taking from his valise the Viking Portable editions of Fitzgerald, Hemingway, Faulkner, Steinbeck and Wolfe. Minnelli certainly missed the irony intended in the original novel, where James Jones stresses that this is not Hirsch's opinion of himself but that of his sister, who had given him the books. Likewise, the subsequent publication of Hirsch's story in *Atlantic Monthly* will only seem a matter of abiding significance to those who regard that magazine as an important arbiter in literary matters.

I don't mean to suggest that the cinema should stick to invented periodicals and books, for these rarely carry conviction. It cannot be denied that a director has much greater control over his material if he does so, yet it is doubtful if this gain in control could compensate for the loss in verisimilitude. For instance, when Hitchcock shows Sean Connery in *Marnie* reading psychiatric textbooks with titles like "Frigidity in Women" and "The Mentality of the Criminal Female" one suspects that Hitchcock has himself invented these titles (or *would* have done if they didn't exist). While the titles serve his simple purposes well, there is something banal or naive about this sequence. In a very real sense the presentation of the books reflects the shallowness of the handling of psychology in the film as a whole.

It is interesting that this cinematic fascination with books should occur at a time when the ideas of Marshall McLuhan are gaining such currency, and that the cinema's greatest display of books should be François Truffaut's *Fahrenheit 451*, which as Truffaut himself pointed out has more literary references than all of Godard's pictures put together. *Fahrenheit* is not only a total rejection of the cinema's traditional attitude to literature but is also, by implication, a counterblast to McLuhan. In Ray Bradbury's novel very few books are actually mentioned by name. Inevitably in the movie we have to *see* the books, and in ways that are sometimes obvious and sometimes extremely subtle, Truffaut achieves an extraordinary power and resonance by his selection and manipulation of titles.

There is a rather touching scene in John Frankenheimer's *The Manchurian Candidate*, that much underrated expression of Sixties *Angst*, in which Frank Sinatra's intellectual confusion is revealed by setting him in a room littered with works of "contemporary significance" through which he has vainly sought the light. In *Fahrenheit 451* Truffaut has taken us beyond this crisis of literacy to McLuhan's "electronic global village" and revealed its nightmare qualities. In the first three-quarters of the film he builds up a situation in which we accept books as characters, and then leads us into his poetic final scene in which characters become human, walking books.

Paradoxically enough too, this rash of references to other arts and other films comes at a moment when everyone is celebrating the notion of pure or autonomous cinema. It is now necessary (or useful) to know far more about the other arts than it ever was in the past when movies really were self-contained. How can one properly appreciate *Paris Nous Appartient* without having read *Pericles*, or recent Bergman films without understanding Bach? And not only that, but working out what the play and the composer mean to Rivette and Bergman. (The relationship between *Pericles* and Rivette's film is somewhat different from that between *Othello* and *A Double Life* or *The Taming of the Shrew* and *Kiss Me Kate*.) Not that this has anything to do with what is pejoratively referred to as "literary cinema", which is generally taken to mean movies that correspond formally to the well-made play or orthodox novel. The term has however always had a note of falsity about it—in the sense that Richard Brooks' film version of *Lord Jim* is "literary cinema", while a more faithful adaptation of Conrad's novel would have resulted in a movie that strongly resembled *Citizen Kane*.

Finally it must be observed that the complexity of a film is not necessarily an indication of its importance, nor the amount of exegesis it demands an index of its quality.

While writing this article I've several times thought of the full-page advertisement for an American book club that appeared in popular magazines a few years ago. It depicted the club's advisory panel (the formidable triumvirate of W. H. Auden, Jacques Barzun and Lionel Trilling) sitting at a table facing an empty chair, on the sturdy leather back of which were the words "This place reserved for the man who prefers books to automobiles." Aesthetically and commercially the cinema has usually preferred automobiles. Godard and Truffaut would find it difficult to state their order of preference.

EXERCISES

on film and literature

1. Until recently, references to books in films have rarely, in French's phrase, "operated on a functional level." Why not?
2. French refers to a scene in a film where a copy of the *Atlantic Monthly* is used to symbolize creativity. Why does French find this to be unintentionally ironic?
3. What precisely is the difference in their attitudes to books of the younger French directors who comprise the "New Wave" and the older generation of Hollywood directors?

on film

1. Why does French point to the types of books referred to in the psychological thriller *Marnie* as an example of the film's "shallowness" in its approach to psychological problems? Can a film which treats a serious topic "shallowly" exert a bad influence on its public?
2. Discuss a recent art film as (or as not) a bad influence on its public.

on structure and language

1. What is the significance of the last sentence of French's essay? Do you find it to be an effectively concluding "punch line"?
2. Both French and Bluestone consider the relationship of books to films. What is the structural difference in their approach to this topic? Which is more critical and evaluative in his approach?
3. Note how the difference in approach determines the differences in tone. Which of the two writers, for example, has more humor?

A POET
AND THE MOVIES

Richard Wilbur

It is hard to say offhand how much one's art may have been tinctured by one's seeing of motion pictures, because watching film is (for me, for most) so much less judicial and analytic than other art experience. The conventions are transparent, the molding of the imagination is insidious. Even the worst movie has much of the authority of the actual, and quite without knowing it one comes out of the theater brainwashed into scanning the world through the norms of the camera. The enthusiasts of the pittoresco at the close of the eighteenth century, rapturously arranging the landscape in their Claude glasses, were conscious of the imposition; the moviegoer walks about taking shots and sequences unaware. The same entrancement characterizes the moviegoer's acquisition of personal style; to put on an Old Vic accent, to ape the gestures of a stage actor or actress—these involve some deliberate imposture, but to smoke like George Raft, to lift the eyebrows like Cary Grant—that is another and more hypnotized order of imitation. The mannerisms of movie stars, unconsciously borrowed and recognized without specific reminiscence, have for us something of the universality of the Italian vocabulary of gestures, though of course they are more transitory.

Knowing how far my mind's eye must have been conditioned by motion pictures, I venture with diffidence the opinion that certain pre-Edison poetry was genuinely cinematic. Whenever, for example, I read *Paradise Lost*, I, 44–58 (the long shot of Satan's fall from Heaven to Hell, the panorama of the rebels rolling in the lake of fire, the sudden close-up of Satan's afflicted eyes), I feel that I am experiencing a passage which, though its effects may have been suggested by the spatial surprises of Baroque architecture, is facilitated for me, and not misleadingly, by my familiarity with screen techniques. If this reaction is not anachronistic foolishness, it follows that one must be wary in attributing this or that aspect of any contemporary work to the influence of film.

But glancing at my own poems, as the editor has invited me to do, I find in a number of pieces—"Marginalia" for instance— what may owe as much to the camera as to the sharp noticing of poets like Hopkins and Ponge: a close and rapid scanning of details, an insubordination of authenticating particulars, abrupt shifting in lieu of the full-dress rhetorical transition. Here is a bit of the poem mentioned:

> Things concentrate at the edges; the pond-surface
> Is bourne to fish and man and it is spread
> In textile scum and damask light, on which
> The lily-pads are set; and there are also
>   Inlaid ruddy twigs, becalmed pine-leaves,
>   Air-baubles, and the chain mail of froth . . .

I notice in the first line of another poem ("Haze, char, and the weather of all souls") what may be an effort at the instant scenic fullness of an opening shot. Move as it may, the picture on the screen gives enviably much at once, and the moviegoing poet, impatient of his prolix medium, may sometimes try for a lightning completeness, a descriptive *coup*. Finally, I wonder if the first four lines of "An Event" are not indebted to trick photography:

> As if a cast of grain leapt back to the hand,
> A landscapeful of small black birds, intent
> On the far south, convene at some command
> At once in the middle of the air . . .

All of the above is doubtful, but there is no doubt about two of my poems, "Beasts" and "The Undead." Each owes something to a particular horror film, in respect of mood, matter, and images.

"Beasts" takes some of its third and fourth stanzas from *Frankenstein Meets the Wolf Man*, and "The Undead" obviously derives in part from Bela Lugosi's *Dracula*. Neither of these films is great art, though the latter comes close, but both are good enough to haunt the memory with the double force of reality and dream, to remind one of a deeper Gothic on which they draw, and to start the mind building around them. One would have to be brooding on a film to produce such a visual pun as "Their black shapes cropped into sudden bats."

THE UNDEAD

Even as children they were late sleepers,
Preferring their dreams, even when quick with monsters,
To the world with all its breakable toys,
Its compacts with the dying;

From the stretched arms of withered trees
They turned, fearing contagion of the mortal,
And even under the plums of summer
Drifted like winter moons.

Secret, unfriendly, pale, possessed
Of the one wish, the thirst for mere survival,
They came, as all extremists do
In time, to a sort of grandeur:

Now, to their Balkan battlements
Above the vulgar town of their first lives,
They rise at the moon's rising. Strange
That their utter self-concern

Should, in the end, have left them selfless:
Mirrors fail to perceive them as they float
Through the great hall and up the staircase;
Nor are the cobwebs broken.

Into the pallid night emerging,
Wrapped in their flapping capes, routinely maddened
By a wolf's cry, they stand for a moment
Stoking the mind's eye

With lewd thoughts of the pressed flowers
And bric-a-brac of rooms with something to lose,—
Of love-dismembered dolls, and children
Buried in quilted sleep.

Then they are off in a negative frenzy,
Their black shapes cropped into sudden bats
That swarm, burst, and are gone. Thinking
Of a thrush cold in the leaves

Who has sung his few summers truly,
Or an old scholar resting his eyes at last,
We cannot be much impressed with vampires,
Colorful though they are;

Nevertheless, their pain is real,
And requires our pity. Think how sad it must be
To thirst always for a scorned elixir,
The salt quotidian blood

Which, if mistrusted, has no savor;
To prey on life forever and not possess it,
As rock-hollows, tide after tide,
Glassily strand the sea.

EXERCISES

on film and literature

1. What technical effects does Wilbur find to be common to both poetry and cinema?
2. To which form does Wilbur feel one responds more passively: theater or films?
3. Why does Wilbur find a cinematic quality in the line: "Their black shapes cropped into sudden bats."
4. Note other cinematic images in Wilbur's poem, "The Undead."

on film

1. Discuss, using examples, the ways in which you feel films may have unconsciously influenced you.
2. On what main point about the way films "work" do Wilbur and Kott agree?

on structure and language

1. Is the relaxed tone of Wilbur's essay in keeping with his attitude toward his topic?

2. Note the terms he applies concerning the effect of films: "insidious," "brainwashed," "hypnotized." This would imply a negative view; yet clearly he is a movie fan. If his terms are not intended to be hostile, how are they intended? And how is this in keeping with his general attitude and tone?

3. And how, finally, is the theme of his poem, "The Undead," in keeping with the theme and tone of his preceding remarks? As we more closely apprehend the poem's theme, may we also apprehend a more serious aim in the whole essay than its tranquil manner would at first suggest?

FILM
and
THE VISUAL
ARTS

There are basic elements which the visual arts share with film: light, color, texture, composition, plasticity, perspective, dimensionality. A painting by Rembrandt and a film like Carl Dreyer's *Gertrud* not only possess such elements but to a degree use them for similar effects. Besides common elements, film and the visual arts employ common styles. The representational paintings of Reynolds or Hogarth or Andrew Wyeth depict the same surface realism as does the average feature film. The abstract expressionism of such artists as Kandinsky or Rothko finds its counterpart in the work of experimental film-makers like Maya Deren or James Broughton.

Films also depend on subjective distortions of space and time, in the manner of the visual arts of this century. The fragmented screen can show multiple actions simultaneously (as in *The Thomas Crown Affair*) in a way which parallels the method of viewing a single subject from multiple angles of vision in cubist painting and sculpture. The flow of blurred images frequently used by experimental film-makers resembles the simultaneous-sequential sculpture of the Futurist, Umberto Boccioni. As Arnold Hauser points out in his essay, the treatment of space-time in film and the modern arts reveals a mutual interaction of influences.

But for all these similarities, the film differs dramatically from the visual arts in being a form which coheres through motion. Traditionally, the painter or photographer—or poet—has been concerned with capturing a moment in time, in order to take it out of time. And his art has served him as the base on which the experience of a moment or a mood in time is held permanent, fixed. We find this motive expressed in Keats' "Ode on a Grecian Urn"; more recently, Frank Conroy summed it up in the title of his brilliant reminiscence of childhood and youth, *Stop-Time*, which is structured as a series of prose snapshots.

A filmed subject, however, means a subject revealed in motion—a stream of mutating images that no traditional art form could hope to duplicate. A film viewer can switch back and forth in seamless sequence between Hiroshima and the act of love, or traverse centuries in seconds ensconced in the armchair of a time machine. Thus film brings a new breakthrough dimension to visual art by spanning worlds and time through kaleidoscopic shifting images. It thereby loses the imaginative contemplation that arises out of a moment fixed in space, but it gains the greater fullness of a varied and explicit imagery. While visual art *suggests* more than film, it *shows* us less; in both cases the scales are not so much balanced as geared to different calibrations.

In his penetrating and cogent essay, "The Film Sense and the Painting Sense," Parker Tyler contrasts and then fuses visual art and the film form. In "Surrealistic Art and the Film" Arnold Hauser notes some of the ways that developments in film have reflected the tendencies and aims of Post-impressionist art; in this perspective, he focuses on film-making as a surrealistic exercise in space and time. In "Art Today and the Film" Rudolph Arnheim takes Hauser's emphases on surrealism further by positing a cinematic ideal in which the "ghostly" world is converted into realistic images. Of this group it is Arnheim who is most concerned to distinguish cinema from the other arts by noting those of its characteristics which are unique and which therefore mark out its own possibilities as an art form. All three authors are distinguished scholars and critics of the fine arts. In the final selection, Joseph von Sternberg, a director noted for his mastery of the techniques of lighting and composition, considers these and related matters from the film-maker's viewpoint.

THE FILM SENSE AND THE PAINTING SENSE

Parker Tyler

There has always been commerce, more or less conscious, between painting and the film. When photography was invented, the major aim was to duplicate the aesthetic effect of painting. Then as the concept of motion was introduced and the movies arrived, the aim was divided sharply between a quest for realities on the one hand and magical fantasy (such as stage illusions) on the other. The very nature of the movies as visible animation suggested adventure rather than formal control, sheer excitement rather than aesthetic emotion. Commercial films have continued to obey this suggestion while serious tendencies in the motion picture have developed the plastic and dynamic senses of the medium in accordance with aesthetic principles. If some enlightened persons are disinclined to consider the movies an "art," it is not only because movies reproduce images mechanically but also because they so seldom, in their instantaneous imagery, suggest the calculated and controlled design of painting.

Because objects in the real world, moving or merely animate, may be faithfully recorded by the film camera, it does not produce on the screen a dynamic effect except in the most elementary sense or a plastic effect except in the sense that the framing may

175

casually create a rough composition. To attain consistent and satisfying plastic and dynamic effects, the camera must be used consciously, selectively, and inventively in regard to *what* it photographs and *how* this is photographed. A rudimentary plastic design such as Mickey Mouse or a highly complex one such as Bosch's *Temptations of St. Anthony* or *Garden of Delight* are "stills," inanimate subjects, which the movie camera, as we have seen, can approach as raw material just as though they were life itself. By thinking of the movie camera as an independent aesthetic agent, distinct from the art work it represents, we can observe its function as an *animator* in a rather strict sense.

D. W. Griffith, in his film *Intolerance*, approached human history as one great mural. His huge panoramic Babylon was approached by the camera inevitably in the way, as happened recently in *The Titan*, Michelangelo's *Last Judgment* was approached: as the complex human collective where the individuals (or "details") must be picked out one by one. Babylon and the Sistine wall as objects were created plastically before the camera faced them, but the camera proceeded to "dramatize" them as though it were an individual spectator, seeing them first in detail and then in ensemble, or vice versa. However, since the camera as a form is literally a series of pictures shown successively, it is automatically adapted to present narrative, or action in quantitative time. Therefore it may move before a congeries of Bosch's imagery as though it were a medieval passion play and similarly may pass before Giotto's murals relating Christ's story in the Arena Chapel and reconstruct the *Massacre of the Innocents* as though it were live action.

In Luciano Emmer's recent *Leonardo da Vinci*, supervised by Francis Henry Taylor, director of the New York Metropolitan Museum of Art, the artist's analytical drawings of birds in flight were animated in the orthodox "Disney" fashion. This cannot be done with other authentic works without a great deal of faking; but an approximation of it has been employed twice in the use of dance drawings by Toulouse-Lautrec. In *Pictura*, named for its producing company, two stages of a kick in drawings of the same dancer are repeated over and over rapidly to give the standard animated effect, while in John Huston's *Moulin Rouge* a sequence of Lautrec's dance-hall figures are run swiftly before the eye and intercut to produce the *impression* of real action in the famous café. Eisenstein, in his *October*, animated three separate sculptures of lions, beginning with recumbent and ending with rampant, with perfect comic success.

Animating a given plastic conception by a great artist may strike one as not only a vulgar but also a criminally absurd idea. Yet in *The Titan*, for an outstanding example, an effect of much subtlety was obtained by passing the camera at close range around the somnolent figures Michelangelo placed before the Medici Tombs. This might be called a *controlled spectatorship* in which the photographic values of black and white within the quadrangular two-dimensional frame contributed an "interpretive" rendering of allegorical sculptures. Signally, too, with the *Bacchus*, the movie camera "narrated" a way of looking that was a way of feeling; the rectangularly isolated views of Bacchus' tipsy face, swiftly modifying each other, and concentration on the little faun, whose presence may come as a surprise, achieve plastic effects virtually impossible without the camera's use. Films, therefore, have meant a new apotheosis of the "detail" in the reproduction of art works.

The Titan's interpretation of the Michelangelo sculptures, bringing three-dimensional art works to the movie screen *as though* they were elements of flat design, refers to an important aspect of the art of the film. This, as Eisenstein has voluminously shown, is the conception of film not as a representation of a three-dimensional world in terms that (like those of sculpture and bas-relief) remind us literally of the third dimension, but rather in terms that remind us literally of the two dimensions of painting. Eisenstein's completed part of *Ivan the Terrible* earned unfavorable criticism as "static" because it clung to single plastic compositions for such protracted periods. Analysis of these compositions shows the lasting effects on Eisenstein of his early experience as designer of abstract-geometric stage sets. Actual motifs of Kandinsky's imagery are discoverable in *Ivan*.

In his unfinished *Que Viva Mexico!* Eisenstein constantly bore testimony to his debt to painting by projecting screen shots that were virtually "stills," carefully composed with plastic values in mind. Interestingly enough, one of the earliest "naif" film makers, the Frenchman Georges Méliès (1861–1938), made his scenes from drawings of which the only *living* element, in the film itself, became the human actors. Showing the same aesthetic instinct for painting, Eisenstein was accustomed to compose his scenes on paper. Essential to many beautiful shots in *Que Viva Mexico!* were the two-dimensional feeling of surface and—of course—the rectangular screen. The latter shape, integral with painting, was always an ingredient of the movies' aesthetic function and apt to operate best in the pretalkie era, since in the talkies the film often tends merely to photograph actors speaking and to follow them about as though they were on a theater stage. This last, indeed, is specifically what Alfred Hitchcock did in *Rope*, thereby sacrificing all opportunities for true cinematic composition in the "still" sense, and making overfluid the kind of "time mural" a movie may be considered in the over-all sense.

Yet if indeed one film trend animates painting, another de-animates life into the still terms of painting insofar as its aim be plastic, two-dimensional composition as a unit in its spatial-temporal art. One may define the film as a plastic, two-dimensional composition which animates itself in a series of mutations, totally replacing one composition at a certain point with another. Style is the element expected to unify so many different compositions. The film, then, is a fused art of time and space. So are, in other respects, mural painting and the narrative easel works of the Renaissance. Technical animation of the popular cartoon kind, while applied approximately to works such as the sequence of Lautrec's Moulin Rouge drawings, actually treats plastic images of dancers *as though* they were live performers and not the central forms in works of a two-dimensional art. What such animation accomplishes, among other things, is a "flashback" impression of the dynamic elements which temporally went into the making of the work.

The technique of the film has allowed us to see, as one continuous movement, a plant growing from seeds below ground to sprouts and leaves above ground and a rose developing from bud to blossom. Analogous to this visual intensification of an objective dynamic process is what the film may do with the progress of a painting's creation. In a documentary on Matisse, we are shown how the artist evolved his conception of a head in a series of sketches from a quasi-naturalistic version to the final form. This was done by superimposing the finished sketches transparently so that an illusion of organic evolution was obtained. Mickey Mouse as well as Lautrec's dancers seem to turn into organic beings before our eyes. But in the case of Matisse's head the element of *mutation* is added; in fact, the animation resides strictly in this element.

The painting-in-motion genre of the film art has been long in existence. The German pioneer Oskar Fischinger animated pure abstract forms in a kind of ballet to music: a dance of optical rhythms. Recently much work of this kind, notably by the Canadian Norman McLaren and John and James Whitney of California, has been done in the experimental film field. The Whitney brothers have invented an extraordinary machine to create their abstract rhythmic patterns, while McLaren and others have worked directly on the film strip, thus dispensing with photography as a means. In such cases as McLaren's, the film frame projected in the theater is a *picture* in the actual sense: literally drawing or painting in movement *as it originally moved*; in this way the film maker has become actually synonymous with the picture maker. Of special interest is a little tour de force by the American Thomas Bouchard in his documentary about Fernand Léger. The distinct formal units of one painting by Léger, having been analyzed, were cut out, painted as in the work, and then by way of the painter's hand (with the camera as witness) placed piece by piece so as to reconstitute the picture. Previously Léger has been shown drawing directly from nature, so that the collage operation of the film, especially since the camera has been stationed directly above, imparts an air of biological magic to what has been hand-created with tools.

A distinctive aspect of the animated cartoons is the absence of motion in the background in contrast with the cavorting figure in front. We sense the background simply as a drawing. It is likewise with the blank ground of the drawing paper or canvas on which, through the film, the designs of artists acquire the "magic" attribute of organic growth. Yet this blank background is not a void but a physical plane surface limited by edges; in this sense, the sides of the paper are equivalent to the sides of the film frame as projected. In the old days when animation was becoming popular, a clown used to be born illusorily from an ink bottle in lines of ink, and the humor of it was his dependence on his creator for things to use, a world to live in, and sometimes even ground to stand on. Lately he has been revived on the television screen. Here is a comic version of the myth of divine creation, and like all myths its elements reverberate in time and space. Thus in 1953 we saw one of the ingenious UPA cartoons, *Christopher Crumpet*, in which properties and backgrounds are created as well as animated before our eyes by an invisible hand, appearing and disappearing as necessary. In a pointed sense, the world is shown here as *man*-created, and this is what, in our urban civilization, the visible world often so largely is.

A great problem of our time is the world which group and individual find to live in and their capacity to change the world according to desires and needs or passively to be changed by it. Imaginatively, work in the experimental film field has contributed insights into the human situation by ingenious exploitation of the film's aesthetic possibilities. The classic advance-guard film, Cocteau's *Blood of a Poet*, has been influential to a great extent. Cocteau devised a basic odyssey: that of the human creator. The narrative fluidity of his film was oriented to definite stages so that the mutating image of the hero becomes the spectator of closed interiors like small stage sets, visible to him only through a keyhole. The final set, the largest of all and equivalent to a small theater, opens into an exterior characterized as cosmic space, where the hero's destiny, and implicitly that of all artists, is finally transmuted into glorious triumph by the artistic instinct.

Maya Deren is an American film maker who has profited richly by Cocteau's example. The chief theme of some half-dozen films by her, made over the last decade, is the odyssey of an individual always engaged in something like an obstacle race and behaving like a somnambulist or one moving through an actual dream. The rhythms are often choreographic and dreamlike, the visual overtones magical and labyrinthine. When, in Miss Deren's *Study in Choreography for Camera*, a dancer begins his movement in a wood, continues it without the least interruption as the scene shifts to a private interior, then to a hall in a museum, then to another interior and back to the wood, reaching his climax with a triumphant sense of dance flow, we have an active self-contained figure seen before a background whose seemingly arbitrary and sudden mutations are independent of his movements and of which he seems quite unaware. This is a parable of the individual's integrity in a changeable environment, not consciously meant as such by the creator, perhaps, but virtually such in any case. Now what gives this dancer his implicit confidence in the continuity of the solid ground required for his steps? It is, I think, the confidence of the artist who essentially creates his own space by establishing some plastic or dynamic rhythm in time and following it through consistently. The ground or "background" he assumes is the basic, limited ground which every artist uses and which implies absolute faith in the future.

Evident in Miss Deren's film fantasies and in conspicuous ones by other young experimentalists whom I shall mention, is the creation of an imaginary visual world in which tension is supplied by the protagonist's effort at equilibrium and control within it, this sometimes emerging in the film maker's own efforts at controlling his medium and creating his style. We see the same basic theme in the adventures of certain cartoon characters, especially in the fabulous feats of UPA's Mr. Magoo, whose trait of short-sightedness combined with sublime self-confidence creates automatically, for the spectator, the tension I mean. Mr. Magoo, as it were, walks the "tightrope" of perilous reality while recreating the objective world in terms of a false mental picture. What saves him from all harm is a miraculous rhythm in chance itself. In this essentially *comic* rhythm lies the ironic falsity involved with human destiny, whose truth is demonstrated individually and collectively by man in the real social world.

The film strip rotating swiftly through the camera projects a limited perspective no matter how often its viewpoint may be changed; this perspective is equivalent to each man's mental image of the world and of those numerous, more or less fanciful, perspectives which inevitably are everyone's subjective possession— the way you or I or someone else "sees life" at some given moment. It is when someone's internal assurance of existence tends to vanish, to represent "spacelessness," that the appetite for life and the future also vanishes. The American experimentalist, Curtis Harrington, has done an eloquent vignette on the subject of suicide. It takes place in a desolate scene by river flats and only two people, a man and his fate (symbolized by a knitting woman), are in it: the brooding man snatches up the dropped ball of yarn and runs with it toward the river, falling and disappearing: only the strand of yarn remains on the ground: the knitter cannot finish her work. The inkline that was the clown's "lifeline," Magoo's implicit "tightrope," and the strand of yarn, all are a kind of navel cord representing the life of the individual which classicism pictured in the hands of the Fates.

Another experimentalist, the American Sidney Peterson, has used distorting lenses to indicate subjective states of mind and emotion as well as to create a visual style. It is not surprising that his *Mr. Frenhofer and the Minotaur* is a surrealistic blend of a love episode with Picasso's Minotaur suite, a story by Balzac about a painter, *The Hidden Masterpiece*, and a verbal sound track employing stream-of-consciousness as found in Joyce's *Ulysses*. Here the odyssey of the artist, first visualized for film by Cocteau, is seen parallel with Bloom's subjectivist journey through Dublin in Joyce's novel. The adventures of the vagabond fool have an ancient tradition in literature and the theater, carried on in American films by such classic comedians as Charlie Chaplin, Harry Langdon, and Jimmy Savo. Another American experimentalist, James Broughton, has wittily reconstructed the style of miming and photography of early film comedy in his *Looney Tom*, who is vagabond fool and clown-Ulysses. Another film by Broughton, *Mother's Day*, is an animated version of the Family Album aptly emphasizing a sense of the picture frame.

The film medium's flexible gamut between subjective and objective is theoretically unlimited, depending entirely on the style, the taste, and the specific aims of the film maker in conjunction with the technical adequacy of his means. In *Fireworks*, experimentalist Kenneth Anger does not hesitate to employ imagery of the viscera to convey spiritual and physical suffering, while *Geography of the Body*, a film by another experimentalist, Willard Maas, is composed of shots of the nude, often taken so close that the body's rondures become abstract and elusively identifiable patterns. Here the optical close-up was carried to its *ne plus ultra* short of microscopy. The inward-goingness of the experimental film is thus as demonstrable as that of lyric poetry or the most subjective psychology of the novel. In experimentalist

Stan Brakhage's work, whether characters speak or only pantomime, the essence of the action (either naturalistic or symbolic)
is invariably *inward* in portent; furthermore, lips moving without
sound create, in the absence of subtitles, an atmosphere of sub-
jectivity.

In an experimental adaptation of Pierre Louÿs' *Psyche*, one
of the youngest American film makers, Gregory Markopolous,
placed close-up and distance images in the same shot to dramatize
the inner mystery of the lovers' relationship as well as to create
the illusion of depth, so that vision holds a psychological dimension (something that appears in painting in Bosch's *Temptations
of St. Anthony*, picturing the saint's hallucinations in the background). Some years ago there was news of a French film maker
who planned to recreate part of Proust's *Remembrance of Things
Past*. Such a film, it seems certain, would be visionary from beginning to end and call upon all the known technical devices of the
film laboratory for indicating states of mind: psychology as shown
in simultaneous montage. In all cases, the basic four-sided screen
of the film is the same constant factor as the four-sided ground of
the painting. I should say that the recently prominent experimental
school in the United States is notably "Proustian" as well as
expressionist and surrealist, inasmuch as the quasi-autobiographic
hero or heroine is usually the psychic as well as the optical center
of the screen. As Proust seems to gather space about his private
person and modulate it with the music of his heartbeat and his
very optic nerve, so in principle does the American experimentalist compose space—with the screen rectangle as his visible limit
—about a sort of cosmic adventurer who is the self.

Many problems of style remain for the experimental film to
conquer and all its young exponents need more taste and imagination, as well as superior means, to accomplish future masterpieces.
Naturally, commercial film has always found more or less close
inspiration in the traditions of painting. Two fairly recent films to
have profited from the painting sense were Carl-Theodor Dreyer's
Day of Wrath and the above-mentioned *Moulin Rouge*, made in
Paris by the American John Huston. Scene by scene, with good
results, the former aimed at a Rembrandtlike chiaroscuro, the
corners of the screen often tapering off into dense shadow. This

element of baroque lighting was sometimes artificially achieved in films by shading the lens itself and spotting images in ovals; this rather crude device, however, seldom approached the emphasis of a style. In Alexander Korda's *Rembrandt*, we sometimes find Charles Laughton as the painter dramatically outlined against snow, as in a Bruegel, or against a daylit interior, as in a Vermeer. With the use of color filters and smoke, Huston caught in *Moulin Rouge* some of the tonal qualities of Lautrec's paintings and was influenced even by Lautrec's visual angles in presenting scenes and persons once portrayed by the artist. As to the experimental field, one may note that in Watson and Webber's pioneer American classic, *Lot in Sodom*, close-ups of faces, both as to lighting and make-up, show the effort to obtain the cubist patterning of modern painting, while in *The Blood of a Poet*, Cocteau drew lines on his female statue's face to reinforce the two-dimensional or "pictorial" art of the film.

In the nonchalant assumption of the usual commercial film that the only necessary formal element is *plot* and that merely conventional "framing" and clear photography are required for plastic values, we find the reason for the vulgar journalistic look and formlessness of standard movie products. The frantic drive of Hollywood cameras to "eat up" space on their recurrent "trips to the moon" directly reflects the general commercial viewpoint toward space as a jungle, a *chaos*, whether void or occupied. Art, on the contrary, is produced by the controlling principles of a *cosmos*, which underlies all casual aspects of confusion and variety and represents destiny as opposed to chance, form as opposed to formlessness. To achieve a meaningful art, the film must invent not only in terms of those formal laws it shares with painting but also in terms of its own exclusive nature; at the same time, in its broad aspects, it gives the former too little attention. Documentaries and newsreels can passively resign themselves to reporting with a clear conscience. Creatively the film must obey a synthesis of aesthetic principles that have existed since the origin of the visual arts. A scrutiny of the animating devices along with the clear-cut procedures of imaginative experimentalists enables us to perceive, very forcefully, how movement may be initiated and artistically controlled within a given space.

EXERCISES

on film and the visual arts

1. Why does Tyler believe painting to be a more serious art than cinema?
2. According to Tyler, the use by the director Eisenstein in his film *Que Viva Mexico!* of "shots that were virtually stills" shows a "debt to painting." In what ways? What is meant today by a still shot?
3. How does Tyler's discussion of the mural painting techniques of Griffith's *Intolerance* help our understanding of the themes of this film?

on film

1. What sort of contrast does Tyler make between films which appeal through their "sheer excitement" and those which appeal through "aesthetic emotion"?
2. Discuss, with examples, films which you feel possess "aesthetic emotion."

on structure and language

1. The essay is developed according to a pattern of similarities and contrasts concerning films and painting, and moves in its range of reference from the relatively easy-to-understand film classics of D. W. Griffith to the experimental and highly abstruse efforts of such "underground" film-makers as Gregory Markopolous and the late Maya Deren. Account for the stages of increasing difficulty in Tyler's own treatment of his material and his style of writing as he progresses from Griffith to Deren.
2. Define what Tyler means when he speaks of the "painting-in-motion genre."

SURREALISTIC ART
AND THE FILM

Arnold Hauser

The great reactionary movement of the century takes effect in the realm of art as a rejection of impressionism—a change which, in some respects, forms a deeper incision in the history of art than all the changes of style since the Renaissance, leaving the artistic tradition of naturalism fundamentally unaffected. It is true that there had always been a swinging to and fro between formalism and antiformalism, but the function of art being true to life and faithful to nature had never been questioned in principle since the Middle Ages. In this respect impressionism was the climax and the end of a development which had lasted more than four hundred years. Post-impressionist art is the first to renounce all illusion of reality on principle and to express its outlook on life by the deliberate deformation of natural objects. Cubism, constructivism, futurism, expressionism, dadaism, and surrealism turn away with equal determination from nature-bound and reality-affirming impressionism. But impressionism itself prepares the ground for this development in so far as it does not aspire to an integrating description of reality, to a confrontation of the subject with the objective world as a whole, but marks rather the beginning of that process which has been called the "annexation" of reality by art.

Post-impressionist art can no longer be called in any sense a reproduction of nature; its relationship to nature is one of violation. We can speak at most of a kind of magic naturalism, of the production of objects which exist alongside reality, but do not wish to take its place. Confronted with the works of Braque, Chagall, Rouault, Picasso, Henri Rousseau, Salvador Dali, we always feel that, for all their differences, we are in a second world, a super-world which, however many features of ordinary reality it may still display, represents a form of existence surpassing and incompatible with this reality. . . .

The new century is full of such deep antagonisms, the unity of its outlook on life is so profoundly menaced, that the combination of the furthest extremes, the unification of the greatest contradictions, becomes the main theme, often the only theme, of its art. Surrealism, which, as André Breton remarks, at first revolved entirely round the problem of language, that is, of poetic expression, and which, as we should say with Paulhan, sought to be understood without the means of understanding, developed into an art which made the paradox of all form and the absurdity of all human existence the basis of its outlook. Dadaism still pleaded, out of despair at the inadequacy of cultural forms, for the destruction of art and for a return to chaos, that is to say, for romantic Rousseauism in the most extreme meaning of the term. Surrealism, which supplements the method of dadaism with the "automatic method of writing," thereby already expresses its belief that a new knowledge, a new truth and a new art will arise from chaos, from the unconscious and the irrational, from dreams and the uncontrolled regions of the mind. The surrealists expect the salvation of art, which they forswear as such just as much as the dadaists and are only prepared to accept it at all as a vehicle of irrational knowledge, from a plunging into the unconscious, into the pre-rational and the chaotic, and they take over the psycho-analytical method of free association, that is, the automatic development of ideas and their reproduction without any rational, moral and aesthetic censorship, because they imagine they have discovered therein a recipe for the restoration of the good old romantic type of inspiration. So, after all, they still take their refuge in the rationalization of the irrational and the methodical re-production of the spontaneous, the only difference being that their method is incomparably more pedantic, dogmatic and rigid than the mode of creation in which the irrational and the intuitive are controlled by aesthetic judgement, taste and criticism, and which makes reflection and not indiscrimination its guiding principle. How much more fruitful than the surrealists' recipe was the procedure of Proust, who likewise put himself into a kind of somnambulistic condition and abandoned himself to the stream of memories and associations with the passivity of a hypnotic medium, but who remained at the same time a disciplined thinker and in the highest degree a consciously creative artist. Freud himself seems to have seen through the trick perpetrated by surrealism. He is said to have remarked to Salvador Dali, who visited him in London shortly before his death: "What interests me in your art is not the unconscious, but the conscious." Must he not have meant by that: "I am not interested in your simulated paranoia, but in the method of your simulation."

The basic experience of the surrealists consists in the discovery of a "second reality," which, although it is inseparably fused with ordinary, empirical reality, is nevertheless so different from it that we are only able to make negative statements about it and to point to the gaps and cavities in our experience as evidence for its existence. Nowhere is this dualism expressed more acutely than in the works of Kafka and Joyce, who, although they have nothing to do with surrealism as a doctrine, are surrealists in the wider sense, like most of the progressive artists of the century. It is also this experience of the double-sidedness of existence, with its home in two different spheres, which makes the surrealists aware of the peculiarity of dreams and induces them to recognize in the mixed reality of dreams their own stylistic ideal. The dream becomes the paradigm of the whole world-picture, in which reality and unreality, logic and fantasy, the banality and sublimation of existence, form an indissoluble and inexplicable unity. The meticulous naturalism of the details and the arbitrary combination of their relationships which surrealism copies from the dream, not only express the feeling that we live on two different levels, in two different spheres, but also that these regions of being penetrate one another so thoroughly that the one can neither be subordinated to nor set against the other as its antithesis. . . .

The emphasis lies everywhere on the uninterruptedness of the movement, the "heterogeneous continuum," the kaleidoscopic picture of a disintegrated world. The Bergsonian concept of time undergoes a new interpretation, an intensification and a deflection. The accent is now on the simultaneity of the contents of consciousness, the immanence of the past in the present, the constant flowing together of the different periods of time, the amorphous fluidity of inner experience, the boundlessness of the stream of time by which the soul is borne along, the relativity of space and time, that is to say, the impossibility of differentiating and defining the media in which the mind moves. In this new conception of time almost all the strands of the texture which form the stuff of modern art converge: the abandonment of the plot, the elimination of the hero, the relinquishing of psychology, the "automatic method of writing" and, above all, the montage technique and the intermingling of temporal and spatial forms of the film. The new concept of time, whose basic element is simultaneity and whose nature consists in the spatialization of the temporal element, is expressed in no other genre so impressively as in this youngest art, which dates from the same period as Bergson's philosophy of time. The agreement between the technical methods of the film and the characteristics of the new concept of time is so complete that one has the feeling that the time categories of modern art altogether must have arisen from the spirit of cinematic form, and one is inclined to consider the film itself as the stylistically most representative, though qualitatively perhaps not the most fertile genre of contemporary art.

The theatre is in many respects the artistic medium most similar to the film; particularly in view of its combination of spatial and temporal forms, it represents the only real analogy to the film. But what happens on the stage is partly spatial, partly temporal; as a rule spatial and temporal, but never a mixture of the spatial and the temporal, as are the happenings in a film. The most fundamental difference between the film and the other arts is that, in its world-picture, the boundaries of space and time are fluid—space has a quasi-temporal, time, to some extent, a spatial character. In the plastic arts, as also on the stage, space remains static, motionless, unchanging, without a goal and without a direction; we move about quite freely in it, because it is homogeneous in all its parts and because none of the parts presupposes the other temporally. The phases of the movement are not stages, not steps in a gradual development; their sequence is subject to no constraint. Time in literature—above all in the drama—on the other hand, has a definite direction, a trend of development, an objective goal, independent of the spectator's experience of time; it is no mere reservoir, but an ordered succession. Now, these dramaturgical categories of space and time have their character and functions completely altered in the film. Space loses its static quality, its serene passivity and now becomes dynamic; it comes into being as it were before our eyes. It is fluid, unlimited, unfinished, an element with its own history, its own scheme and process of development. Homogeneous physical space here assumes the characteristics of heterogeneously composed historical time. In this medium the individual stages are no longer of the same kind, the individual parts of space no longer of equal value; it contains specially qualified positions, some with a certain priority in the development and others signifying the culmination of the spatial experience. The use of the close-up, for example, not only has spatial criteria, it also represents a phase to be reached or to be surpassed in the temporal development of the film. In a good film the close-ups are not distributed arbitrarily and capriciously. They are not cut in independently of the inner development of the scene, not at any time and anywhere, but only where their potential energy can and should make itself felt. For a close-up is not a cut-out picture with a frame; it is always merely part of a picture, like, for instance, the *repoussoir* figures in baroque painting which introduce a dynamic quality into the picture similar to that created by the close-ups in the spatial structure of a film.

But as if space and time in the film were interrelated by being interchangeable, the temporal relationships acquire an almost spatial character, just as space acquires a topical interest and takes on temporal characteristics, in other words, a certain element of freedom is introduced into the succession of their moments. In the temporal medium of a film we move in a way that is otherwise peculiar to space, completely free to choose our direction, proceeding from one phase of time into another, just as one goes from one room to another, disconnecting the individual stages in the development of events and grouping them, generally speaking, according to the principles of spatial order. In brief, time here loses, on the one hand, its uninterrupted continuity, on the other, its irreversible direction. It can be brought to a standstill: in close-ups; reversed: in flash-backs; repeated: in recollections; and skipped across: in visions of the future. Concurrent, simultaneous events can be shown successively, and temporally distinct events simultaneously—by double-exposure and alternation; the earlier can appear later, the later before its time. This cinematic conception of time has a thoroughly subjective and apparently irregular character compared with the empirical and the dramatic conception of the same medium. The time of empirical reality is a uniformly progressive, uninterruptedly continuous, absolutely irreversible order, in which events follow one another as if "on a conveyor belt." It is true that dramatic time is by no means identical with empirical time—the embarrassment caused by a clock showing the correct time on the stage comes from this discrepancy—and the unity of time prescribed by classicistic dramaturgy can even be interpreted as the fundamental elimination of ordinary time, and yet the temporal relationships in the drama have more points of contact with the chronological order of ordinary experience than the order of time in a film. Thus in the drama, or at least in one and the same act of a drama, the temporal continuity of empirical reality is preserved intact. Here too, as in real life, events follow each other according to the law of a progression which permits neither interruptions and jumps, nor repetitions and inversions, and conforms to a standard of time which is absolutely constant, that is, undergoes no acceleration, retardation or stoppages of any kind within the several sections (acts or scenes). In the film, on the other hand, not only the speed of successive events, but also the chronometric standard itself is often different from shot to shot, according as to whether slow or fast motion, short or long cutting, many or few close-ups, are used.

The dramatist is prohibited by the logic of scenic arrangement from repeating moments and phases of time, an expedient that is often the source of the most intensive aesthetic effects in the film. It is true that a part of the story is often treated retrospectively in the drama, and the antecedents followed backwards in time, but they are usually represented indirectly—either in the form of a coherent narrative or of one limited to scattered hints. The technique of the drama does not permit the playwright to go back to past stages in the course of a progressively developing plot and to insert them *directly* into the sequence of events, into the dramatic present—that is, it is only recently that it has begun to permit it, perhaps under the immediate influence of the film, or under the influence of the new conception of time, familiar also from the modern novel. The technical possibility of interrupting any shot without further ado suggests the possibilities of a discontinuous treatment of time from the very outset and provides the film with the means of heightening the tension of a scene either by interpolating heterogeneous incidents or assigning the individual phases of the scene to different sections of the work. In this way the film often produces the effect of someone playing on a keyboard and striking the keys ad libitum, up and down, to right and left. In a film we often see the hero first at the beginning of his career as a young man, later, going back to the past, as a child; we then see him, in the further course of the plot, as a mature man and, having followed his career for a time, we, finally, may see him still living after his death, in the memory of one of his relations or friends. As a result of the discontinuity of time, the retrospective development of the plot is combined with the progressive in complete freedom, with no kind of chronological tie, and through the repeated twists and turns in the time-continuum, mobility, which is the very essence of the cinematic experience, is pushed to the uttermost limits. The real spatialization of time in the film does not take place, however, until the simultaneity of parallel plots is portrayed. It is the experience of the simultaneity of different, spatially separated happenings that puts the audience into that condition of suspense which moves between space and time and claims the categories of both orders for itself. It is the simultaneous nearness and remoteness of things—their nearness to one another in time and their distance from one another in space—that constitutes that spatio-temporal element, that two-dimensionality of time, which is the real medium of the film and the basic category of its world-picture.

EXERCISES

on film and the visual arts

1. What are Hauser's reasons for considering film a Post-impressionist art?
2. How does he tie in the "Bergsonian concept of time" with Post-impressionist attitudes in art and in the film?
3. Which art form does Hauser believe to be most comparable to film, and why?
4. How does Hauser link the space-time continuum to dreams? to surrealistic art? to the film? Can you show how all three linkages are achieved by a similar process?

on film

1. Hauser mentions close-up, flashback, and double-exposure as characteristic cinema techniques. Are analogous techniques available to the novelist? Discuss.
2. Discuss Hauser's idea of the film's unique treatment of space and time with reference to specific films.

on structure and language

1. The first half of this selection is devoted to a consideration of the movement in painting from realism to surrealism. How does this introductory part pave the way to the main points on film made in the latter part?
2. The selection is based on generalization rather than specific instances. No particular painting or film is cited to exemplify a point. Would you have preferred some examples, or do you feel that the author's pausing to give examples would have impeded the smooth flow of his ideas? How smooth is the essay in reading?

ART TODAY
AND THE FILM

Rudolph Arnheim

If the various arts of our time share certain traits and tendencies
they probably do so in different ways, depending on the character
of each medium. At first glance, the photographic image, technically committed to mechanical reproduction, might be expected
to fit modern art badly—a theoretical prediction not borne out,
however, by some of the recent work of photographers and film
directors. In the following I shall choose a key notion to describe
central aspects of today's art and then apply this notion to the
film, thereby suggesting particular ways in which the photo-
chemical picture responds to some aesthetic demands of our time.

In search of the most characteristic feature of our visual art,
one can conclude that it is the attempt of getting away from the
detached images by which artists have been portraying physical
reality. In the course of our civilization we have come to use
images as tools of contemplation. We have set them up as a world
of their own, separate from the world they depict, so that they
may have their own completeness and develop more freely their
particular style. These virtues, however, are outweighed by the
anxiety such a detachment arouses when the mind cannot afford
it because its own hold on reality has loosened too much. Under

such conditions, the footlights separating a world of make-believe from its counterpart and the frame which protects the picture from merging with its surroundings become a handicap.

In a broader sense, the very nature of a recognizable likeness suffices to produce the frightening dichotomy, even without any explicit detachment of the image. A marble statue points to a world of flesh and blood, to which, however, it confesses not to belong—which leaves it without a dwelling-place in that world. It can acquire such a dwelling-place only by insisting that it is more than an image, and the most radical way of accomplishing it is to abandon the portrayal of the things of nature altogether. This is, of course, what modern art has done. By renouncing portrayal, the work of art establishes itself clearly as an object possessing an independent existence of its own. . . .

If we have read the signs of the times at all correctly, the prospect of the cinema would seem to look dim—not because it lacks potential but because what it has to offer might appear to be the opposite of what is wanted. The film is mimetic by its very nature. As a branch of photography, it owes its existence to the imprint of things upon a sensitive surface. It is the image-maker *par excellence*, and much of its success derives from the mechanical faithfulness of its portrayals. . . .

Following the example of painting, the cinema has tried the remedy of abstraction. But the experiments, from Hans Richter and Viking Eggeling to Oskar Fischinger, Norman McLaren and Len Lye, have amounted mainly to a museum's collection of venerable curiosities. This may seem surprising, considering the great aesthetic potential of colored shapes in motion. But since abstract painting is also on the decline, my guess is that once the artist abandons image-making he has no longer a good reason to cling to the two-dimensional surface, that is, to the twilight area between image-making and object-making. Hence the temporary or permanent desertion of so many artists from painting to sculpture and, as I said, the attempts to make painting three-dimensional or attach it to architecture.

The film cannot do this. There seems to be general agreement that the cinema has scored its most lasting and most specifically cinematic successes when it drew its interpretations of life from authentic realism. This has been true all the way from Lumière to

Pudovkin, Eisenstein, and Robert Flaherty and more recently de Sica and Zavattini. And I would find it hard to argue with somebody who maintained that he would be willing to give the entire film production of the last few years for Jacques-Yves Cousteau's recent under-water documentary, *World Without Sun*.

However—and this brings me to the main point of my argument—Cousteau's film creates fascination not simply as an extension of our visual knowledge obtained by the documentary presentation of an unexplored area of our earth. These most authentically realistic pictures reveal a world of profound mystery, a darkness momentarily lifted by flashes of unnatural light, a complete suspension of the familiar vertical and horizontal coordinates of space. Spatial orientation is upset also by the weightlessness of these animals and dehumanized humans, floating up and down without effort, emerging from nowhere and disappearing into nothingness, constantly in motion without any recognizable purpose, and totally indifferent to each other. There is an overwhelming display of dazzling color and intricate motion, tied to no experience we ever had and performed for the discernible benefit of nobody. There are innumerable monstrous variations of faces and bodies as we know them, passing by with the matter-of-factness of herring or perch, in a profound silence, most unnatural for such visual commotion and rioting color, and interrupted only by noises nobody ever heard. What we have here, if a nasty pun is permissible, is the New Wave under water.

For it seems evident that what captures us in this documentary film is a most successful although surely unintentional display of what the most impressive films of the last few years have been trying to do, namely, to interpret the ghostliness of the visible world by means of authentic appearances drawn directly from that world. The cinema has been making its best contribution to the general trend I have tried to describe, not by withdrawing from imagery, as the other arts have, but by using imagery to describe reality as a ghostly figment. It thereby seizes and interprets the experience from which the other visual arts tend to escape and to which they are reacting.

In exploiting this opportunity, the cinema remains faithful to its nature. It derives its new nightmares from its old authenticity. Take the spell-binding opening of Fellini's $8^{1}/_{2}$, the scene of the heart attack in the closed car, stared at without reaction by the other drivers, so near by and yet so distant in their glass and steel containers, take the complete paralysis of motion, realistically justified by the traffic jam in the tunnel, and compare this frightening mystery with the immediately following escape of the soul, which has all the ludicrous clumsiness of the special-effects department. How much more truly unreal are the mosquito swarms of the reporters persecuting the widowed woman in *La Dolce Vita* than is the supposedly fantastic harem bath of the hero in *8¹/₂*. And how unforgettable, on the other hand, is the grey nothingness of the steam bath in which the pathetic movie makers do penitence and which transfigures the ancient cardinal.

EXERCISES

on film and the visual arts

1. What is the distinction Arnheim draws between art as a "tool of contemplation" and art as an "object possessing an independent existence of its own"? In which of these categories does film fall? Explain.
2. Compare Arnheim's views with those of Tyler on the possibilities of an abstract cinema on the lines of abstract painting.

on film

1. Why does Arnheim prefer the first scene of the opening sequence of *8¹/₂* to the scene which follows it? How does his admiration for the steam bath scene of *8¹/₂* tie in with his views of the technical advantages of the film medium?
2. Consider some recent films you have seen from the point of view of their realistic content and the relative authenticity of that content, in the terms posed by Arnheim.

on structure and language

1. Arnheim believes that the "modern mind" is typified by its increasingly "loose" hold on reality. How does this assumption

guide his argument concerning the aesthetics of painting and film?

2. What does Arnheim mean by "detached images"? "the remedy of abstraction"? "authentic realism"? Show how these three terms function as the key phrases in his essay.

FILM
AS A VISUAL
ART

Joseph von Sternberg

Politely, he greeted me with his hat and said, in a soft and somewhat uncertain voice: "Just now, I was able to observe your shadow with inestimable admiration. May I please ask if you care to sell it to me?"
—PETER SCHLEMIHL (VON CHAMISSO)

Goethe's last words were *"Mehr Licht."* He had thought deeply about life and had said things better than most men, but when his eyes grew dim he had only two words to express everything he thought: "More light." The history of light is the history of life, and the human eye was the first camera. It is shaped somewhat like a lens, and the image it sees is reversed as in a camera, and somewhere within the brain it is made upright again.

It took thousands of years for man to create a sensitive surface to hold fast the effect of light and a few more years to pile one image on the other and to apply the principle of persistence of vision to the motion picture. Take away light and you have nothing.

From the skies came the first light, and be it noted that it came from above and not from below (the human face is grotesque when lighted from below), the intensity of the sun blinding the eye and the feeble and eerie light of the moon credited with causing madness. Both sun and moon have left an imprint on man's imagination. The sun, to which we owe life and without which nothing grows, has been exalted, and the moon made by legend the repository of everything that was wasted. To this cold planet Alexander Pope consigned

> The smiles of harlots, and the fears of heirs,
> Cages for gnats, and chains to yoke a flea,
> Dried butterflies, and tomes of casuistry.

Man has always been sensitive to light, and when the sun went down and vanished he curled up to sleep until it returned. Every living thing is sensitive to light. A sudden change of light, such as the passing of a shadow across the surface of a puddle, will cause even mosquito larvae to scatter in alarm. Man worshiped the sun, used the moon to record the passage of time, and the stars to guide him. In the beginning there were only a few sources of light: the sun, the moon, the stars, and the fireflies. In much of the world there is still little else to this day. The last time I was in Cuba I was guest in a hut where the sole illumination consisted of a gauze bag filled with beetles that emitted light from their glowing abdomens.

The proper use of light can embellish and dramatize every object—and that carries us into the province of the artist. The artist's duty and function is to imprison not so much that which he can perceive but that which his skill and imagination can endow with force and power, no matter what the nature of the subject may be. The artist who uses film as his medium must learn to behold and to create, not with the camera but with the eye.

The camera is only an accessory to the human eye and serves principally to frame—to include and to exclude. Within the frame the artist collects that which he wishes us to share with him; beyond the frame is placed what he considers of no value to his thought. It is of great importance to know how to use the camera, for it endows what it gathers with a new and radically different dimension; but it is of far greater importance to know how to use the eye. We cannot see without light, and we cannot photograph without it. Therefore the knowledge of what light means and how it affects what it strikes is the first step in the direction of what photography means.

Every light has a point where it is brightest and a point toward which it wanders to lose itself completely. It must be intercepted to fulfill its mission; it cannot function in a void. Light can go straight, penetrate and turn back, be reflected and deflected, gathered and spread, bent as by a soap bubble, made to sparkle and be blocked. Where it is no more is blackness, and where it begins is the core of its brightness. The journey of rays from that central core to the outposts of blackness is the adventure and drama of light.

The strength of light can be measured; the intensity of moonlight, for instance, is two-hundredths of a unit known as foot-candle. The invention of artificial light is probably man's greatest achievement. For thousands of years there was nothing but the torch, and the feeble flame of the wax candle, and the wick fed by the oil in a clay vessel. Man had to wait a long time before he could harness lightning. The first to use an electric arc in making a photograph was Foucault, who was ingenious enough also to invent the gyroscope. This failed to impress those who preferred the smoky flash from a pan of magnesium powder. The electric arc was discovered in 1801 by Sir Humphry Davy, inventor of a miner's safety lamp. He was an extremely talented man, and Coleridge praised him by declaring that had not Davy been a great chemist he would have been the foremost poet of his age. It took a long time, indeed, to master electricity, considering that it had been mastered by a South American fish some million years ago. The electric eel carries negative and positive plates in its tail, and with this handy battery can stun its prey by bringing head and tail in contact with the skin of another creature.

Each light furnishes its own shadow, and where a shadow is seen there must be a light. Shadow is mystery and light is clarity. Shadow conceals, light reveals. (To know what to reveal and what to conceal and in what degree and how to do this is all there is to art.) A shadow is as important in photography as the light. One cannot exist without the other. The great Alexander threw his shadow over Diogenes when he asked the man who dwelt in a barrel to name his wish. "Stand from between me and the sun!" It is doubtful whether this answer meant that Diogenes craved the sun, as he attempted to achieve the enviable position of craving nothing. More likely he was irritated by a meaningless shadow.

The sun is the brightest light we know. It never ceases to project its rays. Its movement spells night and day, dawn and dusk; flowers open and close according to the strength of its light, insects swarm and mate only when the light is just right. Between the earth and the sun is air. Air is the veil, the diffusion; and when it is too thin the sun becomes destructive, and when it is too thick the sun loses its power. Thick air gathered and arranged by winds becomes a cloud, and when it intercepts the sun the earth can appear to be drab. This is not to emphasize what every child knows but to call attention to the fact that the angle of light and what it has to penetrate affects the appearance of every object.

Light must have a source, a direction from which it travels, an object to bounce against and some remote place where it can hide and become a shadow. The sun cannot be moved, nor can the earth be shifted; all that is left for the photographer to control is his viewpoint and the incidental black box, the curved glass of the lens and the silver emulsion. But with the advent of artificial light, the range of its dramatic power becomes unlimited—along with the margin for error. The more light sources that are used, the more capable the user must be. Lights can be friendly to each other or antagonize each other, or, what is worse, duplicate each other's function, and then the rays are no longer bearers of beauty, but foster confusion. Learn to photograph by beginning with one light; if that one light is mastered, all other lights are mastered as well.

The motion picture began by using one light, the light of the sun, and it followed the sun to California where it shone the brightest and where the clouds were rare—and where it is now used the least. The first studios were built out of glass to permit the sun to enter, but Joshua was not under contract and there was no one to command the sun to stand still. Indifferent to man and his problems, the sun moved, and bit by bit the glass sections were painted black and the sun banished, to be replaced by light that could be relied upon to stand still. Banks of electric arcs and mercury-vapor lamps flickered and flared and spread a ghostly pallor over everything, and the chief qualification of the cameraman was his ability to turn the handle of the intermittent mechanism of the camera evenly. A concave mirror and a high-intensity arc produced the searchlight and brought back the sun into the studio. The photographer now had everything he needed, except one thing—the knowledge required to use what he had. But if he had had that knowledge, this would not have been sufficient either, for the function he was called upon to perform was a subordinate one. He was not in control of the material with which his tools were to deal. His function was to represent something that someone else saw.

It is essential once more to indicate that the motion picture's most important asset is that the images are in motion. This is not so simple as it appears, as movement in this medium does not confine itself to a body or object occupying a different position in space in each successive instant. Motion can also be achieved by altering the position of the camera and by technical manipulation in the laboratory (Alain Resnais' *Last Year at Marienbad*), by jumping backward and forward in time (*The House*),[1] and by the dynamics of montage such as, for instance, the violent flashing of close-ups in rapid order (*Underworld*, 1927), and by dissolves and the shifting of angles.

The white canvas onto which the images are thrown is a two-dimensional flat surface. It is not startlingly new, the painter has used it for centuries; thousands have achieved fame with it, not by copying what was there to see but by investing it with their own personalities and viewpoints, taking what they wanted and discarding what they wished to ignore. Years ago, when this chapter was first discussed with Erich Maria Remarque, he said appropriately, "Whenever I see a painter working in a beautiful landscape I know that he does not know how to paint." One should not bar a painter from placing his easel anywhere, but the point made was that a painter is judged by other standards than by the selection of what is commonly assumed to be beautiful. To mention Cézanne once more, he loved to paint a prosaic landscape very early in the morning because the light was then at an angle; but most of all he favored a clock, an apple, a skull,

---

[1] This is a short and extremely witty film made in the Netherlands. My records fail to disclose the name of the director. It was brought to this country by the industrious George K. Arthur, who, sitting behind me in the dark theatre, distracted my attention by whispering to my wife: "Does he still like his eggs boiled exactly three minutes?"

Incidentally, I take the liberty of suggesting that the directors of full length features adopt some of the superlative qualities often incorporated in many short films. They are made all over the world by many talented experimenters.

or cloth—an object that did not move and could be inspected at length under controlled light conditions. One of my favorite painters, while painting a fish, was asked where his model was, and he answered that he had had it for breakfast. Though undoubtedly the subject matter is of importance to the artist, his primary interest is not quite so obvious. While playing chess with Max Band, he told me that Soutine ransacked Paris for a properly aged canvas and finally, after weeks of desperate search, found an oil of Catherine the Great, which he then promptly covered with his conception of a hanging carcass of a goose.

The painter's power over his subject is unlimited, his control over the human form and face despotic. Not compelled to move it, as in our craft, he can fix the body and expression to his complete satisfaction, and invest every canvas with his own purpose or nobility. His handwriting transferred to the canvas by way of his brush or spade becomes the virtue which distinguishes his work. No one demands that the savage Hogarth be judged in terms of the feverish El Greco, or that Siqueiros, Dubuffet, Miró, Klee, and Burri use the same technique. Rubens painted his nudes until he wished to embrace them, and no one has challenged Renoir because he painted flesh until, as he said, it was tempting enough to make him want to bite it.

The one conspicuous distinction between the image of the painter and the canvas of the film director is the length of time it tarries to be seen. A still life by Cézanne can be studied at leisure (it is perhaps not out of place to mention that Jerome Kern sat in my house for hours, as if hypnotized, before a canvas by Otto Müller, ignoring all else), whereas a film is built out of a succession of mobile images, each replacing the last, though their cumulative effect can be as powerful as the impact of a single canvas, providing that the shifting values are controlled to produce a homogeneous entity.

The artist lauds or glorifies, invents freely when he finds nothing, protests or destroys what he opposes; never does he operate without visible superiority to his subject. His work reflects his opinion, no one else's. Though this is freely acknowledged in the sphere of the arts, it commonly arouses a tempest of fury in the world of motion pictures. This quaint outlook is summed up neatly by Mr. Paul Rotha when he refers to me in his monumental work on films, *The Film Till Now*, "He will perhaps one day make a really interesting film if, that is, he forgets that it is his picture." Apparently it is assumed that the motion picture, in contrast to all other art forms, is a collaborative enterprise, a collective work that must disclose a hundred opinions rather than one. Naturally this is not a standard to be valued, unless the motion picture is to be no more than a mechanical contraption, which, in most cases, it is.

The reason for this is that, with few exceptions, the central force of the motion picture, the director, is not a master of photography, which is the principal element in the transfer of his vision to the screen. The director is at the mercy of the camera. It writes its own language, it transliterates all that is fed into it, and when the director does not control the principal tool of his craft, he has surrendered his most important function. Few agree with this. "When a director dies he becomes a cameraman." This is how the distinguished John Grierson deals with what I consider a prime requisite.

To be master of photography means to be a master of light. We see in terms of light, and our work is reproduced and transferred to a canvas in terms of light. Not even the most ignorant photographer can be unconscious of light, though he may be at a loss as to how it can be put to use. Some hundreds of years ago, according to an old German story, some simpletons built a town hall and forgot to provide for windows, whereupon they formed a bucket brigade and lined up to throw light into the dark building, and when that failed to bring results, they filled sacks with the rays from the sun, and having cut the rays with scissors and tied the sacks, carried the precious light into the building to empty it there. This method is not very far removed from the current system of building sets on our stages where no sensible provision is made for the light problem, unless this phase, also, is guided by the director. He can afford to ignore nothing.

The angle of light spells the difference between the polar regions and the equator; Helsinki and Nairobi differ, as they must, for the shadow that flows from those who walk its streets does not have the same length. The light of London and the light of Paris are entirely dissimilar; and the effect of the sky overhead can seep into every room. All weather affects the light; rain and snow split and deflect it. Light operates only when it hits an object, but the air too is full of solids, as can be seen when it condenses into fog, and it can be made to glow and sparkle.

The director writes with the camera whether he wishes to do so or not, or whether the others permit it or not. He influences and controls the camera as definitely as if he carried it in his pocket and took it with him at night to place it next to his watch beside his bed. The director and the photographer must be one and indivisible; the camera is one of his tools, perhaps his most important one. Somewhere in the *Arabian Nights* a princess is to be won, providing the suitor can identify a certain mysterious object, and failing to do so, his head is added to the pile of the others who had not guessed correctly. Scheherazade tells that the winner took a swift look, recoiled in horror, and cried, " 'Tis the skin of a louse grown large in oil!" The finished motion picture is very much like this mystifying object, and it might be well to inspect its bloated skin before passing judgment on what caused it to appear so puzzling. When I was an assistant director I worked for Mr. Goldwyn, who, one fine day, looked at a film he had initiated. In the silence that followed the presentation, his crisp voice was heard. "Who directed this film?" A man, Windom, stood up. "Who wrote the scenario?" Another arose. "Who was the cameraman?" A third staggered to his feet. "Who was the assistant?" It was my turn now to face him. "Who assembled and cut this junk?" I pointed to my chest. "Who put those actors in there?" Another jumped up. "You're all off the payroll," Mr. Goldwyn said in disgust as he left the room. Had his acumen been as great as he believed it to be, he would have discharged several others also, including himself. There is a reverse to this false diagnosis, for when a film is a success even the man who swept the floor after each scene would quickly be snatched up by a rival studio in the attempt to find the magic formula. But should my opinion be consulted, I would venture to observe that a sound analysis would disclose that the only insect which could have grown the skin in the first place was the director, and no matter how long the skin was soaked to make it monstrous, nothing but the director was its original inhabitant.

There are some directors, among whom I am numbered, who

can and do photograph their own films. I have often preferred to work without an additional interceptor of my ideas, and when I have worked with one—always choosing the best I could find—he used lights and camera positions with precise instruction from me, even when, afterward, he accepted Academy honors for what was to be recorded as a separate function. Where the two functions are separated—and this is considered to be normal—director and cameraman waste time and effort in synchronizing their ideas; and whenever even this synchronization is considered to be superfluous the waste is still greater. The director then sprawls in a chair and waits for the cameraman's function to cease; this can take place only after light has been adjusted for every possible movement of the performers, which movements are not within the jurisdiction of the photographer.

Left to its own devices, the camera is an incisive, vivisecting, and often destructive instrument, and the men behind the camera have devoted much time and effort to appeasing the cruelty of the little piece of glass through which our work is gathered. It dramatizes what it sees, foreshortens and distorts, flattens mass into line, and has its own formula for beauty. And at this point one is again confronted with an intangible ingredient that escapes precise definition, for the word "beauty" describes the most nebulous concept of all.

To be considered beautiful women have tattooed their faces, inserted ivory disks in their lips, deformed their feet, pierced noses with rings, and scarred their bodies. The effect of beauty is anchored in the senses, not in the object, and its power rests in the spectator, and nowhere else. It finds its resonance in odd places, and is conditioned by geography and training. A slide of bacteria can be beautiful to the eye that peers into the microscope, and the philatelist can find beauty in a piece of printed and perforated paper which is meaningless to millions of others. A rice field can be the essence of beauty to one Chinese, but another can find it at the edge of a lake that has no fish, dangling a line that has no hook. "No eye is virgin. . . . In art, as in love, men rarely object to being fooled." [2]

Though beauty can be created, it cannot be put to a test or

[2] Seymour Slive, *Daedalus*, Summer, 1962.

arbitrated; it consists only of its appeal to the senses. Part of the Soviet experiment years ago, as Eisenstein explained it to me, was to abolish art because it was useless. Of course, that theory is not easily put into practice, as this apparent uselessness is the chief virtue of art. There seemed to be a good reason for wanting to abolish art in Russia, for art stimulates thinking, involves the imagination and breeds discontent with what is at hand. René Fülöp-Miller told me that Lenin could not listen to music, and when I questioned this, he produced the following quotation, which I take leave to translate from the original German:

> Lenin to Gorki: I can think of nothing more beautiful than the "Appassionata," to which I could listen every day. It is astonishingly overearthly music. Whenever I absorb those sounds I think with pride and perhaps childish naïveté how wonderful it is what man can accomplish. But I cannot listen to music often, it goes against my nerves, though I would like to indulge in charming nonsense and fondle the heads of those who can in the midst of a filthy hell create such beauty. But this is not the time to caress people's heads; this is the time to let the hands fall in order to split skulls, to split them pitilessly, though the battle against every force is our last ideal—a hellishly difficult task.

Obviously it is easier to kill than to create. Nothing else requires so little talent. There has always been opposition to art, though the customary form this opposition takes is indifference. And nowhere is this indifference more pronounced than in the art of motion pictures.

The film has two instruments with which to fashion art. One is the camera, and the other is the microphone. Both are extremely difficult to use. Every instrument is superior in its inherent potentialities to the human being using it, though there are masters on occasion who can make us feel as if the ultimate in power has been reached. The violin, listlessly held before it is placed against the shoulder, promises more than it ever delivers, and neither the camera nor the microphone have as yet achieved even a small part of their potential. On our stages these two instruments are viewed with reverence, unlike the disrespect given the human element which controls their complicated mechanism. Should something go wrong with the machinery, everyone waits patiently until it is again in order, all sit quietly as if in a church. Not so when anything goes wrong with the human being. The human being is less respected than the machine and treated as if nothing could ever go wrong.

When the microphone first arrived to be added to the tools of our craft, the tyranny of the camera was overthrown. Jolson sang and Garbo spoke, and the crowds came to hear them; the camera was forgotten. No one, except a very few, paid any attention to the important black box with the glass eye, except to cover it with blanket and mattress to hush its noisy insides. It had become an enemy, as its mechanism could be heard by the microphone. Everyone breathed easier when it was confined to a sort of doghouse, from where it could only look out from behind heavy glass plates. One could breathe easier, but not too loudly; to clear the throat, cough, or sneeze was not without consequences. A distant airplane would terrorize the stages as in an air raid.

All eyes were now on the microphone. At first it was held by a distant hand, then it was concealed behind a vase of flowers until it was hung on a long pole to dangle overhead like the sword of Damocles. With one fell swoop the directors and the cameraman were relegated to a distant past, the master of the stage was now a sound engineer, whose eyes were on a dial which indicated the fluctuation of decibels. His earphones were the master instruments, and a nod from him was like a benediction, a shake of his head would stop the camera. No two voices matched either in accent or intelligence, but this was of no importance so long as they could be heard clearly. Since in this early stage of adding sound to the image the mobility of the camera was invalidated, it was, for the time being, a reproductive instrument, as the microphone is to this day; and to reproduce is not to create. Verisimilitude, whatever its virtue, is in opposition to every approach to art.

The voice often is an indicator of the quality of the human being, but it does not often match its exterior, and the appearance of a human being is controlled by light, lens and angle of camera, whereas the voice achieves its effect without being subjected to manipulation. The congenital tendency of the microphone to contradict the camera is not usually recognized by those who use both these instruments. When, with time, the camera mechanism was made to be mobile again, it regained its former facility to be used with skill, but the microphone retained its primitive reproductive stature.[3]

The problem of the microphone has not failed to gain the attention of competent film makers. The harsh roar of a train has been converted into music and many experiments with sound effects have often succeeded in hiding the most flagrant examples of unbearable voices. Intrinsically, almost from its very inception, the sound mechanism was capable of being used with perception. The present system of mixing sound tracks after a film is completed, complicated as it might be, is capable of producing extraordinary acoustic effects. I have never ignored this, and have taken charge of this final phase of film making by doing my own mixing. A dozen separate sound tracks can be fused into one, reducing and augmenting each one at will. As far as the problem of the human voice is concerned, this must be handled on the stage, though by the addition of a commentary, much of the blatancy that comes from the mouth of an actor can be removed.

But sound, important and effective as it is, will always play a supplementary role to the image. Even without the addition of the human voice it is potent enough to expose imbecility. It is also unavoidable to note that the worst damage inflicted by the microphone has been its vitiating influence on what was at one time an international language.

The handling of the problem of sound in films must be subjected to further experimentation, if this has not already been done; dialogue cannot be permitted to carry the burden of plot movement and progression without impoverishing the entire ground gained by the handful of directors who have made it possible for film to be rated as an impressive art form. In contrast to the photographic craft, little experience is needed to manipulate sound; what is required is a new conception of the function of sound, to so manipulate it that it does not become a barrier to the fluid language of the silent image: the silent film which attained

---

[3] *Der Tom wirft keine Schatten* (Sound throws no shadows). I found this written as early as 1930 by Bela Balazs in *Der Geist des Films*.

the enviable power of transferring its content to all races and nations—even to those who could not read and write their own language.

There is no short cut to photographic skill; to master it requires not only theory but intensive practice. Lens, light, material, subject, composition, angle, and the pattern of movement provide a thousand and one pitfalls for the unwary. The ablest painter, sensitive as he is to a single canvas, is helpless to control the ever-shifting, mobile canvas of the motion picture. In Japan the talented Foujita showed me a film he made; it was the work of a beginner. Nor is the still photographer, expert though he may be, who labors for hours to capture a single expression, qualified without thorough training in our craft. However, still photography has one enormous advantage over the motion picture, an advantage which one day will cease; the surface of the finished photography can be controlled by printing manipulation and the interposing of texture through the enlargement process. It is only a matter of time before such manipulation will be incorporated into our work. (Experimenters have already done this.)

The motion picture has capitalized the human being and, not without some justice, has attempted to state that it is a container of everything that is valuable. The camera has been used to explore the human figure and to concentrate on its face as being its most precious essence. In itself, the face is an inspiring mask when not maligned, and our entire history and ancestry has left traces on its surface in ever-varying arrangements no two of which are alike, even as the whorls of our fingertips differ.

The photographer can assume responsibility for his version of the face, and for that matter, for everything that is human, and if he cannot bring to the fore its innate dignity, he should at least conceal what is stupid and shallow—though it is entirely possible that nothing human is either stupid or shallow, but only appears to be so because it is ill at ease and has not found that corner of the world where it can feel comfortable. One Baal Shem Tov, an eighteenth-century sage, was known for his belief that all things, including the lowest acts, had dignity.

Monstrously enlarged as it is on the screen, the human face

should be treated like a landscape. It is to be viewed as if the eyes were lakes, the nose a hill, the cheeks broad meadows, the mouth a flower patch, the forehead sky, and the hair clouds. Values must be altered as in an actual landscape by investing it with lights and shadows, controlled with gauze and graded filters, and by domination of all that surrounds the face. Just as I spray trees with aluminum to give life to the absorbent green, just as the sky is filtered to graduate its glare, just as the camera is pointed to catch a reflection on the surface of a lake, even so the face and its framing values must be viewed objectively as if it were an inanimate surface. The skin should reflect and not blot the lights, and light must be used to caress, not flatten and wipe out that which it strikes.

If it is impossible to otherwise improve the quality of the face, deep shadows must add intelligence to the eyes, and should that not be enough, then it is best to shroud the countenance in merciful darkness and have it take its place as an active pattern in the photographic scale. Before I allow lights to strike a face I light its background to fill the frame with light values, for included in its photographic impact is everything that is visible in the same frame. This principle of containing all values within a frame of values applies also to the human body, and its movement through space is to be as a dramatic encounter with light. But whether face, body, a letter, a toy balloon, or street, the problem is always the same: lifeless surfaces must be made responsive to light, and overbrilliant and flaring surfaces reduced to order, shadows must avoid duplication, and the pattern concentrated toward its primary interest.

Whenever dealing with black-and-white photography, colors in subject matter should be avoided wherever possible, as color sensitivity to light is not revealed by the lens. My sets and costumes are usually made to be without color so that no time need be wasted in assessing their photographic value. The superb virtue of black-and-white photography is that it automatically translates all color to a uniform scale.

So far as color photography is concerned, it is of little value, except for its novelty, unless the artist uses unreal and non-naturalistic color. Color as now used in films is no better than the colored postcards which confront the tourist on every street corner. I am not informed as to the exact time a Henri Matisse needs to determine what colors to use on a single canvas, but it must have been considerably longer than the time used by those who pour color in bucketfuls into the films with firm determination to assault the eye. Of course, most films are of doubtful value even without using color.

A shaft of white light used properly can be far more effective than all the color in the world used indiscriminately. The extensive range of black and white with its numberless variations is capable of producing all the visual drama that may be required. But above all, the greatest art in motion picture photography is to be able to give life to the dead space that exists between the lens and the subject before it. Smoke, rain, fog, dust, and steam can emotionalize empty space, and so can the movement of the camera. The camera can advance and retreat and encircle with or against the action it encounters. It can produce a fluid composition, related to the sum total of all its shifting images and make every movement part of the entire conception. Were I to instruct others how to use the camera, the first step would be either to project a film upside down or to show it so often that the actors and story become no longer noticeable, so that the values produced by the camera alone could not escape study. The camera collects all faults and virtues but is not responsible for them all.

The extraordinary speed with which the eye absorbs visual information must be studied. Slow motion can seem swift in interest, and quick movements can appear to be exceedingly dull. When wielded by a master the camera has no limits to circumscribe its force and power; its limits, if any, are the limits of the human eye.

Its greatest asset, superb and unique, is motion, not only that motion which is always visible, but also that motion which it can transfer to the pulse of the spectator. And in order to master the laws of motion one must have the poet's insight of pause and rhythm. There are some things which cannot be learned, though they can be studied. Among them are the laws of art—and the lawlessness of it, as well.

To quote Goethe once more: "The greatest happiness of man is to explore that which is explorable and to revere that which is unexplorable."

EXERCISES

on film and the visual arts

1. "Shadow is mystery and light is clarity." Discuss the significance of this statement as it relates to von Sternberg's views on what makes an effective film image.
2. What does von Sternberg point up as the key difference in our responses to a painting and to a movie?
3. What does von Sternberg see as the chief motive of both the film-maker and the painter, insofar as they are both artists?

on film

1. What distinction does von Sternberg make between the role of the director and the function of the cameraman in the making of a film?
2. Defend the overriding emphasis von Sternberg places on lighting and composition, on the "mystery" of shadow and the "clarity" of light by citing effective examples of this technique which you yourself have experienced. How important to von Sternberg is plot by itself? Why?

on language and structure

1. What is the point of the anecdote involving von Sternberg and the legendary film producer, Samuel Goldwyn?
2. What is von Sternberg's own attitude to his problems, and achievement, as a director? How does his attitude reveal itself in his diction and tone?
3. "The effect of beauty," writes von Sternberg, "is anchored in the senses, not in the object, and its power rests in the spectator, and nowhere else." It is not likely that von Sternberg had read *The Foundations of Aesthetics,* a volume coauthored by the eminent literary critic I. A. Richards with the psychologist C. K. Ogden and the art esthetician James Wood. Yet the conclusion reached by this team of authorities in their linguistic-oriented study of 1922 is precisely the same as von

Sternberg's: that beauty lives only in the eye of the beholder. Consider some of the ramifications of this point of view, including how it would determine the choices of an artist in developing his material—and the theme of this essay.

FILM
and
MUSIC

While literature and the visual arts interact with film in peer relation-ship, the role of music is distinctly subordinate. Film music serves a virtually completed work and must adapt itself to the work's basic rhythms and shape. Except for film musicals, the score of a film rarely plays a central role.

Despite its secondary role, however, or perhaps because of that, music can affect our response to a film as strongly as any other element in it. Try watching a movie on TV with the sound turned off. You will soon notice that when you view a film without being diverted by music —or by any other sound effects—you actually see much more of what is going on: you more readily observe how the hero taking a punch at the villain in fact misses his target by a clear margin; or you will observe that when the hero and heroine kiss, it is always, as it were, sideways, since film-makers have learned that a kiss directly on the lips does not photograph with enough romantic suggestiveness; and in war movies, you may note how a line of soldiers being mowed down by a machine gun invariably falls in so stylized a manner and rhythm as to give a positively balletic effect. With the sound back on, the same ballet of falling and swooning bodies is transformed into an image of chaos and disorder. (A good example, frequently shown on

TV, is Lewis Milestone's famous film version of *All Quiet on the Western Front*.) There is no question that music in film matters; it affects, materially, the way we see!

Early film music often consisted of adaptations of classic or familiar melodies. As piano accompaniment for the famous silent film, *The Covered Wagon,* for example, a work by Sergei Rachmaninoff was always used. The histrionic and thunderous romanticism of Rachmaninoff's music jelled nicely with the panoramic sweep and uncomplicated heroics of the film, a high-spirited romance-of-the-West saga.

During the 1930s film music shifted from adaptations of a kind which had worked well for silent films to specially composed treatments written after the film was completed. These treatments consisted of a central theme or themes whose variations of intensity stimulated a range of moods. Men like Max Steiner, Alfred Newman, and Miklos Rosza contributed to establishing the styles of such original film scoring, and their manner of handling motif and melody continues to dominate the use of music in most commercial films.

In more advanced film-making, the composer has begun to develop his score alongside the creation of the film, in order to feel the mood of each moment as it takes place. The result has been more atmospheric film scores, as well as more experimental ones, since the music strives to evoke the essence of heterogeneous bits and pieces rather than a limited and clearly signalled number of moods. In this way too, the more serious film composer avoids the dangers of the musical score of commercial films which sometimes tends to nudge responses from the audience not clearly warranted by the actions depicted on the screen. This poke-in-the-ribs effect is avoided by the better scores now being fashioned.

More varied and experimental though it may be, current film music retains its subordinate status. The most effective film scores have been those overseen by directors who have been in a position to exercise firm control over the entire range of tasks and problems which are part of making a film, and who therefore succeed in assimilating the various contributing elements of a film to their own overall conception. Among outstanding film scores is the one composed by Johnny Dankworth for *Modesty Blaise,* directed by Joseph Losey, who commissioned the Dankworth score. Another notable team has been that of director Federico Fellini and composer Nino Rota. Perhaps no director has been so sparing of musical effects as Fellini's great peer in the Italian cinema, Michelangelo Antonioni, whose *L'Avventura* is virtually devoid of musical accompaniment. Instead, it is the sound of waves pounding hollowly on the shores of an island which provides the "music" the director found to be most expressive of his intentions. Other directors who use spare musical scores are Robert Bresson and Roberto Rossellini. It is no coincidence that all three of these directors are more concerned with evoking subtle spiritual and psychological states than with depicting sheer physical action.

As for the attitudes of composers and critics, the essays that follow attest to the exciting opportunities most of them see in writing music for films. Oscar Levant questions the nature of the enterprise itself—in line with his skepticism in general concerning the possibilities of film as an art. Dmitri Tiomkin finds creative satisfaction, as well as the need to compromise, in film scoring and describes some of the technical problems of his métier. George Antheil, an important composer in his own right, defends the new forms of film scoring, while stressing that the basic problem, whether composing for film, or the concert stage, or opera house, or jazz club, is to create music adequate to contemporary reality. And he would clearly include in his conception of reality what Arnheim would call its "ghostly" aspects. Page Cook winds up the discussion with an adverse reaction to some of the more nudging tendencies in recent pop-musical forms.

A COG
IN THE WHEEL

Oscar Levant

It is a tradition in pictures (one of the most stubbornly respected) that nobody in the world goes to hear a movie score but the composer, the orchestrator and other composers. As a kind of compensation, I suppose, they hear every single sixteenth note in the score and are thereafter equipped to discuss its most obscure subtleties. Frequently, however, they have to be told what the picture itself is about.

This has its parallel in another tradition in the movies with which every composer comes into contact as soon as he reports to a studio. It was probably devised by the first producer ever to use a musical score for a dramatic film and runs as follows: If the audience doesn't notice the music it's a good score. This I never could quite understand. It have heard many approving, even admiring comments—not all by composers—on scores for foreign pictures written by Auric, Honegger, Shostakovitch, Prokofieff, Françaix and others. Certainly an audience would not find such contributions out of place in an American picture merely because the characters spoke English rather than French, German or Russian.

Perhaps one of the reasons for the low repute of picture

music may be found in the words that fill the air when a Hollywood score is discussed by those versed in such matters. You never hear any discussion of a score as a whole. Instead, the references are to "main-title" music, "end title" music, "montages," "inserts" and so on, with no recognition of the character of the complete score. It is much as if one would discuss a suit in terms of its buttonholes, pleats, basting and lining, without once considering its suitability to the figure it adorned.

Even so, this represents a considerable advance in the liberty formerly permitted movie composers. It is only within the last half-dozen years that a composer for the movies has been allowed to write anything other than a fanfare at the beginning and end of a picture. In the early days of the talkies the idea of writing music under dialogue was so revolutionary that a number of prominent producers (as, for example, Irving Thalberg) countenanced it only under the greatest pressure, and then but sparingly. They were not merely unfriendly to music; they were actually suspicious of its potentialities.

They made a great fetish, for example, of pointing out the conflict between the so-called "reality" of the movies and the "unreality" of music. Always when a situation seemed to demand a heightening by musical effect they would come back at the composer with the question, "But where would the audience think the orchestra is coming from?" This was supposed to be the stopper for all arguments. When a musical background was absolutely inseparable from an effect they would go to the most extravagant lengths to relate the music to the scene by having a band playing outside the window, or secreting a string quartet behind a row of potted palms or having the sound come out of a radio. Unquestionably it is an additional virtue to make music an integral part of a dramatic situation; but it always seemed to me an example of remarkable shortsightedness that even the best directors and producers could not reconcile themselves to the thought that they were dealing with a completely artificial medium and adapt themselves to it accordingly.

I might mention that one of the few early talkies I remember was the movie version of Barry's *Paris Bound*. My memory of its details is extremely hazy, but I do recall with some clarity a musical score for it by Arthur Alexander. In fact that is the only detail that I do recall eight or nine years after it appeared. The only reason that Alexander had the opportunity to write that score was that a ballet figured in the action, and it is customary, after all, for ballets to have music. In addition, the main character is a composer.

What was particularly preposterous about the producers' attitude was that music has been an accepted accessory of the legitimate theater for generations. I seem to recall, even, that Beethoven wrote incidental music for *Egmont,* Mendelssohn for *A Midsummer Night's Dream,* Bizet for Daudet's *L'Arlésienne* and Grieg for *Peer Gynt.* Nobody peered around and asked, "Where is the orchestra coming from?" when they listened to such scores as these.

The only exception that was made in the early days of sound pictures in Hollywood was in musical comedies, where the girl walked into the room where the boy was seated at the piano. He would say, "Listen to this tune I just wrote . . ." whereupon she would sing it from the second bar on with every word in the lyric perfect. How many times I have envied the telepathic abilities of Jeanette MacDonald, Grace Moore, Lily Pons, Gladys Swarthout and the rest—especially after I found out how long it takes them actually to learn a tune. . . .

The level of musical perception among Hollywood producers is, if anything, slightly lower than their perception of values associated with the other arts. Curiously, the humble artisans who are great music lovers (meaning that they will stand for six hours to hear Gigli in *Pagliacci*) never seem to be the humble artisans who become movie producers.

I recall the plight of one, whose social prestige decreed his presence at a certain Hollywood Bowl concert. It chanced that the important work of the evening was the C minor symphony of Beethoven, which he suffered in silence until the coda of the final movement. This has, as you will recall, what could be described as an 1805 Roxy finish, with the tonic and dominant chords repeated a dozen times, with flourishes. At each insistent recurrence of the tonic he half rose from his chair to facilitate his exit . . . also because he was bored. When the third series of tonic and dominant chords still left him short of the actual end of the movement he turned and muttered, "The rat fooled me again."

On this same program was a two-piano concerto by Mozart, which he dismissed with the terse comment, "It never got anywhere."

Sometime later, after a performance of Ravel's "Bolero" at the Bowl, I received a memo telling me to report the following morning at nine, because "he had an idea." This, apparently, was the one thing he heard during the whole summer that stimulated him. To enhance his position in Hollywood cultural life, he offered a musicale one night at which the invited performers were the Compinsky Trio. They were in excellent form, playing trios by Brahms, Arensky and Franck to the considerable pleasure of the guests. However, just as the applause of the listeners seemed about to result in an encore the host stepped forward—as if anticipating their intention—and said briskly,

"All right, boys—that's enough."

Perhaps his most searching bit of musical criticism was propounded when he said to me dictatorially, "In my opinion"— marking the words carefully to allow the full weight of his thought to rest on me—"the greatest piece of music ever written is 'Humoreske.' "

It was after such a characteristic demonstration that S. N. Behrman said of this producer, "Now I know why he can make those instantaneous decisions—he is never deflected by thought."

That Steiner was able to make any substantial headway against such resistance is a tribute almost as much to his patience as to his talents. From the making of shorts (one of which won him, in some obscure way, the small red ribbon with all the incidental prerogatives of the *Légion d'Honneur*) he progressed to more substantial accomplishments. Possibly the first general notice that was accorded his work came when the Academy Award was bestowed on *The Informer,* with an incidental citation for Steiner's score, though his capacities were recognized in the trade before this, particularly for his work on *The Lost Patrol.* . . .

Despite the vagaries of Steiner he must be credited with the establishment of certain basic principles in movie scoring, particularly through his knack of "catching things" musically. Such is the music, in his score for *Of Human Bondage,* that paralleled Philip's limp. It was almost a crippled theme, so exactly did it correspond to the hesitation in the character's walk. The secret of this derives from Steiner's painstaking study of the scenes for which he is to write music, his mathematical analysis of them in terms of "clicks."

This is a technique now used universally in writing movie music, though six years or so ago it was a novelty. By breaking down the footage of a picture into separate scenes the composer can then calculate exactly the number of seconds for so many feet of film and then write precisely that much music to cover the episode he wants to illuminate. Naturally there is the problem of dubbing the music onto the sound track so that it corresponds to incidents in the picture, but that can be done faultlessly by synchronizing the conductor's beat with the speed of the film.

In a sense this might be described as the "Mickey Mouse" technique, in which every movement of the character on the screen has a complementary bar of music. Steiner is particularly adept at this sort of thing, though his heavy-handed impressionism does not serve him too well in more subjective situations. He is, however, an excellent man on prison-break fogs, and also does a good job of industrial noises. Do you recall the whistles, bells, clanging of doors and other institutional sounds for *Crime School?* The hammer blows and engine noises in *Dodge City?* They were all a part of Steiner's score for these films, and enormously effective. . . .

Steiner's "Mickey Mouse" technique is firmly entrenched in Hollywood, but it also has a robust opponent in another method prevailing in Hollywood, in which the composer doesn't bother to "catch" anything. This might be called the "over-all" or "mood" treatment, in which the endeavor is merely to suggest the whole atmosphere of a sequence with just a few main motives.

Thus, in a triangle picture, you have a "spiritual love" theme, the "other woman" theme, and probably a motive for "conflict." Alfred Newman is a disciple of this school, which derives from Tschaikowsky by way of whole tones. It has always impressed me, however, that the "other woman" theme is generally more exciting, a good deal more enthusiastically written, than the one for the wife. There are constant arguments between the partisans for each method of procedure, the only agreement being that it is more difficult to write in the "Mickey Mouse" manner than in the "over-all" style. On the other hand, it can be contended that a good lush motive for a dramatic situation requires more real creative talent than the other kind of writing.

However, as the increasing prominence of music in pictures has greatly extended the number of employed composers in Hollywood, there is plentiful opportunity for writers of both types. There are now few pictures of any kind that do not utilize music to some degree, and in a considerable majority of them the score is credited to a musician of specialized, if not general reputation. Offhand, in the last year, I have seen films from Hollywood with scores attributed to Richard Hageman, Louis Gruenberg, Ernst Toch, Kurt Weill, W. Franke Harling, George Antheil, Erich Korngold and Werner Janssen, all composers of general reputation; as well as others by such specialists as Steiner, Newman, Stothart, Franz Waxman, Edward Ward, Hugo Friedhofer and Edward Powell, to mention only the more familiar names. Indeed, the methods of mass production have in few other connections been utilized with the skill with which they are applied to the writing of movie scores in Hollywood.

I had an unenviable opportunity to come closely into contact with those methods several years ago during one of my more recent Hollywood intervals. I had tired of living on the periphery of asceticism while studying with Schönberg and sought employment with a movie company, convinced that I could copy as capably from Debussy and Delius as anyone then active in the films.

Through the intercession of friends I was provided with an introduction to an official at M.G.M., whom I had also met on previous occasions at various parties. At one of these, impressed by some fugitive manifestation of talent, he said, "Come to see me. I want to do something for you."

It was after this that I came with the introduction. He looked at me with evident disinterest while he listened to a recitation of my background. Then he shook my hand encouragingly and said,

"Yes. Come back again in two months."

Just what I was supposed to do in this interim was not made clear. But while I awaited the expiration of this interlocutory decree of divorce from my unemployment my friends continued the program of propaganda on my behalf. Finally I was granted a second interview and again rehearsed my qualifications. My prospective employer (so I visualized him) listened with impolite inattentiveness, continuously saying, "Yes? Yes?"

Finally he turned and said, "I'll have to refer you to our music director, Nat Finston."

I had had some dealings with Finston at the Rivoli Theater in New York years before when he was a conductor there. I found him in a commodious office, hung with charts which were his most absorbing possession. Within a few minutes he had led me to the wall (which they covered completely) and begun to explain their significance. Each chart represented a film, and each bore the name of a composer who had been assigned to write the score for it. There was one for Stothart, another for Ward, a third for Waxman and so on. As Commissar of Music for the M.G.M. enterprises, Finston was as closely in touch with the activities of his vassals as the tovarich in charge of a salt mine in the Ukraine.

He then launched into a long exposition of his career at the studio, detailing the chaos in which he found the music department and the perfection of organization that now prevailed.

"I tell you," he said, "it's running like a well-oiled machine."

The phrase appealed to him, and he repeated,

"Like a well-oiled machine. Every man a cog in the wheel."

Then he looked at me severely—running his hands through his thick hair as he did and pacing the room with supervisory strides—and said, "I don't know whether or not you would fit in."

"Mr Finston," I answered, "my greatest desire in life at this moment is to be a cog in the wheel. If I don't qualify it will be because my music is inferior, not because I don't want to be a cog in the wheel."

In response he suggested that I bring in a few scores for him to see.

I came back the next day with my scores, and before I was aware of what was happening we were again busy with the well-oiled machine and how important it was to be a cog in the wheel. The exposition was even more detailed than that of the previous day, though no new territory was explored. The purely scientific pleasure that Finston derived from his creation obviously excluded any interruptions from me. At the end of his discourse he shook his head, implying doubt, and said, "I don't think you'd fit into this well-oiled machine." Then he added as a kind of consolation award, "But any time you want call me up, and we'll have a chat."

It was not until I was outside that I realized that my scores were in the same package in which I had brought them, that Finston had never looked at them.

Two days later I rang up M.G.M. and asked to be connected with Mr Finston. At length I got through to him, and he said brusquely,

"I'm busy. What's on your mind?"

"Nothing," I said. "I just would like to have a chat."

Annoyed but still not quite knowing whether he should show it or not, Finston exclaimed, "Some other time. Not now."

This, in an anecdote, was the history of my career as a composer with M.G.M.

EXERCISES

on film and music

1. What does Levant note about the relationship between the attitudes of early film-makers toward realism and their attitude toward the use of music in film? What does this reveal about the film-makers' idea of "realism"? How would you define this term?
2. How optimistic is Levant concerning the serious possibilities of film music? Compare his view to that of Fuchs on the possibilities open to the script writer.
3. Why does Levant relate the "Mickey Mouse" technique of composing film music with "the methods of mass production"?

on film

1. Cite a film which seems to you to have a "Mickey Mouse" type of musical score.
2. Why were musical comedies exempt from the rules of realism? Among well-known musical films of the past decade are *West Side Story, Star, The Sound of Music,* and *The Umbrellas of*

Cherbourg. Consider any of these or a recent musical film you have seen from the point of view of its realistic elements.

on structure and language

1. Levant is actually concerned with a highly technical subject and its special problems. Yet he is easy to read and both entertaining and serious. How does he gain the general reader's interest and hold it?
2. His attitude toward his subject is negative, yet his tone is neither sour nor superior. How would you describe his tone, and by what qualities does he achieve it? Do you feel this essay is a good example of style expressing the man? Explain.
3. What particular narrative device does Levant share with Fuchs? Note the relative effectiveness of the use of this method in the two essays, and point out one or two significant differences in tone and manner between them.

COMPOSING
FOR FILMS

Dmitri Tiomkin

In the years that I have been composing and conducting motion picture scores, the importance and value of background music have been increasingly recognized. Only a few years ago music was considered a pleasant, unobtrusive reenforcement of a sequence's tempo and mood. Today it is far more.

Screen music is still unobtrusive—for being so is the primary characteristic of any movie score that is good. But screen music is now so artfully and effectively integrated with script, direction and the actors themselves, that it has come to be one of the means of story-telling. It is easy to prove this. Just try to transplant any picture's musical score to similar scenes in another picture. You will find that the transplantation doesn't live.

It is of incalculable value to the composer to be able to sit in on story conferences from the beginning. He will not only better comprehend the total trend, mood or purpose of the story, but he will be able to make suggestions that will enable the music to strengthen and fulfill the story.

For example, at random: consider the point in a story at which a man suddenly, without warning, slaps a woman. Let us say the writers conceived the scene to be with two characters standing together talking by a window. Now sudden violence like a slap in the face has more impact if *something unobtrusive* prepares the audience a second or two in advance. If this split-second preparation is not provided, the mind will resent being taken by surprise. The best "something," it has been found, is music.

When this slapping sequence is discussed in a story conference I might say to the writers, or the director: "I will have to have a few seconds in there just before the slap in order to prepare for it." And we would talk it over and conclude that the man will have to take a few steps in order to slap the woman. This will give me the time I need to presage the violent change of mood.

I have found that a composer will get full cooperation unless his requests alter the story line. Directors and writers know a composer's technical problems. They also know the importance of his contribution.

Not a few writers, and even some directors, have asked me whether a retentive and facile memory of what others have written, or one's own musical inventiveness, is more valuable in scoring a motion picture.

I cannot remember ever deliberately cribbing music from others, except when it was intentional, legitimate, and acknowledged, as in my arrangements of Debussy's music for David Selznick's *Portrait of Jennie.*

Possibly even the most conscientious composer now and then inadvertently uses a fragment of melody that has stuck in his subconscious. But deliberately lifting phrases from the compositions of others is not only musical bankruptcy but incompetent craftsmanship.

Maybe I am fortunately equipped. I was born into a family of concert musicians, and have studied music since I was five years old. When you have thought in terms of music as long as I have it is *easier* to write original music than to bother recalling appropriate bars of music written in the past. After all, scenes and even sequences change so swiftly on the screen that very often there isn't time for more than a couple of measures. It is really *simpler and more effective* to compose than to rummage around in classical music to find something that expresses the idea.

My first scoring of background music, if it can be called that, was when I was accompanist for the great European comedian,

Max Linder. I sat at the piano and improvised all through his act. He was brilliant and unpredictable, and ad libbed freely and frequently. It was impossible for me to arrange and follow a definite score because he never did his act the same way twice. Consequently I watched him and listened to him and learned to divine intuitively what he would do, and thus to improvise what was actually pure mood music. I would even throw in sound effects, such as laughter, at what I thought were the right times.

Linder was one of the truly great comedians of our time. He worked dumb, in the inelegant show business phrase, but his pantomime and his appeal were eloquent. The only comparable artists today are Chaplin, Jimmy Savo, and possibly Cantinflas, the great Mexican clown.

Some gifted comics are so because of blind and blessed instinct, uninhibited by cerebral processes. Not Linder. He had an inspired comedy sense, of course, but he also had an analytical, ingenious mind.

Except for Chaplin, I have never known another comedian who had such an objective view of his own art. Linder was sensitive and responsive to any audience, and could talk audience psychology with the intellectual perspective of a professor. On stage he would introduce a new bit suddenly and without previous thought, but later he could give a profound and apposite reason for having done what he did spontaneously.

My first contact with Linder was typical. A few months before World War I began he was making a triumphant tour that brought him to Petrograd. He arrived in the city by train, but flew from the station to the Astoria Hotel by plane. The effect of such an arrival—especially in 1914—was spectacular.

History is beginning to distort Linder as an eccentric given to flashy public appearances and outré living. But it wasn't self indulgence—merely good business. Like Houdini, he was a showman off-stage too.

Probably because movies were a nearly-perfect vehicle for his pantomime, Linder was enormously enthusiastic over the future of films. Also impatient, because their technological advances seemed to him so slow.

All that now seems to me a far cry from scoring a motion picture, but it was my first step. And from that experience I learned that it was easier, *for me,* to improvise than to recall and use bits of music from the classics or other sources.

After some years of composing symphony and concert music, I became interested in the ballet. It had always been one of my favorite arts, but at that time in my life I became fascinated by the astonishing correlation of sound and sight, of music and movement, that is the essence of ballet.

It was also in this period of my life that I realized, for the first time, how much music contributed to story-telling, or, more accurately, to the transmission of mood to the audience. I wrote considerably for the ballet. My numbers met with varying success. I count this my introduction to the composition of "background music."

After composing for several Broadway shows I fell under the spell of the modern picture camera.

There is a much closer affinity between ballet and movies than casual thought suggests. The story becomes more involved in ballet, for the screen is a more plastic medium, and its story-telling is therefore simpler. Nevertheless, the eloquence of music is as indispensable to film as to ballet.

Sometimes I think a good picture is really just ballet with dialogue.

Dialogue, of course, is of primary importance in determining the genre of background music. It entails problems that must be overcome, and can be overcome only by certain musical techniques.

It is difficult for a layman to realize that speaking voices have astonishing variation in pitch and timbre. It may seem incredible, but many actors' voices, however pleasant in themselves, and regardless of pitch, are incompatible with certain instruments. Clarinets, for instance, get in the way of some voices and magnificently complement others. Further, clarinets may be alien to the spirit of a play, or the characterization of a part.

Some actors have voices that are easy to write for. Actors like John Wayne impose almost no burdens on the composer. Wayne's voice happily happens to have a pitch and timbre that fits almost any instrumentation.

Jimmie Stewart is another actor for whom it is a delight to write music. Paradoxically, his speaking voice is not "musical."

But it has a slightly nasal quality and occasionally "cracks" in a way that is easy to complement. Jean Arthur's voice is somewhat similar.

Just why this type of voice should be easy to write for, I don't know. One might speculate that since these voices have little color in themselves, the complementary musical backdrop doesn't bump into or fall over the dialogue. The mere fact that such voices *are* unmusical gives them an additional definition.

Imagine an actress whose voice has the right harmonics and overtones of a low register clarinet statement. Assume a voice of incredibly pure, round tones. It might be nice to listen to unaccompanied, but it would be a damned nuisance to write for. You'd have to breach the 13-tone chromatic scale and even abandon Standard Pitch before you got a congenial musical background.

The "crack" in Miss Arthur and Mr. Stewart's voices is one of those strangely appealing imperfections, like a single strand of rebellious hair on an otherwise impeccable moonlit coiffure. But don't pursue this appeal of imperfect voices too far, or you'll run into Andy Devine.

Jean Arthur and Jimmie Stewart also illustrate another point: utilizing music to "soften" a face, or to give it qualities it does not have inherently.

This is not necessary with Stewart or Arthur because both have faces that reflect great sincerity. (Frank Capra, with whom I have had the pleasure of working on a number of pictures, once pointed out to me that unless a player has the sort of face that bespeaks sincerity he is not likely ever to become a great star.)

The camera is a merciless, analytical instrument. Even after every artifice of lighting and make-up, the close-up can be cruelly revealing. The composer, by providing pleasant melodic music, can direct attention from what the makeup artist could not hide. And in doing so the composer is surprisingly successful.

To comprehend fully what music does for movies, one should see a picture before the music is added, and again after it has been scored. Not only are all the dramatic effects heightened, but in many instances the faces, voices, and even the personalities of the players are altered by the music.

Because music can add to a personality and even to a player's physical appearance, I paid particular attention to Mala Powers as Roxanne in *Cyrano de Bergerac,* for which I composed and conducted the music. Miss Powers has a lovely, interesting face, but somehow it just didn't look French enough for me. In real life, of course, there are hundreds of thousands of pure-blooded Frenchmen who wouldn't look French. But on the screen a French woman should look like one. Consequently, I used French thematic music for all her appearances in *Cyrano de Bergerac.* By doing so, I like to think, I helped Miss Powers to project the effect of a daughter of France.

While on the subject of typically French music, I would like to point out that much of the music that is accepted as typical of certain races, nationalities and locales, is wholly arbitrary. Audiences have been conditioned to associate certain musical styles with certain backgrounds and peoples, regardless of whether the music is actually authentic.

For instance, all audiences think a certain type of steady beat of tom-tom or tympani drum, and a high, wailing wind instrument performing in a simple four- or five-tone scale, connotes one thing: Indians. I have conducted no exhaustive research into the American Indian's music, but I suspect that this particular stylization of "Indian music" has very little similarity with the genuine article. In the past some composer freely adapted some possibly authentic Indian song, changed and altered it, and came up with the tom-tom effect we all know.

This "conditioned reflex" music, of course, is wholly arbitrary, but it is so effective that sometimes its use is compulsory. I have employed it in any number of Westerns, including Howard Hawks' *Red River,* which, in my opinion, is a classic movie. I have used the "Indian music" that everyone knows not because I am not resourceful enough to originate other music, but because it is a telegraphic code that audiences recognize. If while the white settlers are resting or enjoying themselves, the background music suddenly takes on that tympani beat, the effect on the audience is electrifying. All know the Redmen are on the warpath even before the camera pans to the smoke signals on a distant hilltop. If I introduced genuine, absolutely authentic Indian tribal music, it probably wouldn't have any effect at all.

This musical conditioning underlies much screen composing. But it must not be hackneyed if it is to be effective. In the Indian music mentioned above I never used standard bars and phrases. I simply employed their mood. The idea is to avoid the usual and the trite, and at the same time to retain the basic ingredients of the musical "codes."

The screen composer, like every artist, must work within limitations. No matter how inventive and resourceful he is, he must also be disciplined. He must, to some extent, compromise. For a motion picture is a collective art, and the composer's contribution must enhance, not dominate.

EXERCISES

on film and music

1. What does Tiomkin believe to be the prime contribution of music to a film?
2. In what ways was Tiomkin inspired in his role as film composer by the example of "the great European comedian, Max Linder"?
3. Dramatists often write their plays with a particular star in mind for the lead role, and Tiomkin prefers to write film music the same way. Explain how the film medium thus influences his method of composing.

on film

1. Consider the recent cycle of films centered on youthful heroes like *The Graduate*. How emphatic is the musical background of such films? What type of music is invariably preferred?
2. Do you feel that the musical scores of the youth-oriented films add to the depth and convincingness of their treatment of "how it is"? Discuss, giving examples.
3. Discuss, with examples, films which in your opinion contain notable film scores.

on structure and language

1. Tiomkin notes that film is a "collective art" and organizes his essay from the point of view of his contribution as a member of a team. Explain and defend this statement.
2. For what type of audience is Tiomkin obviously writing? Does Levant seem to be aiming at a somewhat different audience? How does this affect their tone? Which of the two writers seems to you the more defensive, and why?

NEW TENDENCIES IN COMPOSING FOR MOTION PICTURES

George Antheil

I do not consider myself exclusively a motion picture composer for the simple reason that I spend at least three-quarters of every year in composing and performing serious music. On the other hand, I have written a good many motion picture scores for Hollywood films and therefore I may safely say I know most of the problems relating to composing for motion pictures in Hollywood.

The serious composer has only one problem in Hollywood: to sign his name to a motion picture score he can be proud of, musically. But his producer has a different aim in mind: to make sure that he secures a score that fits his picture, enhances its virtues and,—if necessary,—covers its defects. During the past ten years I have seen several composers of international reputation compose music for large—and from the point of view of Hollywood, important—motion pictures. They were never invited back because their scores, although musically beautiful, did not apparently fit the picture. This was not a matter of timing for to compose music to cues divided into so many seconds is not as difficult to do as one might suppose. Nor is it really too difficult to make this presumably fragmentary technique sound like music instead of sound-effects with orchestra.

Though of course it requires both great talent and work to attempt a synthesis of music and visual like the one achieved by Eisenstein and Prokofiev.

DISSONANCE

Previous to my score for *The Plainsman,* Hollywood composers never used prolonged dissonance, though they may have used an "off" chord or two occasionally. It promoted a vogue, and, I think I may safely say, that the tendency to score tense and frightening sequences quite radically became almost *de rigeur* from this time onwards. Both producer and public have come to expect them because, in picture after picture, this has proved to be the most effective kind of scoring. Nowadays, when the score for a picture such as *The Sniper,* which I wrote for Stanley Kramer a few years ago, is from beginning to end in dissonant and even 12-tone harmonies, nothing is said about it because it has come to be almost the expected thing.

On the other hand, the question becomes entirely different when one is called upon to compose music for a picture which *must* emphasize the romantic, tragic, comic or the shades in-between. From the critic's point of view the problem, as I see it, is mostly one of conditioning. We have just gone through a long period in music wherein the serious composer was reacting (as is always perfectly natural in musical history) against what I shall call the "schmaltz" (for lack of a better term) of Debussy, Wagner and Richard Strauss—not to mention Puccini. The vogue of Stravinski, "secco", and the soft-pedaling of untoward emotional stress came in with *The Rite of Spring* (1913) and has continued for quite a long while, 42 years, long enough for us to wish for a change. In the world of advanced serious music that change has been forthcoming: the new lyricism of Prokofiev, Menotti, and Britten seems to turn its back on this antiquated dry-as-dust, anti-emotional school.

In short, in serious music itself, there has recently been an international trend towards what we may roughly call the more "expressive", the human emotions depicted boldly and freely in a new manner. Although it has not yet generally done so, I think that motion picture music, in Hollywood or elsewhere, will soon take note of this fact. Of course, frequently this new type of scoring will shake hands with Debussy, Strauss, Tschaikowsky, and Wagner (to mention only a few of this now "ancient" school) because they too allowed themselves to deal with the same problems. But it will be entirely new, nevertheless, because the men writing this music will be new, living with this age and its problems. In the beginning, however, it will be criticized by those critics who have spent their lives battling for a more dry, less emotional and generally more dissonant "experimental" technique (although what is "experimental" about something that has been proven effective for almost twenty years, Heaven alone knows!).

EMOTION

I have recently completed three one act operas which concern themselves mainly with the problem of love and tenderness, albeit in various moods. It is a problem which interests me because affections and emotions are difficult to express in new music. On the other hand, anyone who knows my early music, *Ballet Mecanique* for example, knows that I am well-aware of the problems of a modern world, and have been aware of them since 1924 when this score was composed. It is, for me at least, a solved problem, and brings with it an unpleasant nostalgia for my youth. I like to feel that we are always marching ahead. It is definitely unpleasant and boring to become a kind of master in one thing early in life, and then go on reproducing that guaranteed element for the rest of one's artistic career. That is why, in motion picture composing, the tender and emotional problems absorb me, as well as the cold and glassy ones which, by now, I can do with my eyes— or my ears—shut. In order to write good, fresh music, one must forever be adventurous, and follow one's inner instinct.

That instinct compelled me to regard with special interest those sequences of a new motion picture in which the emotional is emphasized. In a recent motion picture I have scored *Not As a Stranger*, there were many hospital sequences, operations, moods which, previously, I have shown a knack for scoring. The cold, strange atmosphere of this kind in present-day life is also a part of my equipment as a musician. I probably would have underscored such sequences fairly well if for no other reason than that

I have been able to do so many times before in other pictures. But to have placed such music beneath these sequences—so well-done visually by the director—would have been wrong. It would have made the picture reek of hospital odor—whereas the basic theme of the film was not concerned with hospitals but about the men and women who live and work in them. It was the human side that needed articulation, underscoring, even emotional explanation, rather than the white walls and the ether.

THE CHANGING WORLD

There are many things in present-day motion picture scoring which I violently disapprove of. I disapprove, for instance, of mushy and banal musical sequences as much as any responsible critic does. I hate Hollywood's tendency to score the pictures about antiquity (Greece, Rome, Carthage) à la Rimsky-Korsakoff or mild, early Bartok—I am certain that one could be much more authentic, musically, within the period without antagonizing the great ticket-buying public one whit. I know that I, who love antiquity, would gladly see many a picture of this sort even though it were rather flaccidly made, if it were not for the fact that the accompanying musical score insults me—as I am sure that it does many others. I bewail the tendency of Hollywood to use only large sized orchestras (which, in the main, all sound pretty much alike) instead of smaller, more interesting and colorful combinations. There is a great deal to bewail about Hollywood; but, on the other hand, there is occasionally a resourcefulness and high technique in its scoring which is lacking more often than not in the music of some European film music composers. Many of these latter confine their efforts—and obtain their best successes too—in remarkable atmospheric music; but the main problem of most pictures is to point up the dramatic action, the underlying feeling which, likely as not, they either skip entirely or, if they do attempt, they display an amateurishness which confounds one.

If, in the last motion picture I scored, I would have concentrated upon all the hospital and operation backgrounds—instead of the more deeply emotional and dramatic human beings, I would have done what they most often do. The score, perhaps, would have drawn more attention to itself; but the picture would have been less effective as a whole; and nothing would have been proved about motion picture scoring—if, indeed, I did prove anything.

Our chief and basic problem in scoring for motion pictures today is to find a new approach that would fit our new perception of the changing reality, so as to re-interpret our treatment of the emotional, the lyric and the human. We must approach it in much the same manner as serious modern opera composers approach the new opera. However, and above all, let us not try to win old battles which have been won years ago. How sad is the sight of a man upon an old battlefield, waving his sword, hitting his shield, and crying the old battlecries when, actually, the armies have long ago dispersed while the dead lie peacefully in their graves all around. We would call him a madman—or a charming Don Quixote. There are many real and important battles one should engage in nowadays.

EXERCISES

on film and music

1. According to Antheil, what is the key to writing a score that does not "draw attention to itself"? What is wrong with a score that "draws attention to itself"?
2. Antheil notes that problems of technique alone, or the perfection of technique, tend to bore him. In contrast, what does he emphasize which relates to his emphasis on "dramatic action"?
3. The main job of a film composer, says Antheil, is "to point up the dramatic action." Does this agree with or contradict Tiomkin's view?

on film

1. Antheil is concerned for *human* significance in a film as opposed to tangential matters of decor or landscape or other documentary features. Cite examples of films where you feel the human level of interest and involvement has been lost through overdependence on trick camera angles, or local color,

or an obtrusive musical score, or other forms of lopsided treatment.

2. Why does Antheil appear to feel that dissonant musical effects rather than conventional harmonics are more suited to expressing the deeply human aspects of the contemporary situation? What films can you think of which support his contention?

on language and structure

1. Antheil dubs the music of Debussy, Wagner, and Strauss "schmaltz," in contrast to the "dry" compositions of Stravinsky. Define "schmaltziness" in accord with Antheil's criterion. According to your definition, classify the following (which you may be familiar with as books or films or both) as "dry" or "schmaltz": *A Streetcar Named Desire; Death of a Salesman; Exodus; The Old Man and the Sea; My Fair Lady; Hawaii; Who's Afraid of Virginia Woolf?; Bonnie and Clyde; Rosemary's Baby; Psycho; 2001*. Add freely to the list with other examples of your own.

2. Outline this essay and show by means of that outline how Antheil develops his argument concerning the "dries" and films laden with "schmaltz." Which of these styles does he apparently prefer?

FILM MUSIC AS NOISE

Page Cook

Music has all but disappeared from films. Noise has replaced it.

What was once a functioning part of the cinematic art form has deteriorated into an assortment of auditory effects which derive, when they derive from anything beside ineptitude, from the major and minor neuroses of Western Civilization. Not to mention the no-talent composers who get paid for concocting them.

Hitherto, filmusic never worked *against* a film, but today's "scores" definitely do. It's true the subject matter of most current films could hardly inspire a genuine filmusic composer, and that the characters in today's films are equally uninspiring. But even the worst film doesn't deserve the kind of musical inadequacies that are now being perpetrated.

A film score should relate, in its themes and treatment thereof, to locale, time, plot and characterizations. These relationships are fundamental, and will never be obsolete. The current fashion of imposing *unrelated* sounds on an audience, instead of evoking relevant emotions by means of *related* sounds, is a reversion to the uncouth and even to the barbaric.

Good filmusic sets up in an audience connotations that visuals

244

on the screen cannot supply. That is to say, it enriches the cinematic experience, and hence our lives. Filling ears with clatter merely to prevent one of the five senses from feeling neglected is bad filmmaking and self-defeating. It actually prevents the eye from perceiving as much as it would were the brain not occupied in fending off the irrelevances pouring in upon it through the ear.

Slapping "hard rock" onto a sound track is a truckling to the ignorances of the nihilists among today's young, in the hope of getting *somebody* into movie theatres and drive-ins. In consequence, non-composers, astonished to find so lucrative a market for non-music, do not hesitate to collect fat checks for putting together the idiocies of "pot" music, freak-out blues, and (now old hat) cool jazz.

Neal Hefti is one of the most tasteless of the purveyors of noise instead of music. His "scoring" of *Barefoot in the Park* consists of fragments of jazz that are *never* relevant. His "score" for *Oh Dad, Poor Dad etc.*, which replaced George Duning's score for that film at the last minute, consisted, instead of musical wit, merely of snatches of whatever sounds happened to strike Hefti's fancy.

Quincy Jones was also quite conscienceless in his "score" for *In Cold Blood.* The Clutter family was represented by a melody of *mocking* mush. The actions of the two psychopaths were propelled, of course, by primitive jazz. For the flash-backs of Percy's childhood Jones resorted to blah (weak strings, alto sax meanderings). The scoring of the final scene—the one after Percy's protracted hanging—merely combines a few snorts from the horns with extraneous primary rhythms. To what purpose?

Jones is also responsible for two other banalities: the scores for *In the Heat of the Night* and *The Deadly Affair,* which deploy alienating jazz of the Monk style. The latter also has bossa nova rhythms pointlessly sprinkled throughout its score.

Johnny Keating's scoring of *Hotel* is such insistent din it is a good example of filmusic that works *against* its film. So is his blare for *Robbery,* in which his noise *diminishes* suspense. The opening theme, as the train approaches nearer and nearer, is little more than shriek. Keating's flashy jazz, as opposed to Hefti and Jones' completely addled variety, does connote a few associations, albeit unpleasant ones. Straight jazz, incidentally, is impotent cinematically, which is why it is always hopped-up by some other musical device, however unscrupulous.

Toshiro Mayuzumi's weird sonorities in behalf of *Reflections in a Golden Eye* further prove that his filmusic sense is as vapid as John Huston's directorial one has become.

Lalo Schifrin is another noise-maker whose only aim, it would seem, is to exploit social malaise and individual torment, whether doing so is or isn't appropriate to what is on the screen. His South American rhythms are *always* distracting, but never more so than in his recent scores for *Cool Hand Luke*, *Sol Madrid* and *The Fox*.

For the first he loosed a barrage of snare, kettle and side drums, and highlighted the dramatic and melodramatic phases of that mediocre film with cymbals. For the brutal beating scene he used alternating tempi punched out by xylophone, marimba and snares. The egg-consuming scene is ridiculously underscored with string pizzicatti, which, I suppose, was intended for humor. For Luke's death he played around with multiple chord progressions played by ridiculous horn combinations.

For the degenerate *The Fox* he juggled two semi-melodies— one for the Jill and March relationship, one for March and Paul— and surrounded both with orchestral brawls. He underlined the nude scenes with queasy sounds plus *fanfares!* The full kiss between the two lesbians elicited from Schifrin hysterical rhythms and half-tone key inversions (not quite dodecaphonic). None of the barren meaninglessness of lesbianism is ever intimated by Schifrin's noise.

Francis Lai is also afflicted with the Schifrin syndrome. He augments the slick sounds of the Latin beat with sound slurs and smears that are usually produced by instruments that are untuned or otherwise unkempt. For *The Bobo*, in which a singing-matador (Peter Sellers) is promised a stage booking if he can "make" Barcelona's most notorious whore, Lai uses a pseudo-flamenco *with a beat!* For *Live for Life* he merely regurgitated the boring sounds he wrote for *A Man and a Woman*, i.e., excruciating bossa nova hammered out by a "continental" orchestra.

Ennio Morricone's score for *The Good, the Bad and the Ugly* is littered with metallic *fright sounds.* For *The Battle of Algiers* he and Gillo Pontecorvo (who also wrote and directed that film) concocted a series of sputtering gasps to represent the death agonies of the FLN. Dramatically, most of those sounds were distracting; musically, they didn't exist.

EXERCISES

on film and music

1. How does Cook distinguish between film "noise" and music?
2. How does Cook's criticism of the film scores of Neal Hefti agree with certain of the views on composing for films expressed by Tiomkin and Antheil?
3. On what key point would there be disagreement between Cook and Antheil concerning types of music possible to film? Would Cook fit Antheil's idea of a musical Don Quixote?

on film

1. Why does Cook object to the score of *In Cold Blood*? Does his objection seem valid to you?
2. What types of film does Cook seem antagonistic to? Why? Do you agree with his evaluations?

on structure and language

1. In his paragraph on *The Fox*, Cook uses terms like "degenerate," "hysterical," "barren." These are terms of abuse; note instances throughout the essay where Cook relies on such terms. Do you feel that the frequent dependence on terms of this kind helps or hinders the clarity and convincingness of his exposition and argument. Discuss the problem in general of the use of "loaded" words and phrases.
2. How does one, in one's own writing, draw the line between stridency, which would be self-defeating, and strength of feeling which may serve positively the purposes of good writing. In considering this problem, it may be instructive to compare Cook's style and method with Richard Wilbur's essay. Note that while Wilbur is cool in tone, Cook is intense. Would you say the tone is over-intense? What means of control—despite their differences in other respects—do Wilbur and Cook employ in their writing?

FILM
and
SOCIETY

It is in no small degree that our understanding of the dynamics of a society, of those elements of a society which make it "go," depends on our understanding of its conflicts, both hidden and overt. In the following set of essays, where film is considered in a predominantly social perspective, themes of conflict recur. Most of the essayists focus on the values generated by the social drama, by a scene where various levels of interest meet, contend, and—ideally—mesh in an energizing ensemble of social forces. This kind of focus is exemplified by Robert Warshow's intensive consideration of tragic values in a popular form. In contrast, there is the stunning eclecticism of Marshall McLuhan. Rather than isolate a particular strand of value from his material for the purpose of microscopic examination, McLuhan sets his inquiry in a total field; in this, he is like the influential stage theorist, Antonin Artaud, who insisted that a play script was but one contributing —rather than dominant—element of a "total theater." In an analogous way, McLuhan sees present-day society as a "global village," all aspects of which are inextricably fused together by electronic circuits; McLuhan posits a world where it is impossible not to be tuned in.

We are inescapably tuned in, for example, to images which impinge on our consciousness—and conscience—and so affect our sense of options in conduct, like the images of the Rebel and the Steady which Kingsley Amis defines and discusses. Catharine Sugy is concerned in her essay with what she finds to be demeaning in current images of the Negro, as projected on films and television. And the essay on Westerns by Fenin and Everson is largely devoted to images of right behavior, and the options they imply. In each case we are involved with values, and with values in conflict.

An equal sensitivity to conflicting values controls Pauline Kael's essay on "Movies on Television" which, besides its ostensible subject, is as much about differences in taste and expectation between the middle-aged and college-age generations. David Riesman also touches on the problem of esthetic response but from the standpoint of conditioning anthropological factors. It is from the same point that McLuhan goes to work—but to strikingly different effect: where Riesman in his mode of discussion is historical and chronological, McLuhan is spatial and metaphysical. Yet even from McLuhan's spiralling bird's-eye view of the scene, we can make out points of conflict which he seeks to reconcile by his method, such as the lines ordinarily drawn between "high" and "low" culture.

Susan Sontag is close to McLuhan in the way she tries to steer clear of value judgments. She concentrates instead on psychological conflicts in the audience, on its "tensions." She discusses science fiction films according to the release they bring an audience from its own tensions and anxieties. Warshow is as much concerned as Sontag with the psychology of the audience, but he takes pains to make explicit the values by which he writes. Considering a society in which success in the abstract is made synonymous with heaven, Warshow notes how the terrors—let alone "tensions"—bound to arise from such an equation are both evoked and assuaged through the conventions of the gangster film. And there is perhaps a moral in the fact that it is his essay which most nearly touches home, which is the most universal in implication; for none of us, after all, lives without living near the truths of failure, like the fact that our bodies fail and we die.

THE ORAL TRADITION, THE WRITTEN WORD, AND THE SCREEN IMAGE

David Riesman

The movies, of course, are a boundary-annihilating form, easily transmissible past linguistic and cultural barriers (as well as barriers of literacy). They may also be, as Arnold Hauser suggests in *The Social History of Art*, a democratizing form because of their mobility, the absence of traditional stage conventions and proprieties. Art historians have recently noted that when Renaissance painters shifted the Virgin Mary from front face to profile it marked a decline of Catholic religiosity and a less devout approach to the Trinity. The camera can be even more impudent, and can put aesthetic laws to use in all kinds of ways, leading the audience, as Hauser says, to the events, rather than leading and presenting the events to them, with the voyeuristic intimacy which we can see in such a film as Hitchcock's "Rear Window." A movie can tell its story as though we are telling it to ourselves, or as though we are actually dreaming it; it can force us to identify with its chosen moods and people. The camera, by moving around, subtly invites us to embrace one character and exclude another—to look up and feel awe of a noble man or fear of a villain; to look down and feel contempt or pity. A sidelong glance of the camera alerts us for trouble—a right-to-left pan, reversing the right-handedness

Hermann Weill discusses in his book on symmetry, invests people and places with a spooky feeling. I need not labor the catalogue of the director's powers, aided as they are by the near-hypnotic effect of the concentrated brightness of the screen, while other sights and sounds (save in college-town theatres!) are at a low ebb. The movie is the novel in motion; it is potentially the least rationalistic, the most subjectivized medium. And like the broadcast, the rally, or the fireside council of the tribal chief, it demands attention now, this minute, in this time and at that place; unlike a book, it cannot wait for your mood, or your activity.

Where the movies and the book are both in circulation, the written word and the screen image compete in making our sensibility mobile and empathic, though for many of us even now the movies have pretty well replaced the novel as the powerful medium for anticipatory socialization. Conceivably, when every man has his own movie camera and home projector, and his own movie library as we now have our record collections, he will become more critical and less vulnerable—this being the usual effect of do-it-yourself. Moreover, membership in film societies like the one that I understand is active on this campus can help put moviegoers in the director's place, can help them be more critical of rather than so easily manipulated by him.

But all this betokens a society like ours in which radio and film are cumulative media for the better educated strata—a society in which a certain uneasy balance of powers exists among the media, a society in which the librarians, guided by such men as Paul Bixler, have been vigilant of freedom while the movie magnates have generally failed to fight down their fears of the Legion of Decency and the other censoring groups who ultimately force sadism on the films in exchange for forbidden sex. In the Middle East, where the movies and radio arrive ahead of the book, there is no such balance—though I suppose Turkey comes paradoxically closest where Kemal Ataturk detached the young from even the literate old by imposing the Roman script: here the print-oriented are not simply the students of the Koran but are up-to-date and Westernized.

It is a truism that the revolutions which go on within countries, as the result of the uneven spread of new techniques and ideologies to the different strata, also go on among countries; and we are as accustomed to the term "have-not nations" as to the have-not classes. In microcosm we can watch the dispossession of the elders of Middle Eastern villages who lack access to news and images of alternative ways of life, and of consumer abundance; likewise, some of the very countries whose industrial and cultural development coincided with the Age of Print are now under pressure from those countries whose development begins in the age of the screen image. Print, to be sure, still has prestige all over the world. The Western and Westernized statesmen now old enough to have power have mostly been nurtured on it, or at worst rebelled defensively against it. The model followed by the underdeveloped countries is, of course, profoundly influenced by the past triumphs of print, a process which makes it unlikely that they skip the stage of print entirely. Thus, when it comes to describing what a country would look like where the oral tradition has been fragmented not under the impact of print but of broadcasting and the movies, we are still largely (despite striking developments in India) in the realm of science fiction rather than history.

Let me now go back to the beginning and recapitulate, from a slightly different perspective, the sequence I have here presented in impressionistic and overgeneral outline. First of all, we can see that a preliterate society dependent on the fluid, fugitive nature of the spoken word, may have certain resemblances, in the way its emotions are organized, to a post-literate society which might have moved away from print, or be skipping it, like these peasant communities of the Middle East just mentioned. In both, the encapsulating and isolating possibilities of print are absent; in both, symbols are given weight by their setting, by the local affective color so to speak, rather than by their logicality. But the social structure, of course, is very different indeed. The society based on oral tradition, with its dependence on the memory of the elders, links people together in small tribal groups and in their families. These people may be nomadic, but they are not socially and psychologically mobile in the modern sense; they are led by folk tales and songs to identify with the tribe as it has been and will be, or possibly with a legendary golden age, but they are not incited to imagine themselves outside its comforts and coherence. Sizable kingdoms, as in Africa, have been built on the spoken word, particularly where there are specialists in it, but empires large in space and durable in time require transportable information and some form of permanent record (of which proverbs may be one kind of early approximation). Moreover, the oral communication of a preliterate society tends to freeze the given social structure, though occasionally prophets can overleap the cellular walls of the tribe and bring about new structures. In contrast, a postliterate society would seem almost inevitably fluid, its people on the move, its structure unstable.

In other words, oral communication keeps people together, binds people to each other, while print in our day loosens these bonds, creates space around people, even isolates them in some ways. People who would simply have been deviants in a preliterate tribe, misunderstanding and misunderstood, can through books establish a wider identity—can understand and even undermine the enemies of home and hearth and herd. While the geographic migrations of preliterate peoples have something in common with the incomprehending movement of flocks of deer, the readers of the age of discovery were prepared mentally for some of the experiences of their geographic mobility—they had at any rate left home in imagination even if they had not roamed as far or among as strange people as they were actually to meet. The bookish education of these inner-directed men helped harden them for voyages: they wanted to convert the heathen, civilize them, trade with them—if anyone changed in the encounter, it would be the heathen, while they, as they moved about the globe or up the social ladder, remained very much the same men. The epitome of this was the Englishman in the tropics who, all alone, dressed for dinner with home guard ceremonial, toasted the Queen, and, six months late, read with a proper sense of outrage the leader in the London *Times*. His ties with the world of print helped steady him in his course far from home and alone.

Today, the successors of these men are often other-directed; they are men molded as much by the mass media outside their formal education as by their schooling; men who are more public relations minded than ambitious; men softened for encounters rather than hardened for voyages; if they move about the globe it is often to win the love of the natives or to try to understand their mores, rather than to exploit them for gain or the glory of

God. Meanwhile, as we have seen, the natives (as they used to be called) are themselves in many cases on the move, and the sharp differences between societies dependent on the oral tradition and those dependent on print are tending to be less important with the coming of radio and film. Often the decisive difference is among the peasants themselves within a country now moving out of the stage of oral tradition—differences between those who listen to the radio and go to movies and those who shut these things out as the voice of the Devil or as simply irrelevant for them. In the *Far Eastern Quarterly* (November, 1955), Milton Singer describes the fabulous complexity of such differences in a South Indian province, where all levels of mediation exist between the peasant and the parochial and the Indian and the global. In the Middle East studies it was found that those peasants who listened to Radio Moscow or the BBC or the VOA already had, or perhaps acquired, a different sensibility from those who did not. The former were prepared in the imagination for more voyages than they were likely ever to make. For instance, when these peasants were asked in this study what they would do if they were to become President of Turkey, for example, or where they would like to live if they could not live in their native villages, they could answer the questions; they had a stock of opinions, public opinions, on such matters. But the tradition-directed peasants who were not radio listeners or movie goers could not answer the questions; to the question about becoming President they might say: "... How can you ask such a thing? How can I ... president of Turkey ... master of the whole world!" The very thought appeared sacrilegious. Nor could such people imagine living any- where else, and when pressed some said they would die if forced to leave their village.

Daniel Lerner and I have traced (in an article for *Explorations*) the phenomenon we term "psychic mobility," the fluidity of identification which precedes actual physical movement, but which creates a potential for such movement. In some Lebanese villages, the young bus driver who visits the city or the young storekeeper who has a radio have become the opinion leaders, helping the villages make contact with an orbit in which their elders and chiefs, once looked up to as unquestioned founts of wisdom, now appear small and parochial. Peasants in the same village with the same occupation and the same income—that is, people not distinguishable by the usual demographic indices—are found to differ in their psychic mobility as marked by the degrees and forms of their attention to the mass media. Of course, it may turn out that these newly and unevenly stirred masses are all dressed up in imagination with no place to go.

Despite a certain amount of indirect evidence concerning the new village elite of people who are there first with the most news of the great world outside, these investigations (soon to be more fully reported in a book by Daniel Lerner) are lacking data as to whether peasants who are psychically mobile are isolated listeners or part of a group which mediates the media for them. Paul F. Lazarsfeld, Elihu Katz, and others have made it evident that in America people do not attend to the media as isolated atoms but as members of groups which select among the media and interpret their messages. Indeed, Father Coughlin discovered that he could not organize followers directly by his broadcasts, but needed to set up, as he did in Boston and elsewhere, groups who would listen together—recreating, as it were, the tribal setting. (For one thing, in such a group no one would dare flick the dial.) Similarly, people go to movies in groups—especially the teen-agers who make up such a large proportion of the audience—and formal and informal fan clubs are of course a way of organizing these groups. Again, we see the idiosyncratic elements of print: people do not read in groups (though I suppose one would have to make something of an exception for textbooks and trots, both of which are often books only by courtesy), and the cubicle is as characteristic of the library as isolation is uncharacteristic of a modern movie palace (though the drive-in may in rare cases have brought it back).

Since the Middle East studies are based on interviews with individuals, and not on the observation of groups, we lack any reliable information on this point and tend to interpret the data as if individuals singly began those subtle psychological changes which are reflected in a decision to attend the movies in the nearest town or to listen to the radio in the nearest coffee house. Probably, it is not like that; probably, the moderns who listen and the ancients who don't are each in touch with one another and sustain each other. Lerner in his book links psychic mobility with what Reuel Denney and Nathan Glazer and I have termed "other-direction"; that is, he connects it with the consumer mentality, the concern with others and how they evaluate themselves, the preoccupation with personal relations. It is strange to find something which looks like this urban American communications-conscious outlook in a Lebanese village which has not yet experienced the Industrial Revolution, and we are again struck with the possibility that the age of individualism—the age of the self-starter —may be an interlude between the age of the spoken and the age of the electronic word.

It is too soon, however, to say whether the epoch of print will be utterly elided in the underdeveloped countries, just as, with the coming of electrical and atomic energy, they may skip the stage of coal and water power. Conceivably, the movies and broadcasting will eventually help to awaken a hunger for print, when their own novelty is worn off and when they come to be used as tie-ins with print—as in Lyman Bryson's "Invitation to Learning." Just as the barbarians of Europe in the Middle Ages pulled themselves up by Greek bootstraps, so the nonindustrial countries can for a long time draw on the storehouse of Western science and technology, including the science of social organization; and there are still enough inner-directed men in our society who are willing to go out and help build the armies of Iran and the factories of Istanbul. In this connection, it is striking that the Soviet Union, paying at least nominal heed to the scriptures of Marx and Lenin, has created what is in some ways a replica of the Victorian industrial world rather than the modern consumer world—so that treatises on Marxism and Hollywood movies may be seen as alternative lures to the pre-industrial nations, with national pride voting for steel plants and Karl Marx and personal taste for cars, Coca-Cola, and the stereotype of America. To be sure, Communism may seem the quickest way to the consumers' utopia, with its apparent power to mow down all vested interests, including one's own. (I should parenthetically add that the appeal to the consumer mentality in the East, the appeal of American luxuries, is almost never an intended propaganda move but rather a by-product of media forms coupled with American enterprise.)

In sum, it is apparent that the mass media, like other forms of technological innovation, bring about new polarizations in society and between societies. The readers and the non-readers, the listeners and the non-listeners, may belong to the same economic and social groupings, yet they have different values, different tastes, different turns of mind.

EXERCISES

on film and society

1. Riesman calls movies a "boundary-annihilating" form. In what ways do movies annihilate social boundaries?
2. One result of censorship of films, Riesman claims, is to force "sadism on the films in exchange for forbidden sex." Explain.
3. Riesman applies his famous formulation of the "other-directed" personality (developed in his book, *The Lonely Crowd*) to the individual conditioned more by the mass media than by the reading of books. What are some of the differences he notes between media-oriented and print-oriented people? Which type is more likely to be happy in a "tribal" community? Which would make the better consumer? Which, the better pirate?

on film

1. Riesman sees the movie-going experience as—in contrast to reading—essentially a group activity. When you go to a movie, do you usually go as part of a group, or with a date, or by yourself? If mainly with a date, or with one other friend, would you consider this a type of group activity like charades or a community sing, or more of a private experience?
2. Riesman also stresses the advent of the film club as a social aspect of the film. Does the film club function differently from such former literary groups as the Robert Browning Society or Jane Austen or James Joyce clubs?
3. Riesman suggests that films are more likely to lead to social restiveness and disorder than books. Can you think of evidence for this view?

1. Riesman is concerned chiefly with group behavior rather than individual psychology. Note how, as a sociologist, he applies his knowledge of tribal cultures to elucidating the cultural history of the film.

2. For the most part, Riesman employs specialized knowledge without resorting to jargon. In the context in which they are used here, however, do phrases like "inner-directed" or "other-directed" transcend the level of jargon? Does "inner-directed" mean anything more than independent? And "other-directed" anything more than timorous? Note examples in other books and essays you may be reading of the use of scientific-sounding words to express meanings for which a more conventional, homespun word might be available.

CONTENTS
AND MORAL INFLUENCE
OF THE WESTERN

George N. Fenin
and William K. Everson

*"We'll give them a fair trial,
and then hang them!"*
            —ANONYMOUS

THE HERO

The Western theme, based on the triplex system of the hero, the adventure, and the law, has at all times been fascinating to movie audiences. In the long, sometimes straightforward, but often tortuous road towards development, the motion pictures have presented the theme with different approaches and results. But in its more than fifty years of existence, the Western film has completed, from at least a moral point of view, a first cycle.

The early Westerns, approached in a quasi-documentary fashion, were characterized by sincerity of sentiment and a poetic spirit. Later, the attention of film-makers to the genre jeopardized its freshness, and only William S. Hart's undeniable contributions to realism stressed the morality inherent in the West's history. This was true in the sense that an authentic depiction of this history made the spectator feel he was witnessing not merely casual entertainment but, rather, a serious and dignified visual discussion of an era which had already passed into the nation's heritage.

The epic, which enlarged the Western for audiences with the depths of its research and the advantages of a gradual aesthetic and commercial development in movies, further enhanced the genre's prospects. But studio policies, guided by the public's clamor for more modern, lighter, "escapist" Westerns—the fast, showy vehicles of Ken Maynard and Hoot Gibson, for example— brought about the first fundamental change in the contents and morals of the Western. From now on, the cowboy was not necessarily the successor to the pioneer; he was no longer just the man who toiled hard raising cattle or defending the land barons' privileges, the man whom the Great Cattle Depression of 1886–87 forced to roam the West looking for ways and means of supporting himself. An idealized, whitewashed hero emerged, his character influenced by the various codes of associations, clubs, and groups. This new "hero" reached his zenith the closer he followed Gene Autry's "Ten Commandments of the Cowboy." All promulgated codes of morality are inevitably influenced by current moral trends; and the perfectly acceptable behavior of the Western hero in the Twenties might be considered by some today as the ultimate in un-Americanism. We have a perfect example of this in a mild and quite unimportant Western of 1925 entitled *Shooting Square*. In it, the hero and heroine are to be married, and while they celebrate with a party at the ranch, a cowhand is sent to bring the preacher. The preacher, it turns out, is a Negro. Although he is presented likably, certain aspects of the traditional image of the comic Negro persist. His clothes are ill-fitting and he speaks— subtitles, of course—in traditionally stereotyped fashion. "I'se de preacher," is his first line upon greeting the distinctly shocked gathering. The result is astounding. The heroine almost faints and, indignantly returning the hero's ring, asks him: "How can you treat me like this?" The heroine's outraged father appears to be in a lynching mood, and he orders the Negro from the ranch. The little preacher is bustled out as quickly as possible.

Later, however, the hero (Jack Perrin) restores himself to the heroine's favor, by assuring her that he meant no harm. The line that clinches the reconciliation is: "I didn't know he was *black*." All this is treated casually; the incident is not used to incite racial hatred. Jack Perrin's hero is otherwise absurdly virtuous, possessed in abundance of the nine other commandments.

Today, of course, if such a sequence were included in a film, wholesale picketing would automatically result, and possibly even violence. Later in the film, hero and heroine seek out a white minister, and are then "married" by an apparent preacher, actually an outlaw in disguise; the heroine's discovery that her marriage is illegal provokes a much less concerned reaction from her than did her encounter with the authentic, but colored, minister!

The cowboy-hero, this bulwark of physical and moral strength, was the backbone in the boom of the "B" Westerns in the Thirties. But his influence was felt in the epics that were then being made (*Jesse James, The Oklahoma Kid, Union Pacific, Stagecoach*—all in 1939), and this influence generally continued to be felt in the philosophy and policies of movie producers right through World War II.

It is no surprise, therefore, to notice that right after the end of the War, the ferment of new times began to exert its influence toward a revision of the cowboy cliché. There was a marked move to make the hero a less idealized character; his aims might continue to be those of the chivalrous knight, but he was too much of a realist to achieve those aims chivalrously. The war had destroyed too many illusions.

Bill Elliott was perhaps the foremost exponent of this new "realism" in a series of Westerns made for Monogram and Allied Artists. The Elliott Western saw a number of remarkable changes in the makeup and behavior of the Western hero. In *Bitter Creek*, the hero needs information from a villain and, wasting no time playing the gentleman, Elliott proceeds to beat the information out of him, all the time keeping him covered with a gun. The villain protests: "You wouldn't get away with this if you'd put that gun down!" In the old films, of course, such a taunt would have led to the hero's dropping both gun and belt and proving that right must always win by beating the tar out of his opponent in a fair fist fight. Elliott is not taken in, however; he replies: "But I'm not going to put it down," and proceeds to slug away until the "heavy" gives in and makes his confession.

In *Kansas Territory* (1952) Elliott also resorts to brutal methods to run down the man responsible for the death of his brother, and in at least two films in the series, *Waco* (1952) and *Topeka* (1953), he plays an outlaw for most of the film—not a lawman posing as an outlaw in the time-honored tradition.

Topeka bears a particularly close relationship to William S. Hart's *The Return of Draw Egan* (1916). In both films, the ultimate reformation is brought about not by genuine remorse over a life of crime, but rather through a more sentimental expedient: the love of a good woman. In both films, the hero turns on his former cronies, still hoping to turn the situation to his own advantage, and he "reforms" only late in the game. Elliott had the integrity not to weaken his reformation by a complete transformation. His reformation still works to his own advantage: through services to the community, he is pardoned; he gets the girl, and he keeps any stolen wealth he may have accumulated.

A character even more obviously a product of the war was the near-mystical leader, quite recognizably patterned on Nazi types; however, he did not appear on the screen until the Nazi evil had been effectively minimized for the public due to the cold war. One has good examples of the leader-hero in such films as *Arrow in the Dust* (1954) with Sterling Hayden and *The Last Wagon* (1956) with Richard Widmark. The hero is an outlaw or an Army deserter, frequently a killer. He is reconciled to the fact that he is being hounded, and he is not unduly bitter about it. Given to contemplation, he is convinced his crime was perfectly justified; but unconsciously placing himself apart from other men, he does not overly concern himself with proving his case.

However, fate places him in the position of guiding the destiny of a group of men—in the Western, obviously, the wagon train to be guided through hostile Indian country is the perfect answer. He must maintain perfect discipline, to the point of extreme arrogance, brutality, and ruthlessness; the lives of the group are more important than the life of an individual; the end always justifies the means. Before the adventure is over, the leader-hero has not only proven himself to the group under his command, but has made almost unnecessary and irrelevant any proof concerning his earlier crime. Injurious effects the pioneer leader and the brutal, pragmatic cowboy may have had on youthful audiences were probably nullified by the completely whitewashed Western heroes galloping then on television. Now, however, that television has swung to greater realism, there may well be a far from salutary effect on American youth. Few films, fortunately, went quite as far as did *Jack Slade* in extolling the courage of a killer, demanding sympathy and understanding, if not approval, for his acts. Slade was a colorful historical character of the post-Civil War West, a trouble-shooter for the stagecoach lines, and his very ruthlessness with outlaws brought with it a measure of law and order. Finally, however, killing became an obsession, an obsession fanned by alcohol, to the point that he became a menace to the law he was paid to uphold, and he was finally lynched by vigilantes. In the film version, this bitter end was averted, and he died, almost seeking death in a form of self-atonement, in a fairly fought gun battle. Mark Stevens acted in and co-directed this interesting and powerful film, but in such an overwrought fashion that it was reminiscent of the German film dramas of the Twenties, such as *Warning Shadows* (1922) and that it failed to become the honest portrait of a man and an era that it might have been. It always seemed somewhat confusing in its demand for sympathy for a man whose very actions, including the crippling of a child, made such sympathy impossible.

Generally, the war years left the scars of cynicism and bitterness on heroes, and it was with no surprise that we saw in *The Rawhide Years* (1956), a well-constructed and exciting Western by Rudolph Mate, a hero who is a cardshark, and a heroine who willingly becomes the villain's mistress. These matters are so much taken for granted that the main issue of the film becomes not the regeneration of the hero and heroine, but the elimination of the villain so that the love affair between hero and heroine, presumably now to be sanctioned by marriage, may resume! ...

THE WOMAN

The cult of the super-hero fighting the good fight in a confused and largely hostile world populated by white outlaws and Indian savages, was further developed by the role of the woman.

Originally she was shown as the full-fledged companion of the pioneer, certainly his equal, and occasionally possessed of an inner strength that made her his superior. Later, her image deteriorated into that of a frail creature, forever at the mercy of the lawless element, forever dependent for protection and her livelihood upon the hero. In other words, she ceased to become a plot participant and became a plot motivator; defense of her honor and rights became as important in themselves as the battle between law and lawlessness. Later still, towards the end of the Thirties, she became more self-reliant, increasingly athletic, and conscious of her sex appeal. In the post-war period, this sex appeal became an exasperating and exasperated *leitmotif*, which found its justi-fication in two fundamental exigencies of the motion picture industry: the reaction to the puritanism of the Production Code, exerting an archaic censorship over a depiction of true passion and other legitimate emotions, and the need to stimulate sagging box office returns. Thus the cycle is complete even in this important aspect of the Western: the image of the western women, as rendered by Hollywood, stands confused, between the sentimental and mythological conception of the pure but weak and defenseless female, without any personality of her own, essentially dependent on the hero, and the titillatingly sexual and aggressive heroine.

NECESSITY FOR A LIVING LEGEND

The new moral strength of the Hollywood Western lies in its statement to audiences that life in the old West, notwithstanding the falsely glamorized and savage portrait that Hollywood painted in the past, was hard, monotonous, but also heroic . . . a life that had neither gods nor devils; Hollywood has begun to inform the public that the West was peopled with simple human beings with all their strengths and weaknesses, a folk not very different from those in the audience.

In due time, and with proper care, such a tradition should acquire all the necessary attributes of a living legend, a myth whose authentic example will be accepted by the American nation in its true perspective. Non-American, and specifically European audiences have always approached the Western in an enthusiastic manner, granting even the poorer examples some poetic and realistic foundations which are often baseless. This enthusiastic attitude is often not shared by American audiences who regard the Western naturally, without the emotional enthusiasm for the "foreign" and the "exotic," which is what the Western signifies for the European. These non-American audiences then, kindly disposed towards the Western in any event, have been even quicker to accept and approve the mature changes in the Western format than have their American counterparts.

The combined effects of public taste, the reflections of modern times and the need—now a commercial as well as an aesthetic need—to present the Western in a more adult framework, are all causing Hollywood to take into consideration, both directly and indirectly, the moral influence of their Western product in artistic, social, and human terms. Some of the more dynamic producers of this new school may well know that the vital requirement in their efforts is progression instead of the tested but untrue status quo. The American cinema, on the basis of its past achievements, has the key to a splendid future in developing the fine resources of its epic past. And if the gangster film, the Civil War film, and other branches of adventure in the motion picture, all find their roots in the Western, there is all the more reason to perfect the purest and most original genre of the American cinema.

Such a challenging ideal might in itself bring about a true renaissance in the American cinema, and with it renewed support from the movie audiences of the United States and abroad.

EXERCISES

on film and society

1. The writers note that the hero was a "less idealized character" in Westerns made after World War II. How may we account for this? What does this suggest about the film as a barometer of changing social values and customs?
2. What is meant by the remark that the hero of Westerns in the 1920s might seem today to represent "the ultimate in un-Americanism"?
3. Note the characteristics of the film *Jack Slade* which Fenin and Everson stress. What social and moral problems are raised by this type of film?

on film

1. The authors seem to prefer Westerns which have some "documentary realism." Do you believe that this is essential to a good Western film?
2. To what degree do you share the authors' interest in the Western? Do you feel it is essentially a type of entertainment for juveniles? Or can the form also appeal to adults, and if so, why should that be?

on structure and language

1. "Realism" is a key word in this selection, though its connotations tend to shift according to its context. Thus we have realism as a defining characteristic of TV Westerns; "documentary realism"; and "realistic" as applied to the behavior of a star of Western films, Wild Bill Elliott. What different shades of meaning do you find in these usages? Why do the authors assume that "realistic" is an antonym to "chivalrous"? Do you agree?
2. How much specific detail—concerning, say, acting or plot or style—do the authors give us about the films they mention? Do they offer enough anecdote and example to make their points about the "moral contents" of the films clear and vivid?
3. What factors contribute to the difference in tone between this essay and Riesman's?

THE GANGSTER
AS TRAGIC HERO

Robert Warshow

America, as a social and political organization, is committed to a cheerful view of life. It could not be otherwise. The sense of tragedy is a luxury of aristocratic societies, where the fate of the individual is not conceived of as having a direct and legitimate political importance, being determined by a fixed and supra-political—that is, non-controversial—moral order or fate. Modern equalitarian societies, however, whether democratic or authoritarian in their political forms, always base themselves on the claim that they are making life happier; the avowed function of the modern state, at least in its ultimate terms, is not only to regulate social relations, but also to determine the quality and the possibilities of human life in general. Happiness thus becomes the chief political issue—in a sense, the only political issue—and for that reason it can never be treated as an issue at all. If an American or a Russian is unhappy, it implies a certain reprobation of his society, and therefore, by a logic of which we can all recognize the necessity, it becomes an obligation of citizenship to be cheerful; if the authorities find it necessary, the citizen may even be compelled to make a public display of his cheerfulness on important occasions, just as he may be conscripted into the army in time of war.

Naturally, this civic responsibility rests most strongly upon the organs of mass culture. The individual citizen may still be permitted his private unhappiness so long as it does not take on political significance, the extent of this tolerance being determined by how large an area of private life the society can accommodate. But every production of mass culture is a public act and must conform with accepted notions of the public good. Nobody seriously questions the principle that it is the function of mass culture to maintain public morale, and certainly nobody in the mass audience objects to having his morale maintained.[1] At a time when the normal condition of the citizen is a state of anxiety, euphoria spreads over our culture like the broad smile of an idiot. In terms of attitudes towards life, there is very little difference between a "happy" movie like *Good News,* which ignores death and suffering, and a "sad" movie like *A Tree Grows in Brooklyn,* which uses death and suffering as incidents in the service of a higher optimism.

But, whatever its effectiveness as a source of consolation and a means of pressure for maintaining "positive" social attitudes, this optimism is fundamentally satisfying to no one, not even to those who would be most disoriented without its support. Even within the area of mass culture, there always exists a current of opposition, seeking to express by whatever means are available to it that sense of desperation and inevitable failure which optimism itself helps to create. Most often, this opposition is confined to rudimentary or semi-literate forms: in mob politics and journalism, for example, or in certain kinds of religious enthusiasm. When it does enter the field of art, it is likely to be disguised or attenuated: in an unspecific form of expression like jazz, in the basically harmless nihilism of the Marx Brothers, in the continually reasserted strain of hopelessness that often seems to be the real meaning of the soap opera. The gangster film is remarkable in that it fills the need for disguise (though not sufficiently to avoid arousing uneasiness) without requiring any serious distortion.

[1] In her testimony before the House Committee on Un-American Activities, Mrs. Leila Rogers said that the movie *None But the Lonely Heart* was un-American because it was gloomy. Like so much else that was said during the unhappy investigation of Hollywood, this statement was at once stupid and illuminating. One knew immediately what Mrs. Rogers was talking about; she had simply been insensitive enough to carry her philistinism to its conclusion.

From its beginnings, it has been a consistent and astonishingly complete presentation of the modern sense of tragedy.[2]

In its initial character, the gangster film is simply one example of the movies' constant tendency to create fixed dramatic patterns that can be repeated indefinitely with a reasonable expectation of profit. One gangster film follows another as one musical or one Western follows another. But this rigidity is not necessarily opposed to the requirements of art. There have been very successful types of art in the past which developed such specific and detailed conventions as almost to make individual examples of the type interchangeable. This is true, for example, of Elizabethan revenge tragedy and Restoration comedy.

For such a type to be successful means that its conventions have imposed themselves upon the general consciousness and become the accepted vehicles of a particular set of attitudes and a particular aesthetic effect. One goes to any individual example of the type with very definite expectations, and originality is to be welcomed only in the degree that it intensifies the expected experience without fundamentally altering it. Moreover, the relationship between the conventions which go to make up such a type and the real experience of its audience or the real facts of whatever situation it pretends to describe is of only secondary importance and does not determine its aesthetic force. It is only in an ultimate sense that the type appeals to its audience's experience of reality; much more immediately, it appeals to previous experience of the type itself: it creates its own field of reference.

Thus the importance of the gangster film, and the nature and intensity of its emotional and aesthetic impact, cannot be measured in terms of the place of the gangster himself or the importance of the problem of crime in American life. Those European movie-goers who think there is a gangster on every corner in New York are certainly deceived, but defenders of the "positive" side of American culture are equally deceived if they think it relevant to point out that most Americans have never seen a gangster. What matters is that the experience of the gangster *as an experience of art* is universal to Americans. There is almost nothing we

[2] Efforts have been made from time to time to bring the gangster film into line with the prevailing optimism and social constructiveness of our culture; *Kiss of Death* is a recent example. These efforts are usually unsuccessful; the reasons for their lack of success are interesting in themselves, but I shall not be able to discuss them here.

understand better or react to more readily or with quicker intelligence. The Western film, though it seems never to diminish in popularity, is for most of us no more than the folklore of the past, familiar and understandable only because it has been repeated so often. The gangster film comes much closer. In ways that we do not easily or willingly define, the gangster speaks for us, expressing that part of the American psyche which rejects the qualities and the demands of modern life, which rejects "Americanism" itself.

The gangster is the man of the city, with the city's language and knowledge, with its queer and dishonest skills and its terrible daring, carrying his life in his hands like a placard, like a club. For everyone else, there is at least the theoretical possibility of another world—in that happier American culture which the gangster denies, the city does not really exist; it is only a more crowded and more brightly lit country—but for the gangster there is only the city; he must inhabit it in order to personify it: not the real city, but that dangerous and sad city of the imagination which is so much more important, which is the modern world. And the gangster—though there are real gangsters—is also, and primarily, a creature of the imagination. The real city, one might say, produces only criminals; the imaginary city produces the gangster: he is what we want to be and what we are afraid we may become.

Thrown into the crowd without background or advantages, with only those ambiguous skills which the rest of us—the real people of the real city—can only pretend to have, the gangster is required to make his way, to make his life and impose it on others. Usually, when we come upon him, he has already made his choice or the choice has already been made for him, it doesn't matter which: we are not permitted to ask whether at some point he could have chosen to be something else than what he is.

The gangster's activity is actually a form of rational enterprise, involving fairly definite goals and various techniques for achieving them. But this rationality is usually no more than a vague background; we know, perhaps, that the gangster sells liquor or that he operates a numbers racket; often we are not given even that much information. So his activity becomes a kind of pure criminality: he hurts people. Certainly our response to the gangster film is most consistently and most universally a response to sadism; we gain the double satisfaction of participating vicariously in the gangster's sadism and then seeing it turned against the gangster himself.

But on another level the quality of irrational brutality and the quality of rational enterprise become one. Since we do not see the rational and routine aspects of the gangster's behavior, the practice of brutality—the quality of unmixed criminality—becomes the totality of his career. At the same time, we are always conscious that the whole meaning of this career is a drive for success: the typical gangster film presents a steady upward progress followed by a very precipitate fall. Thus brutality itself becomes at once the means to success and the content of success —a success that is defined in its most general terms, not as accomplishment or specific gain, but simply as the unlimited possibility of aggression. (In the same way, film presentations of businessmen tend to make it appear that they achieve their success by talking on the telephone and holding conferences and that success *is* talking on the telephone and holding conferences.)

From this point of view, the initial contact between the film and its audience is an agreed conception of human life: that man is a being with the possibilities of success or failure. This principle, too, belongs to the city; one must emerge from the crowd or else one is nothing. On that basis the necessity of the action is established, and it progresses by inalterable paths to the point where the gangster lies dead and the principle has been modified: there is really only one possibility—failure. The final meaning of the city is anonymity and death.

In the opening scene of *Scarface*, we are shown a successful man; we know he is successful because he has just given a party of opulent proportions and because he is called Big Louie. Through some monstrous lack of caution, he permits himself to be alone for a few moments. We understand from this immediately that he is about to be killed. No convention of the gangster film is more strongly established than this: it is dangerous to be alone. And yet the very conditions of success make it impossible not to be alone, for success is always the establishment of an *individual* preeminence that must be imposed on others, in whom it automatically arouses hatred; the successful man is an outlaw. The gangster's whole life is an effort to assert himself as an individual, to draw himself out of the crowd, and he always dies *because* he is an individual; the final bullet thrusts him back, makes him, after all, a failure. "Mother of God," says the dying Little Caesar, "is this the end of Rico?"—speaking of himself thus in the third person because what has been brought low is not the undifferentiated *man*, but the individual with a name, the gangster, the success; even to himself he is a creature of the imagination. (T. S. Eliot has pointed out that a number of Shakespeare's tragic heroes have this trick of looking at themselves dramatically; their true identity, the thing that is destroyed when they die, is something outside themselves—not a man, but a style of life, a kind of meaning.)

At bottom, the gangster is doomed because he is under the obligation to succeed, not because the means he employs are unlawful. In the deeper layers of the modern consciousness, *all* means are unlawful, every attempt to succeed is an act of aggression, leaving one alone and guilty and defenseless among enemies: one is *punished* for success. This is our intolerable dilemma: that failure is a kind of death and success is evil and dangerous, is— ultimately–impossible. The effect of the gangster film is to embody this dilemma in the person of the gangster and resolve it by his death. The dilemma is resolved because it is *his* death, not ours. We are safe; for the moment, we can acquiesce in our failure, we can choose to fail.

EXERCISES

on film and society

1. Warshow begins by noting that "America, as a social and political organization, is committed to a cheerful view of life." Why is he careful to qualify his generalization with the phrase "as a social and political organization"?
2. To what sort of view does Warshow continually contrast the "cheerful"? How does he use that contrast in discussing the social implications of the gangster film?
3. In what deep ways, according to Warshow, does the motion picture gangster "speak for us"? How does this tie in with his point about the official "cheerful view of life"?

on film

1. How does Warshow distinguish between the influence and appeal of the gangster film and the Western?
2. Could there be such a thing as a tragic Western? Discuss both of these questions on the basis of the essays by Warshow and Fenin–Everson; then on the basis of films you have seen.

on structure and language

1. Warshow refers frequently to "mass culture," and he clearly intends his essay as an exploration into an aspect of mass culture. What does he mean by "mass culture"? How does that meaning affect the development of his essay?
2. Warshow's style is almost Spartan in its plainness, in its avoidance of fancy writing or personal asides. He hardly ever uses an adjective. Given the highly charged nature of his topic, do you find his style appropriate?

THE IMAGINATION
OF DISASTER

Susan Sontag

Ours is indeed an age of extremity. For we live under continual threat of two equally fearful, but seemingly opposed, destinies: unremitting banality and inconceivable terror. It is fantasy, served out in large rations by the popular arts, which allows most people to cope with these twin specters. For one job that fantasy can do is to lift us out of the unbearably humdrum and to distract us from terrors, real or anticipated—by an escape into exotic dangerous situations which have last-minute happy endings. But another one of the things that fantasy can do is to normalize what is psychologically unbearable, thereby inuring us to it. In the one case, fantasy beautifies the world. In the other, it neutralizes it.

The fantasy to be discovered in science fiction films does both jobs. These films reflect world-wide anxieties, and they serve to allay them. They inculcate a strange apathy concerning the processes of radiation, contamination, and destruction that I for one find haunting and depressing. The naïve level of the films neatly tempers the sense of otherness, of alien-ness, with the grossly familiar. In particular, the dialogue of most science fiction films, which is generally of a monumental but often touching banality, makes them wonderfully, unintentionally funny. Lines like: "Come quickly, there's a monster in my bathtub"; "We must do something about this"; "Wait, Professor. There's someone on the telephone"; "But that's incredible"; and the old American stand-by (accompanied by brow-wiping), "I hope it works!"—are hilarious in the context of picturesque and deafening holocaust. Yet the films also contain something which is painful and in deadly earnest.

Science fiction films are one of the most accomplished of the popular art forms, and can give a great deal of pleasure to sophisticated film addicts. Part of the pleasure, indeed, comes from the sense in which these movies are in complicity with the abhorrent. It is no more, perhaps, than the way all art draws its audience into a circle of complicity with the thing represented. But in science fiction films we have to do with things which are (quite literally) unthinkable. Here, "thinking about the unthinkable"— not in the way of Herman Kahn, as a subject for calculation, but as a subject for fantasy—becomes, however inadvertently, itself a somewhat questionable act from a moral point of view. The films perpetuate clichés about identity, volition, power, knowledge, happiness, social consensus, guilt, responsibility which are, to say the least, not serviceable in our present extremity. But collective nightmares cannot be banished by demonstrating that they are, intellectually and morally, fallacious. This nightmare—the one reflected in various registers in the science fiction films—is too close to our reality.

A typical science fiction film has a form as predictable as a Western, and is made up of elements which are as classic as the saloon brawl, the blonde schoolteacher from the East, and the gun duel on the deserted main street.

One model scenario proceeds through five phases:

(1) The arrival of the thing. (Emergence of the monsters, landing of the alien space-ship, etc.) This is usually witnessed, or suspected, by just one person, who is a young scientist on a field trip. Nobody, neither his neighbors nor his colleagues, will believe him for some time. The hero is not married, but has a sympathetic though also incredulous girlfriend.

(2) Confirmation of the hero's report by a host of witnesses to a great act of destruction. (If the invaders are beings from another planet, a fruitless attempt to parley with them and get them to

leave peacefully.) The local police are summoned to deal with the situation and massacred.

(3) In the capital of the country, conferences between scientists and the military take place, with the hero lecturing before a chart, map, or blackboard. A national emergency is declared. Reports of further atrocities. Authorities from other countries arrive in black limousines. All international tensions are suspended in view of the planetary emergency. This stage often includes a rapid montage of news broadcasts in various languages, a meeting at the UN, and more conferences between the military and the scientists. Plans are made for destroying the enemy.

(4) Further atrocities. At some point the hero's girlfriend is in grave danger. Massive counterattacks by international forces, with brilliant displays of rocketry, rays, and other advanced weapons, are all unsuccessful. Enormous military casualties, usually by incineration. Cities are destroyed and/or evacuated. There is an obligatory scene here of panicked crowds stampeding along a highway or a big bridge, being waved on by numerous policemen who, if the film is Japanese, are immaculately white-gloved, preternaturally calm, and call out in dubbed English, "Keep moving. There is no need to be alarmed."

(5) More conferences, whose motif is: "They must be vulnerable to something." Throughout, the hero has been experimenting in his lab on this. The final strategy, upon which all hopes depend, is drawn up; the ultimate weapon—often a super-powerful, as yet untested, nuclear device—is mounted. Countdown. Final repulse of the monster or invaders. Mutual congratulations, while the hero and girlfriend embrace cheek to cheek and scan the skies sturdily. "But have we seen the last of them?"

The film I have just described should be in Technicolor and on a wide screen. Another typical scenario is simpler and suited to black-and-white films with a lower budget. It has four phases:

(1) The hero (usually, but not always, a scientist) and his girlfriend, or his wife and children, are disporting themselves in some innocent ultra-normal middle-class house in a small town, or on vacation (camping, boating). Suddenly, someone starts behaving strangely or some innocent form of vegetation becomes monstrously enlarged and ambulatory. If a character is pictured driv-

ing an automobile, something gruesome looms up in the middle of the road. If it is night, strange lights hurtle across the sky.

(2) After following the thing's tracks, or determining that It is radioactive, or poking around a huge crater—in short, conducting some sort of crude investigation—the hero tries to warn the local authorities, without effect; nobody believes anything is amiss. The hero knows better. If the thing is tangible, the house is elaborately barricaded. If the invading alien is an invisible parasite, a doctor or friend is called in, who is himself rather quickly killed or "taken possession of" by the thing.

(3) The advice of anyone else who is consulted proves useless. Meanwhile, It continues to claim other victims in the town, which remains implausibly isolated from the rest of the world. General helplessness.

(4) One of two possibilities. Either the hero prepares to do battle alone, accidentally discovers the thing's one vulnerable point, and destroys it. Or, he somehow manages to get out of town and succeeds in laying his case before competent authorities. They, along the lines of the first script but abridged, deploy a complex technology which (after initial setbacks) finally prevails against the invaders.

Another version of the second script opens with the scientist-hero in his laboratory, which is located in the basement or on the grounds of his tasteful, prosperous house. Through his experiments, he unwittingly causes a frightful metamorphosis in some class of plants or animals, which turn carnivorous and go on a rampage. Or else, his experiments have caused him to be injured (sometimes irrevocably) or "invaded" himself. Perhaps he has been experimenting with radiation, or has built a machine to communicate with beings from other planets or to transport him to other places or times.

Another version of the first script involves the discovery of some fundamental alteration in the conditions of existence of our planet, brought about by nuclear testing, which will lead to the extinction in a few months of all human life. For example: the temperature of the earth is becoming too high or too low to support life, or the earth is cracking in two, or it is gradually being blanketed by lethal fallout.

A third script, somewhat but not altogether different from the first two, concerns a journey through space—to the moon, or some other planet. What the space-voyagers commonly discover is that the alien terrain is in a state of dire emergency, itself threatened by extra-planetary invaders or nearing extinction through the practice of nuclear warfare. The terminal dramas of the first and second scripts are played out there, to which is added a final problem of getting away from the doomed and/or hostile planet and back to Earth.

I am aware, of course, that there are thousands of science fiction novels (their heyday was the late 1940's), not to mention the transcriptions of science fiction themes which, more and more, provide the principal subject matter of comic books. But I propose to discuss science fiction films (the present period began in 1950 and continues, considerably abated, to this day) as an independent sub-genre, without reference to the novels from which, in many cases, they were adapted. For while novel and film may share the same plot, the fundamental difference between the resources of the novel and the film makes them quite dissimilar. Anyway, the best science fiction movies are on a far higher level, as examples of the art of the film, than the science fiction books are, as examples of the art of the novel or romance. That the films might be better than the books is an old story. Good novels rarely make good films, but excellent films are often made from poor or trivial novels.

Certainly, compared with the science fiction novels, their film counterparts have unique strengths, one of which is the immediate representation of the extraordinary: physical deformity and muta-tion, missile and rocket combat, toppling skyscrapers. The movies are, naturally, weak just where the science fiction novels (some of them), are strong—on science. But in place of an intellectual workout, they can supply something the novels can never provide —sensuous elaboration. In the films it is by means of images and sounds, not words that have to be translated by the imagination, that one can participate in the fantasy of living through one's own death and more, the death of cities, the destruction of humanity itself.

Science fiction films are not about science. They are about disaster, which is one of the oldest subjects of art. In science fiction films, disaster is rarely viewed intensively; it is always extensive. It is a matter of quantity and ingenuity. If you will, it is a question of scale. But the scale, particularly in the wide-screen Technicolor films (of which the ones by the Japanese director, Inoshiro Honda, and the American director, George Pal, are technically the most brilliant and convincing, and visually the most exciting), does raise the matter to another level.

Thus, the science fiction film (like a very different contemporary genre, the Happening) is concerned with the aesthetics of destruction, with the peculiar beauties to be found in wreaking havoc, making a mess. And it is in the imagery of destruction that the core of a good science fiction film lies. This is the disadvantage of the cheap film—in which the monster appears or the rocket lands in a small dull-looking town. (Hollywood budget needs usually dictate that the town be in the Arizona or California desert. In *The Thing from Another World* [1951], the rather sleazy and confined set is supposed to be an encampment near the North Pole.) Still, good black-and-white science fiction films have been made. But a bigger budget, which usually means Technicolor, allows a much greater play back and forth among several model environments. There is the populous city. There is the lavish but ascetic interior of the space ship—either the invaders' or ours—replete with streamlined chromium fixtures and dials, and machines whose complexity is indicated by the number of colored lights they flash and strange noises they emit. There is the laboratory crowded with formidable machines and scientific apparatus. There is a comparatively old-fashioned looking conference room, where the scientist brings charts to explain the desperate state of things to the military. And each of these standard locales or backgrounds is subject to two modalities—intact and destroyed. We may, if we are lucky, be treated to a panorama of melting tanks, flying bodies, crashing walls, awesome craters and fissures in the earth, plummeting spacecraft, colorful deadly rays; and to a symphony of screams, weird electronic signals, the noisiest military hardware going, and the leaden tones of the laconic denizens of alien planets and their subjugated earthlings.

Certain of the primitive gratifications of science fiction films —for instance, the depiction of urban disaster on a colossally magnified scale—are shared with other types of films. Visually there is little difference between mass havoc as represented in the old horror and monster films and what we find in science fiction films, except (again) scale. In the old monster films, the monster always headed for the great city where he had to do a fair bit of rampaging, hurling buses off bridges, crumpling trains in his bare hands, toppling buildings, and so forth. The archetype is King Kong, in Schoedsach's great film of 1933, running amok, first in the African village (trampling babies, a bit of footage excised from most prints), then in New York. This is really not any different from Inoshiro Honda's *Rodan* (1957), where two giant reptiles— with a wingspan of five-hundred feet and supersonic speeds—by flapping their wings whip up a cyclone that blows most of Tokyo to smithereens. Or, the tremendous scenes of rampage by the gigantic robot who destroys half of Japan with the great incinerating ray which shoots forth from his eyes, at the beginning of Honda's *The Mysterians* (1959). Or, the destruction, by the rays from a fleet of flying saucers, of New York, Paris and Tokyo, in *Battle in Outer Space* (1960). Or, the inundation of New York in *When Worlds Collide* (1951). Or, the end of London in 1968 depicted in George Pal's *The Time Machine* (1960). Neither do these sequences differ in aesthetic intention from the destruction scenes in the big sword, sandal, and orgy color spectaculars set in Biblical and Roman times—the end of Sodom in Aldrich's *Sodom and Gomorrah*, of Gaza in de Mille's *Samson and Delilah*, of Rhodes in *The Colossus of Rhodes*, and of Rome in a dozen Nero movies. D. W. Griffith began it with the Babylon sequence in *Intolerance*, and to this day there is nothing like the thrill of watching all those expensive sets come tumbling down.

In other respects as well, the science fiction films of the 1950's take up familiar themes. The famous movie serials and comics of the 1930's of the adventures of Flash Gordon and Buck Rogers, as well as the more recent spate of comic book super-heroes with extraterrestrial origins (the most famous is Superman, a foundling from the planet, Krypton, currently described as having been exploded by a nuclear blast) share motifs with more recent science fiction movies. But there is an important difference. The old science fiction films, and most of the comics, still have an essentially innocent relation to disaster. Mainly they offer new versions of the oldest romance of all—of the strong invulnerable hero with the mysterious lineage come to do battle on behalf of good and against evil. Recent science fiction films have a decided grimness, bolstered by their much greater degree of visual credibility, which contrasts strongly with the older films. Modern historical reality has greatly enlarged the imagination of disaster, and the protagonists—perhaps by the very nature of what is visited upon them— no longer seem wholly innocent.

The lure of such generalized disaster as a fantasy is that it releases one from normal obligations. The trump card of the end-of-the-world movies—like *The Day the Earth Caught Fire* (1962)— is that great scene with New York or London or Tokyo discovered empty, its entire population annihilated. Or, as in *The World, the Flesh, and the Devil* (1959), the whole movie can be devoted to the fantasy of occupying the deserted city and starting all over again— Robinson Crusoe on a world-wide scale.

Another kind of satisfaction these films supply is extreme moral simplification—that is to say, a morally acceptable fantasy where one can give outlet to cruel or at least amoral feelings. In this respect, science fiction films partly overlap with horror films. This is the undeniable pleasure we derive from looking at freaks, at beings excluded from the category of the human. The sense of superiority over the freak conjoined in varying proportions with the titillation of fear and aversion makes it possible for moral scruples to be lifted, for cruelty to be enjoyed. The same thing happens in science fiction films. In the figure of the monster from outer space, the freakish, the ugly, and the predatory all converge —and provide a fantasy target for righteous bellicosity to discharge itself, and for the aesthetic enjoyment of suffering and disaster. Science fiction films are one of the purest forms of spectacle; that is, we are rarely inside anyone's feelings. (An exception to this is Jack Arnold's *The Incredible Shrinking Man* [1957].) We are merely spectators; we watch.

But in science fiction films, unlike horror films, there is not much horror. Suspense, shocks, surprises are mostly abjured in favor of a steady inexorable plot. Science fiction films invite a dispassionate, aesthetic view of destruction and violence—a *technological* view. Things, objects, machinery play a major role in these films. A greater range of ethical values is embodied in the décor of these films than in the people. Things, rather than the helpless humans, are the locus of values because we experience them, rather than people, as the sources of power. According to science fiction films, man is naked without his artifacts. They stand for different values, they are potent, they are what gets destroyed, and they are the indispensable tools for the repulse of the alien invaders or the repair of the damaged environment.

The science fiction films are strongly moralistic. The standard message is the one about the proper, or humane, uses of science, versus the mad, obsessional use of science. This message the science fiction films share in common with the classic horror films of the 1930's, like *Frankenstein, The Mummy, The Island of Doctor Moreau, Dr. Jekyll and Mr. Hyde*. (Georges Franju's brilliant *Les Yeux Sans Visage* [1959], called here *The Horror Chamber of Doctor Faustus*, is a more recent example.) In the horror films, we have the mad or obsessed or misguided scientist who pursues his experiments against good advice to the contrary, creates a monster or monsters, and is himself destroyed—often recognizing his folly himself, and dying in the successful effort to destroy his own creation. One science fiction equivalent of this is the scientist, usually a member of a team, who defects to the planetary invaders because "their" science is more advanced than "ours."

This is the case in *The Mysterians*, and, true to form, the renegade sees his error in the end, and from within the Mysterian space ship destroys it and himself. In *This Island Earth* (1955), the inhabitants of the beleaguered planet Metaluna propose to conquer Earth, but their project is foiled by a Metalunan scientist named Exeter who, having lived on Earth a while and learned to love Mozart, cannot abide such viciousness. Exeter plunges his space ship into the ocean after returning a glamorous pair (male and female) of American physicists to Earth. Metaluna dies. In *The Fly* (1958), the hero, engrossed in his basement-laboratory experiments on a matter-transmitting machine, uses himself as a subject, accidentally exchanges head and one arm with a housefly which had gotten into the machine, becomes a monster, and with his last shred of human will destroys his laboratory and orders his wife to kill him. His discovery, for the good of mankind, is lost.

Being a clearly labeled species of intellectual, the scientists in science fiction films are always liable to crack up or go off the deep end. In *Conquest of Space* (1955), the scientist-commander of an international expedition to Mars suddenly acquires scruples about the blasphemy involved in the undertaking, and begins reading the Bible mid-journey instead of attending to his duties. The commander's son, who is his junior officer and always addresses his father as "General," is forced to kill the old man when he tries to prevent the ship from landing on Mars. In this film, both sides of the ambivalence toward scientists are given voice. Generally, for a scientific enterprise to be treated entirely sympathetically in these films, it needs the certificate of utility. Science, viewed without ambivalence, means an efficacious response to danger. Disinterested intellectual curiosity rarely appears in any form other than caricature, as a maniacal dementia that cuts one off from normal human relations. But this suspicion is usually directed at the scientist rather than his work. The creative scientist may become a martyr to his own discovery, through an accident or by pushing things too far. The implication remains that other men, less imaginative—in short, technicians—would administer the same scientific discovery better and more safely. The most ingrained contemporary mistrust of the intellect is visited, in these movies, upon the scientist-as-intellectual.

The message that the scientist is one who releases forces which, if not controlled for good, could destroy man himself seems innocuous enough. One of the oldest images of the scientist is Shakespeare's Prospero, the over-detached scholar forcibly retired from society to a desert island, only partly in control of the magic forces in which he dabbles. Equally classic is the figure of the scientist as satanist (*Dr. Faustus,* stories of Poe and Hawthorne). Science is magic, and man has always known that there is black magic as well as white. But it is not enough to remark that contemporary attitudes—as reflected in science fiction films—remain ambivalent, that the scientist is treated both as satanist and savior. The proportions have changed, because of the new context in which the old admiration and fear of the scientist is located. For his sphere of influence is no longer local, himself or his immediate community. It is planetary, cosmic.

One gets the feeling, particularly in the Japanese films, but not only there, that mass trauma exists over the use of nuclear weapons and the possibility of future nuclear wars. Most of the science fiction films bear witness to this trauma, and in a way, attempt to exorcise it.

The accidental awakening of the super-destructive monster who has slept in the earth since prehistory is, often, an obvious metaphor for the Bomb. But there are many explicit references as well. In *The Mysterians,* a probe ship from the planet Mysteroid has landed on earth, near Tokyo. Nuclear warfare having been practiced on Mysteroid for centuries (their civilization is "more advanced than ours"), 90 per cent of those now born on the planet have to be destroyed at birth, because of defects caused by the huge amounts of Strontium 90 in their diet. The Mysterians have come to earth to marry earth women and possibly to take over our relatively uncontaminated planet. . . . In *The Incredible Shrinking Man,* the John Doe hero is the victim of a gust of radiation which blows over the water, while he is out boating with his wife; the radiation causes him to grow smaller and smaller, until at the end of the movie he steps through the fine mesh of a window screen to become "the infinitely small. . . ." In *Rodan,* a horde of monstrous carnivorous prehistoric insects, and finally a pair of giant flying reptiles (the prehistoric Archeopteryx), are hatched from dormant eggs in the depths of a mine shaft by the impact of nuclear test explosions, and go on to destroy a good part of the world before they are felled by the molten lava of a volcanic eruption. . . . In the English film, *The Day the Earth Caught Fire,* two simultaneous hydrogen bomb tests by the U.S. and Russia change by eleven degrees the tilt of the earth on its axis and alter the earth's orbit so that it begins to approach the sun.

Radiation casualties—ultimately, the conception of the whole world as a casualty of nuclear testing and nuclear warfare—is the most ominous of all the notions with which science fiction films deal. Universes become expendable. Worlds become contaminated, burnt out, exhausted, obsolete. In *Rocketship X-M* (1950), explorers from Earth land on Mars, where they learn that atomic warfare has destroyed Martian civilization. In George Pal's *The War of the Worlds* (1953), reddish spindly alligator-skinned creatures from Mars invade Earth because their planet is becoming too cold to be habitable. In *This Island Earth,* also American, the planet Metaluna, whose population has long ago been driven underground by warfare, is dying under the missile attacks of an enemy planet. Stocks of uranium, which power the force-shield shielding Metaluna, have been used up; and an unsuccessful expedition is sent to Earth to enlist earth scientists to devise new sources of nuclear power.

There is a vast amount of wishful thinking in science fiction films, some of it touching, some of it depressing. Again and again, one detects the hunger for a "good war," which poses no moral problems, admits of no moral qualifications. The imagery of science fiction films will satisfy the most bellicose addict of war films, for a lot of the satisfactions of war films pass, untransformed, into science fiction films. Examples: the dogfights between earth "fighter rockets" and alien spacecraft in the *Battle of Outer Space* (1959); the escalating firepower in the successive assaults upon the invaders in *The Mysterians,* which Dan Talbot correctly described as a nonstop holocaust; the spectacular bombardment of the underground fortress in *This Island Earth.*

Yet at the same time the bellicosity of science fiction films is neatly channeled into the yearning for peace, or for at least peaceful coexistence. Some scientist generally takes sententious note of the fact that it took the planetary invasion or cosmic disaster to make the warring nations of the earth come to their senses, and suspend their own conflicts. One of the main themes of many science fiction films—the color ones usually, because they have the budget and resources to develop the military spectacle—is this UN fantasy, a fantasy of united warfare. (The same wishful UN theme cropped up in a recent spectacular which is not science fiction, *Fifty-Five Days at Peking* [1963]. There, topically enough, the Chinese, the Boxers, play the role of Martian invaders who unite the earthmen, in this case the United States, Russia, England, France, Germany, Italy, and Japan.) A great enough disaster cancels all enmities, and calls upon the utmost concentration of the earth's resources.

Science—technology—is conceived of as the great unifier. Thus the science fiction films also project a utopian fantasy. In the classic models of utopian thinking—Plato's Republic, Campanella's City of the Sun, More's Utopia, Swift's land of the Houyhnhnms, Voltaire's Eldorado—society had worked out a perfect consensus. In these societies reasonableness had achieved an unbreakable supremacy over the emotions. Since no disagreement or social conflict was intellectually plausible, none was possible. As in Melville's *Typee,* "they all think the same." The universal rule of reason meant universal agreement. It is interesting, too, that societies in which reason was pictured as totally ascendant were also traditionally pictured as having an ascetic and/or materially frugal and economically simple mode of life. But in the utopian world community projected by science fiction films, totally pacified and ruled by scientific consensus, the demand for simplicity of material existence would be absurd.

But alongside the hopeful fantasy of moral simplification and international unity embodied in the science fiction films, lurk the deepest anxieties about contemporary existence. I don't mean only the very real trauma of the Bomb—that it has been used, that there are enough now to kill everyone on earth many times over, that those new bombs may very well be used. Besides these new anxieties about physical disaster, the prospect of universal mutilation and even annihilation, the science fiction films reflect powerful anxieties about the condition of the individual psyche.

For science fiction films may also be described as a popular mythology for the contemporary *negative* imagination about the impersonal. The other-world creatures which seek to take "us" over, are an "it," not a "they." The planetary invaders are usually zombie-like. Their movements are either cool, mechanical, or lumbering, blobby. But it amounts to the same thing. If they are nonhuman in form, they proceed with an absolutely regular, unalterable movement (unalterable save by destruction). If they are human in form—dressed in space suits, etc.—then they obey the most rigid military discipline, and display no personal characteristics whatsoever. And it is this regime of emotionlessness, of impersonality, of regimentation, which they will impose on the earth if they are successful. "No more love, no more beauty, no more pain," boasts a converted earthling in *The Invasion of the Body Snatchers* (1956). The half earthling–half alien children in *The Children of the Damned* (1960) are absolutely emotionless, move as a group and understand each other's thoughts, and are all prodigious intellects. They are the wave of the future, man in his next stage of development.

These alien invaders practice a crime which is worse than murder. They do not simply kill the person. They obliterate him. In *The War of the Worlds,* the ray which issues from the rocket ship disintegrates all persons and objects in its path, leaving no trace of them but a light ash. In Honda's *The H-Men* (1959), the creeping blob melts all flesh with which it comes in contact. If the blob, which looks like a huge hunk of red jello, and can crawl across floors and up and down walls, so much as touches your bare boot, all that is left of you is a heap of clothes on the floor. (A more articulated, size-multiplying blob is the villain in the English film *The Creeping Unknown* [1956].) In another version of this fantasy, the body is preserved but the person is entirely reconstituted as the automatized servant or agent of the alien powers. This is, of course, the vampire fantasy in new dress. The person is really dead, but he doesn't know it. He's "undead," he has become an "unperson." It happens to a whole California town in *The Invasion of the Body Snatchers,* to several earth scientists in *This Island Earth,* and to assorted innocents in *It Came from Outer Space, Attack of the Puppet People* (1961), and *The Brain Eaters* (1961). As the victim always backs away from the vampire's horrifying embrace, so in science fiction films the person always fights being "taken over"; he wants to retain his humanity. But once the deed has been done, the victim is eminently satisfied with his condition. He has not been converted from human amiability to monstrous "animal" blood-lust (a metaphoric exaggeration of sexual desire), as in the old vampire fantasy. No, he has simply become far more efficient—the very model of technocratic man, purged of emotions, volitionless, tranquil, obedient to all orders. The dark secret behind human nature used to be the upsurge of the animal—as in *King Kong.* The threat to man, his availability to dehumanization, lay in his own animality. Now the danger is understood as residing in man's ability to be turned into a machine.

The rule, of course, is that this horrible and irremediable form of murder can strike anyone in the film except the hero. The hero and his family, while grossly menaced, always escape this fact and by the end of the film the invaders have been repulsed or destroyed. I know of only one exception, *The Day That Mars Invaded Earth* (1963), in which, after all the standard struggles, the scientist-hero, his wife, and their two children are "taken over" by the alien invaders—and that's that. (The last minutes of the film show them being incinerated by the Martians' rays and their ash silhouettes flushed down their empty swimming pool, while their simulacra drive off in the family car.) Another variant but upbeat switch on the rule occurs in *The Creation of the Humanoids* (1964), where the hero discovers at the end of the film that he, too, has been turned into a metal robot, complete with highly efficient and virtually indestructible mechanical insides, although he didn't know it and detected no difference in himself. He learns, however, that he will shortly be upgraded into a "humanoid" having all the properties of a real man.

Of all the standard motifs of science fiction films, this theme of dehumanization is perhaps the most fascinating. For, as I have indicated, it is scarcely a black-and-white situation, as in the vampire films. The attitude of the science fiction films toward depersonalization is mixed. On the one hand, they deplore it as the ultimate horror. On the other hand, certain characteristics of the dehumanized invaders, modulated and disguised—such as the ascendancy of reason over feelings, the idealization of teamwork and the consensus-creating activities of science, a marked degree of moral simplification—are precisely traits of the savior-scientists. For it is interesting that when the scientist in these films is treated negatively, it is usually done through the portrayal of an individual scientist who holes up in his laboratory and neglects his fiancée or his loving wife and children, obsessed by his daring and dangerous experiments. The scientist as a loyal member of a team, and therefore considerably less individualized, is treated quite respectfully.

There is absolutely no social criticism, of even the most implicit kind, in science fiction films. No criticism, for example, of the conditions of our society which create the impersonality and dehumanization which science fiction fantasies displace onto the influence of an alien It. Also, the notion of science as a social activity, interlocking with social and political interests, is unacknowledged. Science is simply either adventure (for good or evil) or a technical response to danger. And, typically, when the fear of science is paramount—when science is conceived of as black magic rather than white—the evil has no attribution beyond that of the perverse will of an individual scientist. In science fiction films the antithesis of black magic and white is drawn as a split between technology, which is beneficent, and the errant individual will of a lone intellectual.

Thus, science fiction films can be looked at as thematically central allegory, replete with standard modern attitudes. The theme of depersonalization (being "taken over") which I have been talking about is a new allegory reflecting the age-old awareness of man that, sane, he is always perilously close to insanity and unreason. But there is something more here than just a recent, popular image which expresses man's perennial, but largely unconscious, anxiety about his sanity. The image derives most of its power from a supplementary and historical anxiety, also not experienced *consciously* by most people, about the depersonalizing conditions of modern urban society. Similarly, it is not enough to note that science fiction allegories are one of the new myths about—that is, ways of accommodating to and negating—the perennial human anxiety about death. (Myths of heaven and hell, and of ghosts, had the same function.) Again, there is a historically specifiable twist which intensifies the anxiety, or better, the trauma suffered by everyone in the middle of the 20th century when it became clear that from now on to the end of human history, every person would spend his individual life not only under the threat of individual death, which is certain, but of something almost unsupportable psychologically—collective incineration and extinction which could come any time, virtually without warning.

From a psychological point of view, the imagination of disaster does not greatly differ from one period in history to another. But from a political and moral point of view, it does. The expectation of the apocalypse may be the occasion for a radical disaffiliation from society, as when thousands of Eastern European Jews in the 17th century gave up their homes and businesses and began to trek to Palestine upon hearing that Shabbethai Zevi had been proclaimed Messiah and that the end of the world was imminent. But peoples learn the news of their own end in diverse ways.

It is reported that in 1945 the populace of Berlin received without great agitation the news that Hitler had decided to kill them all, before the Allies arrived, because they had not been worthy enough to win the war. We are, alas, more in the position of the Berliners than of the Jews of 17th-century Eastern Europe; and our response is closer to theirs, too. What I am suggesting is that the imagery of disaster in science fiction films is above all the emblem of an *inadequate response*. I do not mean to bear down on the films for this. They themselves are only a sampling, stripped of sophistication, of the inadequacy of most people's response to the unassimilable terrors that infect their consciousness. The interest of the films, aside from their considerable amount of cinematic charm, consists in this intersection between a naïvely and largely debased commercial art product and the most profound dilemmas of the contemporary situation.

EXERCISES

on film and society

1. In what ways does Miss Sontag find that science fiction films reflect the anxieties and terrors of their audience?
2. What relationship does Miss Sontag find between science fiction films and social realities?
3. The author suggests that our myths of *apocalypse* provide a main source of materials for the science fiction film, and explain a main cause of its appeal. Why does she find serious political implications in the treatment of the apocalyptic in films?

on film

1. What distinction does Miss Sontag make between the appeal of science fiction films and horror films? Comment on that distinction on the basis of science fiction films and horror films you have seen.

2. The author notes that science fiction and horror films frequently present intellectual types as "liable to crack up or go off the deep end." Would you agree with what these films suggest about "intellectual types"?

on structure and language

1. Miss Sontag is a former professor of philosophy, with a leading interest in the philosophy of esthetics. Cite passages in the essay which suggest her esthetic criteria.
2. Miss Sontag is a formidably equipped intellectual who has ventured into a "nonintellectual" terrain—that of mass culture. Show how this fact influences the diction in her essay.
3. Miss Sontag makes generous use of example to reinforce her points. Her abundant citation of examples contrasts with Warshow, who uses them as sparingly as adjectives. Does the network of examples this essay contains make it more convincing than Warshow's essay?

BLACK MEN OR GOOD NIGGERS?

Catherine Sugy

"Hit him again, man!" The shout comes from somewhere in the predominantly black audience at a 42nd St. theater. And Kirk Douglas's black servant lashes him some more; a close-up shows tears streaming down a face that is very gentle, very black.

The film is *The Way West*, the date Spring 1967. By November there's a change. The black man still belts Douglas, but for a shorter time, without a profile close-up. And without any tears. This time there is no response from the audience.

Why the cut? Who knows? We live in jittery times. But either way, does it really matter? The black man is a servant; he strikes only when he's been ordered to. And as he obeys, he cries. Tearful or tearless, the beating understraps and strengthens, not the old Adam, but the old Uncle Tom.

Race, the uses and abuses of, is back in the public eye. The *New York Times*, *passim*, tries to find where we're all at, racewise, in movies and plays. Mr. Walter Kerr, that most honest of brokers, calls for a "less realistic, more stylized theater in which color is irrelevant" (*N.Y. Times Magazine*, Oct. 15). He is not to be blamed if some see this as mere niche-picking. *Ebony*, organ of black commerce and hair-straightening, exults in the Leslie Uggams hoop-la.

The Teachers' Guide to *Media and Methods* has Professor Manchel of The University of Vermont put the finger on the "new stereotype image of the Negro". The same issue (April 1967) has a Mr. Ned Hoopes, who looks after tv at Hunter College, lauding Bill Cosby's characterization of Alex Scott, black wunderkind of NBC's *I Spy*:

> Scott is the antithesis of the Negro school dropout. A Rhodes scholar and a graduate of an impressive Ivy League College, he provides proof of the benefit to someone from a minority group who takes advantage of school.

And that, somewhere between P.S. 105 and the Harvard Yacht Club, is where Mr. Hoopes is at.

BLACK PEOPLE AS EXTRAS

"I shall try to look like a small black cloud. That will deceive them."—Winnie-the-Pooh

The sincerity of white middle-class support for black civil rights has often been questioned. But that such support is sincere is indicated by the near-universality of black extras in films produced in and around the first half of 1965, that is, at the height of the civil rights drive. In fact, apart from Grade-B potboilers and teen-age surf-rock films, the only all-white film to open in New York City between March and May of 1966 was *Inside Daisy Clover*.

For the most part these black extras appear almost exclusively in middle-class roles: members of a jury (*Madame X*), night-club guests (*Harper*), attending elaborate parties (*Do Not Disturb*), even a Western saloon-keeper (*Gunpoint*). We may assume that an audience is pleased to see blacks in positions of implied social prestige; whether it would be pleased to see them as laboring men or as protagonists in more mundane middle-class situations is something else again.

However, the black extra serves a more immediately political role than the straightforward one of underlining support for civil rights. The extras were included in the first place, not only to capitalize on civil rights support, but also to answer the very real need to think that the racial issue is being absorbed successfully. Were this not so, these extras would have vanished with the movement's collapse—as of course it has collapsed, under the weight of the Vietnam-induced, violence-oriented domestic crisis in the cities.

Has the older use of extras changed in any way? As of the Fall of 1967 they appear less frequently and in different situations —although in early '67 that particular use was spreading even to conventional teen-age films (Elvis Presley's *Spinout*, Troy Dona-hue's *Come Spy With Me*). What change there has been may be credited to the increasing politicization of movies, for it is becoming best either to leave blacks out altogether or to represent them with a small role rather than an extra appearance. Even so, the extra still turns up, often lighter-skinned, discreetly middle-class, the very model of the "spook" figure satirized by black activists.

A brief word on the old Uncle Tom role in its straight form: Till the end of the 40's, a popular black role was that of loving servant, a role that has since been extensively adapted, even though it still shows up undiluted. The Devoted Servant is of course an international figure, tending to appear in the literature of countries with an acute class struggle—the Russian *muzhik* or French *confidante* maid. Admittedly such figures may be useful in the plot of a play or book, but their appeal remains sociological. Often they will point up the hero's goodness—he is kind "even to a servant". And while servants are working-class figures, their devotion is proof that "they aren't all dangerous". Uncle Tom, by his love, gives the dominant classes the certainty both of their virtue and of their survival. He reassures them.

Thus while the traditional approach would be too much for this hyped-up age, the gimmick remains wonderfully alive. At the beginning of *The Trouble With Angels*, Hayley Mills' girl companion bumps into a black train conductor and excuses herself shyly; he smiles and nods. Or in *Come Blow Your Horn* and *A Guide For The Married Man* Frank Sinatra or Walter Mathau stop to pay a black delivery man or flower vendor. The blacks say "thank you".

Everybody's just doing their thing.

BLACK SUPPORTING ROLES

"A Whiter Shade of Pale"—New Song

These could equally well be filled by whites—but this would miss out on the socio-politics. What is most interesting about black support roles is what they are not: male parts follow a rigid formula. And there are few female roles.

To take the second one first: that there should be few roles for black actresses is the result of the stereotyping of women in the general run of American movies. Women are for decoration and sex. This can pass with white actresses; with black women it's more difficult. The folklore that white American men are uncomfortable about black women would seem to be borne out by the emphatic unsexiness of black movie actresses.

As for black male support roles, at first glance the sky's the limit. A Western trapper (*The Professionals*), soldier-convict (*The Dirty Dozen*), gladiator (*Spartacus*), football star (*The Fortune Cookie*), Harlem gangster (*The Pawnbroker*) and a detective (*Penelope*). Social mobility everywhere.

The servant role has changed. Or has it just expanded? Does it, despite the change, actually continue to conform with an image that has supposedly been rejected?

World War Two comes into play here. The servant of the forties became the war-buddy of the fifties and early sixties, (*Oceans 11; The Manchurian Candidate*). There was the added convenience of credibility; servility was, apparently, left behind in Europe or Guadalcanal. And the old war-buddy could be a sentimental figure, while at the same time not being all that close. In other words he fulfilled what seem to be the three absolutes for contemporary black roles: that he not come too close to whites, that he love them, and that he be entirely positive.

Every subsequent part has met these criteria. Like the extra who is a nightclub guest but misses out on the barbecue, the role of detective, athlete, underworld boss, schoolteacher, tells the audience that this black man has made it, without, in the plot, bringing him too near.

And every role shows the black helping whites. In *The Professionals,* the trapper is one of four horsemen sent on a mission to Mexico. There's a lot of fighting and dying, but the only killing our man does is to save his white friends. In *The Dirty Dozen,* the black convict acts with special bravery, kills the villain, and dies. Conspicuously. In *Spartacus* only the black gladiator likes

Kirk Douglas (except of course for the heroine). In *The Fortune Cookie*, the football player voluntarily comes close to becoming Jack Lemmon's servant. He calls Lemmon "my buddy."

And, finally, black roles are wholly positive. No bad, or even complex black people is the rule.

To sum up: these films adapt the "Negro" formula. They present a view meant to be honestly opposed to previous stereotypes. But the formula remains: sexual guilt is sidestepped by turning black women into the most puritanical figures in Hollywood. And the men must be excessively good, in order to calm a fear which, though unformulated, is real.

THE BLACK STAR

"Pale hands I loved beside the Shalimar"—Old song.

The most famous black movie star is Sidney Poitier. He is handsome, sophisticated, gentlemanly, cultured; his occupation—student, bank employee, reporter, detective, teacher—shows him to be boss. He automatically fulfills the first demand on the currently acceptable black, that he help whites feel that their society accepts him. Moreover, in his help to whites, his image again is Uncle Tom refurbished; and his films, although with some elaboration, again emphasize remoteness and victimization.

Poitier has no worries of his own. The plot of each film hinges on white problems and his success in solving them. He is the Black Knight on Westchester Avenue. In *A Slender Thread* he saves a woman from suicide and reconciles her with her husband. In *To Sir, With Love* he teaches teen-agers the middle-class proprieties. In *Lilies Of The Field* he helps build a church for German nuns. In *In The Heat Of The Night* he solves a murder case. And in *A Patch Of Blue* he rescues a blind girl from her slum home. In every picture he is far more wise than the whites. And in every picture, by gentleness and tact, he helps.

But what about the criterion of closeness? Here we may distinguish between black support role and black star role. In the former, particularly if the role is a short one, the black may enter the film in some professional capacity—second detective in

Penelope, secretary in *Doctor, You've Got To Be Kidding.* This is called the natural, or casual entry. But in more substantial support roles, and emphatically in star billing, the black must enter by accident. This is known as the accidental entry—literally true in *The Fortune Cookie,* in which our football player becomes involved by injuring Jack Lemmon during the game.

In the case of Poitier, his lack of substantial ties with the white world is established at the beginning and end of each film. In *In The Heat Of The Night* his involvement becomes almost a parody of the accidental formula. He was just visiting his sick mother in Mississippi.

The last scene in a Poitier film does two things. It shows black-white contact coming to an end; it further shows the divorce to be a result of black decision. In *A Slender Thread,* he is invited by a policeman to meet a woman he's saved. "Oh, no," he replies, gently smiling. In *A Patch Of Blue,* he puts Elizabeth Hartmann into the car taking her to the institution. Again gently smiling and with much shaking of the head and sighing, we infer, as she does not, that it's the last time. And so on. *To Sir, With Love* does have him stay on teaching. But his students have graduated and as the theme song says: "The time has come for closing books/ and long last looks must end/ and as I leave I know that I/ am leaving my best friend." In any event the good teacher image is ideal here, since traditionally this is the person of whom one retains a sentimental memory, without any lasting connection. Rather, in fact, like a servant. Or a war-buddy.

Thus the separation theme is further elaborated in the Poitier films by the act of refusal. This is particularly apposite when there's a romantic angle. (Why, incidentally, are the female leads in Poitier films all previously unknown actresses? Elizabeth Hartmann, Katharine Houghton? Very odd.)

The Poitier-image, then, is the most recent version of the American knight-errant. He appears unexpectedly, solves problems, is always unmarried, has no personal worries, and his background is a mystery. The climax, if that is the word, is reached in *Lilies Of The Field* in which he drives away into the evening, still leading the nuns in song.

THE EVERYWHERE THREAT

"Every Heffalump that he counted was making straight
for a pot of Pooh's honey, *and eating it all*."
—Winnie-the-Pooh (emphasis in the original.)

It should not perhaps be necessary to underline the fact that the films under discussion are made by white men, with white money, for white audiences. And they will reflect in varying degrees the fears, hopes and wishes of these audiences. What, then, is the connection between racial and class animosity? And if there is such a connection, how does it express itself?

One Potato, Two Potato provides something of a text. Here the black lead is middle-class. He works for a corporation, his family resemble solid New England farmers. Like Poitier, in *A Patch of Blue,* he falls in love with a white woman. Unlike Poitier, he marries her and they have a baby; Poitier doesn't even kiss his girlfriend. His wife is his social equal; black militancy—the acid test—is portrayed through his father's pride. There is some sense of the existence of a black collectivity even if it is more or less ignored. *One Potato, Two Potato* was an independent film.

A Patch Of Blue changes all that. It was released in the Spring of 1966, about a year and a half after *Potato.* Poitier's girlfriend is blind, lives in a slum, her grandfather is a terrible drinker, her mother is a whore and a waitress. This is not Poitier's scene. Black militancy this time is represented by his brother, probably since *Birth Of A Nation* the first black who is shown to be really rotten and awful. But then: "We don't agree on race or politics," says Poitier.

The extraordinary performance of Shelley Winters is crucial here. She plays the mother with a rare vulgarity. No heart of gold lurking underneath her whore's chatter, this is the underclass as the middle class really sees it. Naturally she hates blacks as the underclass is supposed to. Naturally the middle class whites in the film are seen to ignore her "racial" outbursts. Naturally Poitier will be beautiful to her daughter and teach her to say "aren't" instead of "ain't", Mozart instead of jazz. Rarely has a film provided such a feast to the bourgeois sensibility: on the one hand, it is positively invited to indulge its hatred of its own underclass

—you just love to hate Shelley Winters—on the other hand it is titillated at the prospect of being told once more that it, at least, is not racist—you just love to love Sidney Poitier—and on the third hand, it is invited to join the consensus of the beautiful people—itself, nice Negroes, deserving poor like winsome, blind Elizabeth Hartmann—against the uglies, the Shelley Winters and the militants and the things that go bang in the ghettos. And the trick is turned by adopting a "liberal" attitude to the secondary problem of race.

On this reading, then, politics is seen as a hardy annual in American films. The image of the Old Tom refurbished as knight-errant provides political sanction for a white middle-class attitude that admits a black man with proper credentials to a share in power. It helps to continue the tradition of ignoring the real roots of violence in the ghettos while allaying fears of that violence. As the white problem becomes more critical, the Poitier films become more popular. *To Sir, With Love* and *In The Heat Of The Night* were released into the heat of the '67 summer, while the older films, particularly *A Patch Of Blue,* are regularly trotted out for re-runs.

However, it is probable that ghetto explosions may not be the deepest source of racial anxiety, since, in the last resort, one-tenth of the population is held to be containable. The real sense of menace comes from foreign revolution. This, accurately, is seen to be non-white. It would require another study to delineate some of the twists and turns that are accompanying the portrayal of orientals in movies—a critical eye might be cast on the early James Coburn efforts, for example. It may be the return of Fu Manchu is upon us. And the connection between the socio-political use of black people and these new substitute-blacks might provide further insight into the heart of darkness that is American racism.

EXERCISES

on film and society

1. The author notes that the frequent appearance of Negroes in films of the mid-sixties was nonetheless "almost exclusively

in middle-class roles." What are the social implications of this? What are its ironic overtones?

2. How does Miss Sugy universalize the Uncle Tom figure in films; that is, show how the political implications of the type go beyond that of race.

3. Explain how the main point of the essay is clearly implicit in its title.

on film

1. If you have seen any of the films Miss Sugy mentions, would you say their treatment of white people is any more serious— or unstereotyped—than their treatment of blacks? Consider any recent film you have seen from the point of view of the way it breaks away—or fails to break away—from stereotypes in its presentation of its characters.

2. On what counts does the author find the treatment of black-white relationships in recent films evasive? Discuss her views on the basis of films you have seen.

on structure and language

1. In this essay a good deal of information and insight is compressed in brief space. What is its overall method of organization?

2. Current idiomatic "hip" expressions are used as a means of ironic counterpoint to the main argument. Cite some instances of this.

3. The rhetorical question is relied on throughout the essay. What function does it chiefly serve?

MOVIES
ON TELEVISION

Pauline Kael

A few years ago, a jet on which I was returning to California after
a trip to New York was instructed to delay landing for a half
hour. The plane circled above the San Francisco area, and spread
out under me were the farm where I was born, the little town
where my grandparents were buried, the city where I had gone
to school, the cemetery where my parents were, the homes of my
brothers and sisters, Berkeley, where I had gone to college, and
the house where at that moment, while I hovered high above, my
daughter and my dogs were awaiting my return. It was as though
my whole life was suspended in time—as though no matter where
you'd gone, what you'd done, the past were all still there, present,
if you just got up high enough to attain the proper perspective.
Sometimes I get a comparable sensation when I turn from the
news programs or the discussion shows on television to the old
movies. So much of what formed our tastes and shaped our
experiences, and so much of the garbage of our youth that we
never thought we'd see again—preserved and exposed to eyes
and minds that might well want not to believe that this was an
important part of our past. Now these movies are there for new

generations, to whom they cannot possibly have the same impact or meaning, because they are all jumbled together, out of historical sequence. Even what may deserve an honorable position in movie history is somehow dishonored by being so available, so meaninglessly present. Everything is in hopeless disorder, and that is the way new generations experience our movie past. In the other arts, something like natural selection takes place: only the best or the most significant or influential or successful works compete for our attention. Moreover, those from the past are likely to be touched up to accord with the taste of the present. In popular music, old tunes are newly orchestrated. A small repertory of plays is continually reinterpreted for contemporary meanings—the great ones for new relevance, the not so great rewritten, tackily "brought up to date," or deliberately treated as period pieces. By contrast, movies, through the accidents of commerce, are sold in blocks or packages to television, the worst with the mediocre and the best, the successes with the failures, the forgotten with the half forgotten, the ones so dreary you don't know whether you ever saw them or just others like them with some so famous you can't be sure whether you actually saw them or only imagined what they were like. A lot of this stuff never really made it with any audience; it played in small towns or it was used to soak up the time just the way TV in bars does.

There are so many things that we, having lived through them, or passed over them, never want to think about again. But in movies nothing is cleaned away, sorted out, purposefully discarded. (The destruction of negatives in studio fires or deliberately, to save space, was as indiscriminate as the preservation and resale.) There's a kind of hopelessness about it: what does not deserve to last lasts, and so it all begins to seem one big pile of junk, and some people say, "Movies never really were any good —except maybe the Bogarts." If the same thing had happened in literature or music or painting—if we were constantly surrounded by the piled-up inventory of the past—it's conceivable that modern man's notions of culture and civilization would be very different. Movies, most of them produced as fodder to satisfy the appetite for pleasure and relaxation, turned out to have magical properties —indeed, to *be* magical properties. This fodder can be fed to people over and over again. Yet, not altogether strangely, as the years wear on it doesn't please their palates, though many will go on swallowing it, just because nothing tastier is easily accessible. Watching old movies is like spending an evening with those people next door. They bore us, and we wouldn't go out of our way to see them; we drop in on them because they're so close. If it took some effort to see old movies, we might try to find out which were the good ones, and if people saw only the good ones maybe they would still respect old movies. As it is, people sit and watch movies that audiences walked out on thirty years ago. Like Lot's wife, we are tempted to take another look, attracted not by evil but by something that seems much more shameful—our own innocence. We don't try to reread the girls' and boys' "series" books of our adolescence—the very look of them is dismaying. The textbooks we studied in grammar school are probably more "dated" than the movies we saw then, but we never look at the old schoolbooks, whereas we keep seeing on TV the movies that represent the same stage in our lives and played much the same part in them—as things we learned from and, in spite of, went beyond.

Not all old movies look bad now, of course; the good ones are still good—surprisingly good, often, if you consider how much of the detail is lost on television. Not only the size but the shape of the image is changed, and, indeed, almost all the specifically visual elements are so distorted as to be all but completely destroyed. On television, a cattle drive or a cavalry charge or a chase—the climax of so many a big movie—loses the dimensions of space and distance that made it exciting, that sometimes made it great. And since the structural elements—the rhythm, the buildup, the suspense—are also partly destroyed by deletions and commercial breaks and the interruptions incidental to home viewing, it's amazing that the bare bones of performance, dialogue, story, good directing, and (especially important for close-range viewing) good editing can still make an old movie more entertaining than almost anything new on television. (That's why old movies are taking over television—or, more accurately, vice versa.) The verbal slapstick of the newspaper-life comedies—*Blessed Event, Roxie Hart, His Girl Friday*—may no longer be fresh (partly because it has been so widely imitated), but it's still funny. Movies with good, fast, energetic talk seem better than ever on television—still not great but, on television, better than what *is* great. (And as we listen to the tabloid journalists insulting the corrupt politicians, we respond once again to the happy effrontery of that period when the targets of popular satire were still small enough for us to laugh at without choking.) The wit of dialogue comedies like Preston Sturges's *Unfaithfully Yours* isn't much diminished, nor does a tight melodrama like *Double Indemnity* lose a great deal. Movies like Joseph L. Mankiewicz's *A Letter to Three Wives* and *All About Eve* look practically the same on television as in theatres, because they have almost no visual dimensions to lose. In them the camera serves primarily to show us the person who is going to speak the next presumably bright line—a scheme that on television, as in theatres, is acceptable only when the line *is* bright. Horror and fantasy films like Karl Freund's *The Mummy* or Robert Florey's *The Murders in the Rue Morgue* —even with the loss, through miniaturization, of imaginative special effects—are surprisingly effective, perhaps because they are so primitive in their appeal that the qualities of the imagery matter less than the basic suggestions. Fear counts for more than finesse, and viewing horror films is far more frightening at home than in the shared comfort of an audience that breaks the tension with derision.

Other kinds of movies lose much of what made them worth looking at—the films of Von Sternberg, for example, designed in light and shadow, or the subtleties of Max Ophuls, or the lyricism of Satyajit Ray. In the box the work of these men is not as lively or as satisfying as the plain good movies of lesser directors. Reduced to the dead grays of a cheap television print, Orson Welles' *The Magnificent Ambersons*—an uneven work that is nevertheless a triumphant conquest of the movie medium—is as lifelessly dull as a newspaper Wirephoto of a great painting. But when people say of a "big" movie like *High Noon* that it has dated or that it doesn't hold up, what they are really saying is that their judgment was faulty or has changed. They may have overresponded to its publicity and reputation or to its attempt to deal with a social problem or an idea, and may have ignored the banalities surrounding that attempt; now that the idea doesn't seem so daring, they notice the rest. Perhaps it was a traditional drama that was

new to them and that they thought was new to the world; everyone's "golden age of movies" is the period of his first moviegoing
and just before—what he just missed or wasn't allowed to see.
(The Bogart films came out just before today's college kids started
going.)

Sometimes we suspect, and sometimes rightly, that our memory has improved a picture—that imaginatively we made it what
we knew it could have been or should have been—and, fearing
this, we may prefer memory to new contact. We'll remember it
better if we don't see it again—we'll remember what it meant
to us. The nostalgia we may have poured over a performer or
over our recollections of a movie has a way of congealing when
we try to renew the contact. But sometimes the experience of
reseeing is wonderful—a confirmation of the general feeling that
was all that remained with us from childhood. And we enjoy the
fresh proof of the rightness of our responses that reseeing the film
gives us. We reexperience what we once felt, and memories flood
back. Then movies seem magical—all those madeleines waiting
to be dipped in tea. What looks bad in old movies is the culture
of which they were part and which they expressed—a tone of
American life that we have forgotten. When we see First World
War posters, we are far enough away from their patriotic primi-
tivism to be amused at the emotions and sentiments to which they
appealed. We can feel charmed but superior. It's not so easy to cut
ourselves off from old movies and the old selves who responded
to them, because they're not an isolated part of the past held up
for derision and amusement and wonder. Although they belong to
the same world as stories in *Liberty,* old radio shows, old phonograph records, an America still divided between hayseeds and
city slickers, and although they may seem archaic, their pastness
isn't so very past. It includes the last decade, last year, yesterday.

Though in advertising movies for TV the recentness is the
lure, for many of us what constitutes the attraction is the dated-
ness, and the earlier movies are more compelling than the ones of
the fifties or the early sixties. Also, of course, the movies of the
thirties and forties look better technically, because, ironically, the
competition with television that made movies of the fifties and
sixties enlarge their scope and their subject matter has resulted

in their looking like a mess in the box—the sides of the image lopped off, the crowds and vistas a boring blur, the color altered, the epic themes incongruous and absurd on the little home screen. In a movie like *The Robe,* the large-scale production values that were depended on to attract TV viewers away from their sets become a negative factor. But even if the quality of the image were improved, these movies are too much like the ones we can see in theatres to be interesting at home. At home, we like to look at those stiff, carefully groomed actors of the thirties, with their clipped, Anglophile stage speech and their regular, clean-cut features—walking profiles, like the figures on Etruscan vases and almost as remote. And there is the faithless wife—how will she decide between her lover and her husband, when they seem as alike as two wax grooms on a wedding cake? For us, all three are doomed not by sin and disgrace but by history. Audiences of the period may have enjoyed these movies for their action, their story, their thrills, their wit, and all this high living. But through our window on the past we see the actors acting out other dramas as well. The Middle European immigrants had children who didn't speak the king's English and, after the Second World War, didn't even respect it so much. A flick of the dial and we are in the fifties amid the slouchers, with their thick lips, shapeless noses, and shaggy haircuts, waiting to say their lines until they think them out, then mumbling something that is barely speech. How long, O Warren Beatty, must we wait before we turn back to beautiful stick figures like Phillips Holmes?

We can take a shortcut through the hell of many lives, turning the dial from the social protest of the thirties to the films of the same writers and directors in the fifties—full of justifications for blabbing, which they shifted onto characters in oddly unrelated situations. We can see in the films of the forties the displaced artists of Europe—the anti-Nazi exiles like Conrad Veidt, the refugees like Peter Lorre, Fritz Kortner, and Alexander Granach. And what are they playing? Nazis, of course, because they have accents, and so for Americans—for the whole world—they become images of Nazi brutes. Or we can look at the patriotic sentiments of the Second World War years and those actresses, in their orgies of ersatz nobility, giving their lives—or, at the very least, their bodies—to save their country. It was sickening at the time; it's perversely amusing now—part of the spectacle of our common culture.

Probably in a few years some kid watching *The Sandpiper* on television will say what I recently heard a kid say about *Mrs. Miniver:* "And to think they really believed it in those days." Of course, we didn't. We didn't accept nearly as much in old movies as we may now fear we did. Many of us went to see big-name pictures just as we went to *The Night of the Iguana,* without believing a minute of it. The James Bond pictures are not to be "believed," but they tell us a lot about the conventions that audiences now accept, just as the confessional films of the thirties dealing with sin and illegitimacy and motherhood tell us about the sickly-sentimental tone of American entertainment in the midst of the Depression. Movies indicate what the producers thought people would pay to see—which was not always the same as what they *would* pay to see. Even what they enjoyed seeing does not tell us directly what they believed but only indirectly hints at the tone and style of a culture. There is no reason to assume that people twenty or thirty years ago were stupider than they are now. (Consider how *we* may be judged by people twenty years from now looking at today's movies.) Though it may not seem obvious to us now, part of the original appeal of old movies —which we certainly understood and responded to as children— was that, despite their sentimental tone, they helped to form the liberalized modern consciousness. This trash—and most of it was, and is, trash—probably taught us more about the world, and even about values, than our "education" did. Movies broke down barriers of all kinds, opened up the world, helped to make us aware. And they were almost always on the side of the mistreated, the socially despised. Almost all drama is. And, because movies were a mass medium, they had to be on the side of the poor.

Nor does it necessarily go without saying that the glimpses of something really good even in mediocre movies—the quickening of excitement at a great performance, the discovery of beauty in a gesture or a phrase or an image—made us understand the meaning of art as our teachers in art-appreciation courses never could. And—what is more difficult for those who are not movie lovers to grasp—even after this sense of the greater and the higher is developed, we still do not want to live only on the heights. We still want that pleasure of discovering things for ourselves; we need the sustenance of the ordinary, the commonplace, the almost-good as part of the anticipatory atmosphere. And though it all helps us to respond to the moments of greatness, it is not only for this that we want it. The educated person who became interested in cinema as an art form through Bergman or Fellini or Resnais is an alien to me (and my mind goes blank with hostility and indifference when he begins to talk). There isn't much for the art-cinema person on television; to look at a great movie, or even a poor movie carefully designed in terms of textures and contrasts, on television is, in general, maddening, because those movies lose too much. (Educational television, though, persists in this misguided effort to bring the television viewer movie classics.) There are few such movies anyway. But there are all the not-great movies, which we probably wouldn't bother going to see in museums or in theatre revivals—they're just not that important. Seeing them on television is a different kind of experience, with different values—partly because the movie past hasn't been filtered to conform to anyone's convenient favorite notions of film art. We make our own, admittedly small, discoveries or rediscoveries. There's Dan Dailey doing his advertising-wise number in *It's Always Fair Weather,* or Gene Kelly and Fred Astaire singing and dancing "The Babbitt and the Bromide" in *Ziegfeld Follies.* And it's like putting on a record of Ray Charles singing "Georgia on My Mind" or Frank Sinatra singing "Bim Bam Baby" or Elisabeth Schwarzkopf singing operetta, and feeling again the elation we felt the first time. Why should we deny these pleasures because there are other, more complex kinds of pleasure possible? It's true that these pleasures don't deepen, and that they don't change us, but maybe that is part of what makes them seem our own— we realize that we have some emotions and responses that *don't* change as we get older.

People who see a movie for the first time on television don't remember it the same way that people do who saw it in a theatre. Even without the specific visual loss that results from the transfer to another medium, it's doubtful whether a movie could have as intense an impact as it had in its own time. Probably by definition, works that are not truly great cannot be as compelling out of their time. Sinclair Lewis's and Hemingway's novels were becoming archaic while their authors lived. Can *On the Waterfront* have the impact now that it had in 1954? Not quite. And revivals in movie theatres don't have the same kind of charge, either. There's something a little stale in the air, there's a different kind of audience. At a revival, we must allow for the period, or care because of the period. Television viewers seeing old movies for the first time can have very little sense of how and why new stars moved us when they appeared, of the excitement of new themes, of what these movies meant to us. They don't even know which were important in their time, which were "hits."

But they can discover *something* in old movies, and there are few discoveries to be made on dramatic shows produced for television. In comedies, the nervous tic of canned laughter neutralizes everything; the laughter is as false for the funny as for the unfunny and prevents us from responding to either. In general, performances in old movies don't suffer horribly on television except from cuts, and what kindles something like the early flash fire is the power of personality that comes through in those roles that made a star. Today's high-school and college students seeing *East of Eden* and *Rebel Without a Cause* for the first time are almost as caught up in James Dean as the first generation of adolescent viewers was, experiencing that tender, romantic, marvellously masochistic identification with the boy who does everything wrong because he cares so much. And because Dean died young and hard, he is not just another actor who outlived his myth and became ordinary in stale roles—he is the symbol of misunderstood youth. He is inside the skin of moviegoing and television-watching youth—even educated youth—in a way that Keats and Shelley or John Cornford and Julian Bell are not. Youth can respond —though not so strongly—to many of our old heroes and heroines: to Gary Cooper, say, as the elegant, lean, amusingly silent romantic loner of his early Western and aviation films. (And they can more easily ignore the actor who sacrificed that character for blubbering righteous bathos.) Bogart found his myth late, and Dean fulfilled the romantic myth of self-destructiveness, so they look good on television. More often, television, by showing us actors before and after their key starring roles, is a myth-killer. But it keeps acting ability alive.

There is a kind of young television watcher seeing old movies for the first time who is surprisingly sensitive to their values and responds almost with the intensity of a moviegoer. But he's different from the moviegoer. For one thing, he's housebound, inactive, solitary. Unlike a moviegoer, he seems to have no need to discuss what he sees. The kind of television watcher I mean (and the ones I've met are all boys) seems to have extreme empathy with the material in the box (new TV shows as well as old movies, though rarely news), but he may not know how to enter into a conversation, or even how to come into a room or go out of it. He fell in love with his baby-sitter, so he remains a baby. He's unusually polite and intelligent, but in a mechanical way— just going through the motions, without interest. He gives the impression that he wants to withdraw from this human interference and get back to his real life—the box. He is like a prisoner who has everything he wants in prison and is content to stay there. Yet, oddly, he and his fellows seem to be tuned in to each other; just as it sometimes seems that even a teen-ager locked in a closet would pick up the new dance steps at the same moment as other teen-agers, these television watchers react to the same things at the same time. If they can find more intensity in this box than in their own living, then this box can provide *constantly* what we got at the movies only a few times a week. Why should they move away from it, or talk, or go out of the house, when they will only experience that as a loss? Of course, we can see why they should, and their inability to make connections outside is frighteningly suggestive of ways in which we, too, are cut off. It's a matter of degree. If we stay up half the night to watch old movies and can't face the next day, it's partly, at least, because of the fascination of our own movie past; *they* live in a past they never had, like people who become obsessed by places they have only imaginative connections with—Brazil, Venezuela, Arabia Deserta. Either way, there is always something a little shameful about living in the past; we feel guilty, stupid—as if the pleasure we get needed some justification that we can't provide.

For some moviegoers, movies probably contribute to that self-defeating romanticizing of expectations which makes life a series of disappointments. They watch the same movies over and over on television, as if they were constantly returning to the scene of the crime—the life they were so busy dreaming about that they never lived it. They are paralyzed by longing, while those less romantic can leap the hurdle. I heard a story the other day about a man who ever since his school days had been worshipfully "in love with" a famous movie star, talking about her, fantasizing about her, following her career, with its ups and downs and its stormy romances and marriages to producers and agents and wealthy sportsmen and rich businessmen. Though he became successful himself, it never occurred to him that he could enter her terrain—she was so glamorously above him. Last week, he got a letter from an old classmate, to whom, years before, he had confided his adoration of the star; the classmate—an unattractive guy who had never done anything with his life and had a crummy job in a crummy business—had just married her.

Movies are a combination of art and mass medium, but television is so single in its purpose—selling—that it operates without that painful, poignant mixture of aspiration and effort and compromise. We almost never think of calling a television show "beautiful," or even of complaining about the absence of beauty, because we take it for granted that television operates without beauty. When we see on television photographic records of the past, like the pictures of Scott's Antarctic expedition or those series on the First World War, they seem almost too strong for the box, too pure for it. The past has a terror and a fascination and a beauty beyond almost anything else. We are looking at the dead, and they move and grin and wave at us; it's an almost unbearable experience. When our wonder and our grief are interrupted or followed by a commercial, we want to destroy the ugly box. Old movies don't tear us apart like that. They do something else, which we can take more of and take more easily: they give us a sense of the passage of life. Here is Elizabeth Taylor as a plump matron and here, an hour later, as an exquisite child. That charmingly petulant little gigolo with the skinny face and the mustache that seems the most substantial part of him—can he have developed into the great Laurence Olivier? Here is Orson Welles as a young man, playing a handsome old man, and here is Orson Welles as he has really aged. Here are Bette Davis and Charles Boyer traversing the course of their lives from ingenue and juvenile, through major roles, into character parts—back and forth, endlessly, embodying the good and bad characters of many styles, many periods. We see the old character actors put out to pasture in television serials, playing gossipy neighbors or grumpy grandpas, and then we see them in their youth or middle age, in the roles that made them famous—and it's startling to find how good they were, how vital, after we've encountered them caricaturing themselves, feeding off their old roles. They have almost nothing left of that young actor we responded to—and still find ourselves responding to—except the distinctive voice and a few crotchets. There are those of us who, when we watch old movies, sit there murmuring the names as the actors appear (Florence Bates, Henry Daniell, Ernest Thesiger, Constance Collier, Edna May Oliver, Douglas Fowley), or we recognize them but can't remember their names, yet know how well we once knew them, experiencing the failure of memory as a loss of our own past until we can supply it (Maude Eburne or Porter Hall)—with great relief. After a few seconds, I can always remember them, though I cannot remember the names of my childhood companions or of the prizefighter I once dated, or even of the boy who took me to the senior prom. We are eager to hear again that line we know is coming. We hate to miss anything. Our memories are jarred by cuts. We want to see the movie to the end.

The graveyard of *Our Town* affords such a tiny perspective compared to this. Old movies on television are a gigantic, panoramic novel that we can tune in to and out of. People watch avidly for a few weeks or months or years and then give up; others tune in when they're away from home in lonely hotel rooms, or regularly, at home, a few nights a week or every night. The rest of the family may ignore the passing show, may often interrupt, because individual lines of dialogue or details of plot hardly seem to matter as they did originally. A movie on television is no longer just a drama in itself; it is part of a huge ongoing parade. To a new generation, what does it matter if a few gestures and a nuance are lost, when they know they can't watch the parade on all the channels at all hours anyway? It's like traffic on the street. The television generation knows there is no end; it all just goes on. When television watchers are surveyed and asked what kind of programming they want or how they feel television can be improved, some of them not only have no answers but can't understand the questions. What they get on their sets is television— that's it.

EXERCISES

on film and society

1. What are some of the differences Miss Kael finds between the social attitudes of teen-agers and their middle-aged parents, based on the movie viewing habits of both groups?
2. How do differences in social attitude affect differences in what each generation expects from films?
3. What do you think of the portrait of her own generation drawn by Miss Kael on the basis of that generation's film fare? Do you find it endearing? depressing? profound? unbelievable? What do you think of her portrait of the "television generation"?

on film

1. The movies and television are both mass media. What does Miss Kael believe to be the key difference between them?
2. What does she note as the difference between seeing a film for the first time on television or in a theater? Discuss using examples from your own movie and TV viewing.

on structure and language

1. Miss Kael is a master of the familiar essay, and this one represents her at her best. What elements make this a familiar, in contrast to a formal, essay?
2. Point out how the author uses autobiographical elements as an organizing principle of her essay.
3. Is her reference to the films of an earlier time as "the garbage of our youth" intended to be entirely deprecatory?
4. Note other phrases and turns of thought throughout the essay which reflect its author's quite open "emotional involvement" with her material. Does this involvement lessen or enhance clarity of expression and force of perception?

A DECADE
OF NEW HEARTBREAKERS

Kingsley Amis

You need not start analyzing sex appeal (thank heaven) to notice that it changes its nature very sharply when it gets from the private to the public domain. The things that attract men and women to one another in their personal dealings are personal things, of which the physical is only a part. It would take an arrant sentimentalist to deny the importance of vigor, individuality, ability to amuse, relative lack of conceit—plus a whole bundle of other stuff that you can shuffle according to taste: some women evidently like their men to kick them around rather, others enjoy functioning as kickers themselves, but both parties would agree that they have to get to know a man to find out whether he would rate as a satisfactory kicker or kickee.

When the man in question is not to be met with in the social circle or at work but can only be glimpsed on a movie or TV screen, heard on a photograph record, read about in a magazine article, the whole philosophy undergoes a huge shift. The nice thing about this shift is that you can never believe it exists for more than two minutes at a time. I can tell myself in tones of utter conviction that what I see and hear as "Marlon Brando" or "Elvis Presley" is nothing but a confection artfully made up by publicity men, script- or song writers, movie or recording-studio directors and such, but I cannot thereby get away from my conviction that these two are persons in the same way that my acquaintances are persons, that Brando would be (I nearly wrote "is") a good man to have along for cocktails, whereas old Elvis would be—not quite so good. And if I can find this difficulty in remembering what I am up to, it must be quite a bit trickier for the girls.

What counts, obviously, is the image these and other such characters present, the other things they seem to fit in with and the part you can make them play in your own private world. (The same goes for politicians, by the way: it doesn't matter what they do, it's how they strike you or don't strike you.) So with Brando it doesn't matter that he is an intelligent, serious man and a gifted actor: the point about him is his imagined role as a wild one, free and violent and full of thrilling rages, perhaps a beatnik who keeps himself shaved and whose conversation is easy to follow. And so with Presley it doesn't matter what he is really like—and in fact he seems quite inoffensive and unremarkable; he has his role as a voice of youth, eager, intense and passionate, bouncing you out of yourself. Such an explanation makes more sense than any would-be psychological patter about "desire to be dominated" or "symbolical fulfillment"; plenty of others make these appeals, but they haven't clicked as Brando and Presley have.

With all their differences, these two have one important thing in common: both are versions of the Rebel, whom I take to be one of the two key figures in postwar social mythology (we shall come to the other in a minute). "Rebel" takes us straight to *Rebel Without a Cause* and James Dean, which is the right direction, isn't it, for wasn't he the lad who got the show on the road? Or was he? Wasn't it rather the timing of his appearance that was important, just when teen-agers were becoming conscious of themselves as a group and looking round for heroes? In any event, the real Dean was soon swallowed up in the mythical Jimmy, dead but immortal like all the best heroes from King Arthur onward. Once again, his high promise as an actor is beside the point; the role was the thing. And this was a role excitingly close to home, available, everyday in its background: high school, parents, jukebox joints, car jags, teen-age group rivalries. It was all just made for the job.

A further likeness of the Dean-Brando-Presley trio and its

imitators is the concentration upon dress and speech. This is not a postwar novelty and is not in itself a teen-age phenomenon, but it is an invariable feature of the Rebel. I have a dose of social history for you now, which sounds horrible when mentioned but is necessary, I feel, to a proper appreciation of what has happened recently. My idea about this whole thing, as you will have gathered, is that the actual looks and personal idiosyncrasies of the various Rebel figures are only important as a framework that can be filled in at need—and this is a social, not a sexual need. I'm sorry to steer away from Elvis' lashes and Marlon's mouth, but I can't undertake to set anybody right about *them*.

The first faint glimmerings of the Rebel image can be detected as far back as Shelley and Byron, one of whom (I forget which) had funny haircuts and the other funny collars. Both of them, but more particularly Byron, performed what was then an unprecedented feat in conveying to the public an image of themselves instead of their real selves—wild, atheistic, antisocial, womanizing, revolutionary. But Shelley died and Byron went into exile before the Rebel could take. He turned up more recognizably later in the century, first in France, then, around 1885, in England, armed with a whole series of eccentricities in dress and a specialized vocabulary, of which the key word was "new." He was the English decadent, the member of the Aesthetic Movement (the first of its kind), the nineties poet.

His innovations were of a kind not difficult to parallel in our own day. The cigarette, until then of lowly status, became fashionable among bright young men. There was a smart color: yellow. The flower in the buttonhole turned into a kind of badge. There were velvet suits with knickerbockers and silk stockings. Open woman-chasing, preferably in squalid conditions, was the mark of any poet of pretension. Drunkenness was de rigueur; one writer of the period met his death through injuries sustained in falling off a bar stool. The stolid, sober world of Victorian London was horrified, which, of course, was the main object of the operation. The bubble was pricked when Oscar Wilde, who had stage-managed most of the business, was jailed for homosexuality—by no means a hallmark of the movement—in 1895. But there had been time for the Rebel's image to become recognizable: he conducted propaganda-in-action against things as they were.

I will not take you through the details of his next appearance just a generation later, in the 1920's (enemy: the world of 1914; weapons: cocktails, cars, phonographs, anti-feminine feminine fashions; key word: "modern"). The difference from its fin de siècle incarnation was the spreading of the Rebel image among people not in high society and not connected with the arts. Today, another generation later, television, advertising, the phonograph and movie boom have completed that spread, and in the process the Rebel image has altered. However, the enemy is still things-as-they-are, for which "respectability" and "parents" and "squares" are other names. The weapons are still stimulants and noise and speed. And there is still a specialized vocabulary, though a new restlessness has precluded any fixed key word: "contemporary" would fit my argument nicely, but not the facts.

All these things clearly tie in with both wings of the postwar/ teen-age/protest movement/attitude/group: both the James Dean fan on the one hand and the qualified *Howl*-howling beatnik on the other—about whom I promise to shut up quickly; I couldn't face reading, let alone writing, another analysis of that generation and what they generate. I will just say that the connections between the two wings, while helping to provide the traditional link between the Rebel and new styles of writing, help to support the idea that it is not what we usually think of as sex appeal that young ladies are saluting when they bow down to Brando. They feel about him the same way as their boy friends do. There is just the accident that the youngsters' new spending power is giving them unlimited access to those fields—TV, movies, records—in which the Rebel is to be seen and heard in something approaching the flesh and in which part of his role has some sexual bearing. If somebody put Jack Kerouac in a film or on a disc we should have a new idol on our hands.

My second key figure, perpetually confronting the Rebel, is the Steady. He is by no means a champion of things-as-they-are, but when they are in real danger he will fight for them. He is Gary Cooper in *High Noon* rallying the town against the forces of anarchy; he is Bogart as Sam Spade hunting down his partner's killer because loyalty and law are important; he is Gregory Peck in *Twelve O'Clock High* pulling the demoralized bomber squadron together by will power. If he appears on records at all he is Bing Crosby, gentle, amiable, a husband-and-father figure. Even before and during the war, when the Rebel was almost completely out of the picture, the Steady tended to be past his first youth, and in recent years recruitment into his ranks has not been easy to spot. The Cary Grants and James Stewarts march on as they did twenty years ago, with only the British actor Jack Hawkins and one or two others to reinforce them. The older Steady's recorded voice is almost silent: Sinatra—a mild and premature Rebel in his early years—seems to have lost interest, and whatever happened to Frankie Laine?

Along with being no longer young, the characteristics of this type of Steady are likewise negative. What he most conspicuously does not have is any mark in clothing or speech such as the Rebel invariably uses to announce himself: a Bogart hat or a James Stewart drawl are utterly inconceivable. It follows that, without being in any full sense an individualist (that's what the Rebel claims to be, though it isn't much of a claim considering how alike they all seem to be), the Steady is incapable of being herded into any movement or group. I fancy that he has more sex appeal, or is thought of much more directly along those lines, than the Rebel. If the entertainment world is partly an escape world, the Steady is at an advantage so far as sex appeal is concerned. You can dream lush dreams of a Cary Grant figure, who turns up only briefly in real life as a boss or a friend of your father's, while reasonable likenesses of Dean and Presley are on hand all the time.

Without delving back into history again—though I should have liked to tell you some stories about how un-Steady some of those Victorian Steadies really were—we can see easily enough that the pendulum has been swinging fairly regularly between Rebel and Steady for some time and that its swings correspond roughly to movements in the general social scene. As we move out of the fifties into the sixties and the rate of change slows up and things settle down internationally (I hope), we can expect that pendulum to start swinging back, away from the Rebel, who has had things pretty much his own way for long enough. In fact, this change is already beginning to take place, though it has been disguised by the fact that, this being an age of youth as never before, the new Steadies are getting started in the Rebel age group, right under the noses of their opponents in the heart of Rebel-land—the teen-age disc-buying public.

If you doubt me, consider the case of Pat Boone, a singer in the old, gentle, Bing Crosby tradition whose personality radiates a smiling, relaxed amiability. Instead of jeans and a funny haircut, he has ideas on teen-age problems. Similarly with Harry Belafonte, whose image is that of domesticity and seriousness, plus a slight exotic quality from his West Indian connections. (The Exotic showed signs at one stage of setting up shop as a third alternative to Rebel and Steady, but since Rudolph Valentino the other two have gobbled up most of him: Yul Brynner, with the funniest of all haircuts, took a couple of recent mouthfuls from the Rebel side, which has had the lion's share. Some of those best settings make the palms and tropic sands, where the old-fashioned Exotic did his stuff, look like the park around the corner.) One very un-Rebel thing about Boone and Belafonte is that older persons can put up with them. Until recently the first qualification of a singer aiming at teen-agers was that his whole personality should be such as to reduce anybody's father to apoplexy: the agent of one of them actually said as much.

I'm afraid I can't think of any new Steady who has appeared on the American screen, but a brief glance at England will show us a good example in Laurence Harvey, whose recent movie *Room at the Top* presented an unheard-of spectacle, the defeat of a Rebel hero in terms that compelled you to judge against him. Coming along nicely too is Dirk Bogarde, an incarnation—perhaps a rather stuffy one—of sympathetic decency. (While we are on England, I might point out that not only do we have our Pat Boone equivalent in Frankie Vaughn—another serious figure, with an interest in youth clubs—but our little Tommy Steele performs the incredible feat of being a Steady version of Elvis. The routines and the style of guitar-toting are the same, but there isn't the nervous throb in the voice or the dark, enigmatic, remote stuff: Tommy is small and blond and he smiles. I don't want to claim precedence for England in this matter; I think it more likely that we've somehow missed our real Rebel phase.)

Finally, the latest reports arriving from San Francisco suggest that even the beatnik stronghold may be beginning to suffer infiltration by Steady attitudes. This is not so surprising as it may appear: no movement that is founded on old-fashioned things like brotherly love and a desire for political and social morality can stay Rebel indefinitely. And if we witness the fall of the idea-producing citadel, what will the poor Rebel do then? Go underground, I suppose, until the 1980's. But I shall miss him. Although he has often been a bore, particularly in his musical incarnations— Elvis makes me want to scream, and even my ten-year-old son is beginning to drop him in favor of Dixieland—I can't help thinking that he is a good kind of person to have around. It isn't a bad thing to be made to scream occasionally.

EXERCISES

on film and society

1. What new sociological difference does Amis note between the emphasis on the "new" in the 1890s and today?
2. What is Amis' point in saying that Brando and Presley—like Byron and Shelley before them—convey "an image of themselves rather than their real selves"? Is it important for us to be able to disentangle the one from the other? How deep a disjunction can there be between the self one projects on the world and the self one takes to be intrinsic?
3. Amis sees Byron as a forerunner of such stars as Brando and Presley. Whom would he see as anticipating Pat Boone? Why does he neglect to give Boone and other Steadies ancestral connections of the kind he establishes for his Rebels?

on film

1. Do you agree with Amis that the Steady is likely to project "more sex appeal . . . than the Rebel"?
2. It is interesting to apply Amis' observation to women stars: Do such eminent Steadies as Julie Andrews and Doris Day project more sex appeal than such a legendary Rebel as Marlene Dietrich? To her generation, Dietrich symbolized a kind of

sexual insolence and independence. Are there actresses among the younger generation who convey similar qualities? If not, what different qualities would seem to be requisite today for a "sex symbol"?

on structure and language

1. Writing in 1960, Amis predicted a swing of the pendulum "away from the Rebel, who has had things pretty much his own way long enough." Has time proved Amis correct in this prognostication? If not, does this vitiate the interest of what he has to say? Note other observations in his essay which subsequent events, like recent developments on college campuses throughout the world, lead us to consider a bit more quizzically than the reader of 1960 may have.
2. "I have a dose of social history for you now, which sounds horrible, but . . ." What sort of style is Amis using in addressing his reader? What is your response to this form of address? What sort of "image" does it give you of Kingsley Amis? Is it more in line with the Rebel or the Steady?
3. Organize a theme of your own around recent exemplars of Rebels and Steadies. For starters, consider in which, if either, category the following would fit: Gregory Peck; Brigitte Bardot; the Beatles; Lucille Ball; Tuesday Weld; Anthony Perkins; the hero of the film, *The Graduate*; Humbert-Humbert (the hero of *Lolita*); Paul Newman; William Buckley, Jr.; Arthur Miller; Art Linkletter; Joyce Brothers.

MOVIES:
THE REEL WORLD

Marshall McLuhan

In England the movie theater was originally called "The Bioscope,"
because of its visual presentation of the actual movements of the
forms of life (from Greek *bios*, way of life). The movie, by which
we roll up the real world on a spool in order to unroll it as a magic
carpet of fantasy, is a spectacular wedding of the old mechanical
technology and the new electric world. In the chapter on The
Wheel, the story was told of how the movie had a kind of symbolic
origin in an attempt to photograph the flying hooves of galloping
horses, for to set a series of cameras to study animal movement is
to merge the mechanical and the organic in a special way. In the
medieval world, curiously, the idea of change in organic beings
was that of the substitution of one static form for another, in
sequence. They imagined the life of a flower as a kind of cinematic
strip of phases or essences. The movie is the total realization of
the medieval idea of change, in the form of an entertaining illusion.
Physiologists had very much to do with the development of film,
as they did with the telephone. On film the mechanical appears as
organic, and the growth of a flower can be portrayed as easily and
as freely as the movement of a horse.

If the movie merges the mechanical and organic in a world of undulating forms, it also links with the technology of print. The reader in projecting words, as it were, has to follow the black and white sequences of stills that is typography, providing his own sound track. He tries to follow the contours of the author's mind, at varying speeds and with various illusions of understanding. It would be difficult to exaggerate the bond between print and movie in terms of their power to generate fantasy in the viewer or reader. Cervantes devoted his *Don Quixote* entirely to this aspect of the printed word and its power to create what James Joyce throughout *Finnegans Wake* designates as "the ABCED-minded," which can be taken as "ab-said" or "ab-sent," or just alphabetically controlled.

The business of the writer or the film-maker is to transfer the reader or viewer from one world, his *own*, to another, the world created by typography and film. That is so obvious, and happens so completely, that those undergoing the experience accept it subliminally and without critical awareness. Cervantes lived in a world in which print was as new as movies are in the West, and it seemed obvious to him that print, like the images now on the screen, had usurped the real world. The reader or spectator had become a dreamer under their spell, as René Clair said of film in 1926.

Movies as a nonverbal form of experience are like photography, a form of statement without syntax. In fact, however, like the print and the photo, movies assume a high level of literacy in their users and prove baffling to the nonliterate. Our literate acceptance of the mere movement of the camera eye as it follows or drops a figure from view is not acceptable to an African film audience. If somebody disappears off the side of the film, the African wants to know what happened to him. A literate audience, however, accustomed to following printed imagery line by line without questioning the logic of lineality, will accept film sequence without protest.

It was René Clair who pointed out that if two or three people were together on a stage, the dramatist must ceaselessly motivate or explain their being there at all. But the film audience, like the book reader, accepts mere sequence as rational. Whatever the camera turns to, the audience accepts. We are transported to another world. As René Clair observed, the screen opens its white door into a harem of beautiful visions and adolescent dreams, compared to which the loveliest real body seems defective. Yeats saw the movie as a world of Platonic ideals with the film projector playing "a spume upon a ghostly paradigm of things." This was the world that haunted Don Quixote, who found it through the folio door of the newly printed romances.

The close relation, then, between the reel world of film and the private fantasy experience of the printed word is indispensable to our Western acceptance of the film form. Even the film industry regards all of its greatest achievements as derived from novels, nor is this unreasonable. Film, both in its reel form and in its scenario or script form, is completely involved with book culture. All one need do is to imagine for a moment a film based on newspaper form in order to see how close film is to book. Theoretically, there is no reason why the camera should not be used to photograph complex groups of items and events in dateline configurations, just as they are presented on the page of a newspaper. Actually, poetry tends to do this configuring or "bunching" more than prose. Symbolist poetry has much in common with the mosaic of the newspaper page, yet very few people can detach themselves from uniform and connected space sufficiently to grasp symbolist poems. Natives, on the other hand, who have very little contact with phonetic literacy and lineal print, have to learn to "see" photographs or film just as much as we have to learn our letters. In fact, after having tried for years to teach Africans their letters by film, John Wilson of London University's African Institute found it easier to teach them their letters as a means to film literacy. For even when natives have learned to "see" pictures, they cannot accept our ideas of time and space "illusions." On seeing Charlie Chaplin's *The Tramp,* the African audience concluded that Europeans were magicians who could restore life. They saw a character who survived a mighty blow on the head without any indication of being hurt. When the camera shifts, they think they see trees moving, and buildings growing or shrinking, because they cannot make the literate assumption that space is continuous and uniform. Nonliterate people simply don't get perspective or distancing effects of light and shade that we assume are innate human equipment. Literate people think of cause and effect as sequential, as if one thing pushed another along by physical force. Nonliterate people register very little interest in this kind of "efficient" cause and effect, but are fascinated by hidden forms that produce magical results. Inner, rather than outer, causes interest the nonliterate and nonvisual cultures. And that is why the literate West sees the rest of the world as caught in the seamless web of superstition.

Like the oral Russian, the African will not accept sight and sound together. The talkies were the doom of Russian film-making because, like any backward or oral culture, Russians have an irresistible need for participation that is defeated by the addition of sound to the visual image. Both Pudovkin and Eisenstein denounced the sound film but considered that if sound were used symbolically and contrapuntally, rather than realistically, there would result less harm to the visual image. The African insistence on group participation and on chanting and shouting during films is wholly frustrated by sound track. Our own talkies were a further completion of the visual package as a mere consumer commodity. For with silent film we automatically provide sound for ourselves by way of "closure" or completion. And when it is filled in for us there is very much less participation in the work of the image.

Again, it has been found that nonliterates do not know how to fix their eyes, as Westerners do, a few feet in front of the movie screen, or some distance in front of a photo. The result is that they move their eyes over photo or screen as they might their hands. It is this same habit of using the eyes as hands that makes European men so "sexy" to American women. Only an extremely literate and abstract society learns to fix the eyes, as we must learn to do in reading the printed page. For those who thus fix their eyes, perspective results. There is great subtlety and synesthesia in native art, but no perspective. The old belief that everybody really saw in perspective, but only that Renaissance painters had learned how to paint it, is erroneous. Our own first TV generation is rapidly losing this habit of visual perspective as a sensory modality, and along with this change comes an interest in words, not as visually uniform and continuous, but as unique worlds in depth. Hence the craze for puns and word-play, even in sedate ads.

EXERCISES

on film and society

1. What does McLuhan mean when he writes: "The movie is the total realization of the medieval idea of change"?
2. Why does McLuhan believe that "the talkies were the doom of Russian film-making"? Note his anthropological basis for this conclusion.
3. What are some of the key psychological differences McLuhan finds between societies whose means of communication is primarily visual and those whose means is primarily oral? How do McLuhan's views on this compare with Riesman's?

on film

1. According to McLuhan, "Whatever the camera turns to, the audience accepts." Do you share McLuhan's belief in the camera's magical powers? Discuss.
2. Like other contributors to this volume, McLuhan stresses the "indispensable" influence of novels as a chief source of film material. Comment on some recent films you have seen derived from novels, according to their quality and effectiveness as adaptations and/or as films.

on structure and language

1. In his last sentence, McLuhan refers to the contemporary "craze for puns." Cite examples of McLuhan's own use of puns. Ordinarily we do not turn to sociological treatises expecting puns and games. What advantages does McLuhan derive from such a play of language?
2. Where Riesman is historical and chronological in developing his material, McLuhan is spatial and metaphysical. Discuss the significance of this distinction. How do their different perspectives and means of presentation influence the way each writer structures such units as the sentence and the paragraph?

FILM
and
ESTHETICS

In this section we turn from discussions of film vis-à-vis traditional art forms to a more general view: to film considered as a form capable of transmuting elements and methods absorbed from the older arts into something unique and complete in itself. In "The Art of the Director," Michelangelo Antonioni expresses his confidence in the film's capacity in this respect. He remarks that he has turned from depicting sentiments to depicting ideas. In line with this purpose, he notes of the protagonist of *Red Desert* (and this is even more true of the hero of his subsequent film, *Blow-Up*) that the crisis she undergoes is "not visible." Thus Antonioni expresses his belief that so visual a medium as the cinema can be called on effectively to render the invisible. In "A Statement," Luis Buñuel shares Antonioni's confidence when he talks of the mystery he anticipates in a great film. The point of Nicola Chiaromonte, however, in "Priests of the Highbrow Cinema" is that films are basically a form of entertainment, whose explicit photographic images exclude the possibilities of either symbolic form or intellectual content. For Chiaromonte intellectual cinema is a contradiction in terms, and he grades down Antonioni and Godard precisely for presuming to *think* with the camera.

329

This brings us to a problem related to that of emotional response touched on in the headnote to Film and Literature: the capacity of the film to entertain ideas. Even in its most subtle effects is a film bound to fall short of the intricate qualification—and intellectual complexity—of a poem or novel of substance? The question leads to further nagging questions concerning the role of ideas in art. Are we agreed on what "ideas" in music consist of, let alone the way ideas work in literature? In taking up the question posed by Chiaromonte, then, you will want first to settle for yourself the significance you would place on the role of ideas in art in general.

At a less intensive theoretical level than Chiaromonte or Antonioni, J. B. Priestley, an elder statesman of cultural criticism, and Jack Kerouac, a leading writer of the Beat Generation, zestfully engage in discussions of particular films. Each of these essays is as free-wheeling in style as it is fully and carefully detailed in reference to the film it considers. Priestley centers on the problem of values; Kerouac's appreciation is primarily esthetic. Both essays are admirable specimens of enjoyable and useful criticism of film as an art.

In "The Impossible Takes a Little Longer," a leading British film critic, Raymond Durgnat, returns us to theoretical matters, which he presents in the light of the basic technical facts of the film medium. His essay, and indeed all of the essays in this section invite you, the student, to define for yourself what you take to be the main features of any art: this means defining, first, you own expectations of a "work of art"; then the criteria by which you decide how nearly your expectations have been met. This done, you will be in a position to offer conclusions on the nature and promise of film in particular—a form (of art? entertainment? junk?) which you have experienced consistently, and at first hand.

It is with your own full participation in it that the inquiry and forum to which this book has been devoted really begins.

THE ART OF THE DIRECTOR: GODARD INTERVIEWS ANTONIONI

GODARD Your three previous films, *L'Avventura, La Notte, L'Eclisse,* gave us the impression of being in a straight line, going ahead, searching; and now, you arrived in a new area, which is called, perhaps, the *Red Desert*, which is perhaps, a desert for this woman but which, for you, is, on the contrary a film about the entire world, and not only about some fuller and more complete world or other: it's a film about the entire world and not only about today's world . . .

ANTONIONI It is very difficult for me to talk about this film now. It's too recent. I am still too tied up with the "intentions" that pushed me to make it; I have neither the lucidity nor the detachment necessary in order to be able to judge it. I believe I can say, however, that this time it's not a question of a film about sentiments. The results (whether they be good or bad, beautiful or ugly) obtained in my previous films are, here, out-dated, null and void. This is another matter altogether. Before, it was the relationship of one character to another that interested me. Here, the central character is confronted with a social milieu as well, and this means I must treat my story in a completely different way. It simplifies things too much (as many have done) to say that I accuse this inhuman, industrialized world in which the individual is crushed and led to neurosis. My intention, on the contrary (moreover, we may know very well where we start but not at all where we'll end up), was to translate the beauty of this world, in which even the factories can be very beautiful ... The line, the curves of factories and their smoke-stacks, are perhaps more beautiful than a row of trees — which every eye has already seen to the point of monotony. It's a rich world—living, useful. As for me, I hold that the sort of neurosis seen in *Red Desert* is above all a question of adaptation. There are people who adapt themselves, and others who haven't yet done this, for they are too tied to structures, or life-rhythms, that are now out of date. This is the case with Giuliana. The violence of the variation, the wedge between her sensitivity, intelligence and psychology and the cadence that is imposed on her, provoke the character's breakdown. It is a breakdown concerning not only her epidermic contacts with the world, her perception of the noises, colors, color personalities surrounding her, but also her system of values (education, morality, faith), which are no longer valuable and no longer sustain her. She finds herself, thus, in the position of needing to renew herself completely, as a woman. This is what the doctors advise and this is what she strives to do.

GODARD What is the explanation for the insert of the episode of the story she tells the little boy?

ANTONIONI There is a woman and a sick child. The mother must tell the child a story, but he has already heard all the ones she knows. She must therefore, invent one. Giuliana's psychology being given, it seems natural to me that this story become, for her —unconsciously—an evasion of the reality surrounding her, towards a world where the colors belong to nature: the blue sea, the pink sand. The rocks themselves take on human form, embrace her and sing sweetly.

Do you remember the scene in the room, with Corrado? She says, leaning against the wall, "Do you know what I'd like? ... Everyone who ever loved me ... to have them here, around me, like a wall." She needs them in fact, to help her to live, because she is afraid she won't be able to arrive at it alone.

GODARD The modern world is therefore only the revealer of an older and more profound neurosis?

ANTONIONI The milieu in which Giuliana lives accelerates the personality's breakdown, but, naturally, the personality must carry within itself a favorable terrain for this breakdown. It isn't easy to determine the causes and origins of neurosis; it is manifested in such different forms, at times going as far as schizophrenia, whose symptoms often resemble neurotic symptoms. But it is by means of a like exasperation that one arrives at encompassing a situation. I have been reproached for having chosen a pathological case. But, if I had chosen a normally adapted woman, there would no longer be a drama, the drama concerns those who do not adapt.

GODARD Aren't there already traces of this character in the one in *L'Eclisse*?

ANTONIONI The character of Vittoria in *L'Eclisse* is the opposite of that of Giuliana. In *L'Eclisse*, Vittoria is a calm and well-balanced girl, who thinks about what she does. There isn't a single neurotic element in her. The crisis, in *L'Eclisse*, is a crisis of the sentiments. In *Red Desert*, the sentiments are a ready-made fact. Moreover, the relationship between Giuliana and her husband is normal. If you were to ask her, "Do you love your husband?," she would answer yes. Until her attempt at suicide, the crisis is underground, it is not visible.

I want to underline the fact that it isn't the milieu that gives birth to the breakdown: it only makes it show. One may think that outside of this milieu, there is no breakdown. But that's not true. Our life, even if we don't take account of it, is dominated by "industry." And "industry" shouldn't be understood to mean factories only, but also and above all, products. These products are everywhere, they enter our homes, made of plastics and other materials unknown barely a few years ago; they overtake us wherever we may be. With the help of publicity, which considers our psychology and our subconscious more and more carefully, they obsess us. I can say this: by situating the story of *Red Desert* in the world of factories, I have gone back to the source of that sort of crisis which, like a torrential river, swelled a thousand tributaries, divides in a thousand arms in order, finally, to submerge everything and spread everywhere.

GODARD But isn't this beauty of the modern world also the resolution of the characters' psychological difficulties, doesn't it show vanity?

ANTONIONI One must not underestimate the drama of man thus conditioned. Without drama, there are perhaps no longer men. Furthermore, I do not believe that the beauty of the modern world in itself can resolve our dramas. I believe, on the contrary, that once adapted to new life-techniques we will perhaps find new solutions to our problems.

But why have me speak of these things? I am not a philosopher and all these observations have nothing to do with the "invention" of the film.

GODARD Was the presence of the robot in the little boy's room benevolent or malevolent?

ANTONIONI In my opinion, benevolent. Because the child, by playing with this genre of toy, will adapt very well to the life waiting for him. But here we come back to what we were just talking about. The toys are produced by industry, which in this way even influences the education of children.

I am still stupefied by a conversation I had with a cybernetics professor from the University of Milan, Silvio Ceccato, considered by the Americans to be another Einstein. A formidable type, who has invented a machine that looks and describes, a machine that can drive a car, make a report from an aesthetic point of view—or ethical or journalistic, etc. And it's not a matter of television: it's an electronic brain. This man, who, moreover, proved to be extraordinarily lucid, never spoke one technical word in the course of a conversation I didn't understand. Well, I went crazy. At the end of each minute, I no longer understood anything of what he had just said to me. He forced himself to use my language, but he was in another world. With him was a young girl, 24 or 25 years old, pretty, of *petit bourgeois* origin—his secretary. Now she understood it perfectly. In Italy, these are generally very young and very simple girls, who have only a modest diploma, who work at programming electronic brains: for them, it's very simple and very easy to program an electronic brain—while it isn't easy at all for me.

Another savant, Robert M. Stewart, came to see me, six months ago, in Rome. He had invented a chemical brain and presented himself at a cybernetics congress in Naples to give an account of his discovery, which is one of the most extraordinary discoveries in the world. It's a very small box, mounted on tubes: it's a matter of cells, into whose composition gold enters, mixed with other substances. The cells are alive in a liquid chemical and they live an autonomous life; they have reactions: if you come into the room, the cell takes on a certain form and if I come in, it takes on another form, etc. In this little box there are only a few million cells, but starting from that, one can arrive at remaking the human brain. This savant feeds them, puts them to sleep . . . he talked to me about all that, which was very clear but so unbelievable that at a certain point I was no longer following him. By contrast, when he gets a little older, the little boy who plays with the robot from earliest childhood will understand very well; he will have no trouble at all in going, if he wants to, out to space in a rocket.

I look at all that with a great deal of envy, and would like to be already in this new world. Unfortunately, we aren't there yet; it's a drama that will last several generations—mine, yours and the generation of those born right after WW II. I think that, in the years to come, there are going to be very violent transformations, both in the world and in the individual's interior. Today's crisis comes from this spiritual confusion, from this confusion of conscience, of faith and of politics; there are so many symptoms of the transformations to come. Then I said to myself, "What does one say, today, in the cinema?" And I wanted to tell a story based on these motivations I was talking about before.

GODARD However, the heroes of this film are integrated with this mentality, these are engineers, they're part of this world. . . .

ANTONIONI Not all of them. The character played by Richard Harris is almost a romantic, who thinks about fleeing to Patagonia and has no idea at all about what he must do. He is taking flight and believes he is resolving, in this way, the problems of his life. But this problem is inside, not outside, of him. All the more true that it is enough for him to meet a woman in order to provoke a crisis, and he no longer knows whether he will leave or not, the whole thing turns him around. I would like to point out a moment in the film which is an accusation of the old world: when, at the breaking point, this woman needs someone to help her, she finds a man who profits from her and from that crisis. She finds herself face-to-face with old things, and it is the old things that shake her and sweep her off her feet. If she had met someone like her husband, he would have acted differently; he would have, first of all, tried to take care of her, then, after that, perhaps. . . . When there, it's her own world that betrays her.

GODARD At the end of the film is she going to become like her husband?

ANTONIONI I believe that, following the efforts she makes to find a link with reality, she ends by finding a compromise. Neurotics have crises, but also moments of lucidity which may last all their lives. Perhaps she finds a compromise, but the neurosis stays with her. I believe I have given the idea of this continuity of illness by means of the slightly soft image: she is in a static phase. What is she going to become? Another film would have to be made in order to know that.

GODARD Do you think that this new world's heightened consciousness may have repercussions on aesthetics, on the conception of the artist?

ANTONIONI Yes, I believe so. That changes the way of seeing, of thinking: everything changes. Pop Art demonstrated that something else is sought. One must not underestimate Pop Art. It is an "ironic" movement, and this conscious irony is very important. The Pop Art painters know very well that they are making things whose aesthetic value is not yet ripe—except for Rauschenberg, who is more of a painter than the others . . . even though Oldenburg's "soft typewriter" is very fine. . . . I like it very much. It believes it is good that all that is coming out. That can only accelerate the transformation process in question.

GODARD But does the savant have the conscience we do? Does he reason as we do, in respect to the world?

ANTONIONI I asked that of Stewart, the inventor of the chemical brain. He answered that his very specialized work, without a doubt, had reverberations in his private life, even including his relationship with his family.

GODARD And must the sentiments be preserved?

ANTONIONI What a question! Do you think it is easy to answer that? All I can say about sentiments is that they must change. "Must" isn't what I mean to say. They are changing. They have already changed.

GODARD In the science-fiction novels, there are never artists, poets. . . .

ANTONIONI Yes, it's curious. Perhaps they think that one can do without art. Perhaps we are the last to produce things so apparently gratuitous as are works of art.

GODARD Does *Red Desert* also help you to settle personal problems?

ANTONIONI While making a film, we live, and nevertheless, we are always settling personal problems. Problems which concern our work, but also our private life. If the things we talk about are not those we were talking about right after the war, it is because the world around us has, in fact, changed and, also we ourselves have changed. Our requirements have changed, our purposes, our themes.

Right after the war, there were numerous things to be said; it was interesting to show social reality, the social condition of the individual. Today, all that has already been seen and done. The new themes we can treat of today are those about which we were just speaking. I don't know yet how we can approach them, present them. I have tried to develop one of these themes in *Red Desert* and I don't think I exhausted it. It is only the beginning of a series of problems and aspects of our modern society and of the way of life that is ours. Moreover, you too, Godard, you make very modern films, your way of treating subjects reveals an intense need to break with the past.

GODARD When you begin or end certain sequences with quasi-abstract forms of objects or details, do you do it in a pictorial spirit?

ANTONIONI I feel the need to express reality in terms that are not completely realistic. The abstract white line that enters the picture at the beginning of the sequence of the little gray street interests me much more than the car that arrives: it's a way of approaching the character in terms of things rather than by means of her life. Her life, basically, interests me only relatively. It is a character that participates in the story as a function of her femininity; her feminine aspect and character are the essential things for me. It is exactly for that reason that I had this role played a bit statically.

GODARD Thus, there is also on this point a break with your previous films.

ANTONIONI Yes, it is a less realistic film, from a figurative point of view. That is to say, it is realistic in a different way. For example, I used the telescopic lens a great deal in order not to have deep-focus, which is for good reason an indispensable element of realism. What interests me now is to place the character in contact with things, for it is things, objects and materials that have weight today. I do not consider *Red Desert* a result: it is a research. I want to tell different stories with different means. Everything that's been done, everything I've done until now no longer interests me, it bores me. Perhaps you, too, feel the same thing?

GODARD Was filming in color an important change?

ANTONIONI Very important. I had to change my technique because of it, but not only because of it. I already had a need to change my technique, for the reasons we've spoken about. My requirements were no longer the same. The fact of using color accelerated this change. With color, you don't use the same lenses. Also, I perceived that certain camera movements didn't always jell with it: a rapid panoramic sweep is efficacious on brilliant red, but it does nothing for a sour green, unless you're looking for a new contrast. I believe there is a relationship between camera movement and color. A single film is not sufficient for studying the problem in depth, but it's a problem that must be examined. I made, for this reason, some 16mm tests. They were very interesting, but I was unable to achieve, in the film itself, certain effects I had found by this means. Up to this point, I've been in too much of a corner.

You know that a psycho-physiology of color exists; studies, experiments have been done on this subject. The interior of the factory seen in the film was painted red; two weeks later the workers were fighting amongst one another. It was re-painted in pale green and everyone was peaceful. The workers' eyes must have a rest.

GODARD How did you choose the colors for the store?

ANTONIONI It was necessary to choose between warm colors and cool colors. Giuliana wants cool colors for her store. These are colors that are less discordant with the objects displayed. If you paint a wall orange, this color will kill any object nearby, while sky-blue or pale green will set the objects off without overwhelming them. I wanted this contrast between warm colors and cool colors: there is an orange, a yellow, a maroon ceiling, and my character discovers that, for her, they don't go well together.

GODARD The film's title was *Celeste E Verde* (Heavenly Blue And Green).

ANTONIONI I abandoned it, because it didn't seem to be a virile enough title; it was too directly linked to the color. Moreover, I had never thought about color in itself. The film was born in colors, but I always thought, first of all, of the thing to be said, this is natural, and thus aided the expression by means of the color. I never thought: I'm going to put a blue next to a maroon. I dyed the grass around the shed on the edge of the marsh in order to reinforce the sense of desolation, of death. The landscape had to be rendered truthfully: when trees are dead, they have that color.

GODARD The drama is thus no longer psychological, but plastic.

ANTONIONI It's the same thing.

GODARD Thus, all those shots of objects during the conversation about Patagonia? . . .

ANTONIONI It's a sort of "distraction" on the character's part. He is tired of listening to all these conversations. He is thinking of Giuliana.

GODARD The dialogue is simpler, more functional than that of your previous films; isn't their traditional role of "commentary" taken by the color?

ANTONIONI Yes, I believe that is true. Let us say that, here, the dialogue is reduced to an indispensable minimum and that, in this sense, it is linked to the color. For example, I would never have done the scene in the shack where they talk about drugs, aphrodisiacs, without using red. I would never have done it in black and white. The red puts the spectator in a state of mind that permits him to accept this dialogue. The color is correct for the characters (who are justified by it) and also for the spectator.

GODARD Do you feel yourself to be closer to the researches of painters than to those of novelists?

ANTONIONI I don't feel too distant from the researches of the New Novel, but they help me less than the others: painting and scientific research interest me more. I don't believe they influence me directly. There is, in this film, no pictorial research at all; we are far from painting, it seems to me. And, naturally, the requirements of painting have nothing to do with narrative content, where one is found in the cinema: this is where the novel's researches join those of painting.

GODARD Did you re-work the color in the laboratory, as is permitted with Technicolor?

ANTONIONI I placed no confidence at all in the laboratory, during the shooting. That is to say, I tried, during the shooting, to put the colors I wanted on the things themselves, on the landscapes. I painted directly, instead of trafficking with color in the laboratory. After that, what I demanded from the laboratory was a faithful reproduction of the effects I had obtained. It wasn't easy, for Technicolor, as you know, requires numerous operations involving the master print: the job was very long and delicate.

GODARD You verified things during the shooting, as you went along. . . .

ANTONIONI Exactly. I believe one mustn't place too much trust in the work that can be done in the laboratory. It's not their fault. It's just that technically, color is still a long way behind.

GODARD In your opinion, does Giuliana see the color as you show it?

ANTONIONI You know, there are neurotics who see color differently. Doctors have done experiments on this subject, with mescaline for example, in order to try to know what they see. At a certain point, I had the intention of having some effects of this nature. But now there is no longer anything of this but one single moment, when you see stains on a wall. I also thought of modifying the color of certain objects and then, the fact of using all those "tricks" very quickly seemed to me to become artificial; it was an artificial way of saying things which could be said in a much more simple way. Well, I eliminated these effects. But we may think that she sees color differently.

It's amusing: at this moment, I am speaking with Godard, one of the most modern talented *cinéastes* of today and, just a little while ago, I lunched with René Clair, one of the greatest directors of the past: it wasn't at all the same genre of conversation . . . he is preoccupied with the future of the cinema. We, on the contrary (you agree, I believe), have confidence in the future of the cinema.

GODARD And what are you going to do now?

ANTONIONI I am going to do a sketch with Soraya. . . . This sketch interests me because I am going to pursue my researches with color, push ahead the experiments I did with *Red Desert*. After that, I'm going to make a film that interests me more. If I find a producer who will let me do it. . . .

(Materials, transcribed from tapes, re-read and corrected by Michelangelo Antonioni.)

EXERCISES

on film and esthetics

1. What assumptions about cinema as an art form underlie the statements of both Antonioni and Godard?
2. Antonioni points out that the heroine of his film is severely neurotic. Why does he choose to build a film concerned with his ideas about the effects of industrialism and technology on

contemporary life around the character and story of an unbalanced person? Why not focus on a healthier, more normal-
seeming type?

3. In point of fact, the unbalanced individual is to be found as
protagonist of many major novels and plays of this century.
Cite some examples. What are some of the reasons which have
led artists to single out this type of character? Do Antonioni's
artistic reasons, as he presents them in the interview, seem
similar to those of the novelists and playwrights you have
cited?

on film

1. According to Antonioni, how does the use of color influence a
film's impact? Cite examples of films you have seen to support
or contradict his viewpoint.

2. What differences do you find between the films of Antonioni
and Godard on the one hand and standard American films on
the other? What similarities?

on structure and language

1. The form of the above selection is that of the taped interview.
How does that form affect the style and organization of this
piece?

2. Notice the types of questions Godard asks. Which type does he
prefer? Which types does he avoid?

3. How obtrusive is the interviewer's presence in the discussion?
Can we make out his own attitude to the interviewee?

4. Antonioni likes to use anecdotes to reinforce his points. Cite
some of the anecdotes he offers. Do you find them to be effective?

5. "Without drama," Antonioni remarks, "there are perhaps no
longer men." What is the significance of this point?

A STATEMENT

Luis Buñuel

In none of the traditional arts is there such a wide gap between
possibilities and facts as in the cinema. Motion pictures act
directly upon the spectator; they offer him concrete persons and
things; they isolate him, through silence and darkness, from the
usual psychological atmosphere. Because of all this, the cinema is
capable of stirring the spectator as perhaps no other art. But as
no other art, it is also capable of stupefying him. Unfortunately,
the great majority of today's films seem to have exactly that purpose; they glory in an intellectual and moral vacuum. In this
vacuum, movies seem to prosper.

Mystery is a basic element of all works of art. It is generally
lacking on the screen. Writers, directors and producers take good
care in avoiding anything that may upset us. They keep the
marvelous window on the liberating world of poetry shut. They
prefer stories which seem to continue our ordinary lives, which
repeat for the umpteenth time the same drama, which help us
forget the hard hours of our daily work. And all this, of course,
carefully watched over by traditional morals, government and
international censorship, religion, good taste, white humor and
other flat dicteria of reality.

The screen is a dangerous and wonderful instrument, if a free spirit uses it. It is the superior way of expressing the world of dreams, emotions and instinct. The cinema seems to have been invented for the expression of the subconscious, so profoundly is it rooted in poetry. Nevertheless, it almost never pursues these ends.

We rarely see good cinema in the mammoth productions, or in the works that have received the praise of critics and audience. The particular story, the private drama of an individual, cannot interest—I believe—anyone worthy of living in our time. If a man in the audience shares the joys and sorrows of a character on the screen, it should be because that character reflects the joys and sorrows of all society and so the personal feelings of that man in the audience. Unemployment, insecurity, the fear of war, social injustice, etc., affect all men of our time, and thus, they also affect the individual spectator. But when the screen tells me that Mr. X is not happy at home and finds amusement with a girl friend whom he finally abandons to reunite himself with his faithful wife, I find it all very moral and edifying, but it leaves me completely indifferent.

Octavio Paz has said: "But that a man in chains should shut his eyes, the world would explode." And I could say: But that the white eye-lid of the screen reflect its proper light, the Universe would go up in flames. But for the moment we can sleep in peace: the light of the cinema is conveniently dosified and shackled.

EXERCISES

on film and esthetics

1. According to Buñuel, what differentiates the impact of the film from that of the other arts?
2. What common purpose does Buñuel ascribe to all the arts? Do you agree with his assumption?
3. Why does he feel that most films made today lack "mystery"?

on film

1. What kinds of things does Buñuel feel the film can express better than any other art form? Cite some films you have seen which depicted those things.
2. What sort of film does Buñuel most dislike? Compare his viewpoint with your own on the basis of the kind of films you dislike.

on structure and language

1. What is the form of Buñuel's "statement": essay, tirade, manifesto, after-dinner speech? Define and explain.
2. What does Buñuel mean by the phrase "free spirit"? How does this phrase tie in with the quotation from the Mexican poet and statesman, Octavio Paz?

PRIESTS
OF THE HIGHBROW CINEMA

Nicola Chiaromonte

A footprint on the sand is the *sign* of a man's passage. The cross is the *symbol* of Christianity. Tears are signs of emotion; words are symbols of thoughts.

A word is a sign only when it is used in a strictly utilitarian way—to indicate or command. In other cases words, even though they have a precise meaning, change with their context. Only in zoology does "horse" signify *equus caballus*. In general discourse it can mean the beast that draws the peasant's cart; the fantastic quadrupeds yoked to Phaeton's chariot; the animals on which Murat's squadrons rode forth; the heroic creature of equestrian monuments; or all these things. The meaning of a word lies not only in its dictionary definitions, but in the host of associations that they evoke. It is not just context that defines and enhances the significance of a word, but syntax and order as well. In the most primitive communication among people words are merely indicative or instrumental. It is in poetry, however, that the symbolic value of words reaches its apex.

Between a sign and the thing it signifies there is the fixed, determined relationship of cause and effect. We see this in the case of the footprint on the sand, the tear on the eyelash, or the trademark of a commercial product. But no matter how closely tied a symbol is to the thing symbolised, the relation is variable, flexible, and free. The cross has become the symbol of Christianity not because of its form, but because the Christians, following St. Paul, at a definite moment in their history decided to adopt the instrument of Christ's torture as their emblem. Similarly, the relation between a word and its meaning depends on its origin, its history, and its usage. Naturally, for a non-Christian or an indifferent Christian, the cross is merely a sign, but for a true believer it evokes the fundamental tenet of his faith: the sacrifice of God-Man. Of course, a word can also be used as a label or as a signal of command. But not by lovers and poets and those who wish truly to commune with others.

A word, then, can be a symbol. A photograph, however, can only be a sign, an unequivocal sign of the passage of a material object before the camera-eye. Similarly, the traces left on a movie film by a motion or a series of motions are also signs. But if a coherent discourse can be considered the "trace" of anything at all, it is the trace of meanings that a human mind in its experience of reality has apprehended and wants to communicate.

To identify a word without penetrating its meaning is utterly useless, and in order to penetrate its meaning, we have to repeat in some way the experience of its discovery. Ortega y Gasset justly observed that understanding a discourse involves our comprehending not only what is expressed in it, but also what is left unexpressed, and what cannot be expressed. Ineffability is an intrinsic condition of language. But the photographic image is an absolutely explicit indicator; and this is both its strength and its weakness. It can show everything that is showable—and nothing else. The emotions it arouses are psychological "effects," in the strictest, most deterministic sense of the word. But an emotion that a word arouses cannot be considered the *effect* of that word. For the emotion immediately provoked by a word does not exhaust its meaning. The mind actively intervenes—clarifying, enriching, interpreting, and perhaps discarding the original reaction in order to comprehend the true significance of what has been uttered.

No trick of montage, no photographic inventiveness—nothing

can change the essential and necessary fact that the cinematographic image is an imprint. Nothing can promote it from the
status of a sign to that of a symbol. It cannot become a kind of
word; it cannot signify more than itself. Nothing can turn a
sequence of cinematic images into a sort of discourse. It can never
be more than a group of pictures that have been juxtaposed for the
purpose of imitating a real event; and the only effect it can have
on the spectator is the evocation of emotions *similar* to those that
could have been aroused by the real event. There is no device or
technique by which a series of cinematic images can pass from the
sphere of the imitative and the external to the intrinsically
different sphere of coherent discourse, through which we endeav-
our to achieve logical order, acknowledging the mind's imperative
to discover the rational in every experience.

If by reason we mean significant order, clear and coherent
expression, then the universe of words (and certainly the universe
of art) is governed by reason. Or, to put it differently, it is ruled by
a necessity other than that of the physical or material world. But
the realm of images is controlled by chance, by the way events and
things happen in reality; and while series of images can cleverly
imitate, reconstruct, and accentuate reality, they do not require us
to ask why things happen the way they do. Reason has no role in
a sequence of images; its place has been taken by actuality, which
needs no reasons. The realm of discourse, however, is entirely
occupied by thoughts and questions. Since one word cannot follow
another without a reason, we cannot avoid asking ourselves why
this is said or that is thought, and what motivates the mind to say
this and think that. In the sphere of language we cannot limit ourselves to the machine-like registration of events, because the mind
cannot function without ordering and evaluating. But images can
only be registered; otherwise, we strip them of their essential
virtue—indisputable evidence. . . .

Our age has been called "the civilisation of the image" and
with reason. It has almost irreparably confused word with image,
as it has confused a presence that is directly perceived with a
photographic or phonographic replica. Caught off guard by the
suggestive power of the new mechanical means of communication,
most people come to believe that an image "says" much more than
a word, and is infinitely more suggestive. Now, it is not surprising

that untrained spectators fall into this trap, but when intellectuals, the guardians of rational language, confound confusion by giving it a theoretical basis, the situation becomes serious. For when, in their analysis of movies, they talk about words and images as if they were identical, they are adding the persuasive power of words to the suggestive force of images, justifying the belief of ordinary people in the reality of their mirages. So it is only natural that makers of films begin to think of a film as a kind of novel or poem, and by the same token begin to consider themselves writers, or even sociologists, moralists, and reformers. They have fallen victim to the cinematic fallacy: the assumption that complex emotions and subtle ideas, which can be expressed adequately only in language, can be rendered in moving photographs. And they turn out films in which they use images as if they were words pregnant with profound, if vague, meanings instead of employing them to create the illusion of a real event.

However, since cinematic images can never have the value of words, no matter how masterly the director's technique nor how sophisticated his intentions, these movies are distinguished by the boredom they arouse in an audience, keeping it interminably waiting for a meaning that is never given. The film time passes emptily, without action or events; this is exactly the opposite of what should happen at the cinema.

If we disregard what we actually see, hear, and feel we can, of course, affirm anything whatever, defend any thesis whatever, and claim to have seen, heard, and felt anything we care to. In the case of the films this is particularly easy, as the cinematic image can blend with, absorb, and adapt itself to practically any meaning we wish to impose on it. The reason is that, never being able to signify anything other than itself, impervious and indifferent to verbal meanings, the cinematic image can support interpretations that are absolutely contradictory. But in order to impose intellectual or symbolic meaning on a succession of images that have been combined in a particular fashion, we are obliged to "read" the film as if it were a series of separate, static, abstract pictures, and not the deliberately continuous, forward-moving composition of images it is supposed to be. That was the Surrealists' way of reading films and also of making them, with results that were at times striking. . . .

What I am saying is that highbrow and arty films, tedious as they may be because of their slowness and their insistent suggestion of hidden ideas, are not essentially different from movies filled with excitement and action. They, too, in the final analysis, present us with a certain number of images to look at. If we are not interested in the meanings the director meant the comings and goings of the characters to have, we can always look at the landscape, try to guess the location of the street the hero is loitering on so long; or scrutinise the furniture in rooms, or the star's clothes. In fact, we do exactly what we do when, obliged to wait for someone or something, we become idle spectators of life. . . .

The one thing a film cannot do is express complex ideas or meanings; and forcing it to do so puts a brake on movement (which is the very essence of the movies) slowing it down to a complete stop in order to suggest a significance that goes beyond the image. But in the movies there is nothing but a void beyond the image. So, for example, an empty street which is supposed to indicate (who knows how or why) the state of mind of a character —to say nothing of the ideas of the director—is simply a static image. It indicates nothing. The picture of an empty street can be superb as photography, but it is only the picture of an empty street. Nor can technical tricks or ideological comment make it say more than it does. What actually happens when a single image is imposed on us for too long a time, is that we are reduced to a state of stupefaction, not knowing what we are supposed to feel. A static image breaks the spell of the movies by betraying the expectation of uninterrupted action that has been aroused, and jolts us from a moving world to a motionless one. The effect is disastrous, for our mind begins to work on its own; either we are completely distracted, or we start associating automatically on the theme, "empty street." But more often we are just bored. And I can think of no worse boredom.

At such moments we become aware of the fact that the movie has the effect, not of directing and ordering the flow of our thoughts around the themes suggested by the pictures on the screen, but of stopping the flow completely, submerging it in a cascade of images. It is as difficult to get back from them to the theme as it is to awake from the effects of a drug. Furthermore, the intellectual cinema uses actors not as sources of actions and gestures but as suggestive and almost inanimate objects. Reduced to the condition of things, actors find it more difficult than ever to express emotions and moods. All they can do is to assume poses.

And the purpose of all this is to escape from the elementary fact that poetry and cinematographic images are at opposite poles. Not only does an image "express without saying," as Dina Dreyfus writes, but it hurdles, so to speak, ordinary discourse in order to achieve an indicatory and emotional force that common words— *les mots de la tribu*—cannot possibly emulate. Obviously, the palpitating image of a thing is infinitely more effective than its verbal label.

Nevertheless, it has nothing to do with discourse and its logical order, where feelings and ideas are mirrored, or with poetry. In fact, the emotion aroused by a cinematic image is similar to that aroused by a spectacle or an event which we happen to witness in real life. For no matter how skilful film directors and actors are, they do not use evocative symbols but images, the indicative unequivocal signs made by the imprint of objects on the screen. Through the cinematic images we can apprehend the world only from the outside, for because of their nature, they are unable to render subjective experience, or to penetrate the world seen through an idea, a conviction, a form, or a passion—which is the world of art as we have always understood it. The cinema can allude to the inner life only to the degree that movements of the body correspond to movements of the soul. But it is obvious that the body can express complex states of mind only very vaguely. We can photograph a motionless person, or a face with a fixed stare, in order to show anguish or sadness. But the image will never render the quality of the anguish or sadness, which is, after all, what matters. The cinema derives its power from its ability to arouse an emotional reaction that is both immediate and certain. Whereas a poem or a novel cannot come alive without the reader's elaboration; its power of suggestion is a construction of his mind, calling into play his sensibility, and his intellectual and imaginative faculties.

It is indeed because they are striving to achieve the allusiveness of poetry, encouraging the spectator to participate in the creation of meaning, that the intellectualistic film directors attempt to use cinematic images as if they were words; thus they keep them in a zone of crepuscular ambiguity, as far removed as possible from their obvious and apparent meaning. But they strive in vain. After all, a cinematic idiom, with its innumerable possibilities does exist, even though it is qualitatively limited. It is the language of signs that describe the external, in all its certainty and completeness. In this language every sign is clear, the meaning of every gesture is immediately comprehensible, and vagueness is excluded by definition.

The resources of the cinema are enormously rich. It has at its disposal a realm where all is explicit and accessible, where act immediately follows on intention, and where real life is magically transformed into a series of clear and definite events. But it is certainly not through the cinema that we can explore what Heraclitus called the "confines of the soul."

Speaking of the relation between thought and image from the point of view of a scientific psychology, Alfred Binet once said that from an idea worth a hundred thousand francs, we get images worth a sou. With images worth a sou, certain movie-makers would like to get ideas worth a hundred thousand francs. The operation, however, cannot be reversed.

EXERCISES

on film and esthetics

1. It is obvious that Chiaromonte's assumptions about the esthetic nature and possibilities of the cinema would not be shared by Antonioni. On what central point would these men disagree?
2. What does Chiaromonte mean by a symbol?
3. What, according to him, are its esthetic values? Why does he feel that the cinema cannot convey symbolism?

on film

1. What is your own opinion about the capacity of the film to articulate and develop ideas? Discuss, with examples.

2. Do the same with the capacity of the film to make use of symbolism artistically.

on structure and language

1. Show how the organization of Chiaromonte's essay is based upon the principle of cause and effect.
2. Chiaromonte's essay is packed with ideas couched in abstract language. Pick out statements which exemplify this. Describe how this practice affects the pace and tone of the essay.
3. Perhaps the two essays in this volume which are the most compressed in their expression and the most unflinchingly intellectual in their approach are this piece by Chiaromonte and the essay by Bazin. Define and compare their tone, diction, and use of rhetorical devices.

NOSFERATU*

Jack Kerouac

Nosferatu is an evil name suggesting the red letters of hell—the sinister pieces of it like "fer" and "eratu" and "nos" have a red and heinous quality like the picture itself (which throbs with gloom), a masterpiece of nightmare horror photographed fantastically well in the old grainy tones of brown-and-black-and-white.

It's not so much that the woods are "misty" but that they are bright shining Bavarian woods in the morning as the young jerk hero hurries in a Transylvanian coach to the castle of the Count. Though the woods be bright you feel evil lurking behind every tree. You just know the inner sides of dead trees among the shining living pines have bats hanging upsidedown in torpid sated sleep. There's a castle right ahead. The hero has just had a drink in a Transylvanian tavern and it would be my opinion to suggest "Don't drink too deep in Transylvanian taverns!" The maids in the Inn are as completely innocent as NOSFERATU is completely evil. The horses drawing the coach cavort, the youth stretches in the daytime woods, glad ... but! ... *the little traveled road!* The castle coach transfers him at Charlie Chaplin speed to the hungry

* *Nosferatu* is the silent film version of Bram Stoker's novel *Dracula;* it was made in 1922 under the direction of F. W. Murnau.

cardinal of vampires. The horses are hooded! They know that vampire bats will clamp against their withers by nightfall! They rush hysterically through a milky dimming forest of mountain dusk, you suddenly see the castle with bats like flies round the parapet. The kid rushes out looking for to go find his gory loss. In a strange wool cap a thin hawknosed man opens the big oaken door. He announces his servants are all gone. The audience realizes this is Count Nosferatu himself! Ugh! The castle has tile floors: —somehow there's more evil in those tile floors than in the dripping dust of later Bela Lugosi castle where women with spiders on their shoulders dragged dead muslin gowns across the stone. They are the tile floors of a Byzantine Alexandrian Transylvanian throat-ogre.

The Count Nosferatu has the long hook nose of a Javelin vampire bat, the large eyes of the Rhinolophidae vampire bat, long horsey mouth looking like it's full of W-shaped cusps with muggly pectinated teeth and molars and incisors like Desmondontae vampire bats with a front tooth missing the better to suck the blood, maybe with the long brush-tipped tongue of the *sanguisuga* so sanguine. He looks in his hunched swift walk like he probably also has his intestinal tract specially modified in accordance with his nocturnal habits . . . the general horrid hare-lipped look of the Noctilio . . . small guillotines in his mouth . . . the exceeding thinness of his gullet. His hands are like the enormous claws of the Leporinus bat and keep growing longer and longer fingernails throughout the picture.

Meanwhile the kid rushes around enjoying the scenery:—little dusty paths of the castle by day, but by twilight?

The Count plunges to sign his deeds with that thirsty eagerness of the Vampire.

The kid escapes over the wall just in time . . .

The scene shifts to Doktor Van Hellsing in sunny classroom Germany nevertheless photographed as dark as Wolfbane or the claws that eat a fly. Then it goes to a gorgeously filmed dune where women's Victorian dresses flutter in the fresh sea wind. Then finally the haunted ship sails down the navigable canal or river and out to sea: aboard is the Count in pursuit of his boy. When they open his coffin a dozen rats plop out of the dirt and slink and bite the seamen on the ankles (how they ever filmed this I'll never know, great big rats) . . . The whole scene on the ship testifies to the grandeur of the horror of Coleridge's Ancient Mariner. Of itself the schooner glides into the port of Bremen with all the crew dead. The sucked-out Captain is tied to his wheel. A disciple of the Count imprisoned in a Bremen cell sees the schooner glide right by like a ghost and says: "The master is here!" Down cobbles deserted at dusk suddenly, like an insane delivery boy here comes Count Nosferatu carrying his own coffin of burial earth under his arm. He goes straight to establish residence in an eerie awful warehouse or armory which made me think: "I shall never go to Bremen if they have things like that! Armories with empty windows! Ow!"

The old Bremen lamplighter is aware of the foolish hallucinations of Bremen folk but he also looks scared as he lights the evening lamp, naturally, as the next day processions carry the coffined victims of the vampire down the gloomy street. People close their shutters. There is real evil swarming all over the screen by now. Nosferatu looks worse and worse: by now his teeth are stained, his fingernails are like rats' tails, his eyes are on fire. He stares from his warehouse window like someone in an old dream. He rises from his coffin at eve like a plank. His disciple who escapes from the prison looks like Mr. Pickwick on a rampage in a chase that has everybody breathing furiously (a masterpiece of breathing), ends in a field, with torches.

At night, by moonlight there he is, the Great Lover, staring across that awful plaza or canal into the heroine's window and into her eye. She waits for him. She wants to save the hero and has read in the "Book of Vampires" that if a victim stays with the vampire till cock's crow he will be destroyed. He comes to her swiftly with that awful quickfooted walk, fingernails dripping. The shadow of the hand crawls like ink across her snowy bedspreads. The last scene shows him kneeling at her bedside kissing into her neck in a horribly perverted love scene unequalled for its pathetic sudden revelation of the vampire's essential helplessness. The sun comes up, you see its rays light the top of his warehouse, the cock crows, he can't get away. He vanishes in a puff of smoke like the Agony of the West. Right there on the floor as the puffing hero arrives too late to save his love.

The creator of this picture, F. W. Murnau, may have drawn a lot of information from the great vampire dissertations of Ranft and Calmet written in the 18th century. Vampire is a word of Servian origin (Wampir),—meaning blood-sucking ghosts. They were supposed to be the souls of dead wizards and witches and suicides and victims of homicide and the Banished! (those banished from family or church). But vampires were also thought to be the souls of ordinary living people which leave the body in sleep and come upon other sleepers in the form of down-fluff! . . . so don't sleep in your duck-down sleepingbag in Transylvania! (or even in California, they say).

Actually, don't worry . . . scientifically speaking, the only blood-sucking bats in the world are located in South America from Oaxaca on down.

EXERCISES

on film and esthetics

1. Few readers are likely to have seen *Nosferatu*. Nearly every reader, however, has seen a horror film—the genre to which *Nosferatu* belongs and of which it is an early example. Does Kerouac's description of *Nosferatu* evoke for you the feeling-tone of those horror films you are familiar with? Do you enjoy in horror movies the qualities which Kerouac responds to in the silent classic he writes about?
2. Does Kerouac's essay serve to reinforce or negate Chiaromonte's esthetic views on cinema?
3. Compare a work of horror fiction like Mary Shelley's *Frankenstein* or Bram Stoker's *Dracula* or a story by E. A. Poe or H. P. Lovecraft with a horror film. Note similarities and differences in treatment. A useful reference guide on this topic is *Horror Movies: An Illustrated Guide* by Carlos Clarens.

on film

1. What does Kerouac assume to be some of the essential characteristics of the horror film as a genre? Discuss his assumptions on the basis of horror films you have seen.

on structure and language

1. The pomposity and solemnity to be found in so much writing on the arts are happily absent from Kerouac's essay. By means of his style, what sort of relationship does Kerouac establish with his reader?
2. What is Kerouac's central purpose in his essay? What is the chief effect of the film on him that he seeks to transmit to his reader? What rhetorical devices does he use to communicate that effect?
3. The style of Kerouac's essay is in striking contrast to that of Miss Sontag. Note some telling differences in their tone, emphases, and general approach to their topic. Both styles are equally appropriate to their material, but which do you personally prefer? Explain and discuss.

THE MAD SAD WORLD

J. B. Priestley

Our more sensible and sensitive film critics have already told us that *It's A Mad, Mad, Mad, Mad World* is not really funny at all, but violent and cruel. I believed them but I felt I had to see it for myself. Having seen it, I have now reached the conclusion that it must be the oddest example of film-making there can ever have been. I never remember before sitting in a place of entertainment and feeling at such complete cross-purposes with the providers of the entertainment. It is as if we belonged to different planets.

The programme, which costs a steep five bob at the Coliseum, is full of information about how the film was made. From its conception to its release, we are told, it took three and a half years, 166 shooting days, 636,000 feet (approximately 125 miles) of exposed film, finally reduced to 21,939 feet—a "running time of 210 minutes, including intermission". Some 1,700 drawings, blueprints and models of the exterior and interior settings were needed. There were 217 items of special effects—" a conglomeration of unworldly devices such as pemberthy siphons, gun powders, squibs and squib hooks, dynamite caps, pulleys, cranes, compressors, popping matches, air rams, hydraulic rams, smoke pots, smoke blowers, cables and wires and opaque paint." For one effect alone, a car going off a cliff in the opening sequence, they had to have "a radio-controlled pilot put together with bits and pieces of electronic equipment they acquired from the laboratories of the California Institute of Technology and nearby aerospace plants." Here, we may say, was our new technological age, nowhere better represented than in Southern California, happily at play. The backroom boys were having fun. And the result is murderous.

Stanley Kramer, the producer-director, is an experienced and courageous film man. He is quoted as saying: "Bill Rose's script was the funniest ever written. If the motion picture isn't the funniest ever made, the fault will lie with the man I see in the mirror." (An odd but perhaps significant way of putting it, for in the mirror we see our outward selves, embodying *our conscious intention*.) We read that:

> He sought to brew an unheard-of mix of on-screen chicanery, calamity, disaster and suspense, requiring more performing talent and behind-the-camera artistry and cunning than any entertainment recipe ever before devised, and to come up with an explosive celluloid of belly-laughs. He aimed to fashion a giant blend of slapstick and whimsy to the end that audiences of all ages, lands and mores would find delirious divertissement.

Even the writer of the programme, we feel, is straining so hard that he may rupture himself.

William Rose, responsible both for the original idea and the final script, is a writer of very considerable talent, an American who spent some years over here and gave us *Genevieve*, surely one of the best comedy films made in this country. Moreover, the cast reads like a convention of film and TV comedians. Never since Hollywood began have so many funny men been assembled by a film producer. And never have funny men been less funny. They all work like whipped blacks at it, and hardly raise a smile. There are some laughs of course, but they are mostly of the shocked nervous sort, in response to yet another realistic catastrophe on the huge screen and a new barrage of amplified sound. We never find ourselves chuckling. Strictly speaking, there is no humour.

Now what can have happened? Where did these experienced film makers, with so much talent and time and money at their command, go wrong? How could they set out to achieve the funniest film every made and end with something that leaves us stunned, repelled, saddened? What became of all the fun that they and we were going to enjoy? To what desert did the river of laughter find its way, thinning out and drying up and vanishing in the hot dust? Why is it that the slapstick films of 35 to 50 years ago are still a joy—often making us laugh more now than they did when we first saw them—when this immensely ambitious new attempt at a comic masterpiece fails so dismally?

Before trying to answer these questions, I will make a point in passing. A few years after the war, a company that not only produced films but that could also distribute them, offered me the chance of writing and co-producing a feature-length slapstick film. Delighted, I said I would do it, and then I retired to the country to consider what I would do. Some days later, I found myself declining the offer. I realised that such a film, to succeed, would have to create for itself an artificial world in which everybody and everything would be ridiculous, as they were in the genuine old slapsticks, in which the very roads and trees, automobiles and trains, were comic characters. I was neither clever enough nor, what was even more important, sufficiently strong-willed and ruthless to create, simply for one film, such a world, so different from ours. Many thanks but nothing doing!

Now this is the trap into which Messrs Kramer and Rose and their colleagues have rushed headlong. Not only have they not attempted to re-create the old artificial world, the dream empire of slapstick, populated entirely by clowns, but they have been at the greatest possible pains and expense, calling on our new technology for all its formidable resources, to show us—in panoramic breadth and full colour—our actual world as it exists today in Southern California. It is there to the smallest puff of dust and can of orange juice. I know that region fairly well, and as soon as the film began, with wide shots of the twisting desert roads, like tape tossed on a moulting hearth rug, I was back there. And I knew that the MAD-4 boys were stuck with it; they could never come out laughing.

Then—at least this is my guess—something else happened. I think they worked so hard and so long at this Super-Jumbo-Comedy that, without being aware of what was happening, they began dredging up out of the dark of their minds more and more disgust and contempt and hatred. A sardonic lama and a communist intellectual, collaborating to attack contemporary American life, could not have done a more ruthless job. It is Southern California on the rack and having its bones broken. It is the American Way drenched in wormwood solution and sulphuric acid. There is in it not a glimmer of affection for anybody or anything. All its huge explosions and bashings are not so much overdone attempts at slapstick as they are the outward and exaggerated expression of an unconscious violence, of disgust and contempt and hatred, once concealed, now boiling over. What it offers us is no "giant blend of slapstick and whimsy", but a savage rejection of contemporary American society and its values and status symbols.

All the people, condemned from first to last to a frenzied chase, are moved by nothing but greed, the hope of getting money without working for it, the fear of missing a soft buck. If all these comedians are never funny (and they aren't) it is because they are not allowed time and space in which to deploy themselves; they are tied to a story-line that is really a fizzing string of fire-crackers. The characters are all contemptible people, inevitably doomed to disaster. They are all screaming their heads off for something they will never be allowed to have and that would do them no good even if they had it. They are loveless, without dignity and self-respect, suspicious and treacherous and stupid; and any society breeding more and more of such creatures is moving away from any true civilisation.

Machinery and property are held in high respect in the American way of life, seen near its peak in Southern California. So in this savagely violent film, more machinery and property are wrecked than ever before. Automobiles, no longer sacred objects, clash against one another, lose wheels and other essential parts, run off the roads, tumble down gorges, fall off cliffs. Aeroplanes are bashed about as if they were cheap toys. A whole filling station is reduced to a heap of boards. Neat rows of canned merchandise, fit for any supermarket, are hurled from their shelves, split open, ruined. The mere existence of a wall, any wall, is a signal for somebody or something to come crashing through it. Nothing is safe from this appalling violence and explosiveness. Even the things that normally try to save life are here a menace to it, so that in the last sequence a gigantic firemen's ladder is transformed by some evil magic into a monstrous catapult, hurling one character after another through doorways and windows far below. And everything that had a kind of dreamlike comic innocence in the old slapstick films now seems menacing, relentless, cruel. This is the world of the nuclear deterrent trying to have fun. It is the high jinks of a ruthless technology. Behind my shrinking gaze and battered hearing, my blood ran cold.

I cannot help suspecting that many of the episodes were chosen not for their comic possibilities but as symbolic presentations of our various predicaments. (In this department it is far superior to the film made out of Kafka's *The Trial*.) As disgust and contempt, hatred and despair, came boiling up from the unconscious, such symbolism was inevitable. It explains the long and wearing adventures of the pair who found themselves locked in the basement of the ironmonger's, together with enormous stocks of explosives, fireworks, fuses and blow-lamps. It explains the episode of the two idiotic youths in the fine private aeroplane, whose owner, a drunk, was unconscious; they did not know how to fly it; while the men in the control tower of the airport were themselves no longer in control. It explains why the good old honest cop (Spencer Tracy, no less) was the craftiest crook of them all. I could go on and on; but why should I? Either you have seen the film or you haven't.

As an attempt not merely to revive but to enlarge, magnify, lengthen and strengthen and bring bang-up-to-date the old slapstick film, demanding a maximum of "belly-laughs", *It's A Mad, Mad, Mad, Mad World* seems to me a huge and appallingly expensive flop, wasting more comic talent than any film has ever done before. But as a savage satire of the kind of society, really a sort of Hell, we are striving so hard to maintain, prepared if necessary for its protection to turn the world into a radio-active cinder, it is in an eye-straining, ear-battering, nerve-shattering class of its own. It makes the blackest of the avant-garde Theatre-of-the-Absurd playwrights seem like tepid protesters playing at charades. And what I wonder now is whether Stanley Kramer and William Rose and their colleagues can go on making motion pictures in Southern California. Purged, purified, free to meditate in peace, they ought to be making arrangements to enter Tibetan monasteries or caves in the Indian forest.

EXERCISES

on film and esthetics

1. Why does Priestley find the film he discusses lacking in entertainment values? On what esthetic grounds does he base his conclusions?
2. To make his point, Priestley discusses past forms of comedy—and past forms of experience. Why does the film violate his sense of his own past, and how is this fact related to his judgment of the film's artistic merits?
3. What does Priestley believe to be the ingredients of good comedy? of good art?

on film

1. Consider a film comedy you have recently seen. Does it tend to "slaughter" its subject in the ways described by Priestley? Or did you find some redeeming features in it, as well as "murderous" faults?
2. What is meant by "black humor"? Notable films in this mode include Chaplin's *Monsieur Verdoux,* Tony Richardson's *The Loved One,* Noel Black's *Pretty Poison,* Lindsay Anderson's *If,* François Truffaut's *The Bride Wore Black,* Stanley Kubrick's *Dr. Strangelove.* Compare and contrast the humor of any of these films or another in this vein, with the gentler form of humor of a situation comedy. Which do you find funnier? Why?

on structure and language

1. Priestley comments adversely on this film in the most generous way possible. What aspects of his style contribute to that generosity?
2. Do the examples of gentlemanly generosity you have noticed give you more or less confidence in the value of Priestley's criticism of the film's esthetic values?
3. Like some other contributors to this volume, Priestley's comments on what he doesn't like about a certain film tell us much about what he doesn't like about contemporary culture in general. Does his clearly not being—nor caring in the least to be—"with it," vitiate his criticism for you?

THE IMPOSSIBLE
TAKES A LITTLE LONGER

Raymond Durgnat

In the early sixties the screen became more fluid than ever in its cutting. The basic reason is a profound change in the whole situation of the medium—a change enforced by the prevalence of television (which, despite the protestations of certain theoreticians, is a branch of cinema, not a sister-art), as well as the spread of home movies. Once upon a time, moving pictures were seen only, or mainly, in "picture palaces", in darkness, with hundreds of other spectators, one's whole attention, strengthened by community feeling, poured into them. The weekly visit to the cinema was an event, an entry into a magic world. In terms which aren't at all Marshall McLuhan's, the cinema is traditionally a "hot" medium, involving one's whole participation intensely. Conversely, if a book annoys or bores you, you just put it down. If a film bores you, you're imprisoned, you writhe and fume.

Now, with TV and home movies, films are frequently watched in semi-darkness or ordinary room illumination, amid the pedestrian surroundings of the home. The sound or brightness may be turned up or down. A little image flickers on the surface of the box. The spectator, once dominated by the medium and its glamour, now dominates it, and often watches half-absently, fitfully, or not at all. TV, and home movies, are "cool" media.

Moving pictures have become almost as common as print. They compel less attention, less emotional energy, less participation. The spectator who once *reacted*, now *notes*. The medium can become more notional, more cerebral, more "abstract", in the sense that ideas are abstract. TV plays often move more slowly than films, needing longer to catch one's full participation; theirs are nearer theatrical rhythms than the cinema's; we talk of TV "plays" even when they're films. On the other hand, other TV genres move very fast, substituting a "notional" continuity of intellectual interest for emotional participation. Ironically, certain TV commercials, especially the early *Dulux Is A Home's Best Friend* series from I.C.I., move with a speed, freedom and whimsicality rivaling that of the cinema's avant-garde. They can exploit a complete emancipation from continuities of space and time. Theatrical "continuity" is utterly exploded. Images are flicked or shuffled through like photographs, not just in an album, but in *packs*.

Dick Lester's *The Knack* (1965), albeit adapted from a stage-play, and Fellini's *Giulietta of the Spirits* (1966) apply this mode to the mainstream story film, using rapid transitions from present to past or future tense (the spectator deduces the tense from his sense of continuity), from objective images to subjective images (daydreams, hallucinations), from simple realism to perceptual "impressionism" and emotional "expressionism" and even negative or subjunctive images (this didn't happen, this might have happened, this would be absurd if it did happen). Where films once had to choose a style and stick to it (only a few films managed obtrusive transitions), now they could be in all styles at once, since what was looked at was known to be an "idea" before it was a "reality".

In these ways the cinema of the *October* Gods is returning to prominence. Marker, Godard, Lester, Kluge, all like Eisenstein, go off into little "essays", and move, not from place to place, but from idea to idea. Yet only a few years back, Karel Reisz, in the pages of *Sight and Sound*, was pronouncing Eisenstein's example a dead end!

Well—that's show-business!

The spate of new styles has utterly exploded old dogmas. Godard, bored with the tedious old habits of showing how your character got from A to B, decided, at the last moment, to cut out all linking shots in *A Bout de Souffle,* and proved all over again that you could "jump" your character from A to B, i.e. make a sudden, uprepared break in "theatrical" space. Every cut is, in a sense, a jump-cut, and all Godard does is defy Hollywood convention; he cuts with no indication of transition, the character doesn't even mutter, "Well—it's time I went", or drop some such hint that this scene is over. Thus, the sense of theatrical sense is further debilitated, and the film can become as casual about place as a novel is, or as film-essays had always been. But it's worth remembering that Griffith cuts just as fast, and jumpily, as Godard's contemporaries.

Paul Mayersberg, clearly startled by jump-cuts, has argued that the cinema was a violence-saturated medium, because the cut tore you from one place to another, inflicting drastic shocks on your nervous system. Remarks as hypersensitive as this aren't rare in contemporary theorising. The fact remains that, as every cutter knows, the run-of-the-mill cut is the smoothest, most invisible way of changing place, and no more inflicts violence on the spectator than a sentence like, "He rose from his chair, shaved, went downstairs and caught a taxi to her house." There are five "shots" and four jump-cuts in that sentence, and it creates a sense of flow, not of jumps. In the same way, the cinema spectator just doesn't see most cuts, because he's looking *through* the image at what's happening in it. Theories which stress the cutting at the expense of the showing can be very misleading. Most cuts are no more violent than replacing one mental image by another; and this is all smooth cutting does.

Much theorizing about "subjective cameras" has gone wrong for similar reasons. "First-person camera" sequences, in which the camera pans and tracks round a room, like an eye, rarely seem as direct and natural on the screen as they should in theory. In fact they're a good way of building up suspense, of making the spectator nervous. The principal reason is that most camera-lens have a field of vision even narrower than that of the optical defect known as "tunnel vision", and part of the weirdness of "subjective" sequences lies in our feeling that we can't see out of the sides, let alone the corners, of our eyes. *Murderers' Row* brings the fish-eye lens to the storyfilm, but the price in optical distortion limits it to gimmick (or expressionistic) status. The way in which we look round a room is most naturally represented, not by the panning close-up (used with very disorientating effect in Dreyer's *Vampyr*) but by some sort of establishing shot, followed by closer views of significant details or configurations. The cuts paraphrase the fact that, even while our eyes turn, our mind doesn't pan over space, it leaps from one point of interest to another, or from one configuration to another. It's then natural to slip in reaction—shots to stop the cuts from "jerking" against one another. Or, again, one might represent the action of the eye by "sweeping" the camera across a room, slowing down to near-immobility at a point of interest, then "swooping" off again; but even then the camera would create a zip-pan effect not noted by the eyes. Theories that the camera can "equal" the eyes fall foul of the differences between (a) the camera's and the eye's optical qualities, and (b) the eye's physical movements and the mind's "editing" of what the eye sees —a process on which gestalt psychology is laying increasing importance. In the last analysis, the cinema is a matter, not of images of the eye, but of images of the mind. Of course, all these effects might be justified by particular moods or situations; our point is that the "mainstream" cinema is not so hopelessly square and conventional as it's often been made out to be, and that it is often far more natural, flexible and resourceful than over-theoretical improvements.

But such experiments in "optical literalism" have become less conspicuous among all the possibilities offered by a "stream-of-consciousness" cinema.

Given this new intellectual flexibility, the cinema is currently exploring a new mode, half-pictorial, half-"abstract", i.e., in a sense, literary—as exemplified by the documentaries of Chris Marker and the half-stories, half-essays, of Godard, his boring sidekick.

Many of these effects are anticipated in Dovzhenko's *Arsenal* (1929) and reputedly are very fully developed in his *Aerograd* (1935). But their current recrudescence is on a much broader front. Through it the story film is acquiring something of the novel's power of discursiveness. And the documentary is experiencing a rebirth. Already in the '30s, Basil Wright's and Harry Watt's *Nightmail* (1935), to some extent, and, even more fully, Basil

Wright's *Song of Ceylon* (1934) had begun to move from the "document" to the essay form, while Thorold Dickinson's *Overture* (1956), a compilation film linking documentary footage from all over the world into one coherent storyline, created a meta-reality, a conceptual reality. It constitutes the link-film between the "Gods" sequence in *October* and the essay form which, with Chris Marker, comes of age. The sequence in *Lettre de Siberie* (1958), where the same sequence is shown several times over, with different music and commentary, as it might feature in a Stalinist documentary, in an anti-Communist documentary, and in a tourist's home-movie, is both an enquiry into Siberia and an enquiry into enquiries; it becomes, in the end, a philosophical meditation on truth and appearance, the documentary to end all notions of documentary as "document". In *Overture,* the image is still "concrete", in that it gives its sense of lived lift to the over-all concept, of co-operation. With Marker's sequence, the image itself is under enquiry, is merely an "idea", a hypothesis. As it is again, in *Alphaville* (1965), where Godard shows us a road, and talks of galactic space, and we "feel" a poetic entity—the contrast is a "montage", in Eisenstein's sense. With all these exciting possibilities to explore, the theatrical aspects of the cinema seem to be in for an eclipse—or, at least, a fallow period. But so long as the cinema depends on acting and acting-out concrete events (rather than on indicating the concrete through words and symbols), that is, so long as it is photographic, it will remain radically theatrical, and Raymond Williams was probably right when in his *Preface to Film,* in collaboration with Michael Orrom, he described the cinema as closest to the theatrical arts (perhaps the two forms are heading for a symbiosis in "total theatre", a promising cine-sideline, with actors stepping from the screen on to the stage and back again).

In any event, progress in the arts is a matter of opening new avenues, not of closing up old ones. For his *Blood of the Vampire* (1958) Henry Cass, who undoubtedly knew how to direct films in more modern idioms, chose to rely largely on long-shots and the longer mid-shots, giving his film an astonishingly archaic quality. With its slow pace, it seems not so much to tell a story as to parade its (hackneyed) story elements before us in chronological order. Yet the quiet, controlled barnstorming of Donald Wolfit (whose stage personality is quite large enough to fill the long-shots with his presence), the evocatively harsh decor (all immobile spaces and brick walls), and a monomaniac colour-scheme (relentlessly dominating us with brick, rust and blood reds), invest these endless "establishing shots" with a looming immovability which at first exists independently of one's boredom and eventually overcomes it. Is this film a rare example of that aesthetic paradox, the film so bad that it's good? I think perhaps we can give it the benefit of the doubt.

The neo-theatrical film continues to flourish, not only in the cinemas, but in the avant-garde. One thinks of Jonas Mekas' *The Brig* (1966)—a film record of an actual performance of the stage-play, owing much of its effect to the camera's perpetuation of the theatrical continuity of space. And Steve Dwoskin's poignant *Alone* (1966), though very fluidly cut, dwells so remorselessly on one girl, on her bed, that the film leaves one with the impression of having been shot in one long take.

What we are watching is, perhaps, the cinema's diversification into a variety of idioms. For the cinema's equivalent is not *literature;* its equivalent is *print.* The cinema is not an art-form. It is a medium, comprising art forms as diverse as print—i.e., ranging from the stream-of-consciousness novel and concrete poetry. It also includes communicating styles which have no connection whatsoever with art (in the usual sense of the word), or even entertainment, and correspond to journalism, technical manuals or textbooks. Soon, perhaps, such a thing as a "film critic" will seem as ridiculous as a "print-critic". There is no art of the cinema. Long live the cinema arts!

EXERCISES

on film and esthetics

1. In what ways does Durgnat believe that films in the sixties have caught up in their techniques to the other arts?
2. Which directors does he cite as being the most artistically advanced from his point of view?
3. What particular new emphasis, as a result, do you find in the films of the past decade?

on film

1. Discuss a recent foreign film you have seen according to how it meets Durgnat's specifications for an "advanced" style. Was your enjoyment of the film enhanced by your consciousness of the techniques it employed?
2. Does your enjoyment of a novel depend on your knowledge of how a printing press works? If not, how valid do you find Durgnat's comparison of the processes of film-making to the printing processes involved in book-making?

on structure and language

1. While Durgnat's style is as compressed as those of Hauser or Arnheim or Chiaromonte or Bazin, it is, however, a more journalistic style. This means that Durgnat makes more concessions to the reader, and is essentially more relaxed in his attitudes. What rhetorical devices and techniques does he make use of?
2. At the same time, Durgnat assumes a wide familiarity with recent films among his readers. Do his rapid-fire references to many films, most of which you may not have seen, make it more difficult for you to follow his thought? Or do you find his encyclopedic approach effective? Does it stimulate you to want to see some of the films he refers to?

POSTLUDE:
FILM
and
THE LIBERAL
ARTS

Besides its other virtues, not the least of which is the vast amount of ground it manages to cover in brief compass, the following essay by the late distinguished art historian, Erwin Panofsky, is exemplary for its poise. Given the widespread and intensely personal interest films and the culture of films have evoked, discussions bearing on them tend to be high-pitched. A turn to the subject of films among a group of people today (no matter what their age or peer-group) is sure to lead to a sudden raising of the voice and heatedness of tone. In its poise—marked by steadiness of tone and lucidity of thought—Panofsky's essay serves to bring this volume to a balanced close. While it is not, of course, to be taken as the last word on a subject relatively new to intensive study and discussion, it offers a survey of the topics considered in these pages, a survey both pioneering (it first appeared in 1934) and of continuing relevance; and as richly informed as it is concisely expressed.

ON MOVIES

Erwin Panofsky

Film art is the only art the development of which men now living have witnessed from the very beginnings; and this development is all the more interesting as it took place under conditions contrary to precedent. It was not an artistic urge that gave rise to the discovery and gradual perfection of a new technique; it was a technical invention that gave rise to the discovery and gradual perfection of a new art.

From this we understand two fundamental facts. First, that the primordial basis of the enjoyment of moving pictures was not an objective interest in a specific subject matter, much less an aesthetic interest in the formal presentation of subject matter, but the sheer delight in the fact that things seemed to move, no matter what things they were. Second, that films—first exhibited in "kinetoscopes," viz., cinematographic peep shows, but projectable to a screen since as early as 1894—are, originally, a product of genuine folk art (whereas, as a rule, folk art derives from what is known as "higher art"). At the very beginning of things we find the simple recording of movements: galloping horses, railroad trains, fire engines, sporting events, street scenes. And when it had come to the making of narrative films these were produced by photographers who were anything but "producers" or "directors," performed by people who were anything but actors, and enjoyed by people who would have been much offended had anyone called them "art lovers."

The casts of these archaic films were usually collected in a "café" where unemployed supers or ordinary citizens possessed of a suitable exterior were wont to assemble at a given hour. An enterprising photographer would walk in, hire four or five convenient characters and make the picture while carefully instructing them what to do: "Now, you pretend to hit this lady over the head"; and (to the lady): "And you pretend to fall down in a heap." Productions like these were shown, together with those purely factual recordings of "movement for movement's sake," in a few small and dingy cinemas mostly frequented by the "lower classes" and a sprinkling of youngsters in quest of adventure (about 1905, I happen to remember, there was only one obscure and faintly disreputable *kino* in the whole city of Berlin, bearing, for some unfathomable reason, the English name of "The Meeting Room"). Small wonder that the "better classes," when they slowly began to venture into these early picture theaters, did so, not by way of seeking normal and possibly serious entertainment, but with that characteristic sensation of self-conscious condescension with which we may plunge, in gay company, into the folkloristic depths of Coney Island or a European kermis; even a few years ago it was the regulation attitude of the socially or intellectually prominent that one could confess to enjoying such austerely educational films as *The Sex Life of the Starfish* or films with "beautiful scenery," but never to a serious liking for narratives.

Today there is no denying that narrative films are not only "art"—not often good art, to be sure, but this applies to other media as well—but also, besides architecture, cartooning and "commercial design," the only visual art entirely alive. The "movies" have re-established that dynamic contact between art production and art consumption which, for reasons too complex to be considered here, is sorely attenuated, if not entirely interrupted, in many other fields of artistic endeavor. Whether we like it or not, it is the movies that mold, more than any other single force, the opinions, the taste, the language, the dress, the behavior, and even the physical appearance of a public comprising more than 60 per cent of the population of the earth. If all the serious lyrical poets, composers, painters and sculptors were forced by law to stop their activities, a rather small fraction of the general public would become aware of the fact and a still smaller fraction would seriously regret it. If the same thing were to happen with the movies the social consequences would be catastrophic.

In the beginning, then, there were the straight recordings of movement no matter what moved, viz., the prehistoric ancestors of our "documentaries"; and, soon after, the early narratives, viz., the prehistoric ancestors of our "feature films." The craving for a narrative element could be satisfied only by borrowing from older arts, and one should expect that the natural thing would have been to borrow from the theater, a theater play being apparently the *genus proximum* to a narrative film in that it consists of a narrative enacted by persons that move. But in reality the imitation of stage performances was a comparatively late and thoroughly frustrated development. What happened at the start was a very different thing. Instead of imitating a theatrical performance already endowed wih a certain amount of motion, the earliest films added movement to works of art originally stationary, so that the dazzling technical invention might achieve a triumph of its own without intruding upon the sphere of higher culture. The living language, which is always right, has endorsed this sensible choice when it still speaks of a "moving picture" or, simply, a "picture," instead of accepting the pretentious and fundamentally erroneous "screen play."

The stationary works enlivened in the earliest movies were indeed pictures: bad nineteenth-century paintings and postcards (or waxworks à la Madame Tussaud's), supplemented by the comic strips—a most important root of cinematic art—and the subject matter of popular songs, pulp magazines and dime novels; and the films descending from this ancestry appealed directly and very intensely to a folk art mentality. They gratified—often simultaneously—first, a primitive sense of justice and decorum when virtue and industry were rewarded while vice and laziness were punished; second, plain sentimentality when "the thin trickle of a fictive love interest" took its course "through some-what serpentine channels," or when Father, dear Father returned from the saloon to find his child dying of diphtheria; third, a primordial instinct for bloodshed and cruelty when Andreas Hofer faced the firing squad, or when (in a film of 1893–94) the head of Mary Queen of Scots actually came off; fourth, a taste for mild pornography (I remember with great pleasure a French film of *ca.* 1900 wherein a seemingly but not really well-rounded lady as well as a seemingly but not really slender one were shown chang-ing to bathing suits—an honest, straightforward *porcheria* much less objectionable than the now extinct Betty Boop films and, I am sorry to say, some of the more recent Walt Disney produc-tions); and, finally, that crude sense of humor, graphically de-scribed as "slapstick," which feeds upon the sadistic and the pornographic instinct, either singly or in combination.

Not until as late as *ca.* 1905 was a film adaptation of *Faust* ventured upon (cast still "unknown," characteristically enough), and not until 1911 did Sarah Bernhardt lend her prestige to an unbelievably funny film tragedy, *Queen Elizabeth of England.* These films represent the first conscious attempt at transplanting the movies from the folk art level to that of "real art"; but they also bear winess to the fact that this commendable goal could not be reached in so simple a manner. It was soon realized that the imitation of a theater performance with a set stage, fixed entries and exits, and distinctly literary ambitions is the one thing the film must avoid.

The legitimate paths of evolution were opened, not by running away from the folk art character of the primitive film but by developing it within the limits of its own possibilities. Those primordial archetypes of film productions on the folk art level—success or retribution, sentiment, sensation, pornography, and crude humor—could blossom forth into genuine history, tragedy and romance, crime and adventure, and comedy, as soon as it was realized that they could be transfigured—not by an artificial injec-tion of literary values but by the exploitation of the unique and specific possibilities of the new medium. Significantly, the begin-nings of this legitimate development antedate the attempts at endowing the film with higher values of a foreign order (the crucial period being the years from 1902 to *ca.* 1905), and the

decisive steps were taken by people who were laymen or outsiders from the viewpoint of the serious stage.

These unique and specific possibilities can be defined as
dynamization of space and, accordingly, *spatialization of time.*
This statement is self-evident to the point of triviality but it
belongs to that kind of truths which, just because of their triviality,
are easily forgotten or neglected.

In a theater, space is static, that is, the space represented on
the stage, as well as the spatial relation of the beholder to the
spectacle, is unalterably fixed. The spectator cannot leave his
seat, and the setting of the stage cannot change, during one act
(except for such incidentals as rising moons or gathering clouds
and such illegitimate reborrowings from the film as turning wings
or gliding backdrops). But, in return for this restriction, the
theater has the advantage that time, the medium of emotion and
thought conveyable by speech, is free and independent of anything that may happen in visible space. Hamlet may deliver his
famous monologue lying on a couch in the middle distance, doing
nothing and only dimly discernible to the spectator and listener,
and yet by his mere words enthrall him with a feeling of intensest
emotional action.

With the movies the situation is reversed. Here, too, the spectator occupies a fixed seat, but only physically, not as the subject
of an aesthetic experience. Aesthetically, he is in permanent
motion as his eye identifies itself with the lens of the camera,
which permanently shifts in distance and direction. And as movable as the spectator is, as movable is, for the same reason, the
space presented to him. Not only bodies move in space, but space
itself does, approaching, receding, turning, dissolving and recrys-
tallizing as it appears through the controlled locomotion and
focusing of the camera and through the cutting and editing of the
various shots—not to mention such special effects as visions,
transformations, disappearances, slow-motion and fast-motion
shots, reversals and trick films. This opens up a world of possibilities of which the stage can never dream. Quite apart from
such photographic tricks as the participation of disembodied
spirits in the action of the *Topper* series, or the more effective
wonders wrought by Roland Young in *The Man Who Could Work*

Miracles, there is, on the purely factual level, an untold wealth of themes as inaccessible to the "legitimate" stage as a fog or a snowstorm is to the sculptor; all sorts of violent elemental phenomena and, conversely, events too microscopic to be visible under normal conditions (such as the life-saving injection with the serum flown in at the very last moment, or the fatal bite of the yellow-fever mosquito); full-scale battle scenes; all kinds of operations, not only in the surgical sense but also in the sense of any actual construction, destruction or experimentation, as in *Louis Pasteur* or *Madame Curie;* a really grand party, moving through many rooms of a mansion or a palace. Features like these, even the mere shifting of the scene from one place to another by means of a car perilously negotiating heavy traffic or a motorboat steered through a nocturnal harbor, will not only always retain their primitive cinematic appeal but also remain enormously effective as a means of stirring the emotions and creating suspense. In addition, the movies have the power, entirely denied to the theater, to convey psychological experiences by directly projecting their content to the screen, substituting, as it were, the eye of the beholder for the consciousness of the character (as when the imaginings and hallucinations of the drunkard in the otherwise overrated *Lost Weekend* appear as stark realities instead of being described by mere words). But any attempt to convey thought and feelings exclusively, or even primarily, by speech leaves us with a feeling of embarrassment, boredom, or both.

What I mean by thoughts and feelings "conveyed exclusively, or even primarily, by speech" is simply this: Contrary to naïve expectation, the invention of the sound track in 1928 has been unable to change the basic fact that a moving picture, even when it has learned to talk, remains a picture that moves and does not convert itself into a piece of writing that is enacted. Its substance remains a series of visual sequences held together by an uninterrupted flow of movement in space (except, of course, for such checks and pauses as have the same compositional value as a rest in music), and not a sustained study in human character and destiny transmitted by effective, let alone "beautiful," diction. I cannot remember a more misleading statement about the movies than Mr. Eric Russell Bentley's in the spring number of the *Kenyon Review,* 1945: "The potentialities of the talking

screen differ from those of the silent screen in adding the dimension of dialogue—which could be poetry." I would suggest: "The
potentialities of the talking screen differ from those of the silent
screen in integrating visible movement with dialogue which,
therefore, had better not be poetry."

All of us if we are old enough to remember the period prior
to 1928, recall the old-time pianist who, with his eyes glued on
the screen, would accompany the events with music adapted
to their mood and rhythm; and we also recall the weird and spec-
tral feeling overtaking us when this pianist left his post for a
few minutes and the film was allowed to run by itself, the darkness haunted by the monotonous rattle of the machinery. Even
the silent film, then, was never mute. The visible spectacle always
required, and received, an audible accompaniment which, from
the very beginning, distinguished the film from simple pantomime
and rather classed it—*mutatis mutandis*—with the ballet. The
advent of the talkie meant not so much an "addition" as a transformation: the transformation of musical sound into articulate
speech and, therefore, of quasi pantomime into an entirely new
species of spectacle which differs from the ballet, and agrees with
the stage play, in that its acoustic component consists of intel-
ligible words, but differs from the stage play and agrees with the
ballet in that this acoustic component is not detachable from the
visual: In a film, that which we hear remains, for good or worse,
inextricably fused with that which we see; the sound, articulate
or not, cannot express any more than is expressed, at the same
time, by visible movement; and in a good film it does not even
attempt to do so. To put it briefly, the play—or, as it is very
properly called, the "script"—of a moving picture is subject to
what might be termed the *principle of coexpressibility*.

Empirical proof of this principle is furnished by the fact that,
wherever the dialogical or monological element gains temporary
prominence, there appears, with the inevitability of a natural law,
the "close-up." What does the close-up achieve? In showing us,
in magnification, either the face of the speaker or the face of the
listeners or both in alternation, the camera transforms the human
physiognomy into a huge field of action where—given the qualification of the performers—every subtle movement of the features,
almost imperceptible from a natural distance, becomes an expres-

sive event in visible space and thereby completely integrates itself with the expressive content of the spoken word; whereas, on the stage, the spoken word makes a stronger rather than a weaker impression if we are not permitted to count the hairs in Romeo's mustache.

This does not mean that the scenario is a negligible factor in the making of a moving picture. It only means that its artistic intention differs in kind from that of a stage play, and much more from that of a novel or a piece of poetry. As the success of a Gothic jamb figure depends not only upon its quality as a piece of sculpture but also, or even more so, upon its integrability with the architecture of the portal, so does the success of a movie script—not unlike that of an opera libretto—depend, not only upon its quality as a piece of literature but also, or even more so, upon its integrability with the events on the screen.

As a result—another empirical proof of the coexpressibility principle—good movie scripts are unlikely to make good reading and have seldom been published in book form; whereas, conversely, good stage plays have to be severely altered, cut, and, on the other hand, enriched by interpolations to make good movie scripts. In Shaw's *Pygmalion,* for instance, the actual process of Eliza's phonetic education and, still more important, her final triumph at the grand party, are wisely omitted; we see—or, rather, hear—some samples of her gradual linguistic improvement and finally encounter her, upon her return from the reception, victorious and splendidly arrayed but deeply hurt for want of recognition and sympathy. In the film adaptation, precisely these two scenes are not only supplied but also strongly emphasized; we witness the fascinating activities in the laboratory with its array of spinning disks and mirrors, organ pipes and dancing flames, and we participate in the ambassadorial party, with many moments of impending catastrophe and a little counterintrigue thrown in for suspense. Unquestionably these two scenes, entirely absent from the play, and indeed unachievable upon the stage, were the highlights of the film; whereas the Shavian dialogue, however severely cut, turned out to fall a little flat in certain moments. And wherever, as in so many other films, a poetic emotion, a musical outburst, or a literary conceit (even, I am grieved to say, some of the wisecracks of Groucho Marx) entirely lose contact with visible movement, they strike the sensitive spectator as, literally, out of place. It is certainly terrible when a soft-boiled he-man, after the suicide of his mistress, casts a twelve-foot glance upon her photograph and says something less-than-coexpressible to the effect that he will never forget her. But when he recites, instead, a piece of poetry as sublimely more-than-coexpressible as Romeo's monologue at the bier of Juliet, it is still worse. Reinhardt's *Midsummer Night's Dream* is probably the most unfortunate major film ever produced; and Olivier's *Henry V* owes its comparative success, apart from the all but providential adaptability of this particular play, to so many *tours de force* that it will, God willing, remain an exception rather than set a pattern. It combines "judicious pruning" with the interpolation of pageantry, nonverbal comedy and melodrama; it uses a device perhaps best designated as "oblique cose-up" (Mr. Olivier's beautiful face inwardly listening to but not pronouncing the great soliloquy); and, most notably, it shifts between three levels of archaeological reality: a reconstruction of Elizabethan London, a reconstruction of the events of 1415 as laid down in Shakespeare's play, and the reconstruction of a performance of this play on Shakespeare's own stage. All this is perfectly legitimate; but, even so, the highest praise of the film will always come from those who, like the critic of the *New Yorker,* are not quite in sympathy with either the movies *au naturel* or Shakespeare *au naturel.*

As the writings of Conan Doyle potentially contain all modern mystery stories (except for the tough specimens of the Dashiell Hammett school), so do the films produced between 1900 and 1910 pre-establish the subject matter and methods of the moving picture as we know it. This period produced the incunabula of the Western and the crime film (Edwin S. Porter's amazing *Great Train Robbery* of 1903) from which developed the modern gangster, adventure, and mystery pictures (the latter, if well done, is still one of the most honest and genuine forms of film entertainment, space being doubly charged with time as the beholder asks himself not only "What is going to happen?" but also "What has happened before?"). The same period saw the emergence of the fantastically imaginative film (*Méliès*) which was to lead to the expressionist and surrealist experiments (*The Cabinet of Dr. Caligari, Sang d'un Poète*, etc.), on the one hand, and to the more superficial and spectacular fairy tales à la Arabian Nights, on the other. Comedy, later to triumph in Charlie Chaplin, the still insufficiently appreciated Buster Keaton, the Marx Brothers and the pre-Hollywood creations of René Clair, reached a respectable level in Max Linder and others. In historical and melodramatic films the foundations were laid for movie iconography and movie symbolism, and in the early work of D. W. Griffith we find, not only remarkable attempts at psychological analysis (*Edgar Allan Poe*) and social criticism (*A Corner in Wheat*) but also such basic technical innovations as the long shot, the flashback and the close-up. And modest trick films and cartoons paved the way to Felix the Cat, Popeye the Sailor, and Felix's prodigious offspring, Mickey Mouse.

Within their self-imposed limitations the earlier Disney films, and certain sequences in the later ones,[1] represent, as it were, a chemically pure distillation of cinematic possibilities. They retain the most important folkloristic elements—sadism, pornography, the humor engendered by both, and moral justice—almost without

[1] I make this distinction because it was, in my opinion, a fall from grace when *Snow White* introduced the human figure and when *Fantasia* attempted to picturalize The World's Great Music. The very virtue of the animated cartoon is to animate, that is to say endow lifeless things with life, or living things with a different kind of life. It effects a metamorphosis, and such a metamorphosis is wonderfully present in Disney's animals, plants, thunderclouds and railroad trains. Whereas his dwarfs, glamourized princesses, hillbillies, baseball players, rouged centaurs and *amigos* from South America are not transformations but caricatures at best, and fakes or vulgarities at worst. Concerning music, however, it should be borne in mind that its cinematic use is no less predicated upon the principle of coexpressibility than is the cinematic use of the spoken word. There is music permitting or even requiring the accompaniment of visible action (such as dances, ballet music and any kind of operatic compositions) and music of which the opposite is true; and this is, again, not a question of quality (most of us rightly prefer a waltz by Johann Strauss to a symphony by Sibelius) but one of intention. In *Fantasia* the hippopotamus ballet was wonderful, and the Pastoral Symphony and "Ave Maria" sequences were deplorable, not because the cartooning in the first case was infinitely better than in the two others (*cf.* above), and certainly not because Beethoven and Schubert are too sacred for picturalization, but simply because Ponchielli's "Dance of the Hours" is coexpressible while the Pastoral Symphony and the "Ave Maria" are not. In cases like these even the best imaginable music and the best imaginable cartoon will impair rather than enhance each other's effectiveness.

Experimental proof of all this was furnished by Disney's recent *Make Mine Music* where The World's Great Music was fortunately restricted to Prokofieff. Even among the other sequences the most successful ones were those in which the human element was either absent or reduced to a minimum; Willie the Whale, the Ballad of Johnny Fedora and Alice Blue-Bonnet, and, above all, the truly magnificent Goodman Quartet.

dilution and often fuse these elements into a variation on the primitive and inexhaustible David-and-Goliath motif, the triumph of the seemingly weak over the seemingly strong; and their fantastic independence of the natural laws gives them the power to integrate space with time to such perfection that the spatial and temporal experiences of sight and hearing come to be almost interconvertible. A series of soap bubbles, successively punctured, emits a series of sounds exactly corresponding in pitch and volume to the size of the bubbles; the three uvulae of Willie the Whale—small, large and medium—vibrate in consonance with tenor, bass and baritone notes; and the very concept of stationary existence is completely abolished. No object in creation, whether it be a house, a piano, a tree or an alarm clock, lacks the faculties of organic, in fact anthropomorphic, movement, facial expression and phonetic articulation. Incidentally, even in normal, "realistic" films the inanimate object, provided that it is dynamizable, can play the role of a leading character as do the ancient railroad engines in Buster Keaton's *General* and *Niagara Falls*. How the earlier Russian films exploited the possibility of heroizing all sorts of machinery lives in everybody's memory; and it is perhaps more than an accident that the two films which will go down in history as the great comical and the great serious masterpiece of the silent period bear the names and immortalize the personalities of two big ships: Keaton's *Navigator* (1924) and Eisenstein's *Potemkin* (1925).

The evolution from the jerky beginnings to this grand climax offers the fascinating spectacle of a new artistic medium gradually becoming conscious of its legitimate, that is, exclusive, possibilities and limitations—a spectacle not unlike the development of the mosaic, which started out with transposing illusionistic genre pictures into a more durable material and culminated in the hieratic supernaturalism of Ravenna; or the development of line engraving, which started out as a cheap and handy substitute for book illumination and culminated in the purely "graphic" style of Dürer.

Just so the silent movies developed a definite style of their own, adapted to the specific conditions of the medium. A hitherto unknown language was forced upon a public not yet capable of reading it, and the more proficient the public became the more refinement could develop in the language. For a Saxon peasant of around 800 it was not easy to understand the meaning of a picture showing a man as he pours water over the head of another man, and even later many people found it difficult to grasp the significance of two ladies standing behind the throne of an emperor. For the public of around 1910 it was no less difficult to understand the meaning of the speechless action in a moving picture, and the producers employed means of clarification similar to those we find in medieval art. One of these were printed titles or letters, striking equivalents of the medieval *tituli* and scrolls (at a still earlier date there even used to be explainers who would say, *viva voce,* "Now he thinks his wife is dead but she isn't" or "I don't wish to offend the ladies in the audience but I doubt that any of them would have done that much for her child"). Another, less obstrusive method of explanation was the introduction of a fixed iconography which from the outset informed the spectator about the basic facts and characters, much as the two ladies behind the emperor, when carrying a sword and a cross respectively, were uniquely determined as Fortitude and Faith. There arose, identifiable by standardized appearance, behavior and attributes, the well-remembered types of the Vamp and the Straight Girl (perhaps the most convincing modern equivalents of the medieval personifications of the Vices and Virtues), the Family Man, and the Villain, the latter marked by a black mustache and walking stick. Nocturnal scenes were printed on blue or green film. A checkered tablecloth meant, once for all, a "poor but honest" milieu; a happy marriage, soon to be endangered by the shadows from the past, was symbolized by the young wife's pouring the breakfast coffee for her husband; the first kiss was invariably announced by the lady's gently playing with her partner's necktie and was invariably accompanied by her kicking out with her left foot. The conduct of the characters was predetermined accordingly. The poor but honest laborer who, after leaving his little house with the checkered tablecloth, came upon an abandoned baby could not but take it to his home and bring it up as best he could; the Family Man could not but yield, however temporarily, to the temptations of the Vamp. As a result these early melodramas had a highly gratifying and soothing quality in that events took shape, without the complications of individual psychology, according to a pure Aristotelian logic so badly missed in real life.

Devices like these became gradually less necessary as the public grew accustomed to interpret the action by itself and were virtually abolished by the invention of the talking film. But even now there survive—quite legitimately, I think—the remnants of a "fixed attitude and attribute" principle and, more basic, a primitive or folkloristic concept of plot construction. Even today we take it for granted that the diphtheria of a baby tends to occur when the parents are out and, having occurred, solves all their matrimonial problems. Even today we demand of a decent mystery film that the butler, though he may be anything from an agent of the British Secret Service to the real father of the daughter of the house, must not turn out to be the murderer. Even today we love to see Pasteur, Zola or Ehrlich win out against stupidity and wickedness, with their respective wives trusting and trusting all the time. Even today we much prefer a happy finale to a gloomy one and insist, at the very least, on the observance of the Aristotelian rule that the story have a beginning, a middle and an ending—a rule the abrogation of which has done so much to estrange the general public from the more elevated spheres of modern writing. Primitive symbolism, too, survives in such amusing details as the last sequence of *Casablanca* where the delightfully crooked and right-minded *préfet de police* casts an empty bottle of Vichy water into the wastepaper basket; and in such telling symbols of the supernatural as Sir Cedric Hardwicke's Death in the guise of a "gentleman in a dustcoat trying" (*On Borrowed Time*) or Claude Rains's Hermes Psychopompos in the striped trousers of an airline manager (*Here Comes Mister Jordan*).

The most conspicuous advances were made in directing, lighting, camera work, cutting and acting proper. But while in most of these fields the evolution proceeded continuously— though, of course, not without detours, breakdowns and archaic relapses—the development of acting suffered a sudden interruption by the invention of the talking film; so that the style of acting in the silents can already be evaluated in retrospect, as a lost art not unlike the painting technique of Jan van Eyck or, to take up our previous simile, the burin technique of Dürer. It was soon realized that acting in a silent film neither meant a pantomimic exaggeration of stage acting (as was generally and erroneously assumed by professional stage actors who more and more frequently condescended to perform in the movies), nor could dispense with stylization altogether; a man photographed while walking down a gangway in ordinary, everyday-life fashion looked like anything but a man walking down a gangway when the result appeared on the screen. If the picture was to look both natural and meaningful the acting had to be done in a manner equally different from the style of the stage and the reality of ordinary life; speech had to be made dispensable by establishing an organic relation between the acting and the technical procedure of cinephotography—much as in Dürer's prints colors had been made dispensable by establishing an organic relation between the design and the technical procedure of line engraving.

This was precisely what the great actors of the silent period accomplished, and it is a significant fact that the best of them did not come from the stage, whose crystallized tradition prevented Duse's only film, *Cenere,* from being more than a priceless record of Duse. They came instead from the circus or the variety, as was the case of Chaplin, Keaton and Will Rogers; from nothing in particular, as was the case of Theda Bara, of her greater European parallel, the Danish actress Asta Nielsen, and of Garbo; or from everything under the sun, as was the case of Douglas Fairbanks. The style of these "old masters" was indeed comparable to the style of line engraving in that it was, and had to be, exaggerated in comparison with stage acting (just as the sharply incised and vigorously curved *tailles* of the burin are exaggerated in comparison with pencil strokes or brushwork), but richer, subtler and infinitely more precise. The advent of the talkies, reducing if not abolishing this difference between screen acting and stage acting, thus confronted the actors and actresses of the silent screen with a serious problem. Buster Keaton yielded to temptation and fell. Chaplin first tried to stand his ground and to remain an exquisite archaist but finally gave in, with only moderate success (*The Great Dictator*). Only the glorious Harpo has thus far successfully refused to utter a single articulate sound; and only Greta Garbo succeeded, in a measure, in transforming her style in principle. But even in her case one cannot help feeling that her first talking picture, *Anna Christie,* where she could ensconce herself, most of the time, in mute or monosyllabic sullenness, was better than her later performances; and in the second, talking version of *Anna Karenina,* the weakest moment is certainly when she delivers a big Ibsenian speech to her husband, and the strongest when she silently moves along the platform of the railroad station while her despair takes shape in the consonance of her movement (and expression) with the movement of the nocturnal space around her, filled with the real noises of the trains and the imaginary sound of the "little men with the iron hammers" that drives her, relentlessly and almost without her realizing it, under the wheels.

Small wonder that there is sometimes felt a kind of nostalgia for the silent period and that devices have been worked out to combine the virtues of sound and speech with those of silent acting, such as the "oblique close-up" already mentioned in connection with *Henry V;* the dance behind glass doors in *Sous les Toits de Paris;* or, in the *Histoire d'un Tricheur,* Sacha Guitry's recital of the events of his youth while the events themselves are "silently" enacted on the screen. However, this nostalgic feeling is no argument against the talkies as such. Their evolution has shown that, in art, every gain entails a certain loss on the other side of the ledger; but that the gain remains a gain, provided that the basic nature of the medium is realized and respected. One can imagine that, when the cavemen of Altamira began to paint their buffaloes in natural colors instead of merely incising the contours, the more conservative cavemen foretold the end of paleolithic art. But paleolithic art went on, and so will the movies. New technical inventions always tend to dwarf the values already attained, especially in a medium that owes its very existence to technical experimentation. The earliest talkies were infinitely inferior to the then mature silents, and most of the present technicolor films are still inferior to the now mature talkies in black and white. But even if Aldous Huxley's nightmare should come true and the experiences of taste, smell and touch should be added to those of sight and hearing, even then we may say with the Apostle, as we have said when first confronted with the sound track and the technicolor film, "We are troubled on every side, yet not distressed; we are perplexed, but not in despair."

From the law of time-charged space and space-bound time, there follows the fact that the screenplay, in contrast to the theater play, *has no aesthetic existence independent of its performance, and that its characters have no aesthetic existence outside the actors.*

The playwright writes in the fond hope that his work will be an imperishable jewel in the treasure house of civilization and will be presented in hundreds of performances that are but transient variations on a "work" that is constant. The script-writer, on the other hand, writes for one producer, one director and one cast. Their work achieves the same degree of permanence as does his; and should the same or a similar scenario ever be filmed by a different director and a different cast there will result an altogether different "play."

Othello or Nora are definite, substantial figures created by the playwright. They can be played well or badly, and they can be "interpreted" in one way or another; but they most definitely exist, no matter who plays them or even whether they are played at all. The character in a film, however, lives and dies with the actor. It is not the entity "Othello" interpreted by Robeson or the entity "Nora" interpreted by Duse; it is the entity "Greta Garbo" incarnate in a figure called Anna Christie or the entity "Robert Montgomery" incarnate in a murderer who, for all we know or care to know, may forever remain anonymous but will never cease to haunt our memories. Even when the names of the characters happen to be Henry VIII or Anna Karenina, the king who ruled England from 1509 to 1547 and the woman created by Tolstoy, they do not exist outside the being of Garbo and Laughton. They are but empty and incorporeal outlines like the shadows in Homer's Hades, assuming the character of reality only when filled with the lifeblood of an actor. Conversely, if a movie role is badly played there remains literally nothing of it, no matter how interesting the character's psychology or how elaborate the words.

What applies to the actor applies, *mutatis mutandis,* to most of the other artists, or artisans, who contribute to the making of a film: the director, the sound man, the enormously important cameraman, even the make-up man. A stage production is rehearsed until everything is ready, and then it is repeatedly performed in three consecutive hours. At each performance everybody has to be on hand and does his work; and afterward he goes home and to bed. The work of the stage actor may thus be likened to that of a musician, and that of the stage director to that of a conductor. Like these, they have a certain repertoire which they have studied and present in a number of complete but transitory performances, be it *Hamlet* today and *Ghosts* tomorrow or *Life with Father per saecula saeculorum.* The activities of the film actor and the film director, however, are comparable, respectively, to those of the plastic artist and the architect, rather than to those of the musician and the conductor. Stage work is continuous but transitory; film work is discontinuous but permanent. Individual sequences are done piecemeal and out of order according to the most efficient use of sets and personnel. Each bit is done over and over again until it stands; and when the whole has been cut and composed everyone is through with it forever. Needless to say that this very procedure cannot but emphasize the curious consubstantiality that exists between the person of the movie actor and his role. Coming into existence piece by piece, regardless of the natural sequence of events, the "character" can grow into a unified whole only if the actor manages to be, not merely to play, Henry VIII or Anna Karenina throughout the entire wearisome period of shooting. I have it on the best of authorities that Laughton was really difficult to live with in the particular six or eight weeks during which he was doing—or rather being—Captain Bligh.

It might be said that a film, called into being by a co-operative effort in which all contributions have the same degree of permanence, is the nearest modern equivalent of a medieval cathedral; the role of the producer corresponding, more or less, to that of the bishop or archbishop; that of the director to that of the architect in chief; that of the scenario writers to that of the scholastic advisers establishing the iconographical program; and that of the actors, cameramen, cutters, sound men, make-up men and the divers technicians to that of those whose work provided the physical entity of the finished product, from the sculptors, glass painters, bronze casters, carpenters and skilled masons down to the quarry men and woodsmen. And if you speak to any one of these collaborators he will tell you, with perfect *bona fides,* that his is really the most important job—which is quite true to the extent that it is indispensable.

This comparison may seem sacrilegious, not only because there are, proportionally, fewer good films than there are good cathedrals, but also because the movies are commercial. However, if commercial art be defined as all art not primarily produced in order to gratify the creative urge of its maker but primarily intended to meet the requirements of a patron or a buying public, it must be said that noncommercial art is the exception rather than the rule, and a fairly recent and not always felicitous exception at that. While it is true that commercial art is always in danger of ending up as a prostitute, it is equally true that noncommercial art is always in danger of ending up as an old maid. Noncommercial art has given us Seurat's "Grande Jatte" and Shakespeare's sonnets, but also much that is esoteric to the point of incommunicability. Conversely, commercial art has given us much that is vulgar or snobbish (two aspects of the same thing) to the point of loathsomeness, but also Dürer's prints and Shakespeare's plays. For, we must not forget that Dürer's prints were partly made on commission and partly intended to be sold in the open market; and that Shakespeare's plays—in contrast to the earlier masques and intermezzi which were produced at court by aristocratic amateurs and could afford to be so incomprehensible that even those who described them in printed monographs occasionally failed to grasp their intended significance—were meant to appeal, and did appeal, not only to the select few but also to everyone who was prepared to pay a shilling for admission.

It is this requirement of communicability that makes commercial art more vital than noncommercial, and therefore potentially much more effective for better or for worse. The commercial producer can both educate and pervert the general public, and can allow the general public—or rather his idea of the general public—both to educate and to pervert himself. As is demonstrated by a number of excellent films that proved to be great box office successes, the public does not refuse to accept good products if it gets them. That is does not get them very often is caused not so much by commercialism as such as by too little discernment and, paradoxical though it may seem, too much timidity in its application. Hollywood believes that it must produce "what the public wants" while the public would take whatever Hollywood produces. If Hollywood were to decide for itself what it wants it would get away with it—even if it should decide to "depart from evil and do good." For, to revert to whence we started, in modern life the movies are what most other forms of art have ceased to be, not an adornment but a necessity.

That this should be so is understandable, not only from a sociological but also from an art-historical point of view. The processes of all the earlier representational arts conform, in a higher or lesser degree, to an idealistic conception of the world. These arts operate from top to bottom, so to speak, and not from bottom to top; they start with an idea to be projected into shapeless matter and not with the objects that constitute the physical world. The painter works on a blank wall or canvas which he organizes into a likeness of things and persons according to his idea (however much this idea may have been nourished by reality); he does not work with the things and persons themselves even if he works "from the model." The same is true of the sculptor with his shapeless mass of clay or his untooled block of stone or wood; of the writer with his sheet of paper or his dictaphone; and even of the stage designer with his empty and sorely limited section of space. It is the movies, and only the movies, that do justice to that materialistic interpretation of the universe which, whether we like it or not, pervades contemporary civilization. Excepting the very special case of the animated cartoon, the movies organize material things and persons, not a neutral medium, into a composition that receives its style, and may even become fantastic or pretervoluntarily symbolic,[2] not so much by

---

[2] I cannot help feeling that the final sequence of the new Marx Brothers film *Night in Casablanca*—where Harpo unaccountably usurps the pilot's seat of a big airplane, causes incalculable havoc by flicking one tiny little control after another, and waxes the more insane with joy the greater the disproportion between the smallness of his effort and the magnitude of the disaster—is a magnificent and terrifying symbol of man's behavior in the atomic age. No doubt the Marx Brothers would vigorously reject this interpretation, but so would Dürer have done had anyone told him that his "Apocalypse" foreshadowed the cataclysm of the Reformation.

an interpretation in the artist's mind as by the actual manipulation of physical objects and recording machinery. The medium of the movies is physical reality as such: the physical reality of eighteenth-century Versailles—no matter whether it be the original or a Hollywood facsimile indistinguishable therefrom for all aesthetic intents and purposes—or of a suburban home in Westchester; the physical reality of the Rue de Lappe in Paris or of the Gobi Desert, of Paul Ehrlich's apartment in Frankfurt or of the streets of New York in the rain; the physical reality of engines and animals, of Edward G. Robinson and Jimmy Cagney. All these objects and persons must be organized into a work of art. They can be arranged in all sorts of ways ("arrangement" comprising, of course, such things as make-up, lighting and camera work); but there is no running away from them. From this point of view it becomes evident that an attempt at subjecting the world to artistic prestylization, as in the expressionist settings of *The Cabinet of Dr. Caligari* (1919), could be no more than an exciting experiment that could exert but little influence upon the general course of events. To prestylize reality prior to tackling it amounts to dodging the problem. The problem is to manipulate and shoot unstylized reality in such a way that the result has style. This is a proposition no less legitimate and no less difficult than any proposition in the older arts.

EXERCISES

on film and the liberal arts

1. Panofsky notes that if movie production were to come to a sudden and complete halt ". . . the social consequences would be catastrophic." Do you agree? What is the significance of Panofsky's point in any comparative view of film in relation to the history and aims of the liberal arts?

2. Later in his essay, Panofsky follows through on his point when he writes: ". . . in modern life the movies are what most other forms of art have ceased to be, not an adornment but a necessity." Has television now become the "necessity" that Panofsky, writing in 1934, saw the movies as being? In

either case, what sort of "necessity" does he mean? Given television, would you say that movies presently serve, as Panofsky says the other arts do, more as an "adornment" than a "necessity" to the general public?

3. Panofsky writes that "the medium of the movies is physical reality as such." This is a key point of his essay and one which remains crucial in current discussions of the cinema. Would von Sternberg or Antonioni be likely to agree with Panofsky's emphasis on "physical reality as such"? Would Chiaromonte be in agreement with this? Or Arnheim? On this question you may be interested to consult Siegfried Kracauer's extensive study, *Theory of Film,* which is in line with Panofsky's view. For a more qualified approach, see Susan Sontag's essay on "Film and Theater" in the *Tulane Drama Review,* Fall 1966, Vol. II, no. 1.

4. In defining the way films work, Panofsky notes ". . . the curious consubstantiality that exists between the person, the movie actor, and his role." What is the significance of his use of the term "consubstantiality" in this context, and what is the general import of his point as it applies to the difference in style and effects between film and theater?

5. Panofsky organizes his essay according to the chronology of the film's development from its early phase to the present. At the same time, note how he intertwines with his exposition a developing argument concerning the esthetics of the film, and the place of films and the liberal arts in the modern world. Discuss his argument on the basis of your own reading about and experience with film.

LIST
OF
RECOMMENDED
FILMS

The films are grouped according to the topic divisions; where possible, I have listed films discussed or referred to in the essays. Selections were determined in part by what I knew to be readily available through distributors. I have also preferred titles relatively inexpensive to order. In some cases, I have cited lesser known signficant—and discussion-sparking—works rather than those more widely known, especially in the case of features frequently shown on television. Since the essays concentrate mainly on feature films, I have chiefly noted that type of film, though some shorts and other types of experimental and educational film have been included. Student discussion tends to get off to a quicker start, as well as to prove more extensive, when it is in response to a feature-length film. I have selected films which open avenues to extensive and engaged discussion and writing, and have sought variety among times and places and nations and genres and levels of seriousness, though no film has been included which is not a top example of its kind. As the note to each listing may suggest, the placing of a film in "Rhetoric" when it might as easily have been placed in "Society" or "Music" largely depended on the relation of one or another of its elements to a particular topic. The listing according to category remains, however, somewhat arbitrary and the instructor could of course make use of the works in each group in any ways or combinations he preferred. BW signifies a film in black and white; C, in color.

FILM AND RHETORIC

Broken Blossoms (1919)—BW—120 min.—Museum of Modern Art Film Library

D. W. Griffith's affectingly intimate rendering of a star-crossed romance. The film shows the various techniques of continuity, suspense, and audience involvement which Griffith either perfected or invented —like the iris, the full shot, the close-up, the panoramic shot, the crosscutting of shots—and over which, by the time of this film, he was in full command.

Breathless (1959)—BW—90 min.—Brandon

Made by Jean-Luc Godard, this is a key innovative film. Unlike those of Griffith, Godard's young lovers aren't especially tender blossoms—though their story is an equally compelling one. And in contrast to the smooth flow of Griffith, this film's jumpcuts and lack of transitional sequences are in keeping both with the fragmented and hectic sense of experience the films seeks to transmit, and with the "Protean" nature of its characters.

Beauty and the Beast (1946)—BW—90 min.—Brandon

Fantasy in film by the fabled poet and film-maker, Jean Cocteau. The film offers a contrast, in its softness of focus and tone, to the drier, analytical style of Godard. Cocteau's published diary on the making of this film is on all counts rewarding reading.

Zero de Conduite (1933)—BW—44 min.—Brandon

A work by a tragically short-lived prodigy of film-making, Jean Vigo. Childhood and schooldays are envisioned surrealistically and with great power and intensity.

Bed and Sofa (1927)—BW—109 min.—Brandon

This film by Abram Room is in its plot a standard love triangle; in effect, it is a masterpiece of the Russian cinema and a landmark of film realism.

La Strada (1954)—BW—107 min.—Brandon

Frederico Fellini's parable in a contemporary setting, which marks the movement of the Italian cinema beyond neo-realism.

Psycho (1960)—BW—109 min.—Contemporary

Perhaps the best known—and most notorious—of Alfred Hitchcock's shockers. Hitchcock propels his characters beyond the realms of romance (whether bitter or sweet) into the regions of madness and sudden evil. He is as skilled as Griffith in editing a film and telling a story and as tough-minded as Godard.

FILM AND LITERATURE

Adventures of Mark Twain (1944)—BW—130 min.—Brandon

A sympathetic and realistic portrayal of Twain's life and times, directed by Irving Rapper.

All the King's Men (1949)—BW—109 min.—Brandon

The films of the late Robert Rossen have come to be increasingly esteemed. This adaptation of Robert Penn Warren's novel on the rise and fall of a political demagogue is ranked among Rossen's best.

Accident (1967)—C—90 min.—Columbia Cinematheque

Directed by Joseph Losey and scripted by Harold Pinter, this film merges the talents of a leading film director with those of a leading playwright in a provocative treatment of contemporary life. It is discussed in this volume by T. J. Ross.

The Big Sleep (1946)—BW—114 min.—Brandon

Based on a novel by a master of the hard-boiled detective genre, Raymond Chandler, this screen version by a master of the commercial cinema, Howard Hawks, results in a smoothly crafted and highly entertaining film. Like *All the King's Men,* it also raises basic questions concerning the comparable, contrasting, or parallel qualities and functions of the work of entertainment and the work of art.

To Have and Have Not (1944)—BW—100 min.—Brandon

Humphrey Bogart meets Lauren Bacall in a film based on a novel by Ernest Hemingway, scripted by William Faulkner, and directed by a contemporary and friend of both writers, Howard Hawks.

Lord Jim (1965)—C—100 min.—Twyman

Richard Brooks directed this sincere and fairly faithful film rendering of Joseph Conrad's famous novel about an anti-hero striving to become a hero.

Occurrence at Owl Creek (1964)—BW—27 min.—Contemporary

A short film by Roberto Enrico based on a short story by Ambrose Bierce. The camera is used to add further shock effects to the strong, shocking qualities of the original—with a resultant twist of meaning and moral closer to contemporary attitudes than to those of Bierce's time.

Ivan the Terrible, Parts I and II (1944–1946)—BW—90 min. each—Brandon

Eisenstein is to the Russian cinema what Griffith is to the American. *Ivan* represents his last completed and most freely esthetic achievement before he fell foul of the censors. The film strikingly juxtaposes moments of personal intimacy and public grandeur; nobility and madness; pomp and terror. The pace is leisurely and there is frequent use of looming close-ups.

Richard III (1955)—C—155 min.—Brandon

Considered by many to be Sir Laurence Olivier's most successful filming of Shakespeare, *Richard III* centers, like *Ivan the Terrible,* on a heroic villain of history and legend. The respective treatments of Eisenstein and Olivier offer interesting contrasts in style, emphasis, and tone.

Hamlet (1948)—BW—153 min.—Twyman

Olivier's controversial Freudian interpretation. James Agee's extensive review in *Agee on Film,* and Mary McCarthy's in her *Sights and Spectacles* provide a full complementary discussion of the film in which the main questions posed by it are raised.

Throne of Blood (1957)—BW—105 min.—Brandon

A much-praised adaptation of *Macbeth* by Japan's foremost filmmaker, Akiru Kurosawa. The concentration is on film rather than literary values, as J. Blumenthal notes in his essay on the film included in this volume.

FILM AND MUSIC

Frantic (1958)—BW—90 min.—Brandon

A suspense thriller by a leading director of the New Wave, Louis Malle, with a jazz score composed and played by Miles Davis.

Dr. Strangelove (1964)—BW—120 min.—Royal International

Stanley Kubrick's satirical film is another of the key works of the past decade. In its use of music to provide ironic counterpoint to the screen image—a characteristic shot is that of a flight of bomber planes taking off to the tune of "Try a Little Tenderness"—the film is in keeping with the dissonant mode of black humor, a mode which came to the fore at about the same time this film was being made.

Afternoon of a Faun (1952)—BW—10 min.—Brandon

Dance in film. Hans Richter directed this film in which music and motion brilliantly blend.

The Ballet of Romeo and Juliet (1954)—C—96 min.—Brandon

The music of Prokofiev, the plot line out of Shakespeare, the dancing by Ulanova, and the corps de ballet of the Bolshoi Theater of Moscow—in another apt blending of forms where color is added to music and dance and drama.

Forty-Second Street (1933)—BW—90 min.—Brandon

The archetypal film musical of an earlier decade, directed by Lloyd Bacon. The plot is absurd; the musical production numbers, arranged by Busby Berkeley, are of an all-stops-out scale and flamboyance.

Gold Diggers of 1933—BW—90 min.—Brandon

Another of the musical extravaganzas whose production numbers were arranged by Busby Berkeley. Mervyn Leroy, the director, proved equally adept with gangster films. While for many viewers of middle age, the entertainment values of both the early musical and gangster genres remain undiminished, is this equally the case with younger viewers?

A Visit to Pablo Casals—BW—20 min.—Irving Lesser

A Visit to Marion Anderson—BW—20 min.—Irving Lesser

A Visit to Artur Rubinstein—BW—20 min.—Irving Lesser
The above series was directed by Jules Dassin.

FILM AND THE VISUAL ARTS

Carnival in Flanders (1936)—BW—90 min.—Brandon

Set in sixteenth-century Holland, this film by Jacques Feyder is famous for the strong period flavor it succeeds in capturing through a treatment which is leisurely, sympathetic, and "painterly." Events and scenes are depicted as in a series of tableaux. The cast includes one of the notable figures of the French theater in this century, the late Louis Jouvet.

Gertrud (1965)—C—90 min.—Contemporary

No carnival spirits here but rather the toils and anguish of a doomed love. Again, the focus on an earlier period in its texture and pace and mood is sensitive, detailed, and painterly in effect. The director, Carl Dreyer, was a leading figure among Scandinavian film-makers.

Red Desert (1965)—C—100 min.—Janus

A film by Antonioni. The director, as deeply versed in the fine arts as he is in the cinema, here uses color both to esthetic and psychological purpose. The hidden moods of the heroine are reflected in the colors visible on the screen.

Under the Black Mask (1958)—C—50 min.—Brandon

This is one of a series of art films directed by Paul Haesaerts. A pictorial exposition of Congolese sculpture with a background of authentic African music. Commentary in English.

From Renoir to Picasso (1959)—C—32 min.—Brandon

A film by Paul Haesaerts which makes use of diagrams, split screen, and animation. It is generally rated among the best art teaching films.

Mark Tobey: Artist (1951)—C—20 min.—Brandon

The artist comments on his own work, with the camera serving his presentation.

Rubens (1947)—C—45 min.—Brandon

Directed by Paul Haesaerts. The camera functions as expositor, as the artist is considered in the intellectual, social, and aesthetic contexts of his age.

The Acropolis of Athens (1964)—C—30 min.—Contemporary

Stunning close-up views of the Acropolis.

FILM AND SOCIETY

Ikiru (To Live) (1952)—BW—140 min.—Brandon

Directed by Akiru Kurosawa, this compassionate and realistic film combines themes central to such works as Arthur Miller's play, *Death of a Salesman,* Leo Tolstoy's novella, *The Death of Ivan Ilyich,* and Ingmar Bergman's film, *Wild Strawberries:* face to face with death, man is led to face the nature and meaning of his life—and of the society in which he led his life.

Morgan (1966)—BW—97 min.—Columbia Cinematheque

The anti-hero runs rampant through this celebrated British satire. Direction by Karel Reisz.

Diary of a Country Priest (1951)—BW—90 min.—Brandon

A film on faith and compassion as spare in form as it is powerful in effect. Based on a novel by George Bernanos and directed by Bernanos' friend and admirer, Robert Bresson, himself one of the most admired directors of the contemporary French cinema.

The Crime of Monsieur Lange (1935)—BW—90 min.—Brandon

Romantic love versus the social order in a film which combines the realistic with the farcical, the comic with the absurd. Its director Jean Renoir is one of the undisputed major figures in world cinema.

Les Carabiniers (1965) and *Le Petit Soldat* (1960)—BW—70 min. each
—New York Review Presentation

Concerned with the loss of identity through the experience of war, these are among Jean-Luc Godard's most controversial and disturbing films.

The Grapes of Wrath (1940)—BW—128 min.—Brandon

Like the novel by John Steinbeck on which it was based, John Ford's screen adaptation became famous as a powerful treatment of social themes.

The Sound of Trumpets (1960)—BW—90 min.—Janus

We have heard much about the Organization Man. This film by Ermanno Olmi depicts in a low-keyed graphic way the moulding of an Organization Boy.

Fahrenheit 451 (1966)—C—111 min.—Twyman

A free adaptation of Ray Bradbury's classic of science fiction, in which the eminent film director François Truffaut pays homage to the vitality and values of book culture and the enduring importance of those values to a free society.

The Thing (1951)—BW—87 min.—Brandon

One of the most smoothly done—and most frightening—of science fiction films, with James Arness cast as The Thing.

I Am a Fugitive from a Chain Gang (1932)—BW—90 min.—Brandon

A strong characteristic gangster film of the thirties, directed by Mervyn Leroy and starring Paul Muni. It invites comparison with a characteristic film of recent years like *Cool Hand Luke,* which stars Muni's contemporary counterpart in style and image, Paul Newman.

Bend of the River (1954)—C—91 min.—Twyman

A good example of the Western by one of the best directors of this genre, Anthony Mann. James Stewart and Rock Hudson star.

Virginia City (1940)—BW—120 min.—Brandon

Randolph Scott versus Errol Flynn versus Humphrey Bogart, with Miriam Hopkins standing by. An exhilarating example of the nonadult Western. The direction by Michael Curtiz is unpretentious and deft. Musical background by Max Steiner.

Carmen Comes Home (1951)—BW—120 min.—Brandon

When we think of the Japanese film, we do not ordinarily think of comedy, yet this film directed by Keisuke Kinoshita is one of the most brilliant satirical comedies of our time. Beneath its quiet surface of events concerning a night club dancer's return on a visit to the village of her birth, the more problematic aspects of the relationship of the arts to society are probed and defined.

FILM AND ESTHETICS

L'Avventura (1960)—BW—120 min.—Janus

This film by Antonioni is virtually a *summa* of the themes and techniques of the advanced cinema since 1960.

The Golden Coach (1952)—C—102 min.—Brandon.

A film created as an homage to the world of the theater by Jean Renoir, with color photography by Claude Renoir and a musical score adapted from Vivaldi. It is a film which seeks to take full advantage of, even as it celebrates, the various arts of which the film partakes.

Children of Paradise (1940)—BW—193 min.—Contemporary

Like *The Golden Coach,* the subject of this film is the world of the theater. The theme—suitably—is romantic love which is considered, like the theater itself, in light of the play and conflict of illusion and reality, art and truth, life and death. In its treatment and articulation of its themes, the film may be closely compared and contrasted to that of similar themes and concerns in *L'Avventura.* The film's script is by the poet Jacques Prevert, its direction by Marcel Carné, a major figure in the French cinema with whom Antonioni at the beginning of his career was briefly associated.

Man of Aran (1934)—BW—62 min.—Brandon

One of the famous films of Robert Flaherty in which documentary techniques are used for the purpose of creating a "poetry of the cinema."

The Brig (1966)—BW—60 min.—Film-Maker's Cinematheque

A performance of an Off-Broadway play about a day in a marine stockade, filmed "live" with a hand-held camera. The result is a film which takes on a harrowing dimension of its own as a unique statement on a universe totally dominated by, and submerged in, the "rules" of force and terror. The film's creator, Jonas Mekas, is a founding father and leading publicist of the New American (sometimes called Underground) Cinema, and his film is itself among the best to have hailed from the Underground.

On the Edge (1949)—BW—6 min.—Contemporary

Made by Curtis Harrington, this experimental film seeks to suggest a state of mind in abstract images.

Tartuffe (1925)—BW—60 min.—Brandon

A silent film adaptation of Moliere by a major director of the twenties, F. W. Murnau. Questions concerning transmutations from a linguistic into a visual medium are here clearly raised.

Finnegans Wake (1965)—BW—97 min.—Film Canada Presentation

Produced and directed by Mary Ellen Bute, this is an interesting venture in finding equivalents for the freight of meanings carried by Joyce's "Portmanteau" language.

Repulsion (1966)—BW—90 min.—Columbia Cinematheque

A film by Roman Polanski in which the director seeks to project the interior world of madness. How successful is the film in depicting an interior state of mind? On this question, it is interesting to compare the depiction of psychosis in this film with the depiction of neurosis in *Red Desert*.

Life Begins Tomorrow (1950)—BW—87 min.—Brandon

A film directed by Maurice Védrès which combines documentary techniques with those of *cinema-verité*. The musical score is by Darius Milhaud. The camera follows a young Everyman as he has a series of interviews on the theme of freedom and responsibility with such men as Jean Rostand, J. P. Sartre, Le Corbusier, Picasso, and André Gide.

ADDRESSES OF DISTRIBUTORS
OF FILMS LISTED ABOVE *

Brandon International Films, 221 W. 57th St.
Columbia Cinematheque, 711 Fifth Ave.
Contemporary Films, 267 W. 25th St.
Film Canada Presentations, 1 Charles St. East, Toronto 5, Ontario, Canada
Film-Maker's Cinematheque, 83 E. 4th St.
Irving Lesser Enterprises, 527 Madison Ave.
Janus Films, 24 W. 58th St.
Museum of Modern Art Film Library, 11 W. 53rd St.
New York Review Presentations, 250 W. 57th St.
Royal International Films, 711 Fifth Ave.
Twyman Films, 329 Salem Ave., Dayton, Ohio

* All are located in New York City unless otherwise noted.

SELECTED BIBLIOGRAPHY

Agee, James. *Agee on Film: Reviews and Comments* (paperback ed.). Boston: The Beacon Press, 1964.

Arnheim, Rudolf. *Film as Art* (paperback ed.). Berkeley, Calif.: University of California Press, 1966.

Bentley, Eric. *The Life of the Drama* (paperback ed.). New York: Atheneum Publishers, 1967.

Bergman, Ingmar. *Four Screenplays.* New York: Simon and Schuster, Inc., 1960.

Brownlow, Kevin. *The Parade's Gone By.* New York: Alfred A. Knopf, 1969.

Clarens, Carlos. *Horror Movies.* Berkeley, Calif.: University of California Press, 1968.

Duras, Marguerite. *Hiroshima Mon Amour: Text for the Film by Alain Resnais.* New York: Grove Press, Inc., 1961.

Durgnat, Raymond. *Buñel. New York: Doubleday & Company, Inc.,* 1968.

Everson, William K. *The American Movie.* New York: Atheneum Publishers, 1963.

Gessner, Robert. *The Moving Image.* New York: E. P. Dutton & Co., Inc., 1968.

Huss, Roy, and Norman Silverstein. *The Film Experience.* New York: Harper & Row, Publishers, 1968.

Jacobs, Lewis. *The Rise of the American Film* (paperback ed.). New York: Teachers College Press, Columbia University, 1967.

Kauffmann, Stanley. *A World on Film.* New York: Harper & Row, Publishers, 1966.

Kracauer, Siegfried. *From Caligari to Hitler: A Psychological History of the German Film* (paperback ed.). New York: The Noonday Press, 1959.

Langer, Susanne K. *Problems of Art.* New York: Charles Scribner's Sons, 1957.

Leahy, James. *The Cinema of Joseph Losey.* New York: A. S. Barnes & Company, Inc., 1967.

Lindsay, Vachel. *The Art of the Moving Picture.* New York: Crowell-Collier and Macmillan, Inc., 1915.

Lowenthal, Leo. *Literature, Popular Culture, and Society.* Englewood Cliffs, N.J.: Prentice-Hall, Inc., 1961.

Mayersberg, Paul. *Hollywood: The Haunted House.* London: The Penguin Press, 1967.

McCarthy, Mary. *Sights and Spectacles.* New York: Meridian Books, Inc., 1957.

McVay, Douglas. *The Musical Film. New York:* A. S. Barnes & Company, Inc., 1967.

Ramsaye, Terry. *A Million and One Nights: A History of the Motion Picture* (paperback ed.). New York: Simon and Schuster, Inc., 1964.

Renan, Sheldon. *An Introduction to the American Underground Film.* New York: E. P. Dutton & Co., Inc., 1967.

Ross, Lillian. *Picture.* New York: Holt, Rinehart and Winston, Inc., 1952.

Sarris, Andrew. *Interviews with Film Directors.* New York: The Bobbs-Merrill Company, Inc., 1967.

Schumach, Murray. *The Face on the Cutting Room Floor: The Story of Movie and Television Censorship.* New York: William Morrow & Company, Inc., 1964.

Spottiswoode, Raymond. *A Grammar of the Film.* Berkeley, Calif.: University of California Press, 1962.

Stern, Seymour. "The Birth of a Nation: 1915–1965," Special Griffith Issue, *Film Culture,* 1965, no. 36.

Thorp, Margaret. *America at the Movies.* New Haven, Conn.: Yale University Press, 1937.

Wolfenstein, Martha, and Nathan Leites. *Movies, A Psychological Study.* New York: The Free Press, 1950.

Wollen, Peter. *Signs and Meaning in the Cinema.* New York: Doubleday & Company, Inc., 1969.

Wood, Robin. *Hitchcock's Films.* New York: A. S. Barnes & Company, Inc., 1966.

Wood, Robin. *Howard Hawks.* New York: Doubleday & Company, Inc., 1968.

INDEX

411